Living Lightly

ALSO BY WALTER AND DOROTHY SCHWARZ
Breaking Through: Theory and Practice of Holistic Living (1987)

ALSO BY WALTER SCHWARZ
Nigeria (1966)
The Arabs in Israel (1969)
The New Dissenters: The Nonconformist Conscience in the Age of Thatcher (editor)
(1989)

ALSO BY DOROTHY SCHWARZ
A New Horse for Many (1979)
Simple Stories About Women (1998)

Living Lightly

Travels in
post-consumer society

WALTER AND DOROTHY SCHWARZ

Jon Carpenter

Our books may be ordered from bookshops or (post free in the UK) from
Jon Carpenter Publishing, 2 The Spendlove Centre, Charlbury, OX7 3PQ,
England

Please send for our free catalogue

Credit card orders should be phoned or faxed to 01689 870437
or 01608 811969

Our US distributor is Paul and Company, PO Box 442, Concord, MA 01742
(phone 978 369 3049, fax 978 369 2385)

First published in 1998 by
Jon Carpenter Publishing
2 The Spendlove Centre, Charlbury, Oxfordshire OX7 3PQ
☎ 01608 811969

ISBN 1 897766 44 0

Printed in England by J. W. Arrowsmith Ltd., Bristol
Cover printed by KMS Litho, Hook Norton

Acknowledgements

• •

Thanks to everyone who helped us with encouragement, funding, addresses, interviews, reading draft chapters and hospitality. We never realised until we started our travels what a fund of kindness and generosity exists among strangers who become friends.

In the UK: Nic Albery, Tessa Blackstone, Peter Bunyard, The Catalyst Collective, Sheena and Julian Clover, Simon and Suzanne Campbell-Jones, Maurie Cohen, Sharon Cromarty, The Daiwa Foundation, Simon Fairlie, Mark & Diana Fisher, the Findhorn Foundation, Sven Gigold, Herbie Girardet, Teddy Goldsmith, Peter Harper, Colin Hodgetts, Patrick Holden, Liz Hoskin, Intermediate Technology, Keveral Farm, Satish Kumar, Sue Lo, Julia Meiklejohn, Norman Myers, June Mitchell, George Monbiot, Helena Norberg-Hodge, Angela Oels, Alison Parkes, Len Peters, Ed Posey, Jonathon Porritt, Jules Pretty, John Seymour, Tariq and Nighat Shabeer, Diana Sherwood, Caroline Walker, Tracey Whittaker, Benjamin and Amina Zephaniah.

In the US and Canada: Arnie Anfinson, Cecile Andrews, Albert Bates and many others at The Farm, Joanni Blank, Brent Cameron, John and Camille Clark, John and Diana Carroll, Guy Dauncey, Marco Donners, Diana and Robert Gilman, Trauger Groh, Susan Heath, Sarah Knott, David Korten, Julia and Brian Laforgia, Marjorie Marquette, Sister Miriam MacGillis, Rainu and Paco Neogy, Bruce Seligman, Sam and Elisabeth Smith, Stuart and Lynette Staniford-Chen, Abigail Summers, Ben and Sonja Walter.

In India: Abu and Psyche Abraham, K. R. Datye, Ulhas Gore, Alan Herbert, Marti Mueller and many others at Auroville, the Pattenkar family, K. J. and Mani Roy, Sonny and Maggie Thomas, Sarojini Vittachi.

In Australia: Jenny Allen, Annie and Rory Barnes, Bobo and John Bryant, Emily and Michael Field, Di and Michael Fitzjames and Chloe, Lea Harrison, David Holmgren, Jill Jordan and many others at Manduka, Max Lindegger and many others at Crystal Waters, Bill Metcalf, Brian and Chris Pelerman, Bob Taylor, Chris and Teresa West.

In Japan: Richard Evanoff, Masahiro Fukushi, Kumiko Goto, Takashi Iwami, Shigeki Mariyama, Tomoko Masunaga, Masahiro and Ahiro Matsushima, Professor Minimada, the Morita family, the Olinda family,

Nobhito Orita, Simon and Masako Piggot, Goichi Terachi, John and Masako Watts.

In Holland: Paul Dijkstra and many others in the VAKgroep.

And lastly a big thank you to our supportive family, Ben and Fredy, Habie, Tanya, Zoe and Zac and to our editor and publisher Jon Carpenter who had faith in a big book.

Contents

• •

The authors.

Foreword

· ·

by John Vidal

Some of humankind's greatest revolutions may be taking place right under our noses. Massive global economic forces and market-led developments in science and technology are together sweeping into every crook and cranny of the world. The communications revolution is changing the way we interact with each other; the technological revolution is redefining how we work and move; and the biological revolution is beginning to alter for ever the way we understand life and our place in the world. Coincidentally, but linked, we are fundamentally changing the ecology of the earth that sustains all life. All this is leading to deep fragmentation of societies, cultural mayhem, disappointment or frustration in the way we live and intellectual, spiritual and social turmoil.

Yet this newly globalised world of finance, trade and industry, travel, sport, agriculture and entertainment represents supreme progress for only a few. The revolutions are largely exclusive and elitist, being imposed by the few on the many with no consideration of the value or importance of what they are replacing. They come with a terrible human and ecological price tag. The only things not on offer in the global supermarket are values, wisdom, continuity, harmony, mutuality, happiness, co-operation, neighbourliness, security, compassion and richness of culture.

The emerging new global order seems economically and socially seductive. Scientists, business, the media and politicians are quick to say it offers us more choice, greater opportunity and new horizons. We are told there is no other way and that the global marketplace will bring new knowledge, new access to places and each other, undreamed of wealth, longer lives and better environments. We are promised a further, faster, fitter future.

But, of course, this is a contrick. Globalisation for most of us is proving to be the greatest thief of all time, stealing our time, our values, and our potential. Choice for some is lack of choice for others. One group's wealth can mean lower quality of life for all. One sort of apple on sale in all supermarkets inevitably means thousands of other varieties are not grown. One sort of media can lead to one sort of thought, one definition of success means many sorts of failure, one system of anything — science, agriculture, medicine or production — will always diminish rather than increase the whole.

The new global order is increasingly intolerant of anyone who begs to differ. Driven by visions of wealth and control, rather than being a response to people's universal needs, it has an ugly tendency to bypass natural justice, to be authoritarian, triumphalist and fundamentalist. Anyone disagreeing with the new orthodoxy of today's globalising world can expect to be dismissed as luddite, naive, irrational, reactionary or plain ignorant.

In the face of such powerful forces, it would be easy to give up. But no. Every revolution has its opposition and its rearguard and there is nothing stronger than people working together.

Dorothy and Walter Schwarz have spent the past three years gathering first hand evidence of resistance to globalisation from the frontlines of change. Their book is a chronicle of hope, a record of practical survival and individual and community improvement, and proof not only that that there are real options open to people, but that a significant global counter-movement is developing to challenge the orthodoxy of globalisation.

This is not a DIY manual for the millennium or even an alternative lifestyle directory. It is a genuinely inspiring global report, showing clearly how common humanity and consideration for others brings its own rewards, is flourishing in the unlikeliest of places, and how people everywhere are wising up to what is going on.

New groups are finding ways to express what centuries of humanity have found valuable and cohesive, new ways to organise themselves and new ways to celebrate diversity, imagination and individuality. These groups are in the vanguard of real change and I dare say that in time, their contribution to society will be recognised as a powerful and important forerunner to a better future for all.

(John Vidal is Environment Editor of *The Guardian*)

Introduction

● ●

Happiness, like love, justice or beauty, is notoriously hard to quantify but easy to recognise. In our travels on four continents we met people who have rejected the glamour of consumer society in order to follow their vision of a simpler life — and have grown happier. They have found a better model for living at this turn of the century — a time when a handful of multi-national companies have grown more powerful than governments, the gap between the rich and the poor widens year by year, and the competitive demands of an endlessly expanding global economy have come to rule our lives. More and more people experience the world as becoming uglier, dirtier, less healthy and less just. In rich countries, people appear divided into those who work too hard to enjoy their prosperity, those who work, full-time or part-time, for pitifully low wages — and those who have no jobs at all. As a result, more individuals are becoming interested in alternatives.

How can we speak of 'living lightly' in the Third World, where most people are poor? In India we found boundless enthusiasm for Western-style comfort and affluence, and we found people resentful that well-off travellers from a rich country should tell them not to become rich. They are right. You can't tell someone who wants a refrigerator that they can manage with an ice-box, particularly not when you've always had a fridge yourself. But we found that here, too, individuals and groups had begun to question the benefits of the global economy and of so-called economic development. Since the end of the second world war, millions of rural people who were poor by industrial standards but led viable lives have become destitute, as the forests which nour-ished them for centuries are cut down, water supplies are drained off for industrial use or polluted, fish stocks are depleted by mechanised foreign ships, homes and lands are drowned by a gigantic new dam. 'Development' of this kind forces farmers off their land into cities where neither sufficient work nor adequate infrastructure awaits them. As a result, there are people in the South (as we prefer to call the Third World) who are experimenting with different approaches to development. In tune with the ideas of the Living Lightly culture in the North, they are seeking home-grown solutions.

The pioneers in this book are changing themselves. They act on the micro-level, at the grass roots. Most are practical people; some are technological wizards who invent sustainable solutions for living better with less, and who network with each other across the world by e-mail and through the Internet. They already belong to the twenty-first century. They hope that the tiny islands of better living which they inhabit will provide examples which will eventually supplant the norms of unfettered global capitalism which rule us today. Their hope is not in revolution but in persuasion by example.

What is original about such groups? Malcontents and misfits have always been around; we had more in the sixties than today. Nor is there anything new about middle-aged folk like us lamenting that the world 'ain't what it used to be'. Dropouts and prophets of doom have rarely changed events. What is new is that small groups of Living Lightly people are now part of an articulate and increasingly purposeful global culture which promotes values that run counter to those of the mainstream. We found such groups in the USA, Europe, Australia, India and Japan, with the same aims, the same ideology — and using a similar vocabulary to describe it.

The words that matter are empowerment, community, sustainability, consciousness (their word for a new awareness), and energy (their word for the spiritual power of group feeling, not sources of mechanical power). In different continents, in North and South, they envisage and practise similar solutions: eco-villages (self-reliant and convivial communities), permaculture (a more productive and sustainable way of organising homes and gardens), CSA (community supported agriculture), LETS (trading with a local currency), cohousing (living in your own home while sharing basic facilities), and downshifting (voluntary simplicity). They rarely talk about the environment, which they often see as a luxury protected by privileged people for their own enjoyment: they are more interested in a world which allows everyone a good life.

In India we visited pioneers with their own vision of what 'development' should mean. Not content with protesting against large dams which tend to benefit the rich, they were building small dams. We found scientists, engineers and social activists introducing equitable water distribution and organic farming into groups of villages. They were not trying to return to a primitive past; they want technology to serve the needs of living beings and of the planet.

The Living Lightly people hold values which are based on a conviction that life has meaning beyond the visible and measurable. Such perennial values continue to enjoin reverence for all life, human and non-human, and therefore exclude the sort of exploitation practised in the deforestation of the Amazon region, in a motorway destroying a beauty spot, and in other profit-making exploits in the name of development. Such values reinstate notions of community, beauty in architecture, local self-reliance and living in a bioregional economy.

Living Lightly pioneers believe that the emerging global market is in effect a new world empire worshipping false gods of consumerism and greed. They think the empire will eventually disintegrate, as others have. In anticipation of that collapse, islands of refuge must be prepared. Whether a world-wide financial crash or an ecological catastrophe happens or not, these experiments will serve as beacons lighting a route to the next century. The techniques of sustainable living will have been perfected and tested in readiness for a time when consumption has been uncoupled from greed and returned to its primary purpose of fulfilling need.

Warnings of catastrophe can be exaggerated. Bigots and fundamentalists also talk about islands of refuge against Armageddon. But in the past a few lonely prophets of doom were proved right. The moral prophets of the Old Testament warned that a society with no communal morality was doomed, and so it proved. The new Green prophets aren't that different. Voices like Wendell Berry's or Gary Snyder's in the USA or John Seymour's in Britain are part of an unbroken tradition of prophetic writing. And their prophecies are listened to and validated by movements in ideas, linked world-wide on the Internet. There is a U-turn in what progress means.

We, Dorothy and Walter, were young adults in the Sixties, when the poet Philip Larkin wrote: *Sexual intercourse began/ In nineteen sixty-three/ (Which was rather late for me) / Between the end of the Chatterley ban / And the Beatles' first LP.* We rejoiced that progress was inevitable — not only in sexual liberty but also personal freedom, prosperity, technology, and fun. We believed unquestioningly in economic development, expressed in roads, factories and large dams, certain that these artefacts meant material benefits for everyone. We spent much of the sixties in West Africa, much of the seventies in India and much of the eighties in France. Walter was a journalist and Dorothy had babies.

Returning to Africa in the eighties and to India in the nineties, we found the expanding middle classes had immured themselves in oases of prosperity, surrounded by deserts of poverty. In one of the newly popular motels on the Delhi to Agra road, the surrounding lawns, harshly emerald, are watered by sprinklers while outside the gates the eroded hills can no longer support the poverty-stricken, water-starved villagers. Such a waste of water in a drought-prone area should be a criminal offence. It is not. 'Development' now seems little more than a window dressing for economic colonialism.

It sounds crazy to claim that economic development *impoverishes* the poor but we have watched it happen. Along India's south-west coastline, industrial prawn cultivators — a new breed of entrepreneurs who operate in many other countries as well — pump a mixture of seawater and fresh water into inland ponds to breed prawns for the luxury markets of Europe, USA, and Asia. Their exorbitant demand on fresh water runs village wells dry. Brackish water seeps out from the ponds, ruining farmers' fields for miles around and poisoning mangrove swamps where fish breed. So these regions, already poor by industrial standards but plentifully endowed for farming and fishing, are being ruined: thousands have had to leave their villages. Protein is being systematically taken from the poor to serve a luxury market abroad. That is foreign aid in reverse — the rich robbing the poor. The prawn-breeders usually have government backing because they earn dollars and constitute 'development'.

We are convinced, after our journeys among the post-consumerists in North and South, that people would be happier in a thriving local economy, providing basic food and livelihood for all, than the global one which changes food into a commodity, destroys jobs, devalues cultures and devastates the human and natural environment.

We are less brave and adventurous than the Living Lightly pioneers, but like many others in the North we yearn for re-involvement in community, for fresh, wholesome local food and for a less destructive lifestyle. As we see urban households shrinking, children degenerating into a spiral of crime and rows of grannies banished to old-age homes, we want to rediscover, or re-invent, the extended family which is still the norm in much of the South.

In every place that we visited we found people who, having emerged from the materialistic paradigm, were working with an amalgam of new and old traditions which has attracted the label New Age. We met educated people who had joined a private rebellion against conventional intellect — people for whom the certainties of reductionist science are outdated. In Queensland we found a lawyer using the theory of Cabalistic numbers; in New England, a farmer was sowing seeds in relation to the phases of the moon; at the Findhorn Community in Scotland, members feel the beneficial presence of nature spirits. Exchanging science for magic appeared to us a dead end. But look deeper and you can see the hunger people express to return to a more natural way of living and thinking. Underlying such attempts is the conviction that reductionist science does not hold the only, or indeed, the best answer to the questions human beings ask. Who am I and why am I here? Belief in science-based 'progress' has fuelled most of the dying century's developments, from the hydrogen bomb to the computer chip. Along the way, many moral guidelines were discarded. However, if someone wants to leave the conventional path of modernity, they need guidelines. Religion is one, pschyotherapy another, Eastern spiritual practices a third. Conventional religion does not easily nurture this popular spiritual quest. That its fringes are lunatic should not blind us to the significance of New Age thinking and behaviour — young people living in trees to save them from felling; city dwellers digging community gardens to drive drug-pushers off vacant lots; doctors in Bombay leaving highly paid city jobs to work among forest tribals.

Thinking about consciousness and awareness became important for us. This is what the post-consumerist movement is about: consciousness of nature and of ourselves, and awareness of the crisis inherent in the unique moment of history in which we live. Hitherto people could always find a frontier (part of the American Dream is based on the idea of an endless one). There seemed a limitless supply of forests to cut down, rivers to dam, new markets to infiltrate, empty seas, deserts and jungles in which to dump our wastes. This frontier has disappeared — although many people, especially in the US, continue to act as if it still exists. The planet is finite and it appears to be ailing. Global warming is not fantasy, nor are floods caused by cutting down forests or encroaching deserts imaginary.

We don't pretend that we met or even read about more than a tiny fraction of people who live lightly. We encountered failure as well as success. But we found the pioneers, and their children, exciting, because they lived more intensely, with more awareness and spirituality, more mutual caring, more fun and in some cases more danger.

Not everyone has the courage of the Living Lightly pioneers, but anyone can go some of the way. Albert Bates, a seventies trailblazer of communal living, whom we found running eco-village courses at The Farm in Tennessee, described Living Lightly as being: ...*as simple as getting up at sunrise or as difficult as eating fruit and vegetables in their season. It might mean for you — travelling less, putting down roots and working to protect and restore a piece of the earth that means something to you. It may mean changing your job or career in mid-life and redirecting your money and energy towards solving a tiny portion of the problem. If you are a parent, you might want to teach your children values that include caring for the earth and a consciousness of their impact upon it.*[1]

As we set out to discover people who have broken out of the straitjacket of the consumerist life, we ourselves have made no radical lifestyle changes. Our youngest child, Zachary, complained: 'You say so many different things but you actually do less than the average person because you go around so much in airplanes. To help the environment be Green on a scale of ten you lot would be about ONE. Mum says all the time, oh, if only people could be vegetarian, but then she still eats bacon. She says, oh God, why buy new clothes when you can make do, but her cupboard's full of shoes. I think that's bad. You should either shut up or put up.' We sympathise with Zac's view. He is young. There is no middle way for him. We, older, do our best in our native surroundings. To live lightly in its purest form would mean a return to a hunter-gatherer society — a silly proposition. In between, there are infinite choices.

The following pages describe initiatives — tiny pieces of a jigsaw so gigantic that no one book can ever describe the whole. If some readers are encouraged to add another piece, our book will have succeeded. Meanwhile, these ventures are part of a movement which is in continual flux. A young community struggling to survive may, six months later, have 'arrived'; or it may have folded. These are snapshots not posed photographs; they give a partial but we hope an unprejudiced view. We have added an appendix of addresses to enable readers to make their own enquiries.

Some of our American characters could be considered too affluent to qualify as living lightly, at least in the eyes of the less well-off. But we still take them seriously because, having rejected the values of a consumerist lifestyle in the richest and most wasteful country in the world, they provide an example which can influence others in both the North and the South. As one of their admirers out it: 'They redefine what the good life is. We all need to be a part of this conversation'.

At the other end of the scale, some of the people we write about, mainly in the UK, are criticised as too idle, or too scruffy, or too ready to draw benefit handouts, at least by those who work harder and wash more frequently. We don't agree because, by rejecting the competitive business ethics most of us live by, they provide a valid interpretation of the ills of our society and remind us of deeper values we tend to forget.

Each chapter describes a different set of experiences — except Chapter 8 in which we set out the case against the global consumer economy, and Chapter 17, in which we reflect on the role of computers and the Internet in a Living Lightly context. Criticism of the global economy forms the underlying theme of our book, the viewpoint shared by the people we write about and the justification for the changes in lifestyle which they have made. Can these 'islands of success' survive? Are they replicable for the rest of us? These are the questions we were asking ourselves on our travels. Come with us on our journey ...

Note

1   Albert Bates in *Shared Visions – Shared Lives*.

Part 1 : More or less radical lifestyles

1
Downshifting — upgrading

●●●

'**M**y only possibility' of having some effect somewhere is to walk my talk.' So Arnie Anfinson walks his talk. His clothes are second-hand. He feeds kitchen waste to worms which he breeds in a bag outside his back door for use in his vegetable garden. He is proud of household appliances got for nothing: an oven which broils but does not grill, a toaster which has to be tied down with elastic. His shelves carry a selection of *Tightwad Gazette*, *Penny Pincher Times* and the *Use Less Stuff Report*.

Arnie is retired — he is almost eighty — but neither age not physical handicap (he has an artificial leg) have slowed him down. His self-imposed mission keeps him busy — a mission to spread the ideas and practice of voluntary simplicity through face-to face contact and through the Internet.

The base line of voluntary simplicity is the belief that over-consumption must be curbed to preserve both our natural resources and our sanity. Simplicity or frugality aren't new ideas in the United States. They have a respected history going back to the first puritans. Arnie sniffs: 'Buying stuff and the security that goes with it doesn't add *anything* to the joy of my life. I will not buy a new item if I can get it second-hand.'

He occupies the bottom half of the modest house which he owned until he sold it to his daughter Daphne, who lives in the top half with her family. Arnie lives on $800 a month — $300 to spend and $500 in rent to Daphne. 'I could afford to buy a new car: I don't want that. I even feel a little guilty when I drive my old one just because I can play the game of wooden leg.'

Being an ailing old man does not deter him from frugality even over health. 'If you're going to live frugally you can't afford to be going to MDs regularly. I am potentially my own best doctor because we're all unique, and most chronic illnesses are related to mental or emotional states. I realise I haven't been having enough fruit partly due to my frugality and I can put that right. I'm well situated: haven't got more than twenty years and I've got Medicare; I don't worry. So many of my friends are fussing about nursing homes and all that. What I aim for is when the times comes, when I figure I cannot

Arnie Anfinson.

contribute or get around, I'm going to let go.'

Arnie lives in Seattle on the western seaboard. Seattle's citizens, prosperous from the presence of lavish employers including Microsoft and Boeing, far away enough from the east coast and not yet caught up in California's excesses, are reputed amongst Living Lightly people to be seriously and successfully involved with sustainable living initiatives. We found its reputation well-deserved. There are Sustainable Seattle initiatives in both private and public sectors, business, cafés, communities. We have come here to explore the concept of voluntary simplicity and how it affects individuals' lifestyles. Arnie is our host. He knows everyone in this growing movement, identified in at least one survey as a major trendof the nineties, with hundreds of devoted adherents in the Seattle area alone. He estimates that in Seattle around twenty study circles are active at any one time, with up to twenty people in each.

Arnie claims he was 'tightwad' most of his life and his frugality is rooted in his family background. 'My parents were homesteading in North Dakota; we lived in a sod house. I was born with a club foot. We never became middle class. My father became a jack of all trades. We often moved. Always pretty poor.'

In those days there was little emphasis on affluence in the US, any more than in Arnie's Scandinavian heritage. 'My mother had this biblical thing — it's *good* to be poor.' Arnie followed the American dream, won scholarships to college and studied aeronautical engineering. One leg was amputated below the knee when he was in his twenties; he has myalitis in the other. He

---

Voluntary Simplicity is one of the top trends of the nineties. By the year 2000, fifteen percent of people in their thirties and forties (the baby boomers) will be part of a 'simplicity' market — low-priced, durable gardening and home products that are short on slickness and status.   · Trends Research Institute of Rhinebeck NY, 1995.

never complains. He worked in Panama during the war as a meteorologist, spent eighteen years in Fiji on various assignments, married an Australian women and had four children.

'The Fijian way of life was pleasant, easy-going, people lived in their village with rules and enjoyed security. Right now, people in the older group in voluntary simplicity still have that kind of tradition in mind.' Arnie's first step into grassroots action was in the peace movement. 'And then we saw that we couldn't change attitudes about war until we had changed attitudes about money: the two are closely related.'

Twice a week he does voluntary work at the New Road Map Foundation, the unofficial headquarters of the voluntary simplicity movement. He took us in his battered car to the big suburban house in north-west Seattle where Joe Dominguez and Vicki Robin run the Foundation with a few full-time colleagues and many part-time volunteers.

The New Road Map Foundation

An ancient bus called The Ultimate Vehicle is parked in the front garden as a memento. Joe and Vicky, the downsizers' gurus, lived in it as they went around the country giving the first pioneering seminars on how to manage your money so that you can afford to live simply. The courses were so successful that they were sold as audiotapes and formed the basis of the book, *Your Money or Your Life*. The book sold half a million copies in three years — even though the authors frugally advised people to get it in the public library. Using the book's profits, Joe established the New Road Map Foundation as a charitable foundation to disseminate his ideas. The house is run as a four-person community; all day long it hums with volunteers sending out VS course tapes, or the VS book, or VS newsletters, or operating the VS Internet page.

Joe with a heavy moustache and spectacles, and the younger Vicki, long-haired and fresh-faced, are a popular double act and appear regularly in TV talk shows.[1] Dominguez was a Wall Street stock analyst until he retired at thirty-one to teach others to others to follow his example. 'My ideas struck a chord in all sorts of folk — from yuppies to people on welfare — who felt they weren't managing money or getting value for things. These are old American values: good use of

In a random survey of 800 people taken in 1995, 28 percent had downshifted — voluntarily cut back income over last five years to reflect changes in priorities. 35% had upshifted. 82 percent agreed that 'we buy and consume far more than we need'. 88 percent agreed that 'protecting the environment will require most of us to make major changes in the way we live'.
· *Merck Family Fund Report*, 1995.

money, good bargains, and lack of ostentation. Addictive mass consumerism didn't come in until the late forties.'

He found mothers were the first to see that ten dollars earned weren't worth an hour less with their children. 'Even little kids learned that an hour more with Mom was worth giving up ten dollars worth of toys or gadgets.'

This personal impact of VS works on the local level; it has repercussions on the global. Vicki declared, 'Lowering consumption in North America is the single most important thing that can happen on this earth. Right now we are transforming the planet into products and then into waste. We are doing this to ourselves.'

With many homilies and a sprinkling of jargon, Joe and Vicki taught their students how to enhance their savings until they reached financial independence (FI) so they can live off the interest while leading lives of voluntary simplicity (VS). No complex investment strategies are needed: 'Just buy Treasury Bonds, which cut out the middleman and are patriotic. We encourage people to save, not to speculate.'

As an apprentice downsizer your first step is to find out how much money you have earned in your life and compare it with assets and liabilities now. That shows you how much effort you have wasted. Step two: work out your net hourly wage and keep track of every cent of expenditure with the help of a notebook. 'Ask yourself: did I get fulfilment, satisfaction or value in proportion to life-energy spent? How might expenditure change if I didn't have to work? Learn to choose quality of life over standard of living. It's cool.'

> When you simplify your life you do fewer (or none) of the things you don't like to do and more of the things you enjoy. And you seek out and nurture only those people and relationships which enhance your life. This is not about deprivation, this is about choices.
> · Charlene Macmahon in *Tightwad Gazette* (40,000 subscribers), Leeds, Maine.

The cardinal rule is: buy what you need and don't go shopping; service your appliances; do it yourself; buy in bulk in sales — provided it's something you really need or want; buy used; don't go into debt on credit cards; walk and cycle. Joe spells this out for us in late October, Christmas glittering already in the Seattle shopping malls.

Modestly, Joe claims only partial credit for the rise in the US savings rate from three to five percent in the last five years. Despite the growing anti-consumerist influence of the Voluntary Simplicity movement, the corporate economy has not yet tried to strike back at him. In fact, several big companies quite like him and send their employees on VS courses. 'They know that more

Vicky Robin and Joe Dominguez.

staff buy-outs (voluntary redundancies) are on the way; it's in their interest that people increase savings and it's in the national interest too: our savings rate is much too low.' Joe thinks loss of consumer custom through VS is only a drop in the ocean for the corporations, who make most of their profits abroad.

Joe expects the long-term benefits of the VS trend to accumulate, when a less consumerist future restores a sense of community. 'As the movement spreads there will be more people per household, more co-operation in repairing and maintaining household goods, more car pools, tool sharing, and women having lovely parties for exchanging clothes.'

Joe is sanguine that a change in values, demoting shopping from its place as the favourite American pastime, can be and is being achieved as the old American core values come back: 'Good use of money, good bargains, and lack of ostentation. This period of conspicuous consumption began in the late forties, now we're returning to normal.'

Thinking of our teenage son and his insatiable desire for new trainers we ask Joe: what if the kids suffer peer pressure to consume?

'Just say no to them; it's good for their character.'

Joe and Vicki both manage to live as they choose on low incomes by US standards: Joe on $5000 a year and Vicki, who runs an aged Volvo, on $7000.

Vicki thinks of her life as a success: 'Not because of the best-selling book but because I feel I'm living my life authentically — using it for what it was designed for. The book and the tapes pay for most of what we do here — the actions, mailings and campaigns.' She says simply: 'I have these faculties and gifts. How can I direct them so that the world is more beautiful and more loving? Just imagine a world where people's needs were met. It would not be a homogenous world. We are all different people with different experiences.'

She wants people to develop an attitude that leads to maximum joy using minimum means, in local and small-scale economies in which people could 'change' from being a nuisance to being a resource. 'If you do frugality skilfully, you will begin to interact skilfully. My sense is that we would create a harmonious dance. Some are drawn to dance, others to act.' Like Jo, Vicki has chosen to be childless and doesn't regret this both because of world population pressure and because the ideas of voluntary simplicity are easier to adopt without children.

Arnie's meeting

Arnie believes in putting on a sweater instead of turning up the heating, but for tonight there is a heater which he switches on at the last possible minute. This is the fortnightly voluntary simplicity support group which he hosts in his open-plan living room. He has reluctantly been persuaded to replace worn-out chairs with rustic, second-hand armchairs. The study groups are the one of the most valued activities of his life.

> Hi, Schwarzes, Are you having anything in UK like BUY NOTHING DAY on Friday, Nov. 21st? As you probably know, this is the day after Thanksgiving and the busiest shopping day of the year — all the 'bargains' to lure us to part with our money for STUFF we don't need! The NRM (New Roadmap Foundation) people, and many others are congregating at the Westlake Plaza. Vicki and John DeGraaf and others will be Affluenza doctors, giving help with this disease à la Lucy in the Peanuts cartoon.
> · E-mail from Arnie, 20 November 1997.

A dozen people turn up, dressed in nondescript but not hippie clothes — slacks, jeans and sweaters. Two people knit throughout the proceedings, giving the evening a wholesome tinge. No snacks or drinks, not even tea or coffee. The procedure — everyone speaks in turn — is familiar, so they need no moderator.

Linda, single, in her late thirties, has come to the group for the second time. 'Like a lot of people I'm waiting to make the changes and I'm still buying things. But there's a struggle going on: I don't *need* these things.' She says she would like to live in a community or a cohousing group (see next chapter) instead of a condominium as now, but doesn't know how to go about it. She has followed the VS course on audio-cassettes. Still working for the US & West telephone company, she plans to retire in three years. Already, her new skills have saved money and opened opportunities, enabling her to help nieces and nephew through college. Her aims are clear; she's anxious to learn from the group in cutting down expenditure and working less to free herself for other activities.

David, more experienced, is somewhat chic in his fawn slacks and he shows off hand-sewn brogues bought for nine dollars in a thrift shop. (We saw thrift shops all over America. Their merchandise is donated and sold for charities.) This kind of inverted ostentation is common in voluntary simplicity. Cathy, in the same vein, produces a magazine showing $1000 outfits and boasts she has seen the same clothes for $20 in a thrift shop.

Cathy, a Japanese woman of forty, wants to retire at forty-five and with this aim follows the voluntary simplicity routine. Her husband and family aren't enthusiastic about the new direction her life is taking and she comes to Arnie's circle for support. 'People at work criticise me for wearing old shoes. But I guess they like me all the same.'

Ed in an old jacket and old baggy trousers has come for the first time. He has a ruddy face and a forthright manner. His job, in a store selling luxury limousines, displeases him; he gets hassled at work for driving a down-beat 1981 Honda. Now he has read *Your Money or Your Life* he wants to cut his four-day week further. A new career in art work and a simpler life beckons. He pays $920 rent a month for a house which he says he doesn't need. 'I'd be happier in a trailer.' Everyone is delighted with Ed on his first appearance. This is not the sort of group where a newcomer needs to feel apprehensive.

Only the newcomers talk earnestly about voluntary simplicity philosophy; Arnie's group is two years old already and the old-timers prefer to take the ideas for granted and swap energy-saving tips and anecdotes showing off their frugality. Much discussion ensues on whether David should have bought shoes in the thrift store. Sue says you must have shoes that fit. Jacque, David's wife, tells a story: a friend asked how she could bear to buy second-hand sheets. Her reply: 'Every time you got to a hotel you're using second-hand sheets.'

Ed says he has chosen not to have children. This is politically correct in voluntary simplicity circles. It is a policy encouraged by the New Road Map Foundation, all four of whose directors are childless. We listened to diatribes against too many children in some discomfort, since we have five.

Bob, a long-standing voluntary simplicity supporter in his sixties, tells how he makes beer the cheap way, starting with grain — and then uses the spent grain for bread making. His wife owns a house that they have split into three, renting off the ground and first floors in two apartments and living in the basement which they have converted into living quarters. It is unspoken but understood that voluntary simplicity is born out of affluence. How many of us own our own houses?

Julia recalls the high income she used to earn working for a construction company. Visiting Nicaragua in the course of her work has changed her values. 'I saw what a sense of community those people had and how separately we live here.' Her lifestyle changed; she has become a master-gardener with an organic practice.

Evelyn, in sweater and jeans, is one of the knitters. She says working in insurance gave her too much money so, in desperation, she started collecting teddy bears. Then she read The Book (as the *Your Money or Your Life* is reverently called) and realised: 'I don't have to sell insurance. I hate it.' So retiring from work, she returned to university and then started living 'at a very low standard but I still felt very wealthy. All of us have a good lifestyle.' Her mortgage is paid off and she feels she has stepped into a 'culture of independence.' She wants to go further. 'I'm starting to see the cost of having to support my house, the dogs. I'm thinking of sharing accommodation or moving to a small apartment. I'd like to do some writing. There's so much opportunity to help people in charities.'

Evelyn remarks that voluntary simplicity can be difficult when one is attacked by neighbours and family. 'When you drop out of the consumer culture you are giving them an implied reproach.' She wants to live more communally but her house cannot conveniently be divided . She sees co-housing as an attractive alternative: 'Sharing people's expertise, gardening and so on, with support for the old as well as for children.'

As Linda burbles some more about how she's bought used things and finds it wonderful, all this self-congratulatory chat begins to irk us. Daringly, we ask if people don't sometimes become killjoys. Might there be a pathological element in Voluntary Simplicity?

There is a pause.

The men react defensively.

I made the switch to frugality after years of wanton waste! My former 'high-powered job', shopping and dining out, mindless following of trends and fashion, has been replaced by a stay-at-home-mom career, volunteer work in a homeless shelter, and a surprising ability to be creative and inventive. As I look at the unbelievable cast-offs we receive at the shelter — excellent clothing, household goods, furniture, etc. — I realise just how much this society consumes needlessly. Thank goodness my kids recognise this too, and think carefully about their own spending and acquisitions. Short term rewards of tightwad living are great: long term rewards are immeasurable.
· Sybil (letter in *Tightwad Gazette*).

When people balk at being asked to give things up, it isn't enough to say it will help the planet, you have to offer something in return to fill the void that people are filling with products and spending. Someone who gets a high from shopping isn't going to sign up for voluntary simplicity, even if they believe it is right. What I see the movement offering people is community and the inter-connectedness with others that so many media sources (and others) have identified as missing in modern American life. I wonder if this will make it especially appealing to the 20-nothing or Generation X crowd. I'm in my 20's and find that most of the data on the 'trend' of voluntary simplicity is about babyboomers. I think this movement needs to be intergenerational to really work.

· Carisa, in VS Chat Line on the Internet.

Arnie: 'I may go too far sometimes but I feel good about that.'

Ed: 'I'm thinking about eating beans and rice every day and I feel good about that.'

But the women consider the question. Jacque agrees there's a danger in adopting an all-or-nothing approach. Cathy volunteers: 'We just bought a brand new car,' as if to challenge everybody to be shocked. Not to be outdone, Evelyn informs us she's going on a trip to the UK in January and later on a cruise with her mother because that's what her mother wants. Her comment: 'If you make it all so deadly serious, you lose the ultimate purpose.'

The meeting finishes at nine p.m. precisely. Some more gossip, handshakes and people walk off into the snow. Arnie switches off the electric heater. It has been a successful meeting.

The celebrated Heitmillers

David Heitmiller and Jacque Blix are members of Arnie's circle who, as exponents of downshifting, are rapidly becoming superstars of the VS movement. They have appeared on TV and articles have been written about them in *The New York Times* and *Esquire*. Now they are writing a book. They sit side by side on a white leather sofa like two experienced gurus; he is fifty and she is forty-six. They need little prompting.

David: 'We went through this heavy-duty yuppie phase in the mid-eighties, then achieved financial independence one year ago. When we got married in 1986 it was right at the very peak of what we call the yuppie period and we were each making $50,000'. He was an executive with National and West; she was with I.T. & T. 'We had two kids at home. It was mind-boggling when we think back. We were just talking about it this morning: in November 1985 I bought a brand new Jeep Cherokee four wheel drive: the very first week we took a trip in it to Oregon and Jacque flew back to go to a wedding and there was a snowstorm — that was the pace of life. Pretty soon it started to feel very empty.'

Jacque: 'It was fun but not the having-to-go to work part. I spent a lot of Sundays on an aeroplane and all those hours I spent worrying about work. Insecurity was something that came from me internally. I was reluctant to give up what I had because it seemed to me there was this either/or kind of thing, either destitute or in great money.'

David: 'Things started to happen about 1988. Jacque took a leave of absence to go back to college, my daughter was an exchange student in Argentina and we went down there — my first trip to a non-English speaking culture. I started thinking differently after that. I saw people not so absorbed in the money-making and material stuff. In my job, I liked the technology for a long time but the work became more and more abstract, you couldn't see the result. There was no reward other than the pay-check. And then in the late eighties and early nineties the company started to downscale and people who were left had to work harder. In 1990 I turned forty-five.' (Like many voluntary simplicity followers, it was a mid-life crisis that pushed David into action.) 'I became interested in writing and started taking community classes in writing, and I started writing about my own past experiences and emotions.'

Jacque: 'I read an article about a woman who had a nice life with four little kids on very little money and then I stumbled across the *Your Money or Your Life* tape.'

David: 'Jacque came home talking about this woman who lived on $600 a month and I thought: she must live in a dog house! We were living in a four-bedroom home and the mortgage alone was $1300 a month. Jacque persuaded me to go with her to a VS study circle. It was a new way of thinking.'

Jacque: 'We didn't sell our house right away because prices were low. We sold our second car, went over our budget with

How can we reach the mainstream consumers, those 93 percent of American girls whose favourite pastime is shopping? My sixteen-year-old brother, wearing his Thursday pair of trainers, assured me that his classmates know about the environmental and social problems caused by their purchases, but those problems are remote and concern for them is not fashionable. He grandly stated: 'You have to use consumer culture to counter consumer culture.' The message, he argued, must come through channels that youngsters can relate to: girlie magazines, role models such as film and sport stars, and advertising. If youngsters' role models began not only to espouse but also to live a lower consumption lifestyle, the popular media could turn the issue into something exciting. Wearing an old pair of trainers, eating Fair-Traded goods and recycling could become the in-thing to do. Such a climate could pave the way for policy reforms to become more politically acceptable. We need to develop strategies that allow the creative consumer in each of us to transform sustainable consumption into fashionable consumption and thus fashionable consumption into sustainable consumption.
· Tanya Schwarz in *New Economics Foundation Newsletter*, March 1998.

a fine tooth comb, got rid of cable TV, boat, stopped buying two new suits a year. After eighteen months we said we didn't miss that stuff at all: we were actually happier, had a couple of garage sales, gave a lot of stuff away to friends, started looking for an exit passage at work.'

David: 'Downsizing gave me the chance: I got a good severance deal — nearly a year's salary in all. We had cranked up a voluntary savings plan with the company. We have bought health insurance although some VS people don't do that. Joe and Vicki take just a catastrophe-only policy. The big reward is having time. I do Habitat for Humanity two days a week — building homes for the working poor — and Big Brother for Fatherless Boys — four hours a week. Community clean-up once a year. Cycling: one a year a week-long tour, sometimes for charity.'

Jacque: 'My parents were pretty thrifty when I grew up but that was more upwardly-mobile thrifty: they saved to send me to ballet school and things like that, so I knew the mechanics of thrift but the motivation was different.'

David: 'In the late sixties there was this rejection of societal norms — suddenly it was a status symbol to be poor and drive an old car and live in a decrepit apartment. I was following the trend, and then as soon as I married my first wife I fell back in line with the American dream.'

Jacque: 'Our expenditure has come down to $1900 a month. We bought this place so don't have rent.'

We were doubtful about the actual simplicity of this lifestyle. What the Heitmillers call simple living would to most Europeans, let alone anyone further east or further south, appear luxurious. They own their house, still have a car, TV, dishwasher, washing machine and dryer. Aren't they gradually re-adopting the yuppie style they had abandoned? They politely disagree.

Jacque: 'Voluntary simplicity could give people a sense of their own power and abilities and help them have more control. True there's a baseline of food and shelter that everybody needs; after you have that — then you can get into VS. Our culture is so abundant in so many things that can be got for so little money, so there are ways to get round those perceived deprivations. Take clothing. We were in this thrift store in quite a modest neighbourhood; they had a bag sale on clothing — you could take a big paper grocery bag and fill it up with clothes for five bucks. I've got fifteen items in a bag of clothes which comes out at about 35 cents each. I used to pay $35 for one shirt.'

David: 'We found that our example, not talking about it, made people start to ask questions. Under the surface of their lives a lot of people are empty or dissatisfied. All this stuff isn't making them happy but they don't know how to get out of that mode.'

David and Jacque have made a virtue out of necessity. The issue of down-sizing is here to stay. Jobs which were once guaranteed for life have vanished. The corporations, looking for efficiency, shed workers and middle managers where they can. What are these workers to do? Chase ever-decreasing job prospects? Or alter their lifestyle so as to remove themselves as far as possible from the grip of the corporations, finding a gentler, easier way of life, as the Heitmillers have done? VS as they live it doesn't overturn their bourgeois comforts but it does mean a change in attitude, to accept *enough* instead of always *more*.

Life in a cupboard

The VS message can be interpreted with wide variations in lifestyle. Bob and Jody live in a converted basement.

'Some people consider it extreme,' says Bob. 'We don't. Both my wife and I are what are called blue people — living in a small space. This is the way you live when you're on a boat.'

Average American working hours rose by 165 per annum for employed mothers, and 222 hours (an extra six weeks) for single parents between 1968 and 1993. In a survey, 30 percent of North American adults said they experience 'high stress nearly every day' and a majority said they get 60-90 minutes per night less sleep than they should. Between 1960 and 1986 the time parents made available to be with their children fell by 10 hours a week for whites and 12 hours for African Americans.
· Juliet Schor, *The Overworked American.*

We had met Bob in Arnie's support group. His part-Norwegian wife Jody was away visiting her family. They've converted the basement of Jody's house into an apartment modelled on the Norwegian boats both are used to: the two of them sleep in a cupboard-like space with no windows. We found it claustrophobic. Bob loves it.

A common theme for older members of voluntary simplicity circles is the thirties' depression. Bob remembers it vividly — his family jobless and depending heavily on a substantial vegetable garden. 'People were aware of their community, neighbours knew each other. Now nobody wants to have anything to do with a street person; in those days you used to have them in for a sandwich — you'd find jobs around the house so you could give them something to eat. Most people today don't even know who their neighbour is.

'If we had another depression all that would change in a big hurry. There is space in the towns and cities to grow food, probably enough to feed the whole population.' Bob says his state pension at $700 a month is more than he can spend because their tenants' rents pay for their modest lifestyle.

Bob prospered in business until one day in 1970: 'I started looking up that growth mountain and asked myself where it stopped. My wife thought I was crazy. I broke up with her about it. I gave her power of attorney for everything and left with two suitcases and $100. My security was in me.'

When Bob remarried, he and Jody wanted somewhere congenial to settle and chose Seattle. 'We were already living simply but we had a lot to learn, like getting along at Christmas without this gift rush. You find ways of exchanging not giving gifts. We give gifts of time: Jody and I give each other two days.'

Bob declares their lifestyle has a positive impact on their neighbours. 'We have an old car and an old camper for recreation. I garden and neighbours come and look and now some of them garden too. Many people in their twenties and thirties grow gardens and have little cars and maybe part-time jobs. They find that more civilised than having two people in a household working forty hours a week: that's uncivilised.'

Other VS people tell similar stories: they want to reject the worst excesses of consumer society. Janet Luhr is the editor of Seattle's voluntary simplicity newsletter. We invited her to meet us in the Honeybeare, the popular café-cum-bakery that provides a meeting place for VS people. On Saturday morning they were queuing up to choose their cakes and coffee, buy loaves and desserts — some to take home and some to eat there. Janet insists on buying her own snacks: treating one another is not done in VS.

She was raised to live within her means. 'My dad was an airline pilot, comfortably off but never a consumer.' She married a lawyer; her first VS crisis was a fight when she wanted to close their credit card account. He won.

> **How to change your life in ten easy steps (UK)**
>
> **1** *Bank with an ethical bank and get an ethical pension*
> * Contact: Holden Meehan independent financial advisers (0171 404 6442); Triodos Bank (1117 973 2874); Co-operative Bank (0345 212212
> **2** *Join Your Local LETS scheme or set one up*
> * Contact: LETSLink, 2 Kent Street, Portsea, Portsmouth PO1 3BS. (01705 730639)
> **3** *Buy organic food*
> * Contact: The Soil Association, 86 Colston Street, Bristol BS1 5BB
> **4** *Garden organically*
> * Contact: Henry Doubleday Research Association, Ryton on Dunsmore, Coventry, CB7 3LG
> **5** *Buy Fairtrade products*
> * Buy products with Fairtrade label with minimum packaging, not tested on animals. Contact: 0171 405 5942
> **6** *Use the car less or lift-share*
> * For short journeys cycle, walk or use public transport. Contact: Freewheelers (lift-sharing agency (0191 222 0090); Sustrans (6,500 mile cycle network) (0117 929 0888)
> **7** *Holiday wisely*
> * In the UK or, if you go abroad, book with a tour operator who has clear environmental and social policies. Contact: Tourism Concern, Stapleton House, 277-281 Holloway Road, London, N7 8HN (0171 753 3330)
> **8** *Live near your work*
> **9** *Reduce your household waste, energy and water usage*
> * The Home Energy Efficiency Scheme provides grants for pensioners and the unemployed for loft-insulation, draught-proofing, hotwater tank jackets and energy advice (Freephone 0800 181667)
> * Take it easy. Get an action-at-home kit to change your lifestyle. Contact: WWFN for a global action pack. WWFN-UK, Panda House, Weyside Park, Godalming, GU7 1XR
> **10** *Build an ecologically designed house or renovate your current one*
> * Contact: The Ecological Design Association, The British School, Slad Road, Stroud, Gloucs, GL5 1QW (01453 765575 Fax: 01453 759211); Walter Segal Self Build Trust, 57, Chalton Street, London, NW1 1HU (0171 388 9582); Ecology Building Society (01535 6359833)
> (Special Report — 'How to Live in the New Millennium', *The Guardian* 5/4/97)

'Then we got into the whole business of mortgages, interest payments on credit-card balances — I hated it. He was working around the clock, working and spending. I look at that period as an aberration.' The marriage broke up over this issue. Now she does not use a credit card except for travel. She still has the mortgage to pay off and shares her house with her sister. Her two children, aged eight and ten, are her only problem in living simply. 'So far I'm amazed how much influence I have with them. I live quite middle-class but they don't watch TV at home. When they ask for things like toys or for me to buy a fancy car I say: OK, but then I'd have to work harder and spend less time with you. They really understand that.'

Janet buys clothes second-hand but won't go as far as second-hand shoes like David. She thinks people like Amy Dacyzyon, who edits *The Tightwad Gazette*, overdo their frugality. 'Saving and recycling every button, every piece of paper, taking the lids off things and turning them into something else. When you go to the extreme it puts other people right off.'

Spreading the message

When Cecile Andrews opened a VS workshop in a Seattle community college in 1989, only four people registered. Three years later, the same workshop brought in 175 takers. Now she is in demand all over the US, appears on TV and has just brought out a book: *The Circle of Simplicity – Return to the Good Life.*

Her enthusiasm bubbles over; she is big, untidy and charismatic. Her pretty house on a hilltop has a garden full of tame rabbits which infiltrate the house in which she lives with her science writer husband. 'A lot of people live more simply than I do but I've become prominent because for the past two decades I've been an educator.' Spreading the word she believes in so passionately means that she earns about half the salary she once had as a schools administrator.

Cecile finds receptive audiences everywhere. 'A lot of people discover they never *liked* shopping anyway. It is like being hypnotised, following the direction of some vile genie. We're like kids in a candy store, eating everything we can until not only does nothing taste good, but we get sick and begin a search for something more nourishing.'

We try to identify with her but find it difficult. We see the funny side of all these earnest discussions among affluent people about buying second-hand suits. Have the VS people ever thought about *real* hardship: the hardship of walking seven kilometres to fetch water or living in a tin shack inside a rubbish dump? But then we reflect: if you are born white middle class and North American, and you become aware of the irrational, unfair and profligate way the earth's resources are used, what exactly are you to do? When Cecile advocates voluntary simplicity she doesn't dwell on the implications for world trade or for energy use, but concentrates on the personal benefits for the affluent individual, insisting that a simpler lifestyle leads to a happier one. In addition, she is aware, like the other VS lifestylers, of what our shopping culture is doing to the environment.

But Cecile has her critics. This letter appeared in the local paper:

'Dear Cecile, I've been following your column in the *Seattle Times* for quite a while now, and I've often wondered whether you lived in the same world that I do. You seem to be totally ignorant of the basic laws of economics. If your ideas were taken to their logical conclusion, all of our lives would be much poorer. If we in the 'rich' countries stopped buying the products of all those 'underdeveloped' countries of the world, all of their people would starve, instead of some of their people. We cannot return to the time when we all lived off local products only — the world simply runs on international trade. (Would you like a diet without pepper or nutmeg, or a house without chrome faucets or copper plumbing, both metals being mined abroad?) Yes, we can try to make that trade fairer, and that includes countries like Japan opening their market to US products. But retreating into our shell and 'buying local' is not the way to go about it.'

This letter was much discussed in voluntary simplicity circles. Most down-shifters feel they would be better off with *less* foreign trade, allowing people in rich and poor countries to produce more of what they need.

> The industrialised fourth of the world uses fifteen times as much paper, ten times as much steel and twelve times as much fuel as the rest of the world. American houses are twice as big as they were forty-five years ago; we have more shopping centres than high schools; we drink more soft drinks than tap water. In our time-starved lives we turn to environmentally expensive conveniences: prepared food, disposables, clothes dryers and kitchen appliances. We're using up nature.
> · Cecile Andrews in *The Circle of Simplicity*.

Other critics of VS say it is only relevant in the prosperous US and Canada. Elsewhere too few people could manage any sort of financial independence before their normal retirement age. And who, apart from North Americans, would want to discuss their spending habits with strangers in a study circle? Cecile replies that even if this movement were only for the well-off it would still be worthwhile. 'But VS goes deeper: it is an attempt to redefine what the good life is; we all need to be a part of this conversation.'

But what is the good life? For Arnie it means: 'Family; community; self-made entertainment; dedication to one's passionate goal.' Wasting energy is, for him, incompatible with that good life, hence the importance of repairing the oven instead of buying a new one, staying at home in your family or community instead of restlessly seeking entertainment elsewhere. Arnie is convinced that 'unless we in the North do not quickly spread the word to the South that life is more fulfilling when one lives simply, we will not have breathable air, drinkable water, food fit to eat or sunshine fit to bathe in. Try to imagine two billion Chinese living and consuming as we do!' Arnie's favourite quotation is from Lao-Tzu: 'He who knows enough is enough will always have enough.'

Downshifting Britons

Soon after Polly Ghazi and Judy Jones published *Downshifting: The Guide to Happier, Simpler Living*, giving a British slant to the VS idea, their book had enough mainstream appeal for recommendation in the Mind and Body section of a national book club. Where the USA leads, Europe follows. Journalists Ghazi and Jones show that even in Britain, less affluent than the United States, there is a growing urge to downshift amongst people who have altered their lifestyles to provide a higher quality of life. They tell of Daniel and Bel who gave up the rat race to run a five hectare smallholding in Wales, of Paul who gave up property development to retrain as a counsellor, and many others.

Ghazi and Jones quote British research by the Henley Centre for Forecasting in 1996, suggesting that one working person in eight had either taken a crucial step towards downshifting or was thinking of doing so. A much higher proportion reported that they were cutting back on spending and were seeking more balance in their lives.

Our own experience confirms the Henley survey. Among our friends we notice a growing distinction between rat-race people and downshifters. In a neighbouring farmer's family, one daughter becomes a high earner, her husband also working, while her sister chooses a simpler lifestyle, a lower salary working for a voluntary organisation, and their younger brother simply drops out and spends his summer road-protesting.

It is easy to poke fun at VS when it becomes an obsession (how many uses for an empty sardine tin?) but we found that Arnie and his friends in Seattle posed questions for us too: how hard are we prepared to work, how much of our leisure and family time are we prepared to sacrifice in order to satisfy artificial 'wants'?

Note

1   We write with great sadness that a few weeks after our last visit to Joe Dominguez and Vicki Robin in December 1996, Joe died. We had wondered why he seemed a bit abstracted and irritable. Nobody told us that he was suffering from terminal cancer.

2

Living together apart

●●●●●●●●●●●●●●●●●●●●●●●●●●●●●●●●●●●●●

One solution for people who dislike the endless cycle of consumption that fuels the global economy, as we saw in the previous chapter, is to put into practice the Green slogan — *Live simply, so that others may simply live*. Another solution is to design your living environment yourself. Simple living is only possible in a correctly designed environment. You cannot conserve heat in a draughty old mansion (The Small School; see Chapter 16). You can't do without a car if there's no other access to the shops (Crystal Waters; see Chapter 7). You can't give your kids the freedom of the streets if cars and lorries drive fast through your neighbourhood (see Chapter 8). Cohousing eases such difficulties. How does it work? A self-selected group chooses to share a site for building their individual homes, or they may retrofit an existing building or group of homes and remove dividing walls and fences to create a common space. The resulting estates, designed and managed by residents, are intentional neighbourhoods, where people are committed to living as a community. The physical design — a common garden and playspace free of cars, a common house for shared meals and meetings, toolshed, laundry and library in common — helps to promote friendliness and neighbourliness.

Living in a cohousing doesn't imply that you have quit mainstream society. It's more of an adaptation. Cohousing has affinities with the wider movement for intentional communities (see Chapters 13, 14 and 15); the basic difference is that each household maintains its financial autonomy and its separate dwelling, thus minimising the pressure of people living too close together. Cohousing satisfies a need we feel for closer community while allowing us that personal privacy we have been brought up to expect.

The cohousing movement began in Denmark in the seventies with a group of friends who found that available housing was not meeting their needs. One of them, an architect named Jan Gudmand-Hoyer, went on to describe their ideas in a national newspaper. The movement spread to Sweden, Germany, Holland, Australia, New Zealand, Canada — and the US where some two hundred projects were finished or being planned in 1997.

Life in a modern consumer society is more isolated and lonelier than life used to be, and many of us wonder if human beings were meant to live like that. Families, until the industrial revolution in the North, were economic units, as they still are in the South. Parents and children worked the farm or shop or weaving shed as a group. In a village the blacksmith lived beside his forge, a grocer lived above his shop and the village postmistress only had to step through from the back room to sell her stamps. Yes, there could be claustrophobia, narrowness of opinion, backbiting and other horrors of village life, but a face-to-face society brought benefits of security, of shared self-reliance, that we, in our isolated apartments and bungalows, still mourn.

Cohousing is a grassroots movement that re-establishes community — albeit a community planned by its members, not one that has grown up over time. Although co-houses are generally somewhat smaller than individual homes, residents find that the provision of shared facilities in the common house and the larger amount of shared grounds an adequate compensation. Cohousers claim that the design of their houses facilitates a higher quality of life.

In this respect it's not new. People have lived in tightly-knit communities for longer than they have lived in isolated nuclear families. Cities originally grew up over time as interlocking communities, like Lombard Street in the City of London where the Italian bankers from Lombardy in the fifteenth century lived and worked. Much city housing was constructed in rows or terraces. Even in the US where individualism flourished earlier than elsewhere, early Philadelphia and early Boston contained streets of row-houses. It is economical to cluster dwellings together and proximity promotes interaction between neighbours.

The separation of work and home began with the growth of transport in the nineteenth century when the well-to-do, later copied by the less well-to-do, went to live in the suburbs. From his suburban house surrounded by its well-kept lawn, the visible sign of his prosperity and his detachment from his neighbours, the male worker travelled to his office leaving the female to perform 'house' work at home. But housework never attained the same prestige.

How to start your own cohousing

The typical cohousing community has 20-30 family homes clustered around a central pedestrian street. Half way along the street is a larger building: the common house. Here residents, if they wish, eat together several times a week, and here they meet to discuss their common concerns and manage the shared enterprise. They may share other facilities in the common house such as office space, workshops, laundries and playrooms.

Planning a new cohousing group in Oakland, California.

A project begins when interested people meet. Typically in the US, they attend a slide show by a cohousing group. Next the group tries to agree on a vision of what kind of community they want to build. 'At this point the going starts to get tough,' says a guide in the cohousing web-site. The search has begun for a site — undeveloped land or an urban site suitable for renewal. 'The group must form a legal entity and contribute money to purchase the site. Then they must find professionals to help them to design their community. Next the group must convince a bank to make them a loan, and find contractors to build. Along the way, the group has to learn to work together. Typically groups make decisions by consensus and become expert at doing it quickly. Many groups put time and effort into how they resolve disputes and handle personality conflicts. They are likely have a range of fun activities together such as camping trips, parties, and potlucks. In the end, their success will be measured as much by the quality of the community they build as by the quality of the buildings.'

You do not have to be deep-Green or an alternative person to live in a cohousing scheme. There are many advantages. Professional or business people love coming home from work to find a communal meal has been cooked for them and their children have been cared for in an extended 'family'. Because of shared meals, parents can spend time with their children that normally is spent cooking and cleaning. Cohousing promotes a large group of surrogate siblings that can meet casually in common play areas. On-site day care and informal baby-sitting between neighbours is easily arranged. For single parents, having other adults to share the events of the day while eating dinner in the common house can be a way out of loneliness. For elderly people, neighbours in the sense they once knew them can be their lifeline.

Retrofit in N Street, Davis, California

The slow, scenic Amtrak train from Seattle rattled into Davis. We found our way to N Street. From the outside you see a row of box-shaped, single-storey, fifties-style houses — pleasant, high-density, neither degraded nor smart. The streets are tree-lined with cars in the driveways. Inside, you enter a different world: a green oasis with zigzag pathways among orange, almond and lemon trees. A twelve-metre bishop pine dominates the garden. Twelve suburban houses and twelve suburban gardens have lost the fences that used to divide them. The resultant garden area is 300 by 30 metres The kids' play area with swings and slides is in the centre. Free-range hens have their own enclosure sheltered with bushes and trees. Only one house, in the middle of the communal garden, remains separated. It is owned by a recluse who refused to join the scheme, but he allowed his fence to be replaced by a black-berry hedge.

We got to know Stuart and Lynette (he's from England, she's Chinese-American) by browsing the Cohousing Network's Internet pages. Cohousers are keen on the Net because it is an ideal way for new groups and potential members to contact each other. N Street's own site gives the e-mail address of a contact person for visitors. That's Stuart.

Davis is the right place for cohousing. This Californian university town was the original home of the anti-war movement. The city council was 'greened' in the seventies. Since then the students have been running the bus system (they even drive the buses which include red London double-deckers still marked: Number 13, Golders Green via Strand and Charing Cross); there are wide cycle lanes though not as well used as those in Holland. Like Maleny in Australia (see Chapter 11) Davis is a town of co-operatives — an artists' co-operative, housing co-operatives, students'

> Most Americans don't know their neighbours. If you ever think the people over the wall seem like nice folks and wish you could get to know them better, there are things you can try. Options range from just asking them over for coffee once in a while to organising a neighbourhood association with street parties and potlucks. Or you can go all the way and take the fences down and start living as a community.
> · Stuart Staniford-Chen in *Urban Ecology*.

co-operatives, day-care co-operatives, business co-operatives, a big food co-operative and bakery. The presence of so many co-operatives give an underlying feel to the town of sympathy with and support for many of the visions that Living Lightly people are trying to establish. If you believe that hemp should be grown as a crop for building, clothing, soap and its many other uses, you can open a shop without hassle in Davis, as someone has done.

Lynette says with affection that Cohousing doesn't make things simpler: it makes them more complicated. She points out that the laundry, the workshop, the sauna and the hot-tub (known as the 'cannibal pot') are sited in different spots — in people's private houses or just outside. 'So all the time we have to move around the place, and move around each other. We use the hot tub only in winter, naked. It's designed for five but eleven have squeezed in.' Lynette and Stuart share their home with two singles, a man and a woman. In that respect it's not that much different from any student or young professional workers' household.

N Street residents are proud of their recycling skills. The hot tub, the compost bins, the hen house are all constructed from the discarded fence timbers. The common room is simple and utilitarian with Formica-topped tables and assorted trestle-chairs. A bookshelf lines a wall behind the dining tables. This house doubles as living accommodation for two tenants: the upstairs rooms are private.

A member at home in N Street.

Cohousing addresses a number of social trends that have been growing in the last quarter of the 20th century: the time-crunch and stress experienced by all kinds of families as more and more women have entered the workplace, the increasing number of singles (many of whom feel isolated in conventional housing), and the increasing number of people over sixty (many of whom have a need for sociability and mutual support as well as the mobility to move to places where Cohousing is being established). In general... Cohousing constitutes a reaction to automobile-centric development patterns that discourage the kind of pedestrian interaction that used to be the norm in small town and 'urban villages' of the US. Also, for many people, I believe that Cohousing is attractive because it provides a social context in which it is possible to scale down and simplify one's life.

· Don Lindemann, Editor-in-Chief, *Cohousing* (personal communication with the authors).

Our second evening at N Street was a common-meal day and around the table members told us that the good company of these suppers was the best part of living here. It's an economy because buying in bulk and cooking for larger numbers is cheaper. The meals are uncommonly good. Whoever's cooking takes it as a challenge to produce the best.

N Street people are environmentalists; their project has made little demands on energy. Since their houses were already there, they did not have to cut down any trees or build over agricultural land. On the outskirts of Davis, we saw farms being cut up to provide housing estates on the conventional model of a single residence each on its own private lot.

The N Street garden shows permaculture influences (see Chapter 7) even if it is not a model plot. All food wastes go either to the compost bin or to the chickens. Many residents grow as much of their own food (behind their houses or in the common garden) as time allows. The community is dotted with fruit trees. Everyone keeps old lumber and cardboard for re-use. Stuart says: 'We began by re-using our houses, and we are committed to re-using everything else we can. This comes right down to the crockery and cutlery in the common kitchen: all of it came from thrift stores.'

N Street's pioneering example of a retro-fitted cohousing scheme has inspired imitators, including Ongoing Concerns in Portland, Oregon and Erie

Cohousing communities offer some prospect of reducing their residents' dependence on automobiles. A common expectation of Cohousers is that they will spend less time driving children around the town in search of playmates. Car-pooling, and even car sharing, is a reasonable prospect among households that have already managed the co-operative effort of creating their own housing.

· Bruce Coldham in *Cohousing*, Fall 1995.

St. in Cambridge, Massachusetts. We tried to imagine people pulling down fences in Britain but found it difficult. In London districts, many rows of old workers' cottages could be ideal units for a cohousing, but they have become too valuable. A few years ago, on a green field near our home in Essex, a property developer built six houses. Built to high specifications and selling at £80,000 each, designed for middle managers or high-salaried employees, each has a tiny fenced-in garden, windows staring into the house opposite. Six lawn mowers for six handkerchief-sized lawns. There is neither real privacy nor shared space. The site is euphemistically called 'The Paddocks'.

In N Street the houses had little value to start off with. Stuart is convinced that in the US the example can be more widely followed. 'You don't have to do it all at once: just get started by buying or even renting the house next door and taking the fence down.'

N Street members include several university people who find its arrangements ideal. Marco bikes to his job on campus in the bio-chemical laboratory. He searched desperately for housing until he found at N Street the lifestyle he always wanted: 'The nuclear family thing was never fulfilling for me.' His girl friend lives in a nearby housing co-operative. He says the amount of chores

Where fences used to be: the common garden at N Street, Davis.

Another view of the N Street cohousing.

in a cohousing is about the same as in a private apartment unless you volunteer for more. Not content with the common garden, he rents some space in the community garden at the end of the street.

We offered to help Brian and Laurie Rivers who were rebuilding their house, almost doubling its size to 650 square metres, adding a bedroom and a big loft where they were storing dozens of boxes of accumulated objects — just like all of us out there in the mainstream. Now they have the largest house in the group, with a spacious open-plan sitting room and L-shaped kitchen, leading to a dining area and adjoining office space. An orange tree and vines are outside the back door and children from the whole group are playing outside.

Brian and Laurie say the drawback of cohousing is the time-consuming meetings which they *ought* to attend once a week, though it is not compulsory. Committee work takes three hours every month. Laurie is the community's treasurer and he's the one-man committee for fixing things. They were given a two-year lease in 1990 on condition they tore down their fence. Three years later the group all bought their houses; Brian has a thirty-year mortgage and borrowed separately for the improvements.

It was late November. Coloured lights already adorned the Davis downtown shopping area. Brian and Laurie were preparing recycled Christmas gifts: the N-Street custom is to give new gifts inside the family but recycled ones for everyone else in the community. These gifts are wrapped and numbered and people draw lots. On the Saturday before Christmas there's a dessert potluck, at Easter, a potluck breakfast and Easter-egg hunt. In summer there are open-house tours, and celebrations for the anniversaries of the fence-tearing. There is a back-to-school ritual, an Equinox celebration, a Day of the Dead at Halloween with people telling stories about dead friends, a Thanksgiving dinner. These rituals and celebrations grew up spontaneously. 'We take part or not,' said Laurie. 'Usually we do.' Brian and Laurie like to attend most of the common meals; there are fifteen a month.

Children love this extended-family living but parents can have reservations. Brian and Laurie, perhaps the most conventional members here, complain that their ten-year-old girl had too many distractions and too few boundaries. They find they need to schedule family time — they like family bike rides — so they can be alone as a unit. There was a lot of discussion about whether kids should have the right to wander anywhere, and compromises were arranged, leaving some private areas out of bounds. N Street has sixteen children under eighteen among thirty-five adults. Half are from parents now separated and spend weekends out of the community with their other parents.

Brian and Laurie find living in N Street cheaper: their water bills are only a third of the mainstream average. 'We value used things over new things: nurse our old car instead of replacing it, save wood pieces for heating: most of our stuff is re-used.'

Kevin Wolf is the founding father of N Street: it was his perseverance and shrewdness over money that turned the houses from rented properties to permanent community assets. An alert, confident man aged forty, with a dark, trimmed beard, Kevin is proud of having used capitalism to develop a non-capitalist community, bending and subverting its cumbersome rules, growing almost surreptitiously. He studied theoretical ecology at the Davis campus.

The modern, single family detached home, which makes up 67 percent of the American housing stock, was designed for a nuclear family consisting of a breadwinning father, a homemaking mother and two to four children. Today less than one quarter of the US population lives in such households. Rather, the family with two working parents predominates, while the single-parent household is the fastest-growing family type. Almost a quarter of the population lives alone and this proportion is predicted to grow as the number of Americans over the age of 60 increases. At the same time, the surge in housing costs and the increased mobility of the population combine to break down traditional community ties. These factors call for a thorough re-examination of household and community needs and the way we house ourselves.
· Kathryn McCamant and Charles Durrett, *Cohousing: a Contemporary Approach to Housing Ourselves.*

Now his vision goes far beyond N Street. He sits on the board of the Davis food co-operative and runs a Water on Line page on the Internet to get citizens' input for solving California's water problems. Information is power, he says. 'If people knew what was going on they wouldn't put up with it'. When the banks' rules stood in the way of the group's property acquisition in N Street — forbidding borrowed down-payments — Kevin got the members to pass the money to their relatives who would then 'gift' it, which made it eligible.

The development of N Street was not originally planned — it simply happened. In 1986, Kevin's new partner, Linda Cloud, was able to buy the neighbouring house (number 724). However, the seller also owned number 732 and, worried about his property values, persuaded Kevin and Linda to put option money down on 732 as part of the purchase agreement on 724. Subsequently, they were to buy 732 also; it was already occupied by tenants who were interested in the nascent community.

At this point, other people became excited about the project and began a pattern that has continued ever since: buying or renting adjacent houses on the block, taking down the fences, and joining in the fun. Fence-tearing-down parties became a community institution. Linda read Kathryn McCamant and Chuck Durrett's book *Cohousing*, and said: 'Wow! That's what we are!' Kevin says: 'That's when the vision started. Once you can name something you have power. There was no Cohousing in the US at that time. We contacted the authors who came to a slide show at the Village Homes co-operative in Davis. This was 1989. A developer went too and that was how Muir Commons, the first Cohousing, got started.'

Kevin wants N Street to grow. He plans to turn buildings at the edge of the property into apartments, with a mini-common-house, increasing the membership. He believes in high density living as an ecological necessity. These radical ideas are becoming more widely accepted as even in the enormous spaces of America, ribbon development is ruining natural environments and decimating the remaining wilderness. Kevin says: 'California must stop converting agricultural land into housing units. I'm in a minority on this and people want to stay as they are. I'll take it step by step as I always have. In the end this whole area could be a Cohousing. A community like ours should operate as a bank, lending or buying shares, allowing people to put down money on new houses or new storeys, paying off the mortgages with rentals. Garages could be converted into apartments. When people have access to capital they get rich.'

A text-book design at Doyle Street

The cohousing concept reached North America in the late eighties. Two architects, Kathryn McCamant and Chuck Durrett, who had visited the Danish communities, began touring the US and Canada giving slide shows about this new way to live. They founded the Cohousing Company in Berkeley, California, to promote the concept and advise new groups. They wrote the only comprehensive text book: *Cohousing: A Contemporary Approach to Housing Ourselves*. Then they put their theories into practice and rebuilt Doyle Street as a cohousing community with twelve residential units. The site, an abandoned factory in Emeryville, a district of Oakland, California, could not have been less promising.

A brewery dominates the straggly street of anonymous, sprawling factory and office blocks, a street barely humanised by a cafe and a few shops. At first sight the cohousing complex looks industrial too, a set of box-like structures with corrugated tin sides painted blue. When you drive in the effect is more domestic: two L-shaped levels with neat front doors, flowers in pots and shrubs: an oasis of domesticity. A dog wanders around; there are scattered children's toys on the paving stones.

We are going to stay with Joanni Blank whom we've met through the Internet. After the homespun, recycled interiors at N Street, her apartment seems luxurious with white fitted carpets, soft armchairs, gleaming bathroom. The common house at Doyle Street is more upmarket too; wine and sherry appear at the common evening meal. Table cloths are in use. This is cohousing middle-class style.

The text-book design at Doyle Street Cohousing.

Chuck and Kathryn are lively and sociable and laugh a lot. 'Our motivation for doing that book was that we wanted to live this way. We were members of a dining club in San Francisco in which we ate by turn at each others' houses to save the chores. More and more we came up against the frustrations of young couples with children when both parents work. We had to find a way of sharing without compromising privacy.'

After their year's study in Denmark of the system known as *bofaellesskaber,* Chuck and Kathryn coined the word cohousing. Now Chuck finds the lifestyle works for him: 'It actually facilitates my individualism. I play water polo two nights a week: that is freedom.' When he is out at the pool, Kathryn and their five year old daughter are surrounded by neighbours who are also friends. They also cite the cost saving when energy use is properly designed. At Doyle Street, Chuck estimates that people's living expenses are between $100 to $200 a month less than if they lived separately.

A drawback often cited by critics of cohousing is that it can take years to get a project off the ground. Not so, says Chuck, who is definitely an optimist. He believes that the skills needed to co-operate develop during the difficult preliminary planning period. He cites a Danish failure when the co-housers moved into a ready-made site; after six months the project collapsed because the group had never bonded.

Joanni Blank met us at the railway station in her small car. She herself is small, red-haired (not natural); the vivid and varied life she later described had rubbed off the hallmarks of her age. For her, cohousing is a step into a new kind of relationship, intimate and uninhibited. To look at, she could have been anyone; she turned out to be a sex therapist and writer who has become a crusader for the joys of masturbation. Not that Joanni sees cohousing as necessarily linked with sexual habits, but she points to a relationship between sexual and social inhibition.

That perspective makes her less optimistic than Chuck and Katie about the future of the movement because, in her view, most people are not ready for the intimacy and co-operation involved. 'People don't necessarily see intimacy as desirable. They are fearful of connecting with each other, afraid to get close. If somehow people could *try* it! My sex stuff is not scary: it could help. There is also the class problem: people have this American ideal of going up in the world, having their own house with four walls, not to have ever again to share a room with their little sister.' In a wider context, Joanni sees cohousing as 'not turning away from society but a balancing act to stop us going nuts with the global economy.'

Joanni wears the COYOTE tee-shirt shirt of the prostitutes' union: Call Off Your Old Tired Ethics. She trained in health education and worked in family planning. In women's groups she got involved with sex counselling, learning on the job. 'We trained them how to masturbate, eventually trained a bunch of therapists how to do it.' She obtained her licence in sex therapy. Dealing with clients, Joanni came up against problems when she told woman to buy sex toys. She approved of vibrators but found most places which sold them 'gross'. So she opened a more congenial store where women could browse unthreatened and unembarrassed. We visited. The atmosphere is open and genial. Plexi-glass stands display the various sex-toys grouped in subject areas. The carpet is soft grey, the assistants female and friendly. Joanni insists that sex toys should be a universal pleasure. Meanwhile there are only two other stores like this one in the USA. She would like to sell a franchise in the UK if we could find a suitable woman to run the store: we have not yet succeeded.

Showing that we were less inhibited than Joanni's image of us, we shared our first hot tub with Chuck, Joanni and friends. The fibreglass, electrically-heated tub, which belongs to everyone, is on the roof of the apartment block, behind a discreet wooden fence. They were worried that we might object to being naked. We said sniffily that we had been 'skinny dipping' while they were all at kindergarten. It wasn't a cold night — a Californian November is like an English April — and we lowered ourselves into the hot water with relief. And then the magic happened. There are few things more relaxing than constantly hot water, the gentle chat of new friends and the stars above. We stayed in too long for first-timers and afterwards felt faint for a few minutes. Then, we slept deeply and peacefully as Joanni said we would.

We helped prepare that evening's common meal in a well-designed modern kitchen, separated by a high ledge from the community room. The whole complex has an upmarket but unfussy air, as suitable for conviviality as for business. The shared sitting room has good quality pine chairs and expandable tables that serve many configurations of diners or conference members. There is room for all seventeen adult members, their one teenager and four children. At one end, settees are arranged before a TV and video. A wall of bare brick and glass separates the room from the communal workshop/bicycle shed. Potted plants are vigorous and well-watered. A wooden staircase goes up to a children's play area. People say the workshop should have been smaller; it is under-used because the group can afford outside labour for its odd jobs and construction projects. Even the cleaning of the common house is done by a paid person.

There is no guest room, no teens room, no hobby room — as there are in many other cohousing projects. Most of the members here are busy professionals. The site has no space for a garden: just a kids' sandbox under the stairs. Two dogs and five cats.

We were not the only foreigners sniffing around cohousing projects. Graham Meltzer from Brisbane University was researching the environmental sustainability of cohousing. He showed us the results of his questionnaire for Doyle Street: people were concerned about the environment but did not support the Sierra Club and had not made a mission statement; site steward-ship scored well because they had recycled an existing building; high density of occupation was also a plus point, while transport scored badly because nearly everyone went to work, and to shop, by car. Plenty of bicycles were in the shed but rarely used; buses were inconvenient. There is no formal car-pool but some sharing is done. Energy: there is no solar or wind power though wiring has been done for solar batteries. Few people care about water use: there is no low-pressure showering, no mini-flush loos and no grey water recy-cling. People refuse to turn down the water heating level. There is no policy for organic produce in common meals.

None of this adds up to a positive image for environmentally friendly living. But we felt that that the cohousers had taken some positive steps, particularly in terms of their personal relationships. Asked about 'relation-ships' Joanni says: 'The community isn't as bonded as I hope Oakland will be (a new cohousing project she hopes to join). We had a retreat once and every-body hated it.' Joanni tells us that most people at Doyle Street don't see cohousing as part of a social change movement. 'We don't talk about politics or religion: I think we should.' She, Chuck, Kathy and one or two other ideal-ists are the exceptions.

Yet there are important 'family' aspects to this community. There's a 'grab-bag' annual gift party around New Year and a Thanksgiving dinner. Around fifteen people and some kids attend most of the three common meals a week. Michelle the teenager is the only real vegetarian. Meat is on the menu on some evenings but there is always a vegetarian version or alternative.

Once a month is work day for maintenance; the maintenance committee decides between gutter or oven cleaning, patio washing down, furniture in the common room, etc. Everyone must sign up for three work days a year and there's always one 'coach' who co-ordinates and buys materials.

We saw one of the great benefits of community in the old-fashioned sense, sad though it was. Margaret, a divorced woman in her sixties, is suffering from terminal liver cancer. She has elected to stay in her apartment for as long as she can. Her neighbours run her errands. They are not her 'blood' family but they are fulfilling that role. Margaret is going through her illness with a touching dignity.

Doyle Street is a community catering for individuals. An eccentric Chinese member lives alone, his room barely furnished, piled to the ceiling with old magazines. Joanni says: 'He doesn't know he doesn't belong — so he belongs.' Judy's marriage broke up and she could no longer afford the larger apartment on the first floor so she swapped with Stephanie who has moved to the ground floor. She finds living alone is so much easier in Doyle Street than it would be elsewhere. There's one fundamentalist Christian, one Republican. Pets are the most divisive issue. Joanni says that 'Not enough privacy' is people's commonest fear when joining but it is rarely realised.

To live in cohousing involves meetings. The Doyle Street Condominium Association meets monthly over supper in the common house. Decisions are taken by consensus. For the meeting we attend, the dining room tables, made of extendable teak, have been joined together to form an impressive board room surface. Boxes of bought-in pizzas are provided, which people eat as they arrive.

Joan arrives, very confident as chairman; makes no apology for being late. A quorum has now assembled. Joan, just in from her professional work, seems irritated at first at having more 'business' to do at home. But soon the mood lightens; people laugh and wise-crack. Affection and mutual trust surface: there is, after all, a community here. At the end they all agree it was a good meeting. Chuck says to us: 'Good meetings happen when the people who take part don't like meetings.'

A covered street at Windsong

Fans of the growing cohousing movement enthuse over Windsong, near Vancouver, Canada. It has taken five years in the planning but now it's up and running with thirty members in thirty units and a waiting list.

Windsong at first sight looked like any other housing development. The pine-hilled farmland had been bulldozed for sprawling housing developments which stretched for kilometres, neither beautiful nor ugly — 'ticky-tacky boxes' of Bob Dylan's song. From the highway you saw a small apartment block: a large building of yellowy brick, a visitors' parking lot, a glass door with a list of names and unit numbers to be dialled for admission.

We called Jerry Kilganan's number. As she led us through a spacious entrance lobby, the differences became apparent. Although the common kitchen still lacked tiles and cupboards, the communal dining room was already in use. Jerry said the common meals were already a total success, with a 'pot luck' every evening. Sometimes everybody came, the other night only half a dozen. When the kitchen is finished, regular meals will be cooked for whoever signs up.

Jerry, a retired social worker, is Windsong's treasurer and a member of the governance team. She said she enjoyed the inter-generational aspect of living here. She showed us the craft room, the children's playroom, the teenagers' room, and then we walked down one of the two covered streets — Windsong's main showpiece. Balconies, street lights, tables and chairs in the street give the impression of convivial small town in southern Europe. House fronts are painted in pastel shades. Steeply sloping glass frames form the street's roof; the concrete underfoot feels soft and silent. This idea of glassing in the main street was first tried in Denmark and it works extremely well. Everyone is proud of it. The street is cold in late November, and reported very hot in summer. Cost restrictions excluded levered windows which could have regulated the climate.

Windsong sits on a rise overlooking a stream which has now been flooded by the action of beavers. This is a conservation area; we soon understood why the scheme was built as a single building with underground facilities. The environment authorities had stipulated that the cohousing must be separated from this special area — which restricted the project to using only a quarter of the two and a half hectare site, forcing the planners to go underground at a higher cost. Only a quarter of a hectare is left over for the community garden, as yet uncultivated.

Kimron Rink's workshop adjoins the underground car park. He is a young urban ecologist who runs a design company. He is a 'mentor' at the Insight Out team at Virtual High (see Chapter 17) and he is so enthusiastic about cohousing that he intends to set up more schemes with more emphasis on sustainable energy, water use and waste. 'The next generation of cohousing will have proper eco-planning from the start, with solar and wind energy using heat pumps to store summer sunshine for winter, biological waste purification, greenhouse window-boxes, etc.' He is glad the environmental restrictions forced Windsong into its compact and layered shape which has a lighter footprint than a more spread-out plan.

Howard Staples, a radio engineer, occupies an attractive two-room apartment. In his open-plan sitting room you see out frontwards into the street and back, over his balcony, to the trees overlooking the river. With two small children, Howard is enthusiastic about his new life at Windsong. He looks forward to a share of a common vegetable garden. 'I've done enough lawn mowing in my life, just to make the garden look nice for the neighbours.' In their old home the kids often used to be bored; now they were out of the apartment sixty percent of the time. 'My daughter chooses her own baby-sitter.'

Howard found a negative side of cohousing in differences over parenting philosophies which led to behaviour not approved by all. Another was the immense effort and risk incurred by a limited number of founding members.

Ten families had put the bulk of their life savings into a venture that could have foundered at any moment over planning difficulties or unforeseen technicalities. 'And then what happens is that each lot of new people coming in is more conservative in their ideas because they have to save money.' Options for the future, like installing levered windows over the covered streets, may have to wait a long time for this reason. However, Howard suggested that risk problems could be minimised by teaming up with a developer — a practice that may grow as public housing funds dry up.

Like most cohousers, Howard believes some sort of communal living will become inevitable in his lifetime as mainstream society runs short of food, housing and energy. 'People living here are slightly ahead of others in lifestyle patterns: one third of the families are vegetarians; many get the New Road Map Foundation newsletter on voluntary simplicity.'

Howard said the group ended up 'more communal than when it started.' The underground parking lot now doubles as a kids' skateboard rink. 'Being under one roof has made a big difference: we use our common rooms, including the laundry, much more than at the Bainbridge Island cohousing where people have to go outdoors to reach the common rooms. People here can linger after meals and talk. Life is easy and good — we have ballroom dancing.'

On that upbeat note we left cohousing. Still in an experimental stage, it remains a solution for those with at least some capital or steady income. It is still something of a luxury for salaried people, although some rental cohousing schemes have been started. As more successful projects are completed, newcomers have more examples to imitate. Because cohousing involves no radical lifestyle change, its ideas can be adopted by those who are prepared to take some steps towards a living lightly society. In the next two chapters we look at solutions undertaken by radicals who as individuals or groups are prepared to go much further.

3

Squalor and magic

●●●

So far, we have been in the company of moderates, mostly middle class, who've taken one step into a new culture of living more lightly. We now move into more radical territory. Two British groups, one rural and one urban, reclaim an ancient right of access to land which the industrial society has taken away. In a secluded wood in Somerset, England, we've shared the adventures of settlers at Tinkers Bubble; and we've pitched our tent in a communal squat on a derelict site owned by the Guinness brewery in central London, ironically called, after the Guinness slogan, Pure Genius. Both groups want to expose and defy the unjust restrictions on the use of land and establish that citizens have a basic right of access to land; both groups make their point by living their lives according to their beliefs.

At the centre of each venture is an intellectual with the leadership qualities to move people to action. Simon Fairlie, a journalist who has been active in road protests and served as an editor of *The Ecologist*, is a founder member and permanent resident at Tinkers Bubble. George Monbiot, an investigative writer and broadcaster on the global misuse of land, inspired a movement of direct action called The Land is Ours (TLIO) and was one of the originators of the Pure Genius squat.

Most land in Britain is inaccessible, both to a rambler and a would-be rural settler. Planning laws, originally designed to stop the invasion of the coun-

---

The land is our most fundamental resource. All of us depend on it for homes, food and livelihoods, a sense of place and a sense of belonging. It is our common inheritance. Even though we no longer possess it, all of us are affected by the way it is used. Today just a tiny handful of landowners and developers decide how the land is employed. As a result development takes place not for our benefit but for theirs. Our role is to highlight ordinary people's exclusion not only from the land itself but also from the decision making processes affecting it, and to campaign and facilitate other people's campaigns to put this right.

· The Land is Ours, Web Page at www.envirolink.org/uk/orgs/tlio/

tryside by urban developers, also serve to keep off benign initiatives, including low-cost organic farming by young people who want to live on their land and experiment with low-impact habitation, using local materials for houses that blend with the landscape. The land is effectively reserved for industrial farmers who are involved in the destructive processes which the Living Lightly reformers seek to mend. If you want to farm a piece of land sustainably and settle on it, living lightly and building lightly, can you solve the problem by buying it? You can buy a one-hectare (2.4 acres) field for about £5,000 but you cannot build a house and live on it, unless your land is already used for residential purposes or designated 'development land' — which costs up to £100,000 or more a hectare when it becomes available. If you erect a wooden hut or a tipi on your *own* land you are 'changing its use' from agricultural to residential and the planners will defeat you.

Tinkers Bubble

Simon Fairlie and a group of friends — travellers, writers and road protesters — bought ten hectares of woodland, four hectares of apple orchard and two hectares of terraced land near Yeovil in Somerset — on a hill named Tinkers Bubble after the stream that rises in the woods. Their intention was to build low-impact housing and live there by harvesting the Douglas fir, replacing felled trees with native trees appropriate to the site, coppicing the hazel and earning additional income from larch, vegetables, apples and livestock. But local residents in an area of prosperous rural retreat feared these unconventional newcomers. The result: the Tinkers Bubble people were refused planning permission and have had to live from month to month in temporary shelters with the legal status of campers.

Dorothy writes: With Walter away in India I paid a first visit to Tinkers Bubble, determined to have no preconceived notions, although dreading the hardships of camping in November. Tinkers Bubble had been established for eighteen months and was preparing for its second winter. Simon said on the phone to give him some notice as he wants to 'warm the bender'. What did he mean? Will I find a welcome in such a frugal place? I've also read press cuttings about local hostility — a pub owner was quoted complaining the Tinkers Bubble women would sneak into his lavatories. Was I heading for a suitable place for our research — a success story, viable, sustainable and replicable?

The village of Norton, Somerset is NIMBY (Not In My Back Yard) country, manicured lawns, grey stone houses, nobody about. Where do the inhabitants of English villages live? I accost a tweedy pedestrian with Labrador at heel, who answers, 'Oh them? You won't find *them*. Swinging up in the trees somewhere, I expect.' In the discouraging dusk the fir trees look threatening; the wood is huge. Where is the camp? I take my torch and find a farm house sideways to the lane with nine cars parked in the drive and a deserted air. A rosy-checked countrywoman, straight out of a TV butter advertisement with matching Archers' accent, tells me: 'Too far up, m'dear. You'm must look fer 'em further down.'

Setting off with bundles of bedding into gloomy woods, I am glad to have Leah, my German Shepherd; any malefactor won't know that her size is in inverse proportion to her courage. She growls. Someone coming downhill through the pines, carrying two jerry cans, asks my name, says I am expected and offers to take my bedding roll. The gradient becomes one in four. Michael, who cannot be more than a few years younger than me, is impervious to the slope. We climb past a couple of tethered goats and a small orchard with grazing sheep beneath the trees and terraced vegetable gardens. The apples from the orchards are nearly all stacked in boxes. The place looks tidier than other communes we've visited where litter lies scattered like confetti.

The Bubblers wanted to pitch their tents and build their houses next to their terraced gardens down in the valley. Local people objected so they have to live on top of the hill, out of sight. As we climb, a couple of fires glow through the dark. The wood seems no longer threatening but welcoming. Some dozen or so tents and benders, the open-air kitchen and a tarpaulined lean-to are set among fir trees. Michael shows me where I am to sleep. It is a yurt — a modern yurt made by an English craftsman following traditional nomads' designs. I've only ever seen pictures of yurts in *The National Geographic*. It is circular, made of white canvas with a dozen mattresses placed around the walls and worn carpets and rugs covering the plastic ground sheet. In the domed top, plastic panels serve as windows. A wood stove made from a recycled gas canister is already lit. On a plank stands a jug of spring water and a bowl of apples. A squat candle emits a warm orange light. A few minutes to hang my clothes up on the struts of the yurt, stoke the stove and drink a glass of spring water and I feel as though, if not in another country, at least in another time.

The quiet is overwhelmed by the irruption of four children, who make as much noise as forty: Karen, who will be twelve on Sunday, her ten-year-old brother Michael and two small sisters of eight and three, Rebecca and Tasha. The children are friendly — kids who live with lots of adults and don't have much canned or plastic amusement. Karen is delighted to see me, especially as I have brought a tin of chocolate biscuits. The children proceed to finish the biscuits while Karen explains about the Bubble. She has obviously done this many times before. Between mouthfuls of chocolate, she says, in the tone of a patient tour guide: 'We came here in winter two years ago. We didn't have a good apple crop that summer but we did this year. We had to store them. We've turned an old reservoir into an apple store. Now we've made shelves. My Mum is Louise. Andy is my Dad. His name is Andrew but you mustn't call him that. My Dad's family are OK about us living up here. My Mum's family aren't. My Mum's mum won't even talk to her. I love living here. I can walk around as much as I like. I always hang around with adults. Only about two of my friends from school come up here and they really love it.'

The children drift off and I go out of the yurt into a starlit evening — no one around. Someone has left a pile of split logs outside the yurt and I feed the burner. Then Michael (who helped me up the hill) comes and sits inside on one of the mattresses and talks about himself, which he does readily enough as if he were speaking about someone else. He has a grizzled beard and wears a woolly hat. Why are woolly hats a uniform in Green circles? Michael doesn't consider himself as hippie or ex-hippie. He was a businessman and a tea-planter in Sri Lanka, now he describes himself as a gardener. When his business folded in the seventies' recession — 'I had time to reflect, and I became a sort of recluse.' He fulfils a role of wise elder in the growing extended family here.

Michael is in revolt against the way land is managed in Britain, which he sees as an evolution of the industrialisation of agriculture in the eighteenth, nineteenth and twentieth centuries. 'People have become redundant: we're at a point where machines make other machines and redundant populations are stuck in the cities. We have got to repopulate the countryside. Tinkers Bubble is an attempt — but it's a series of compromises because we must not offend our neighbours, the community is too poor to do it any better way and we haven't money to build proper houses. In Sri Lanka, when someone marries the community builds them a house.' Michael is convinced many people would live in rural simplicity if they were given the right education, help and gentle encouragement. He sees travellers and road protesters as representing the future.

It is sometimes difficult to dispel the feeling that the countryside lobby is collaborating with the development industry in carving Britain into two: an urban zone within which almost any kind of development is permitted somewhere, and a rural zone where (in theory) nobody but large-scale farmers are allowed to do anything... Neither camp seriously confronts the question that lies at the root of the whole problem: what is it that makes modern development so unbearable and destructive that we are placed in the impossible position of wishing to flee our cities and yet having to fence off our countryside?
· Simon Fairlie, *Low Impact Development*.

Over the four days I spend up on the hill, I often watch Michael, wearing his woolly hat, carrying Tasha, the youngest Chant child, on his shoulders. The grubbiness that some of the Bubblers affect has not touched him. He stays clean in a situation where every drop of water has to be carried up a steep hill and heated in a black pot swinging over an open wood fire. He spends some of each week in his flat in Bristol.

First impressions of yurt life: the floor is well-insulated and the top loftier than my bedroom at home. The lack of running water disquiets me.

Keeping clean is not something that bothers Karen's mother Louise. At first sight I find her alarming — a practically shaven head with three tiny pigtails knotted with beads dangling over her forehead. A couple of missing side front teeth make her look older than her thirty years. She has a round, jolly face and is dressed in several brightly-coloured cotton layers ending in black tights and heavy boots, obviously sensible when you live out of doors as much as she does. She has black-rimmed fingernails and a smell I remember of mountain villages in India where the cold traps old sweat into an aroma rather like tobacco. Not actually unpleasant — gamy.

She sits chatting with Steve and Simon around an open fire under a tarpaulin where the Bubblers do the cooking. A wooden dresser stands out of doors with a fishing net suspended behind it full of tomatoes and onions. The tarpaulin keeps out rain, some wind but not the cold. It is picturesque and surprisingly practical. The lean-to also doubles as larder with metal cabinets and wooden cupboards opening to disgorge loaves of bread, bottles of home-made pickle and margarine in catering quantities.

The blackened pot pivots gently on its chain and the stew bubbles. Louise generally cooks but tonight she's off to the pub with her girl friend Claire and Steve will cook. The dish is home-grown vegetables, well-spiced and seasoned followed by a rabbit that one of them ran over that morning. The home-grown spinach was tossed in butter. I have forgotten, since I so rarely eat them, the taste of freshly gathered organic vegetables.

A lanky grey bitch appears, but the two bitches don't fight. The Lurcher, Star, and Leah sniff bums, wag tails and wait for food as if they have known one another for years. This is surprising since Star has ten three-day-old puppies in Steve's tent. Is this strange amity between the bitches an augury for human relations up on the hill?

There are five men, two women and four children and a shifting population of visitors. I ask why the sex ratio is so skewed. Various opinions are offered. 'No bathroom puts people off,' says Louise. The Bubblers own a ram pump for bringing water up to the site but haven't yet connected it.

Simon disagrees. 'Loads of blokes settle on a farm and then can't find a woman to stop there. I've come to the conclusion, although it is non-PC to say so, that women make nests, men chop down trees. Look at it this way — women have more incentive to bring up kids in an economic environment. Since the Dongas left we have had an unbalanced community.' The Bubblers first arrived with the Dongas, a group of travellers who have adopted a tribal way of life, and the two groups camped together for several months. Tinkers Bubble was founded not only as a sustainable rural settlement but as a place where tribes of travellers and road protesters could rest up.

Claire says that it is all social conditioning. She is a nineteen-year-old road protester who has dropped out of college. She wouldn't mind living up here but 'there is more that needs doing outside. I'm not into farming but protesting. And besides my parents wouldn't approve.'

Claire and Louise leave on their pub jaunt, leaving me with the two Steves and Andy. We sit on logs around the fire and smoke. It feels primeval. I think of all the past generations who have sat around open fires. Andy, the Chant kids' father, is a quiet, watchful man — a contrast to the vociferous Louise. He is concerned over Karen's cough and makes her take an infusion of euca-lyptus leaves and hot water. He doesn't speak to me readily and later I learn that he objects to my taking notes. He has been a bricklayer for ten years but he and Louise now live on Income Support. They are both thirty. I tell Andy how strangely beautiful it seems to live in a tent on top of a hill. He nods. 'I was bought up a Catholic. I don't believe any of it any more but there is a feeling about this place — a sort of magic.' He falls silent.

That night, the three eldest Chant children bring their duvets and share my yurt which could sleep a dozen in comfort. We fall asleep in the warmth and hear the owls hoot. When I wake at four to go out into the stars for a pee the stove is out and the yurt is freezing. I put on two extra sweaters and fall asleep until a gong bangs me awake at 7.30.

'The tea gong,' says Karen, bright-eyed and bushy tailed as kids are first thing in the morning. When I stumble out, not wanting to be the last, I find I am the first after Steve, who has lit the open fire and made tea. Amazingly comforting, a chipped mug of tea at seven-thirty out of doors in November. In daylight the camp is tattier than I had noticed at dusk. Bottle tops and cabbage leaves mixed in with pine needles. Not as bad as a park before the sweepers have arrived but I find that my middle class notions of propriety would prefer to sweep up the litter. I ask whether the paths get muddy in the winter and how do they cook in the lean-to. With difficulty, I'm told. Nobody complains in my hearing about any hardships. Whether it is because I am an outsider or whether it is because that's their social dynamic, I don't yet know.

My first visit to the latrine passes off — what would be the right word —

Samson sharing Simon's snap.

successfully. A pit has been dug and privacy protected by a wattle hedge. The Bubblers dig a pit, use straw to cover individuals' faeces and then fill in and move the shelter on. Everyone pees out of doors. A system that is perfectly environmentally friendly. I feel squeamish that no washing water is obviously in sight around the shit pit but find, next to the cooking lean-to, a basin, water, soap and towel. Hurdles are set up to protect piles of timber, giving the settlement the look of a half-dismantled film set for a Western.

Since their arrival in January 1994, some of the original settlers — Simon, Andy, Louise and Michael — are still here almost two years later. The two Stevens are one year and seven months into the scene. Both are attractive men in their mid-thirties; I wonder about their apparent celibacy. Later I am told by several people that Louise herself forms a barrier which makes it harder for other women settling here; being so dominant she frightens them off. Emma, Simon's girl friend, re-appears on my second day. She is an English graduate of twenty-nine, and a road protester. A vivid, dark woman, who dislikes the media. 'It's not you personally — you are very charming,' she says doubtfully. 'We don't need any more publicity and the less we get the more likely we are to slip through the planning net. How would you like someone asking questions while you are having your breakfast?' Actually I wouldn't mind at all if anyone were genuinely interested but I take her point and resolve to be tactful. Although she doesn't say so, the lack of a bathroom must irk Emma. She has set herself up a little cleaning stall in the marquee that she shares with Simon.

The Bubblers have a sheet of instructions for visitors. The first night's hospitality is free, subsequently, you pay £1.50 a day for food and you're asked to help with work or chores, so on my first morning, after breakfast, I decide to do last night's washing up. A black cauldron is boiled over the fire and two large enamel bowls are set on a U-shaped wooden table with racks to one side and a draining board. There is no soakaway so you have to pour the dirty water into a ditch. Once I start, washing up for twelve people is easier than it looks. Nothing is dried. What happens when it rains, as the U-shape is fully out of doors? No one says.

Something puzzles me after less than twenty-four hours up here: how are people motivated to work after they have walked away from the wage structure? Simon never seems to stop working but the others spend a lot of time just sitting. The Bubblers are not catastrophically lazy — neither are they industrious. It would not have been very time-consuming to have constructed a wooden roof over the washing up area in the months that they have been here. A lot of jobs are left undone because nobody has got around to doing them; most of the apples are harvested but too many are rotting on the ground and will not be usable for cider much longer. This is November: daylight is short but Steve did not emerge from his tent until after ten and then he was going shopping with Louise. Is this a deliberately relaxed response to the protestant work ethic? I would have to be here for longer than a few days to decide. The ram pump has been sitting there, uninstalled for three months because the apples had to be harvested. The pump is the next-but-one item on the communal work programme. The next item is to finish the round house, a wooden structure with a canvas roof for meetings and meals and shelter in bad weather. It has been three months in the building.

I am torn between admiring the amount of time people sit around or stay in their tents just jawing, and anxiety that wood needs to be chopped, laundry folded and paths swept. My days here make me question our own work ethic. Much of what we consider housework does not exist here — no furniture to dust, beds to make, surroundings to prettify. Does that leave everyone longer time for meaningful discussions or purposeful activity? It does not seem to. The level of petty quarrelling appears as high as in a suburban semi: *Why has someone taken my tea strainer? Where's the bloody shovel? Keep those dammed kids quiet.* A disappointment. Emma told Simon, 'I've got to get away. All these people are making me feel mentally ill.'

However, when they are not actually arguing, or cross, everyone at the Bubble speaks charitably of others. When I ask people why they don't work more than two days a week on communal projects they seem to find the question genuinely puzzling. 'We have our own projects to do,' they reply. Tinkers Bubble is not a full-time occupation for everyone.

Every month, the settlers hold a meeting for themselves and any other Tinkers Bubble shareholders who want to come. There are about ten of us. Theo and his lady, who own a wood, listen and make no comments. The meeting begins at noon and continues with interruptions for blazing rows and tea breaks until six. The management plan for a five-year cycle is well thought out and organised. It is written in a big black book kept in Simon's marquee. The committee meeting itself is similar to any other. Animosities surface, hidden agendas are glimpsed but not aired. Some people talk too much. Emma is the chairperson and brooks no time-wasting.

Steve wants to run electricity off a windmill. They have bought one but it is not yet installed. Simon wants to continue with paraffin lamps. Afterwards Steve says: 'I get so mad at Simon. He's a romantic and thinks he is going back to the old ways but he doesn't realise how bloody polluting paraffin is and how benevolent sun and wind power are.' The meeting breaks up without agreement, but after a thirty-minute tea break, resumes as if nothing had occurred. The Bubblers are British bred and educated; however much they want not to be, they are still acculturated to the English formalities. Naturally, the consensus procedure doesn't work as well here as we saw it in a group in Australia which had been together for many years.

I've been sitting outside for a couple of hours and once again my work ethic starts to itch. Already November — why don't the Bubblers finish the round house? It must be so dreary here when the weather is too bad to sit out. Yet they only work on communal projects on Tuesdays and Saturdays. On Saturdays, people who are members of the Trust and who don't live here, and anyone who wants to help, come to work on communal projects. At this rate I can hardly imagine when they will get the round house finished.

Louise says that when some farmers in Malawi were shown a video of life at Tinkers Bubble they roared with laughter. They could not understand how rich Westerners could give up so much. 'I did get depressed last winter,' said Louise, 'and I thought of applying for a council house but then the kids didn't want to leave.' The more I talk with Louise I realise that her brusque manner conceals a kind and loving nature.

We are sitting around the second camp fire when a couple of policemen, in shirtsleeves, helmets tucked under their arms, puff into sight. They have found the trek up the steep hill even harder than I had. The clear, cool sunshine of early November has continued. The policeman are jovial and after a mug of tea, divulge their mission. One of the Bubblers has been seen in a Yeovil factory, rummaging in a skip and removing several cardboard boxes. The factory owner has made a complaint. His main grudge was not that the skip had been rifled but that he was not asked. 'No one minds you lot recycling. You ought to have asked permission.'

Invitations to play ping-pong on the table next to the fire are given and accepted. The elder policeman, Norton's local constable, tells me he has far more trouble with drinking offences than with drug offences. 'People up here are fine.' The two bobbies leave. 'We get on fine with him,' says Simon.

Simon took me to the old apple orchard where the two work horses, a small cob mare and a large shire gelding, are grazing. Simon is besotted with the gelding; he hand feeds it daily and paints its huge hooves with salt water. Finding a blacksmith to shoe a shire horse is difficult in this region. The last one they had charged £70 a set and will not come in winter.

Locals object that Tinkers Bubble spoils their amenities and that if the Bubblers are granted planning permission, many other settlers will descend. The Bubblers argue that their low-impact dwellings without roads or electricity have exactly the opposite effect: they regenerate the land and use it sustainably, living so frugally that other newcomers would be deterred. I believe them. It is unimaginable to conceive of people in large numbers living with such a lack of material comforts. To live as they do, you have to change your mindset and they have.

In the middle of the weekend, I drive to Yeovil with Karen to buy her a birthday present. The contrast between Tinkers Bubble and Yeovil pedestrian shopping area is startling. What *are* all these things in the shops? Who needs them? Two opposing ideologies are present at the same time and today I am not sure which one I admire and want to follow. The shops *are* pretty with their myriad coloured piles of baubles but they are also stuffed with goods superfluous to anything anyone needs. Their seductiveness affects us all, even Karen, so totally different to the consumer-orientated kids that I am accustomed to. I buy her two puppets and a mug with her name on.

Being here reminds me of the summer of 1972 that I spent with my children in a lonely cottage in Snowdonia. I decided not to wash for the whole two-months holiday to see what happened. Our skins and hair regained their natural oiliness. I don't know whether we smelt or not. It was hot and we were bathing in streams and waterfalls every day. It was delightful but Habie got sores round her mouth.

As I walk away through the fir trees I see the two Steves, sitting with mugs of tea around the open fire. The glamour of Tinkers Bubble strikes me once again: the harmony of the benders amongst the trees. Such a lack of physical comfort is at once constricting and liberating. I have brought with me the mistaken idealistic thought that if someone gives up a materialistic lifestyle they give up the moans and groans of day-to-day living. Up there they haven't. In spite of the gentle way people have of expressing themselves, there is a continual undercurrent of personality conflicts.

And I can see a schism in their aims. They want to work the land in a sustainable fashion, yet they do not want constraints. They live in an extended family yet they are not related to one another. The bonds of consanguinity, except for the Chant family, are conspicuously absent. When Emma told me, 'I can't stand people around me all the time,' she was voicing a difficulty that almost every Western-educated person feels. With my puritan Judeo-Christian work ethic, it bothered me that communal work days were only twice a week when there was so much that needed to be done. If they are to succeed the Bubblers must find a solution to the structural problem of living in a group which tries to function without a leader.

By the time this book goes to press the Bubblers are still on site. They remain optimistic. The government has changed and they hope that a new attitude to people returning to the land will evolve. Simon Fairlie, the two Steves and Michael (of the woolly hat) are still there and another single woman, Kate, has joined them with her horse, goat and dog.

Now that there is a proper bathroom made with wooden planks and shingles, Michael hopes more women will join. The problem as he sees it is that the present Bubblers are over thirty, while the new wave of road protesters are much younger. 'Women over thirty are used to having had a job, they are less prepared to share a kitchen and bathroom and do without a washing machine.'

Louise, Andy and the children, who braved out two winters on the hill, still keep their goat and grow their vegetables at the Bubble, but the family is installed in a council house in a nearby village.

The round house is now finished with an upper gallery for guests to sleep and a cooking range for winter cooking.

Simon has had to compromise with his aspirations for minimum technology. The Bubblers now have a share in a portable steam engine so that they can cut planks and use them to sell or for building. They are still hanging on there.

Pure Genius

The saga began on May 5, 1996. The television and the newspapers reported that The Land Is Ours, a new direct-action group, had seized thirteen prime Thames-side acres near the heart of London and set about creating a village to demonstrate green urban living. Several hundred squatters arrived by chartered coach and invaded an empty industrial site in the Conservative flagship borough of Wandsworth. The site had been a gin distillery and oil depot, left flattened and derelict. The owners, the Guinness brewery, were waiting to sell it to a developer for a supermarket and a luxury apartment block, but the project was opposed by the local council and planning permission had not been given. George Monbiot, spokesman for The Land is Ours, was quoted as saying, 'The landowner and the developers have had their chance and they've blown it. Now it's our turn. The market isn't delivering the sort of development people need.'

We have visited the squat a few times. Now we bring a tent and the dog Leah, and stay a few days. We find the main gate closed but visitors are welcome through a small gateway, with signs saying: COME & BE HAPPY, WELCOME HOME, CITIES ARE FOR PEOPLE NOT PROFIT. Above the entrance is Guinness' own slogan PURE GENIUS.

We set up our tent amongst a mass of buddleia bushes, just behind a disused jetty on which someone has started building his house. A new banner invites passing vessels to 'Free Mooring'. Leah can't stop tail-wagging, with six hectares of securely walled land to run around in, several other dogs and no officious people to tell her she should be on a lead. Anarchy feels wonderful.

Eva and Kira inside their bender, made from scrap metal.

The site has an air of a tatty fairground — flags, balloons and painted signs, stone-edged paths marked out amongst the builders' rubble, small circular raised vegetable plots (one or two with a few brave plants donated by well-wishers), a children's play area bright with painted stones and slides and swings.

Permaculture has started in a small way. On the raised beds, the irrigation is cleverly managed with plastic pipes and empty plastic drink bottles. You pour the water in and it seeps through the pipes. Various arches and wire sculptures decorate the area.

Assorted wooden houses are being built from recycled wood, donated timber and what you can find in skips all over town. Stacks of old clothes, piles of furniture, and an assortment of food and building materials have been left at the entrance by well-wishers. Lorries drive up filled with sacks of compost and earth for the vegetable beds. The site dwellers dress in keeping with the fairground image — shaved heads, dreadlocks and plenty of woolly hats although it is full summer.

Green Dave, who walks around in a semi-transparent sarong which allows anyone to see he has discarded underpants, has almost finished his house, built on two levels entirely from scrap wood. Brendan has just finished his own, Indian-style house. A shanty town is growing up. George Monbiot waxes enthusiastic: 'This is what we want to see. These houses are a bit tacky and I would not trust them in a high wind, but they really are low-cost houses for people who would not be housed otherwise.'

The occupation began as a successful publicity exercise but the people it recruited are not operating as theoreticians or agitators: they are citizens of a different society. George has support from many other groups — the Rainbow Tribe, the Dongas, the Men and Women of the Trees at the Newbury Bypass demo, and a score of alternative groups who have made rejection into a way of life. Many call themselves anarchists.

We thought we would be energetically digging permaculture beds or helping paint new buildings, but by the time we have spent a day on the site we have got into the prevailing mood of hanging out. In the event, all we do is talk to people and sneak off to the pub for chips because we find the communal meals inedible — stale bread and a stew of everything (mostly garnered from supermarket skips) thrown in together, which, like a mixture of too many paint colours, ends up brown.

In the gorse bushes behind the roundhouse the compost lavatories have two wooden seats, one for shit and one for urine. The first batch of compost has already been removed, sanitised in its layers of earth and neatly labelled: 'This is all your turds from the compost toilet 26th May 1996'. Instructions on how to turn the pile are added; it will be ready to use in 9-12 months. The toilets only have sheets of plastic instead of walls but like most objects on the site are gaily decorated with splashy designs and flags.

In this tiny, nascent community we find many contradictions. Squalor in the kitchen, and the unpleasantness of the petty thieving. We put down a purse with £30 for a few minutes while we help with the washing up. It disappears. Next morning Green Dave reports that a collection of handcuffs and an alarm whistle, reserved for use in the event of a sudden eviction, have been stolen. Bill says loyally that kids from the town must have been pilfering but Dave thinks some member feeding a drug habit has done it. Later that night, John Pendragon comes to our tent and hands over a jam jar full of copper coins and silver, mostly ten pence pieces. 'We had a whip round for you,' he says. The collection yields £22 and seven pence.

When Twig, in his floral leather waistcoat, blows the conch for sunset, he says he is 'Saluting Muvver earth', just as he did at the Twyford Down road protest and at Glastonbury and at Stonehenge. It is a tender moment and a feeling of peace and sanity settles over the evening. Someone points out a hawk across the evening sky. A little while later Concorde flies overhead on its evening run from New York. The site lies in the flight path from Heathrow; when the aeroplanes are stacked up they come over every one or two minutes. There is a helicopter pad a few hundred metres down the wharf. On the opposite bank is a squat and smug-looking new Sainsbury's store. Next to the Pure Genius site a brand new block of luxury flats lies empty because the rent is unaffordable. The river is dirty and scummy. In the evening we see two herons.

The residents constantly remark how beautiful they find the site which seems an exaggeration for this polluted wasteland. Yet there is beauty: the yellow-flowering gorse, buddleias and the wild rambler roses, the flights of geese, and the long sweep of the Thames. They are seeing the site with their inner eye — not as it is now with areas of crumbling concrete and rusty iron pegs coming out of the ground but as it might be — a village in the centre of a city with food growing, and flower gardens.

Every couple of days the community meets, sitting in the wooden walled roundhouse on salvaged settees or squatting on the threadbare carpets. About forty people are grouped round the central pillar which is decorated with candle holders, its base protected by small stones and fenced by cut poles as if it were a shrine, an effect enhanced by lit joss sticks. The community has endless hassle from its fluctuating and uncontrollable population: there are no enforceable rules in their illegal settlement, and no power to exclude the unwelcome.

The topics go round as personalities clash. A couple of older guys in their late fifties or even more, several heavily pierced teenagers, early twenties and late twenties. A few children wander in and out. Green Dave, who now sports a Crocodile Dundee hat as well as his sarong, tells the meeting: 'We're too diverse to make a single group; we should have little communities grouped around a headquarters and the whole thing should be considered a bio-region.' He argues vehemently in his East London accent. His points are practical. 'We got every class here, middle class and working class. Basically we are all lazy. Let people build something. They can have a mess inside their space. If you mess up outside, you clean up. And you must clean the bogs. Everyone has got to learn everyone else's ways.'

Nobody supports his wish to split up into smaller groups. A local Wandsworth man, a carpenter in his sixties, says with some irritation, 'Get yourselves a time limit for meetings. I've come for the cause. You are all lovely people. Charming all of you but now I am going off to work.' A young girl

Rainbow George tending the stone spiral.

bites her lips, twists her hands and then stands up and makes an inspirational speechette about caring for the earth. The issue of last night's fight is aired and resolved. By the time the meeting breaks up, nothing practical has been decided. It is not easy to work consensus in practice. Pure Genius admits no gurus, no leaders — so things are done at a slow pace without timescales or schedules and hardly any duty rosters.

John Pendragon is a veteran of alternative living and one of the squat's unofficial spokespersons. His waist-length fair dreadlocks are mixed with grey, his multi-coloured clothes reminiscent of the Rainbow tribe of whom he was once a member. He complains that George Monbiot and friends have 'abandoned the baby much too soon.' A movement of intellectuals have set up this audacious and illegal community and then, after a week of fanfare in the media, left it in the lurch.

George tells us later that he and his friends in The Land Is Ours never intended to stay. 'The policy was to let the people on the site do their own thing, while we remained part of the wider community that Pure Genius represented.'

A hundred serious demonstrators settled here in the first week; in the second week these were replaced by the curious, the homeless, the far-out, the drugged, the unstable and the dishonest. However, a small group of genuine communitarians — Brendon from Australia, Anya from Holland, Bill the engineer, Laura and Dan with their two vans and one mobile telephone, the Dragon himself and three or four others — form the nucleus of a community that can survive, at least until eviction day and no doubt beyond, in another place.

Can Pure Genius be a launch pad for an alternative economy? Bill the engineer doesn't think so: alternative economies are always going to be crushed by the mainstream money system — and his view is supported by the way the community lives, marginally and precariously off stale bread and discarded supermarket vegetables retrieved from skips. Most of the citizens of this new polity are on benefit.

John Pendragon, somewhat older than most of the others, has experience of communities over twenty years. He was in the big festivals and the celebrated squats. Once he worked for the Green Party, then he was drawn to animal rights. He sees himself as 'the catalyst in the creative interaction that takes place here,' and reacts strongly against Green Dave's idea of dividing into groups. 'That's just what's wrong with most places,' he argues. He trashes the famous Findhorn community in Scotland (Chapter 14) because he says it costs £100 a week to stay there (actually it costs more). 'And in Tipi Valley in Wales when I was there people started putting fences up. That's the problem. That is what society does: divide and rule. There is a flag flying here on this site which says FREE LAND. What do we mean by free? Once you go over the limit, that is chaos.' The Dragon's arguments go back a long way, to all the peasant revolts of our history, and as such they are unanswerable. 'You start to say "My land — I'll protect it." That's society since the enclosures. Divide and rule.'

The Dragon hopes, claims and declares that this time there *will* be real community. His tone is gentle, prophetic. He is trapped in his story, he wants us to believe in a life that has been a microcosm of anarchist, communitarian, Green-tinged dissent. In his youth he went overland to India, then to South America. He describes himself as a poet and story-teller who had Irish parents. He is convinced that after the period of calm which followed the hippie revolt of the sixties, 'people in the nineties are breaking out again.'

Bill the engineer's house, made entirely of donated off-cuts of planks and salvaged windows, is almost finished: he sleeps in it and it has a lockable front door. He works full-time in the Wandsworth Borough Engineering Department. Exhausted after a day in the office and an evening working on his house, he hunkers down on his floor to talk.

He has prepared a detailed planning application for the alternative eco-use of the Pure Genius site — for a mixed-use area with small enterprises, work-shops, homes with green spaces, cafés, restaurant, theatre. The entire site would be managed on permaculture principles: no private cars, a circular bus route, self-built houses. 'It will be the first of its kind in Europe, with its own energy, sewage treatment. Guinness will get the publicity. Some people in the Council are interested in principle but they keep this squat at arm's length. They could be right: our squat is a protest and a protest is not sustainable.'

Bill has travelled in South America and Eastern Europe, and everywhere found similar aspirations: in his view, the alternative movement is alive and spreading. He is thirty, comes from a small Wiltshire village and considers himself an ecologist by nature and temperament. He wants Pure Genius to show what ordinary people, left to themselves, can do. His idea of an urban community involves permaculture, building with recycled materials, group enterprise, debate, education and integration with the local community. Easy to visualise the ideal; hard to imagine it realised in the present social and political climate.

The site has drawn young people, some confused, others curious, yet others disappointed and a few pursuing their aims with single-mindedness. The only common denominator is their wish for a simpler way to live. But practicalities overwhelm them.

Caroline, with several rings in her nose, is living on the site with her best mate and their two dogs. 'We keep coming and going. I get bored in one place. We had a caravan but someone smashed it.' She thinks she knows who (someone coming off hard drugs) but she won't make an issue of it. 'Might get smashed up myself.' Berenice talks in a whisper and complains that she suffers from irritable bowel syndrome. 'I believe in the site totally. I am a real anarchist. Some days I wake up full of optimism.' Today is clearly not one of those days. 'I veer between misery and happiness. I can't get on with the Council. I have been trying to arrange for a compost delivery. We have not got a vehicle and when I ask they won't lend one.' Her voice drops in despair. 'I wish people would be more helpful.'

Alison is eighteen. Thin, dark and intense. In September she starts a course in performing arts. 'I'll stay here until then. It's the most exciting thing I've ever done.' The idea of eviction obsesses her. 'We have had a meeting to decide where we will be when the bailiffs come. I'll be up one of the trees with a camera. If you have a camera they won't try anything.' She and her father live in a council flat in Kingston. 'I've chosen to live here. It is about sharing. They don't *share* outside.'

Seeing Laura packing up her van (she's unsure whether she and Dan will return) we fret that the more stable elements are leaving. She will be taking the site's only mobile telephone. Her van is comfy, lined in wood, full of books. 'In the first week there were loads of people here. The locals put them-

Charlotte plants up seedlings in the teepee greenhouse.

selves out to help.' She is a traveller, spending time with friends all over. Like her, other travellers move onto the site for a few days and then move on. She says many have moved to France, but now the French police are harrying them.

Green Dave is passionate about the house he is building from a Norwegian design: wedge-shaped, passive-solar heated. The roof slopes steeply on one sweep from the high end to the low, the water is filtered through gravel and sand down through the roof which will be turfed. A ladder will access the bed platform under the highest part of the interior.

Dave is a fruitarian — or will be when he has grown all the fruit he needs around his house. He is lean, earnest and energetic. He has little to do with his birth family in the East End. 'My campaign friends are my family. I have found my niche. It is not natural to eat cooked food, cooking is an energy use the world cannot afford; mankind must place itself in the natural system, we must be part of the reproductive system, like squirrels.' He will grow vines up the side of the house. He will eat seeds as well as fruits, and grains, pulses, nuts, mushrooms. Dave draws no dole and needs no money. He tried drawing benefit but they told him his manner of dress showed he was not seriously looking for work. He builds his house from cast-offs, even bent nails which he straightens. 'I'm self-educated. I read for myself: Gandhi, Kropotkin, William Morris.'

Green Dave designed and built most of the community roundhouse from materials brought in by demolition contractors and chipboard from DIY stores bought with donations. He owns the roundhouse's windmill and generator. A donation of thousands of candles from a candle factory up the road was helpful. However, Dave thinks all these gifts can create the wrong attitudes among people. Charity isn't the answer.

The afternoon is sunny. Children are playing on home-made swings. Anya is tending a tiny flower-bed in front of her yurt. Anya's yurt is gorgeous. Unfortunately it's not closed in with canvas or felt but plastic sheeting. That's the building material she finds in the skips. At the entrance, a genial mermaid painted on chipboard welcomes you in. Inside, Anya has created a witty fairy-land with artificial flowers woven into the supporting trellis. Showing us around, she says, 'I'm a nest builder.' She is a German who grew up in Holland and studied architecture. Her strong, frank personality radiates an integrity that reminds us of our own Tanya. She would like to work on ecological buildings but can't find a suitable job. She joined the site from the beginning and intends to stay until the end of the summer or until evicted.

'The eviction notice drove me a bit paranoid,' she say, but so far she is enthu-siastic about the site. 'It's hard enough when a group of people who know each other decide to form a co-operative. We don't know one another. Too many people come and go. There is a lot of will to make things work. I never expected the locals would accept us. They give us their time and materials. Two schools want to make contact and do biology and geography projects.'

Brendan, a burly, genial Ozzie, has just built his first real home — a six-sided roundhouse made from scrap materials in a North American Indian design. He has found his first real community and he is happy. He had been living in London squats when he saw the The Land is Ours newsletter and came to the planning meeting for the present venture. 'At twenty-one I wanted to see some places. I came to London, got a job, then I was in Spain, France, Egypt, Jordan, Syria and Turkey. I didn't like Britain: life here is dead, and I can't claim any benefit here; anyway I don't like taking money off the govern-ment. Working one day a week is enough for me: I can earn £50. I'm a sign writer by trade: I plan to return to the Middle East in October, then Pakistan, maybe Australia. In Turkey I lived in a small beach community — it was down to only four in the winter before we were thrown out: that was good while it lasted.

'This is different. It's political. Here we're dealing with society's problems — homelessness, drugs, theft. Nobody's forcing anyone to do anything: people come for a few days and move on. But for some it's a great place. Lawrence, who's helping me build and is right now asleep inside the house, has been on the streets for eight years: now he feels this is home. I'm going to look after him. He'll be building his own house. There's another Laurie here, just separated from his wife after thirteen years: he was very high and a big drinker: now he's healing here.'

Brendan draws a sharp distinction between drifters and stayers. 'People who come just to get pissed get fed up with the hassle and move on. There's a core of people really into what's going on, they're like a family to me. If we get evicted we'll regroup somewhere — we don't know where. I've never built a house like this before, it's a big learning experience. I was tidying the round-house this morning — just conscience, nobody told me to. There's no work rota. But there's a core of people — Pendragon is like a big Daddy, he's wise and experienced, has been in so many communities: he's not busy with his hands but he checks on things, who's coming and who's going and who's doing what. Bill's another core member: he's technical and practical, a do-it man. Then Laura and Dan, George in the green bus — they're from the Rainbow Tribe.'

The next evening a public inquiry into the planned supermarket develop-ment held a local session in a church hall and we joined the squatters in canvassing door-to-door to encourage local people to come. Nobody wants the supermarket. The inquiry had a homely village atmosphere with children running in and out; around fifty people, mostly local residents, spoke up in defence of the spaces and houses they needed. The inspector who chairs the inquiry, an apparently sympathetic woman with a ready smile, wrote every-thing down.

Wendy, a local resident, said she wants to keep the site as it is. 'The eco-village is brilliant. Pure Genius is bringing a sense of community to Wandsworth.' A twelve-year-old boy complained that the community gardens he used were now closed. He loves to go and play on the site. 'Pure Genius is great for kids.' Everyone clapped. Several mothers from tower blocks complained that their kids have no play areas. They want gardens.

Adrian from Pure Genius brought in the visitors' book and read out comments: 'Great place but the news said you were gypsies' — 'This is liberty!' — 'The best use of land in Battersea. Good Luck!' — 'Here you can light fires and sit and talk. You can't do that in a public park. It is an example to the rest of London. In the centre of London you have created an environ-ment that people go on holiday to find.' A boy aged eight had written: 'I love this place better than any Safeways. Please let it stay.'

On our last visit to Pure Genius, just before we left for the States, the site had been in operation for four months. It was a cold September day. We had heard that the community was experiencing problems. When we arrived, Green Dave was having a violent altercation with the person keeping the gate. Lots of, 'Don't you fucking well tell me what to do.' 'I fucking well will.' Like two sparring dogs of equal ferocity the argument stalled without any conclu-sion. Dave plonked himself on the settee parked beside the gate. We invited him to the pub. His leg was in plaster from falling off a wall. He looked ill — tired and stressed. He said: 'I've built this place up and look at it. It's meant to be a shining example. We're meant to show self-government. People walk in and see the communal place is a pig sty.'

Dave has lost sympathy with George Monbiot's views. 'For me, the present situation is extreme, while a lot of academic people like Monbiot are reformist. They want to stay within the system and incorporate Green ideas.' Dave says bitterly, 'You can't build an ecological house with solar panels and all the rest of it for less than £20,000 downpayment. We can't afford that. For the working class, ecology is a luxury. We're dealing with inner-city life here: too many people are here. All their benefit money goes on alcohol and drugs'. Dave, like many Vegans we speak with, expresses his opinions with great violence. We worried that eating out of skips as he does, he was becoming undernourished.

> What Pure Genius achieved does not end on this piece of blasted land. All over Britain, communities are waking up to the fact that neither government nor conventional developers are going to help them. Credit unions, LETS schemes, self-build projects, city farms and gardens, Permaculture and community education remain almost invisible to the people who think they are running this country. While the Government watches the dead leaves blown across the water, beneath the surface Britain has begun to flow the other way. This is the way the world begins again: not with bang, but a whisper.
> · George Monbiot, in *The Guardian*, 4 September 1996.

Dave lets us buy him a plate of chips and eats a piece of bread after he has scraped off the butter. His fragile hope that the site may become an eco-village growing its own food is fading fast. 'It was meant to be an example for the people of Wandsworth. I've worked out that one person can feed themselves off a quarter of an acre.' When we point out mildly that there isn't enough land for high-rise flat dwellers to have a quarter-acre each, Dave snaps that roads can be broken up and planted with orchards. Do most flat dwellers want their roads turned into orchards? Dave decides we are on the wrong side and stops talking.

At the site John Pendragon is waving in a lorry delivering a free load of scrap wood. He is also harassed but much cleaner than when we last met. He is possibly going back to live with his ex-wife and their three children. 'We're invaded by social problems. Around forty people still live on site but only about a quarter of those really work for the community. There's a nucleus of about a dozen but generally only six or seven on site at any one time.'

The problem he spells out is the same one we saw when we first came. There is no structure, no organisation, no chain of command. John says many people who pass through the site are homeless and some have mental health problems.

As we left, we got talking to a girl traveller sitting at the entrance of her van. Half her hair was shaved, the rest in pink-dyed dreadlocks. Her van was full of bright cushions and magpie-collected objects. She looked perfectly happy.

The end of Pure Genius happened at dawn on October 15 — five months and a week after the beginning. We were in the US and read the details in newspapers. Twelve bailiffs broke down the barricades, pulled people off roof-tops and dragged them from trees as more than one hundred police officers stood by. About fifty residents and visitors were removed from the site. Some people destroyed their own houses and left quietly, others resisted eviction for several hours after climbing on top of the roundhouse and onto a gantry leading to a disused jetty. They had been warned by leaks from the police that the eviction was imminent.

4

Wombats and home-cured ham

● ●

At the age of eighty-three John Seymour has written a novel, *Retrieved from the Future*, which encapsulates most of the ideas of this book. He is uniquely placed to make up a story about the collapse of our civilisation and its replacement by a peasant society using only human-scale technology and living simply. He has been a soldier, sailor, hunter, explorer, farmer, self-sufficiency pioneer, teacher of right livelihood and an author with a command of English that apparently allows him to write straight off into his final draft. We love and admire John as a resourceful and wise man, preaching what he practises and practising what he preaches with humour and good living and good company, never lecturing or sermonising, modest, always ready for a drink and a song.

We have known John for several years. We met first at a Hampstead gathering of good Green people. He was then in his mid-seventies — an amiable giant with a presence and a charisma that dominates any room. Like many thousands of people who enjoyed the sixties, we had read his best-seller *The Fat of the Land,* his account of running a small-holding in Suffolk with his wife Sally. John was a guru for many of us, although by the nineties his message of sustainable living went largely unheard.

Some years later, he was staying with us in Essex. We were trying to start a herb garden next to the kitchen door. 'Leave it to me,' said John. He double dug the patch of weedy grass slowly, methodically, wasting not a movement. Enthralled as we were by the no-dig ideas of Permaculture and Fukuoka's *One Straw Revolution,* we were unconvinced of the benefits of old-fashioned double digging. Today, four seasons later, on our heavy clay soil, John's corner is still the most productive part of our garden. The herbs left uncut provide feeding grounds for seven species of butterflies, damson flies, ladybirds and more bugs than we know the names of.

Talking with him about people to visit for this book, he suggested a family living in North Wales, whom we wouldn't find on any list of organic farmers or smallholders. 'If you want to see how a family *can* live sustainably, go and see them. They've got it right. They are private people and they are *doing* it — not talking about it.' A recommendation from John Seymour wasn't to be taken lightly. (Unlike the rest of the people we visited this family didn't want us to use their real names, so we call them the Coopers.)

Daniel and Suzanne Cooper

Dorothy writes: Daniel's directions were both vague and precise at the same time. His letter said: 'When you leave the B road do not take the left fork down to the river but continue until you come to a wooden bungalow painted white. Park opposite and walk up the track. Ty Newydd is on the right.' Lanes were precipitous and narrow, houses sparse in the landscape. Sheep and scrubby oaks behind dry stone walls. Not a rich countryside. What if I met a tractor coming the other way? I didn't. And soon enough the wooden bungalow appeared with a non-motorable track leading steeply upwards opposite.

The Coopers' house is set longways to the track. A stone-paved yard, a suspicious black and white sheepdog and a flock of farm hens clucking. Cherry trees, grown larger in that sheltered spot than is usual in North Wales, were dropping orange leaves. Next to the house, a stone-walled garden displayed clumps of emerald green vegetables. A pig grunted from a nearby field and two goats bleated — the scene reminiscent of a cheerful Brueghel, with ancient tractor replacing wooden wagon.

The young woman chopping wood with three young children tumbling around her like puppies must be Suzanne. She had the clear complexion of a non-city dweller and a smile that reached her eyes. She offered tea, home-made scones and home-made jam. Reserved at first, she soon gave out a warmth and a friendliness that you rarely find when you meet a stranger. Daniel was away replacing batteries for the generator. Suzanne was plucking a cock for supper. She hoped I would enjoy him. 'Poor fellow, he drowned in the water butt trying to get a drink so we shall eat him tonight. He's quite a fattie.'

We snatched moments to chat. Suzanne was the youngest of what she calls 'a stable middle class family.' After Oxford Polytechnic she landed a plum job with an English wine-maker, travelling to fairs and trade shows. 'It was glamorous alright but never what I wanted, all that PR bit and wearing smart suits. It was a false world.' She laughed. 'My boss liked my off-beat image. I loved the English wine scene but I didn't want to sell the wine.'

She met Daniel through a mutual friend and they lost sight of one another for some years. When they met again in their late twenties, he was already

> We must teach children to sing, to play instruments, to make instruments, to paint, to weave, to pot, to sculpt, to carve, to make up songs, to compose poetry. These are the activities that make for happiness, for integrated people, for the true culture as opposed to imposed culture.
> · John Seymour, *Retrieved from the Future.*

living at Ty Newydd in a caravan. Suzanne moved in and found what she was searching for. 'I wanted to build a nest. Daniel has the ideas but they run away with him. I'm not a pioneer, I've always been practical. Being here fulfils my creative side. In the society that I've left behind there wasn't room. I'm the youngest of the family. I always felt inferior with so many clever older brothers and sisters. Here I can be myself. Maybe you could say that I'm hiding away. I don't think so.'

She taught herself to make baskets and her products are sought after as examples of traditional craft. Canes sorted according to colours, shapes and sizes are kept in the long low room that the Coopers are converting into their new living room. Now she teaches basket making. 'It makes me go out and meet people, a lovely way to natter over basket weaving. There is nothing that I really miss from that other world. When we first moved up here, I used to go and visit friends and family. Since the children, I don't really feel the need to go out. People tend to come, want to come. We have friends in London, living the rat race to the full, who feel the need to come.'

Without a mortgage, a car or a job, Suzanne feels she has escaped dependence on the wider economy. 'Getting enough money to keep all these things going doesn't rule us. We need to raise very little — we are saving ourselves a lot of money just by being here. Last week I bartered a log basket for twenty rabbits — a good bargain as long as the rabbits don't all arrive at once. Daniel has to do a few boring jobs for income but by and large we don't *have* to do things for money.'

Their house, originally part of an estate, had been leased to two old ladies who kept it as a bird sanctuary. Barn owls nested there. 'We said we were keen on wildlife, so the estate sold us the freehold and a little land around the house. My Dad is a solicitor — from his point of view it seemed a nightmare: we had no planning permission to restore the house, and still haven't. For years whenever someone official looking drove up the track, we were petrified.' Over the last ten years the couple have restored the stone house and are restoring a separate wing, originally part of the main house, using local materials — wood, stone and sand.

The herbs are in pots on windowsills, onions in strings. The room where Suzanne weaves her baskets smells of linseed and resin. Two Rayburn woodburning stoves bought second-hand provide hobs and ovens, hot water and warm rooms. This was cosier than our own all-electric household, but it wasn't shirtsleeves temperature in November. Suzanne is convinced this is healthier. Just as well, as neither she nor Daniel have much sympathy with doctors. To keep really warm they chop wood.

'But then you see,' says Daniel, 'I don't mind chopping wood.' He is slight, sandy-haired with a gentle smile; he's almost always in motion. They are not on the electricity grid nor connected to mains water. Cisterns and hosepipes collect their water from the roof and the steep fields. 'We made a conscious choice that we would run a small windmill — enough for a couple of electric lights but not enough for all the techno-gadgets.' When there is enough sunlight, four home-made solar panels add to their power supply. Their grey water runs off into a willow bed for Suzanne's baskets. They have a radio and they don't miss television. The light bulbs are supplemented with lamps and candles.

I slept each night in a raftered room with white plastered walls. The beautiful dormer windows with their stained glass panels were made by Daniel's sister. And you can, if you need extra light, use a paraffin lamp.

Lisa, Joe and Micky, aged six, four and two, were born at home. Suzanne says: 'I'm still reeling from Micky. But now the children are more handleable, we can go on courses and give courses.' Daniel wants the children educated at home because schools don't teach the right values. I suggest this arrangement

The Coopers' farm in North Wales.

might deprive the children of the advantages of mixing with their peers, but he says they meet plenty of other kids anyway and he is hoping his community will expand. Suzanne doesn't enter the argument and she keeps a small smile going; I feel that school may not be such an impossibility eventually. We also disagree amicably over vaccinations and innoculations for children: we had done ours, they would not do theirs.

They decided, on principle, to install a compost toilet — a comfortable mahogany commode with a metal bucket under the seat. Sawdust is sprinkled over the wastes and the bucket is emptied into a compost pile. What seems primitive to the sanitised city dweller is in fact both practical (no smellier than a flush toilet) and environmentally friendly. On the shelf in the toilet outhouse is a collection of tree books and farming manuals. Suzanne remarks that city folk are edgy about the loo at first but get rapidly used to the arrangement.

Daniel thinks that Greens talk too much theory and don't do enough gardening. 'Take those permaculturalists: they all want to be designers. You hardly ever see a flourishing permaculture plot. They don't get down and do it. I just plant and grow and learn from my mistakes. I'm no great expert.'

Maybe not. But to my jaded palate, eating salad and vegetables in November that were pulled out of the soil in time for lunch, bore no relation to what I normally eat. The south-facing garden of only a hundred square metres was flourishing with beds full of salads, greens, parsnips, carrots and leeks.

Daniel's dislike of Green theorising does not prevent him from holding strong opinions. He condemns rural society, with its systematic degradation of the land, its protection of privilege through European Union subsidies and its oppressive planning procedures. He has planted 1500 trees and takes pride in the friends and neighbours who constitute a small local counter-community. Criticising consumer society for its pressures on people to buy what they neither need nor want, he refrains from buying anything he can do without

---

Cut that land (exhausted as it is) up into a thousand plots of ten acres each, give each plot to a family trained to use it, and within ten years the production coming from it would be enormous ... The motorist wouldn't have the satisfaction of looking out over a vast treeless, hedgeless prairie of indifferent barley — but he could get out of his car and wander through a seemingly huge area of diverse countryside, orchards, young tree plantations, a myriad of small plots of land growing a multiplicity of different crops, farm animals galore, and hundreds of happy and healthy children.
· John Seymour, *The Fat of The Land.*

or can make for himself. He is dismissive of environmental agencies, NGOs and government departments. 'I plant more trees comparatively than any institution. This society is in a bad situation and nothing is being done to get us out, and that makes me cynical.'

A couple of years back, the Coopers sold their car. They found it a liberating experience. Daniel said, 'We became locally based. Once you become local there are things you see that you had never noticed before. I don't feel that I've given up anything. I absolutely love it. Of course I can go away. Tom (a young man who lives on a caravan on their property) looks after the animals. And we travel by train.'

Gareth and Rod, friends who have settled nearby, have both kept cars which the Coopers can borrow, contributing to expenses. 'Realistically, I have to say that the less money I have, the happier I feel,' Daniel says. 'You know the feeling you have when you come home with a bucket of milk?'

'No, it's not a feeling I know.'

'It's a shame that it can't be communicated. That's why I want to teach by example. I'm really not into starting movements, newsletters and that stuff. I must maintain a strong sense of ordinariness. I think I've got the answers but it can't be put about. If you set up an organisation, things stultify. I am an incurable optimist. If there is a need, a mutual need, then things will happen.' The evidence of what happens, what the Coopers have built up over ten years, lies all around us.

The cash flow Daniel reckons he needs is less than £100 a week, including supplementary food, stock and building materials. Their own fruit and vegetables, goats, chickens, pigs and geese feed them throughout the year, and they aim to pay, by their skill and labour, for what they still have to buy. There is a growing cash income from Suzanne's baskets, from Daniel's hazelwood fence hurdles and the days he puts in on the neighbouring farms, drystone walling (a skill he taught himself), haystacking and treeplanting. But the Coopers' aim to be self-supporting is not yet fully realised. Suzanne's father helps with irregular but sizeable cheques.

Although they need little money for the paraphernalia of the middle class lifestyle they have abandoned, the Coopers have still benefited from the larger economy. Suzanne inherited a legacy from her grandfather, which enabled them to buy the ten hectares of hillside — including the wood — above their farmyard. This steeply sloping land was for sale at £5000 a hectare, a comparatively high price which they were willing to pay. They call their land the mountain.

For Daniel the mountain is a spiritual entity. They need not have bought it. It is not part of the equation of his self-sufficiency. Trees are his passion and he is visionary about the necessity to replant. The four hectares of mixed broadleaf take up so much of his labour that it makes the difference between a gracious life and a life with never enough time. His passion for trees and the need for an income combine when he works as an occasional tree feller on one of the local estates. When a tree falls or becomes very old, he offers to take it out and plant saplings and protect them with a stock fence.

'Trees die and if they are not replaced the wood itself dies. Whether it is in fifty years or five hundred depends on how we manage. In this countryside the woods are not managed. Stock are allowed to graze so they never regenerate. I feel a responsibility to try to keep them alive.' Daniel's own trees are now four to five years old, sturdy and healthy. They have been cared for with tree guards and rides connecting the areas, using mostly the summer labour of friends and neighbours. A landowner's planting grant covered the cost of buying the saplings.

We looked out onto the valley facing the homestead. From the kitchen garden the view is of green hills, wooded slopes and a couple of homesteads. 'There used to be double the inhabitants living here only a hundred years ago — a dozen dwellings where you are looking now.' Daniel, in spite of owning ten hectares, doesn't think of himself as a landowner, nor as a farmer. 'I did not intend to get land. But I feel that if something is meant to be — it happens. That's how it has been here all along.'

He implies that there is a spiritual side to his world view but declines to pontificate. 'Religion must have been invented for people in high-rise blocks. It's all here, isn't it?'

The Coopers share their land with two friends, both single for the present. Tom and Rod live in caravans on the hill. Tom is planning to buy the quarter-acre site he lives on and continue with his vegetable terracing and planting fruit trees. He has advertised in the Green press for a companion and is negotiating visits with several young women. The problem of planning permission will arise when he wishes to build a low-impact dwelling where his caravan stands.

Rod is a cheerful Brummie with a feather in his pigtail. He works weekends as warden in an hostel for the homeless and during the week he digs in his vegetable garden and works on the forge that Daniel has set up. He was forging door handles and window catches for the new wing of Daniel's house. His caravan has no running water so he comes to the Coopers for his bath. Not that often — he doesn't like baths.

Social relationships between the established family and the two bachelors were mutually supportive. Daniel said: 'If I broke my leg, Tom would look after the animals. What I've done is invest in community instead of BUPA.

And if Rod or Tom got ill, we would look after their chores. There is much more security in that sort of long-term community. Of course we all gossip about one another, that's village life. But it isn't big-city alienation. We would love it if more people arrived here who are sympathetic to what we are trying to do.'

The Welsh farmers respect Daniel because they see him hard at work and employ him in stone-walling and tree care. Daniel says: 'They aren't Welsh farmers: they are my neighbours. I hate what they are doing to these hills, grubbing out hedges and overgrazing to get the hill subsidy for sheep. In some cases they even fill in streams so that they can get more land for ploughing'.

Daniel runs a small wood business on the patch of flat land near the road where he has stored planks and timber. This is to be the site of the barn he plans to raise in the winter. 'We'll run a barn-raising course and we expect to get the roof on the barn during the course. The course fee of around £20 a day will pay the tutor's salary and everyone's food.'

Daniel and Suzanne work long hours but don't consider themselves as working as much as living. It is restful to watch the pair of them work in harmony. Gender stereotypes do not seem to affect them: either will chop wood, cook the dinner, feed the pigs or read to the children. They stop readily for coffee or tea when people drop in. Caitlin, a sixty-year-old woman who farms alone, comes in to arrange a barter in which Daniel will repair fences for her in return for twenty bales of straw. She tells an involved tale of how her boar climbed the wire of his enclosure with the agility of a cat and it took her two days to coax him back in with a trail of food.

I wondered if others could follow the Coopers' example. A few other families have settled in this valley and those adjoining, living similar lifestyles. Daniel replied: 'One thing is, you must not start too big. A lot of people get land — maybe five acres, and they do this, do that; they run into trouble and they're stuck and they leave. When I first came to Wales lots of people were running a smallholding. After a while I found they did nothing; they were stoned a lot of the time. We started small, with a quarter-acre, some hens and one goat. With too much land and not enough experience you get stuck; your fences fall down, your stock gets loose.' Daniel quoted an Eastern saying as summing up his own lifestyle. 'A Guru said: I chopped wood and I fetched water. I became enlightened. I chop wood and fetch water.'

We both visit the Coopers eighteen months later, in the spring. Daniel has finished building the second part of his stone house, Suzanne has plastered the walls. All the wooden fitments in the new kitchen area are hand-made out of elm. Now the house covers the area of the original dwelling. It is a hand-finished, wood-furnished stone dwelling at peace with itself. Daniel still has not applied for planning permission. The family has moved from the cramped living area, now turned into workspace, into a low, oak-beamed living room, warmed at one end by a Rayburn and the other by a wood fire. The two elder children have been sent to school. Suzanne explains that it was no longer practicable to teach them at home. The parents were too busy. Daniel is regretful but resigned. The two eldest, who walk down the track each morning to catch the bus, love school. The little one, Micky, spends his time with either parent, while they perform their tasks. It seems a gentler way to grow up than going to the child minder while your parents work in an office.

What is that elusive quality of life that everyone wants and few people attain? Have the Coopers found it? Daniel has had doubts. 'Last summer I got so depressed I almost wanted to pack it all in.' Gareth, the nearest neighbour, had started renting his barn to a rock band. They played full volume five nights a week. The thrumming floated up the track. Daniel couldn't bear the noise. He and Gareth quarrelled bitterly after a decades-long friendship. And Tom in the caravan moved away to be with his girl friend but rented out the caravan. Caravan tenants wasn't what Suzanne had envisaged when they sold Tom his plot.

So even in this Arcadia the problems of noise and neighbours take hold. Daniel says they reached a compromise. Gareth has tried to sound-proof the barn and Daniel to reconcile himself to the noise. Sometimes he has felt that their life on the hillside has been too perfect; he has felt ecstatic for weeks at a time.

Daniel still does not consider that he and his friends live in any extraordinary way. 'We are just ordinary,' he says. Like John Seymour, he desires passionately that people should take back some of the skills that have been lost in consumer society. He acknowledges that the majority would not want to live the way he does. What he can't understand is why they don't take a few small steps: 'Make their own bread, grow a few veggies. It is so easy and so satisfying.'

We were full of talk about communities and projects we were visiting. Daniel didn't want to know. There was too much talk and not enough action. How does he want to convince people? He doesn't. He does not belong to any organisations. He is living the life. Like many of the Living Lightly people, Daniel does not think our consumer society can continue indefinitely. When and if it crashes, he believes he has shown another way.

Even so, there is no way you can live entirely outside the money economy. For the first time since they moved in, the Coopers have considered applying for Family Credit in addition to the Child Benefit they already receive. Their income is low enough. All the money left over from buying the mountain is finished apart from a National Savings nest egg. However, their joint decision is, 'No, let's manage,' and it has left them happy. Suzanne has begun giving basket-making courses; Daniel works regularly a couple of days a week for local farmers.

Daniel says that they could have set up their sustainable life without the help of Suzanne's legacy which they used to buy the hill. Suzanne isn't so sure. It seems to us that if you want to live a sustainable life, you will probably need some subsidy, whether it is from state, family or charity. The Coopers have made a choice — to live more simply than the rest of us. They have consciously removed themselves from the rat race. And it works. In that elusive pursuit of happiness they are among the most successful people we met.

Wombat people

There is another way of returning to the land — not aiming to change your lifestyle as much as to rescue a degraded environment and restore as much as possible of its natural life. That is what Wayne and Cheryl Donald have done on their remote and degraded land in South Australia, two hours' drive northwards from Adelaide. The Donalds have sacrificed their living standards and devoted their lives to stopping and reversing the decimation of wildlife in general, and of the hairy-nosed wombat in particular.

They used their savings to buy 243 hectares of abandoned cattle country. They bought the land in bits and pieces over seventeen years. They have lived on it for fifteen. Their sole ambition for their land is to leave it alone and save it for its endangered native species. Especially the wombats, nocturnal creatures so shy that they are hardly ever seen.

Wombats look and behave like small bears, with a similar shuffling walk, but their legs are shorter and their backs broader. They live in burrows, sleeping by day and venturing out in the late evening and early morning. In Tasmania, wombats are larger, with short ears, coarse fur and naked muzzle. Here in South Australia the hairy-nosed wombat (*Lasiorhinus latifrons*) has a silky fur and sharply pointed ears.

The Donalds are not your typical middle-class environmentalists. Neither has been to college. Both have modest jobs — Cheryl is a cook and a play group supervisor, Warren works in a local winery. They live in relative discomfort and have to put up with the local redneck farmers who think of them as hippies and maliciously tear down their fences and complain against them to the police on petty grounds.

Surely wildlife cannot be preserved by individuals buying large chunks of land for no other purpose than conservation? It can in Australia — one of the few places left in the world where an individual, without being rich, can obtain land. Maybe not very fertile land — but land nevertheless.

Friends brought us from Adelaide. After an hour's driving past wheat fields each as large as a small European town we stop in Truro and drink iced coffee. The bakery menu is pies, pies, more pies and sticky buns. In this heat it seems an odd choice of patisseries. Alison asks whether any of us wants to use the public toilet. 'Cheryl's toilet is outside and behind a curtain. I can't hack it.' We'll be able to hack it. We're going to India next week.

We cross the Goyder line, beyond which farming has been recognised belatedly to be destructive and unprofitable. It is a notional line named after the geologist who worked out its latitude. Beyond the line, sheep and cattle with their sharp cloven hooves strip off the topsoil and small white rocks about the size of tennis balls appear. That is what happened to the land that Cheryl and Wayne bought.

The Donalds and their two children live in a converted steel barn, closely shuttered against the killing summer heat. It is 42 degrees centigrade outside at noon and 31 inside — even under the ceiling fan. This is not a welcoming land. Yet people live here. Wayne is connected to the main grid electricity; he'd like to have a solar house but doesn't have the cash.

With a holding of a size that in a more favoured agricultural community would make him wealthy, Wayne struggles to make ends meet. The majestic gums of temperate rainforest don't grow here; the bush is called mallee — slow-growing, gnarled trees, resembling olive trees. Because cattle have been removed from the land for nearly twenty years, the mallee has started to regenerate. There is no danger of bushfire with these stubby trees; the saltbush, with its prickly leaves to resist drought, is fire-resistant.

When they first came, the Donalds thought of breeding pigs on eight hectares of cleared space next to the road. But they found four species of birds which build their nests on the ground that would have been eliminated by pigs. So they decided to leave the land alone. Because the land is declared a sanctuary, the government pays for the access road and fencing, and taxes are reduced.

The children go to school further afield than the local school because the local kids, egged on by their parents, tease them as hippy kids. Unlike most Australian environmentalists, the Donalds have a cat. She lives enclosed in a wire pen and when she dies, she won't be replaced. Cats have become a major threat to native wildlife which has no resistance against cats who run wild.

When the rain comes it's heavy. The spear grass grows up to your thighs. In the arid scrub surrounding us now, it is hard to imagine that the flowers Wayne has photographed with such skill and love had bloomed after rain. He shows us slides of the wildlife he has observed on his property. To get his first photo of a wombat he stayed out all night to catch it at dawn. 'Wombats get into trouble in the drought. We tried to feed them with Lucerne hay and stock fodder but it never worked.'

The Donalds have become self-taught experts on wildlife: 'You see that tree, the same pair of parrots have been nesting there for fifteen years.' Wayne checks the wombat warrens on his land on his way to work and keeps a diary of all sightings. 'They don't always manage to rear their young. Young wombats can't digest dry summer grass and unless we have three good years in a row they die. But luckily wombats live to be thirty so they can breed again.' Wayne rummaged around in what was to us indecipherable bush and came up with a wombat skeleton, fur still attached. 'Sorry it is a bit stinky. A young wombat. Must have died in the hot weather.'

There is a four-thousand hectare wombat sanctuary near his property. To form a corridor to his own sanctuary, Wayne bought a small block of land adjoining and gave it to the sanctuary. To increase the sanctuary still more, he has influenced a friend living in the area to buy a parcel of land and let it regenerate.

At his boundary fence we could see the difference between his land and that of his neighbours. His is covered in salt bush and mallee and the neighbours' land is burnt and barren. A white horse stood on red-baked earth covered in white stones, without a single tree for shade. Each enormous field contains heaps of stones collected and piled up by ever-hopeful graziers. When the land is first cleared it supports cattle for a couple of years, then the quality and quantity of grass degrades slowly and surely and the profits diminish. A perfect example of modern agriculture impoverishing a fragile eco-system that had existed in balance for thousands of years.

Wayne tried to explain the values that he lived by. 'I've struggled with religion all my life; it's too much of a mishmash of values. I am interested in reincarnation. Have you read James Lovelock's *Gaia Hypothesis*?' He had Fukuoka's *One Straw Revolution* on his shelf — the Japanese no-dig philosophy of organic gardening. 'You do what you can, what you want and need to do.' And then he showed us an eagles' nest in a 400-year-old mallee tree.

When it is cool enough the children play outside. There is one rule: they must wear gumboots to go to the compost loo, twenty yards from the house. 'Snakes leave you alone — if you leave them be,' said Cheryl. Was she lonely, on this isolated piece of bush, mocked at by many of the locals? She wasn't, but she thought the family might have to return to Adelaide in a few years for their children's high schooling.

In the evening a band of kangaroos came to drink outside their window.

We were allowed to watch but only standing well back from the window. Wayne does not want the kangaroos habituated to people.

Wayne insisted we must see a wombat. As dusk fell we went on a search around the warrens. We had almost given up. 'There he goes,' whispered Wayne. A blunt-nosed, grey furry creature just visible for a few seconds. As it sensed our presence, it disappeared down into its tunnels.

Part 2 : Better farms, better food

5

Who eats what and why?

●●●

Food is a juicy topic which unites and divides us all. Without good food our health suffers, so does our quality of life — obvious enough for poor people in poor countries, but applicable to us, too. If our beef is suspect because of a BSE outbreak, and our fruit and vegetables are chemically treated during growth and sprayed again with post-harvest fungicides to preserve them for their journey half way round the world to our supermarket, then we have been deprived of standards of taste and health we used to enjoy.

In rich North and poor South alike, farmers are forced off their farms because farming itself has been replaced by industrial agriculture, a game only industrialists can play successfully. Such food is apparently cheap and varied; well-off consumers are offered an exciting choice of gaily packaged, high-quality food from all over the world at low cost. But the food is not as cheap as it seems because of the hidden environmental, health and social costs.

Skilful advertisements convince us that we have more choice — an illusion. The dozens of biscuit and cookie varieties on the shelves are merely recombinations of the same ingredients and preservatives. Of the 10,000 new food products launched on the European market annually only one thousand survive the year. Meanwhile, thousands of local varieties of fruit and vegetables have disappeared, replaced by a few which have been developed for their uniform appearance, not for their taste and quality. Young people in the affluent North rarely experience the taste of fresh food their parents used to enjoy. Profit has become the driving force behind the food industry. The proponents of genetically engineered food assure us that it is necessary to increase yields and feed larger

Six thousand varieties of apple have been recorded growing in the UK, today only nine dominate in our commercial orchards. Apples are imported from Europe, New Zealand, Chile, the US and South Africa... The UK could produce a much greater variety of apples, reducing imports, increasing biodiversity and saving energy on packaging and transport.

· Food Miles Action Pack, S.A.F.E. Alliance.

populations. The dangers are not mentioned or glossed over and so is the hidden agenda that such foods are highly profitable to the multinational corporations that market them and potentially ruinous to millions of small farmers.

Eating in the global market is unhealthy. Northerners are eating a diet containing excessive amounts of protein, saturated fat, cholesterol, pesticide residue and not enough fibre. This diet creates spiraling medical costs. A report by the US Surgeon General estimated in 1988 that sixty-eight percent of diseases in the US were diet-related. Other rich countries have the same problem and the South is going the same way, as millions of Chinese and prosperous South Asians move into protein-rich diets. So far the prevailing diet among Asians is still high in plant foods and low in meat, poultry and dairy products, resulting in a very low incidence of the diet-related diseases prevalent in Western culture. However, when these Asians migrate to the North and adopt the high-fat, high-protein, low-fibre diet, they incur the same incidence of heart attacks, strokes, arthritis, breast cancer, colon cancer, osteoporosis, diabetes, asthma, gallstones and obesity. If lifespans are shorter in the poor countries, that is partly because of lower standards of hygiene and housing, and lack of access to the market in food, and partly because infant mortality figures are lumped in with adult figures. If a child in the South survives into adult years, life expectancy is not very different.

The problem of meat

For centuries, and still today, eating meat has the status of luxury food. Does it still make sense to eat meat? Sound reasons of land-use and morality as well as health suggest not. The grain and soya needed to produce the meat, poultry and dairy products eaten by the average American each year is enough to feed seven people on a meatless, non-dairy diet. To feed the world's current population on an American-style diet would require two and a half times as much grain as the world's farmers are currently growing. As developing countries turn to meat, more forests are cut down to provide grass, while twenty million people die every year of malnutrition and starvation.

Are there moral or ethical reasons not to eat animals? In Peter Singer's classic, *Animal Liberation,* he puts forward strong arguments. He introduces the concept of what he calls 'speciesism' — an affliction as prevalent and as pernicious as racism — that because we are superior in some respects to animals we have total rights over them.

Singer asks us to imagine that Martians invade the earth and proceed to enslave, exploit and eat human beings, acting towards us as we do to other species. Our human lives become a hell of fear, captivity, pain and early death.

FOOD FACTS

• In 1985 North Americans were consuming half the grains and potatoes they did at the turn of the century, 33% more dairy products, 50% more beef, and 280% more poultry. This shift resulted in a diet with one-third more fat, one fifth less carbohydrates, and levels of protein consumption far exceeding official recommendations. (Committee on Diet and Health, National Research Council 1989)

• Livestock consume 90% of soy, 80% of corn [maize] and 70% of grain grown in the US, and half of the world's grain harvest. (USDA Agricultural Statistics 1989-91)

• Global cattle population doubled in the 40 years to 1989 (FAO Yearbook 1989) Fowl population quadrupled. (New Scientist)

• 64% of US cropland produces livestock feed, only 2% produces fruit and vegetables (USDA Agricultural Statistics 1989)

• 78 calories of fossil fuel are expended to produce one calorie of protein from beef; only two calories of fossil fuel are used up for one calorie of protein from soybeans (David and Marcia Pimental, Food Energy and Society, London, Edward Arnold 1979)

• 33% of the world's grain and 70% of the United States' grain are fed to livestock.

• Every steak has the same global warming effect as a 25 mile drive in a typical American car.

• Livestock production uses excessive amounts of water, accounting for more than half of the US water consumption.

• In 1996 there were 15 billion cattle, sheep, goats and pigs in the world, out-numbering people by almost 3 to 1. The amount of land these animals graze on could feed millions who are now undernourished or actually starving.

(From Earthsave pamphlets)

As we protest to the more intelligent and technologically superior Martians that we are sentient beings, we argue that they don't need to eat human flesh to live and, indeed, they might be healthier if they did not. They agree, and admit, as a compassionate species, that their treatment of us isn't as good as it might be. However, they insist that we have no moral argument. We belong to a species both different and inferior. They treat us, they point out, much the same as we treat other species. They cannot see why they shouldn't factory-farm our children and munch them for breakfast after the cereal.

These Martians are right: we humans feed, fondle and cherish our pets and, without a qualm, relegate other domestic animals, who are as aware and intelligent, to factory farms, where they endure a short, brutal life and a grotesque slaughter, after which we are quite happy to eat them and give Fido one of their bones.

Singer observes that children frequently express horror at the origin of their dinner. In a South Indian meat market, our ten-year-old Zachary saw a kid taken from its mother and butchered with a razor. It bled to death before his horrified gaze. Zachary stopped eating meat for six years. However as he goes through high school with his peer group, none of whom are vegetarians, he has gradually lost his initial empathy for the animal and eats McDonalds with the rest of the gang.

The two middle girls became vegetarian as young children. We were living in rural France. Sadly, our combined efforts to produce some degree of self-sufficiency failed. Our milch goat went dry and devastated the neighbour's rose beds. Pigeons ate all our cabbages. Our ducklings were eaten by water rats. The fox carried off our chicks in broad daylight; the remaining pair drowned in their water bowl. Our jack and doe rabbit appeared infertile so we asked a neighbour to kill our doe, being too squeamish ourselves. The skinned carcass was lying on the kitchen table when the dog discovered five blind babies carefully hidden *underneath* the rabbit hutch. We reared three of them with fountain pen fillers dropping milk into their mouths. One survived into jack rabbithood but later broke his neck jumping off the kitchen table. At that point Tanya gave up eating animals and fish and has never gone back to it. She had to pay a price for her principles when she was traveling in the jungles of meat-hungry Brazil and had to survive on tins of condensed milk while her Amazonian Indian friends hunted their succulent dinners. Her younger sister, Zoe, suddenly stopped eating meat because she no longer liked the taste. As she grew up she stopped dairy produce, too. She doesn't drink milk because, 'I'm not a baby cow.' Ben, the elder son, living in Paris, once briefly considered eliminating meat on the grounds that feeding grain to cattle is not the best use of grain, but, swayed by his surrounding culture — a French butcher's slab is an art form in itself — never adopted the idea.

We, the parents, belong to the growing section of people — more than one third according to some polls in Britain and the US — who are undogmatic vegetarians. We no longer buy meat or poultry for a mixture of reasons — concern over the appalling conditions of animals reared in factory farms; to save money; and because so much of the meat and poultry available in British stores is of indifferent quality and not necessarily safe. We live as well and as healthily without meat, although we do eat fish, mostly when entertaining, occasionally share Zachary's bacon, and accept meat when we are guests. We eat meat to avoid bother or embarassment, not because we crave it.

How many vegetarians are there? Accurate research is difficult because it vegetarianism has become fashionable and politically correct. *The Vegetarian Times* produced a poll in 1997 suggesting that seven percent of Britons considered themselves vegetarian; other figures suggest one in eighteen. All these percentages have been creeping up, year by year, for two decades. The proportion is highest — up to ten percent — among children and young teenagers.

Should we, come to that, eat any animal products at all? That more radical question is leading more and more people to become vegans. We can be sure veganism will continue to grow — especially with the support of such persuasive vegans as the British performance poet Benjamin Zephaniah, who told us that his abhorrence of exploiting animals arose out of a sympathy for the underdog.

'I went to one of these schools where I was the only black kid and every day it was like this, when you are the only black kid no one wants to talk to you, so you get friendly with cats and spiders. I look at a spider, I still do it, and I say: is that spider going shopping, wandering around going to find the family food? I mean I was only six or seven, it seemed animals were better than humans. Then I was about eleven years old; we had meat, I never really liked meat. I was talking with my mother over dinner: where does the meat come from? I got it from the butcher, silly boy. Where does the butcher get it from? He got it from the farmer, you silly boy. Eat your dinner. Where did the farmer get it from? The farmer got it from the cow. Where does the cow get it from? You silly boy — it IS the cow. That moment I connected.'

Talking Turkeys

Be nice to yu turkeys dis Christmas
Cos turkeys just wanna have fun
Turkeys are cool, turkeys are wicked
An every turkey has a Mum.
Be nice to yu turkeys dis Christmas
Don't eat it, jus keep it alive,
It could be yu mate an not on yu plate
Say, Yo! Turkey I'm on your side.

I got lots of friends who are turkeys
An all dem fear Christmas time,
Dey wanna enjoy it, dey say humans destroyed it
An humans are out of dere mind,
Yeah, I got lots of friends who are turkeys
Dey all hav a right to a life,
Not to be caged up an genetically made up
By any farmer an his wife.

Turkeys jus wanna play reggae
Turkeys jus wanna hip-hop
Can yu imagine a nice young turkey saying,

'I cannot wait for de chop'?
Turkeys like getting presents, dey wanna watch Christmas TV,
Turkeys hav brains and turkeys feel pain
In many ways like yu an me.

I once knew a turkey called Turkey
he said 'Benji explain to me please,
Who put de turkey in Christmas
An what happens to Christmas trees?'
I said, 'I am not too sure Turkey
But it's nothing to do wid Christ Mass
Humans get greedy and waste more dan need be
An business men mek loadsa cash.'

Be nice to yu turkeys dis Christmas
Invite em indoors fe sum greens
Let em eat cake an let em partake

In a plate of organic grown beans,
Be nice to yu turkeys dis Christmas
An spare dem de cut of de knife,
Join Turkeys United and dey'll be delighted
An yu will mek new friends 'FOR LIFE'.

Benjamin Zephaniah

'A year or so later I got hold of a little booklet of some kind — saying things like the human animal is the only animal that drinks other animals' milk. Yes, we're the only animals to drink milk after infancy. The thing was that humans had to force themselves to digest milk. I was a bit of a strange kid. Years and years later, someone said to me: you are a vegan. I remember getting agitated. I wondered should I defend myself? Were they insulting me? Like calling me a nigger — calling me a vegan? What are you callin' a vegan? Me? No, you are. It's someone who doesn't eat dead animals and that was it. It was really as simple as that. So I realise that I come from a different angle and I find myself in a lot of vegan talks, in conflict with a lot of people. I tell people it is a cheap food, it should be for the masses. Someone said to me: come and talk at this vegetarian seminar 'cos I know that you can reach the black community.'

Vegan Delight

Ackees, chapatiies
Dumplins an nan
Channa an rotis
Onion uttapam,
Masala dosa, green Callaloo
Bhel an samosa
Corn an aloo.
Yam an cassava
Pepperpot stew,
Rotlo an guava
Rice an tofu,
Puri, paratha
Sesame casserole,
Brown eggless pasta
An brown bread rolls.

Soya milked muesli, bean curd
Soya sweet sweeties
Soya's de word

Soya bean margarine
Soya bean sauce
What can mek medicine?
Soya of course.
Soya meks yoghurt
Soya ice cream,
Or soya sorbet
Soya reigns supreme,
Soya sticks liquoriced
Soya salads
Try and soya dish
Soya is bad.

Plantain an tabouli
Cornmeal pudding
Onion bhajee
Wid plenty cumin,
breadfruit an coconuts
Molasses tea
Dairy free omelettes
Very chilli.
Ginger bread, nut roast
Sorrell, paw paw,
Cocoa an rye toast
I tek em on tour,
Drinking cool maubi
Mek me feel sweet, What was dat question now?
WHAT DO WE EAT?

Benjamin Zephaniah

'What do we eat?' Benjamin asks in his poem. Can the ten billion people we expect on earth in the twenty-first century live on the kind of food we are eating now — cultivated plants that have been selected and bred? We found a radical answer on a farm in Cornwall run by Ken Fern, his wife Ariadne and members of their collective. Ken argues that our vegetables depend on cultivated plants which have to be replanted every year, weeded and watered. He asks: What if we could live, like many wild animals do, on perennial plants? All we need to do is find them, identify them, collect and distribute the seeds.

Plants for a Future

Down a steep Cornish hill, up a steep hill past hollyhocked gardens and grey stone cottages, you reach a five-barred gate with a hand-painted sign: PLANTS FOR A FUTURE. (PFAF) Inside, a couple of caravans, a wooden shed, two polytunnels and a display of plants for sale — an impressive array of common perennials and herbs that we recognise and many that we don't. Stretching away into the distance, plant beds and screens of trees, an initial impression of cherished plantations. No-one around.

Eventually, we find Dawn sitting beside a rose bed having her lunch which is mainly rose hips, which she opens to eat out the sweet centres. She wears a nose ring. 'Help yourselves to blackberries and apples,' she says.

A ring in the nose, along with unlaced boots and woolly hats, appear to be the signals of a willingness to go against the mainstream. Dawn was catering for festivals until she grew more interested in growing food. 'At a festival recently, lots of people were talking about really important issues. About land. A lot of poor people who couldn't buy land discussing getting together to buy some. Eco-village is the new buzz word.' The members of PFAF are keen to start such a village; Dawn says that when they do, the whole project will move.

PFAF is a community of eleven members. They want to live on the site, using the garden shed for a while until they can build their homes — but planning laws rule this out. So they live elsewhere and come in to work on the ten

---

MISSION STATEMENT FOR PFAF

There are 20,000 known species of edible plants in the world and yet, over the centuries, we have become increasingly dependent upon fewer and fewer species to provide our food. Indeed fewer than 20 species of plant provide 90 percent of our plant foods. We now see huge areas of land devoted to single crops and an increasing dependence upon chemical fertilisers, insecticides, fungicides and herbicides. There is the constant threat of new diseases or of chemical-resistant insects evolving and this could wreak havoc in such large areas of single crops. A changing world climate would also cause major disruptions in agriculture with many important food-growing regions such as the north American grain belt becoming incapable of producing their traditional crops. Clearly a greater diversification is urgently required. Just compare a huge area of wheat with an area of natural woodland. This woodland receives no chemical fertilisers or sprays yet year after year it produces lush growth; it is alive with a great diversity of plants and animals quite unlike the wheat field which can support very few species. The quality and depth of soil in the woodland is maintained or improved yearly while erosion and loss of soil structure make cultivation of wheat increasingly difficult.

· Ken Fern.

hectare site, which they call The Field.

The plans for the eco-village are on hold, while PFAF members look for a local council somewhere in the country who would provide them with free or low-rent land. They don't have much capital but they are ready to issue loan stock to purchase a suitable property.

The site is divided on permaculture principles into zones, with those needing most care near the entrance and the tool shed. There are corridors of wilderness for wildlife habitats, although any rabbits have to compete with Ken's wife Ariadne for the dandelions — they are one of her favourite salad ingredients.

The sale of plants through mail-order is hardly a commercial success. 'We have to fight to make Ken sell — he prefers to give them away,' Dawn says. The pamphlets Ken writes are sold at cost price. Sympathisers are invited to join Friends of PFAF for a fee of £10 (low-income £6), giving them the chance of coming in to help when they feel like it. 'We could afford to pay ourselves a wage of £50 a week for two months this summer during May and June, but now we're back on benefit.' The benefit question was one we came across in many different situations. Are you justified in allowing the state to support you while you work on projects you believe benefit the whole of society? Many Living Lightly people believe that they are. Ken accepts the need of some PFAF members to claim benefit.

Sitting in a polytunnel surrounded by luxuriant vegetation, Ken told us his story, quietly proud of achieving as much as he has with no financial backing, working entirely from passionately held convictions.

'I was in my twenties, my first wife was pregnant — and she gave me some meat to eat with nipples on it. I gave up meat. Within two years I gave up all animal products.' He was a London bus driver, but what he wanted was to grow

Oca: a South American tuber that has an acid-lemony flavour when first harvested, but becomes very sweet and can be eaten as a fruit after having been left out in the sun for a few weeks.

Quinoa: a South American plant with an edible seed. This seed contains a complete protein so it is an ideal part of the vegetarian or vegan diet and can be used in all the ways that rice is used. As a bonus it produces its own bird deterrent!

Reichardia picroides: a Mediterranean plant with mint-flavoured leaves that are produced all-year round and are an ideal salad ingredient. There are many hundreds of medical plants that can be grown in temperate climates and there are probably a good deal more with properties as yet undiscovered.

· From Ken Fern's plant labels at PFAF.

Ken Fern at Plants for a Future.

his own food on a two-acre field he had bought. 'I tried to grow all my food in my field but I soon saw how much hard work it was with all that weeding and annual planting. I became convinced there must be a better way. Then I read Robert Hart's *Forest Gardening*. I started thinking about perennials. I became obsessive.'

He joined a vegan co-operative project and in 1985 met Ariadne, who is a botanist. They found the site for The Field and started work in 1989.

'The main difference between permaculture and us is that we have no animals. The argument that you need farm animals to provide manure is rubbish: compost does the job just as well much more cheaply and practically.'

While we stroll around the mixed borders, he chooses particular leaves and flowers and insists that we try them. After an initial recoil, we were munching saltbush, lily flowers and campanula flowers with relish. Unlike the majority of cultivated food plants, most of these species have never been selectively bred to increase size and yields, reduce bitterness, increase sweetness, etc. Yet many are delicious, as different from commercial food as wild strawberries from cultivated ones. Ken's small son eats the plants, too. He is as cheerful as his father and also on the thin side. This reminds us of India where you never see a fat peasant. 'When I was fifteen,' says Ken, 'I had arthritis and I was a heavy meat eater. After my diet changed I never suffered again.' We remark that throughout our travels we have gathered plenty of anecdotal evidence that lessening meat consumption improves health. And the harmful effects of the excess fat eaten in milk products is too well documented to doubt.

Ken is aware that his vision of replacing much of the world's agriculture by perennial plants sounds far-fetched. He defends it on practical grounds and has expressed his ideas in a recent book (see Bibliography). He is sure that a start can be made now. His vision could be relevant to urban gardeners who use up their space on lawns, flower beds and herbaceous borders without bothering to plant even a year's supply of herbs, salads and root vegetables. 'Just one patch of garden will provide twenty different species to pick in the middle of winter. One person can provide all their food from one acre of land. We don't want to go back to being hunter-gatherers but we need to be gatherers.'

Ken Fern is not alone; his vision of mankind's future diet is shared by Wes Jackson, a researcher and writer who has devoted his life to the quest for more abundant and sustainable sources of food. Wes is convinced that the best future for humans is to develop perennial grain plants, since seventy-six percent of all human calories come directly or indirectly from grains. At the Land Institute in the American Mid-West at Salinas, Kansas, Wes and a research team are developing 'a sustainable grain agriculture', grown in mixtures, for human and animal consumption. Using the prairie native to their region as the model, Land Institute researchers are trying to use genetic diversity to solve all the problems that beset modern agriculture and which are currently being tackled with chemicals: soil building, fertility and pest management. The Land Institute team is also raising livestock and growing conventional annual crops using organic methods and renewable energy. Wes believes it can be done within eighty years.

Ken Fern and Wes Jackson are pioneers. Their views are extreme and not readily accepted. What role is there for people who want to live lightly and grow organic food? How can they live? Is it enough to be 'lacto-vegetarian',

---

I became a vegetarian when I was sixteen after seeing old milch cows sold off at a market. Gradually I realised that we didn't need to eat any animal products. I am lucky that my husband, who is a teacher, and both my children aged eleven and nine, are also vegans. Veganism is no longer a handicap in our lives. When people meet me and find that I'm not New Age or particularly alternative they're quite surprised. Now my kids go to McDonalds and have a vegan burger. I don't think they are handicapped by their different eating habits. I don't approve of the violence of some of the animal liberationists. I came to veganism through Gandhian ideals of non-violence.
· Annette White, vegan (to the authors).

as the more moralistic vegans call the milk-and-cheese eaters? Can a community live by growing organic food? Is it moral to live on social security benefits as an unofficial 'wage' for looking after land and improving the human diet? In Cornwall, close to Ken Fern's Plants for a Future, we visited Keveral Farm, an organic farming commune where a fluctuating population of around fifteen were living, working, idling and, above all, arguing about these problems. Their hopes, ideals and frustrations struck us as a microcosm of the issues raised in this book.

Keveral Farm

Keveral Farm has been a commune since the seventies. Now a housing co-operative owns the house, and a workers' co-operative runs the twelve hectares of mixed woodland, fields and gardens. When we visited in late 1996, members were growing about thirty percent of their food — not much when you consider how much land and labour is available. They intend to do better. Work is voluntary, not organised in a structured manner. The emphasis is on the quality of life; work is only 'good' if it is part of the positive and holistic redefinition of one's life. In practice such principles lead to rows over potatoes needing harvesting and seedlings wilting through lack of water. As a result, dedicated core members struggle to meet the practical needs of the group while others work sporadically or not at all. Personal income comes mainly from social security benefits and some outside jobs, some income from forestry grants and sale of produce to the Monkey Sanctuary nearby, and some local trading in fruit and vegetables.

The farm lies at the end of a rutted and potholed track, its courtyard dominated by piles of scrap timber, derelict cars and vans. Marigolds and herbs in pots and beds relieve the mess outside the house. There are more potted plants in the litter-laden courtyard that leads to the kitchen. Above the farmhouse roof, a weathervane in the shape of a goat swings in the breeze. Later we find this was forged by a member called Moth, who disapproves of goats unless they are wild.

Inside the farmhouse, whitewashed walls are discoloured; a scruffy, stone-flagged kitchen is greasy with blackened cooking pots. The dining room with bacon hooks in the ceiling holds a cramped table seating a maximum of twelve in a community of fifteen which also has to feed WWOOFers (Willing Workers on Organic Farms) and guests for most meals. But there is plenty of room around a huge hearth behind the table; some people are always happy to sit and chat and drink while they wait for a place at the table. Just sitting around is a common activity at Keveral.

Gareth, one of Keveral's members, took us down a track with fine views, past caravans and cottages where members live, past vegetable gardens with two polytunnels, to the campsite. Here we pitched our tent. A van load of Dutch eco-travellers had taken the last of the level sites, so we rolled onto each other during the night and rain seeped in. But the sun rose, the sleeping bags dried out, and by the second night we had grown used to the slope.

Breakfast in the farmhouse is good: Oak's home-baked bread, honey, Nescafé — and powdered milk because Gareth has not yet milked the goats. Gina had instituted a grab bag in the kitchen for household chores, with jobs inscribed on cards, but the scheme hasn't run in yet, someone told us. 'It's the summer, everyone feels like they want to be on holiday.'

> 'I have more freedom here in a community than living in a town. If I need personal space I go up to my house in the woods. When I see four battleships from Plymouth cruising by I feel fine about my benefit. If everyone gave up their job and claimed benefit it would bring about the collapse of the whole system which is causing the destruction of the planet. I believe the climate upheaval will crash the world's economy: there will be floods, earthquakes, no more petrol — it will all go pop! I see it happening in the next five years.
> · Gareth, aged 25 (speaking to the authors).

We sense a feeling of unease in the atmosphere: members are worried and unsure how a community can face the harsher economic climate of the nineties. Oak is ready to explain the difficulties: administration is one of his responsibilities and after six years he is the longest-term resident. Oak is tall, a lean man of thirty-six with a high forehead under a Mohican-style haircut. He wears boots without laces — badge of rural alternative living — and radiates uncertainty, rarely venturing a categorical answer or statement. 'No-one is obliged to work; it's too easy for people to just take it easy here. Keveral could be a brilliant place to live — and it's been improving over the years. But often it's energy-draining and soul-destroying, with conflicts blowing up. It can be even worse when they don't blow up — problems and issues that we put to one side and forget about, hoping that they will go away.'

He explains that all of the eight long-term members belong to a workers' co-operative which has no guidelines on how much work is expected. Applicants to join have to be acclaimed by consensus after a three-month probation. 'We don't want to exclude people, but we have to admit we're not financially viable; we're dependent on the state and while we're in that position we can't really prove anything to anyone.'

Oak is responsible for, and proud of, 2000 trees planted here over six years, but he says, 'I've taken it all on myself and haven't been very good at getting other people involved.' Many trees are suffering and the forest would benefit by more clearing of undergrowth. He had come to Keveral Farm for a more sociable life and opportunities to care for land. 'I've learned a lot. It's the conflicts on smaller issues that take time; just now it's veganism versus animal husbandry. Moth is so strong on veganism that he's thinking of leaving but he's a very useful member of the community as a blacksmith and mechanic.'

Three years earlier Oak had drawn up a list of six urgent tasks for the community — tasks which could well apply to many of the communities we visited later:

- ❧ More self-sufficiency in food and materials
- ❧ Recycling and alternative energy
- ❧ More support for other communities and projects
- ❧ That Keveral should be educational, progressive and radical
- ❧ Encouraging diversity in activities and land use
- ❧ Achieving financial self-sufficiency

Sadly, Oak admitted that little progress had been made on any of his points. Materials for a solar-heated shower had been bought but not erected, children's' camps had been successful but the community took no responsibility to educate its own children, workshops and craft activities were still in the planning stage and enlarged outlets for vegetables were being sought.

Ed, who is in charge of the vegetables, is determined that the business should make the community self-supporting, and that Keveral Farm should become a happy home for him, his German partner Marta, two-year-old Eamonn and another child on the way. He complains of frustration over the absence of a work ethic and harassment from vegans who object to Eamonn's milk in the communal refrigerator.

Ed, in his forties, detested the nine-to-five routine of mainstream life. 'The thought of living in a nuclear family was quite horrific. We wanted to get out of the city because of Eamonn; we wrote to thirty-five communities.'

The dispute over veganism turned quite nasty. One day Ed found ANIMAL MURDERER scrawled over the fridge, and a note saying he was 'raping the goat' by milking it. He says: 'I

I believe we could have a very rosy future here because there is so much potential for earning our living at the farm — from camping, courses, organic fruit and vegetables, woodland products, maybe a holiday caravan or two, the camping barn, the forge, crafts, maybe a farm-shop, charcoal, organic herbs, healing therapies, etc. etc. But first we have to do all the preparation to make it possible for everybody to survive here when the time comes, because we are all in it together.

· From *Like One Big Happy Family!* — Ed's vision statement at Keveral Farm.

could of course buy dairy products from the shop but that would be taking ten steps back from my vision of getting away from all those horrors.'

Much of the tension about veganism died down when Moth, fiercest of the vegans, stopped eating in the communal kitchen, although the meals there are vegan, and started eating where he lives, by his forge. Moth has shoulder-length hair and intense eyes and is never seen around without his dog.

'I was an Animal Rights activist. I've been a hunt sab. I support Plants for a Future; it was through Ken that I came down to Cornwall. Now this place is turning towards farming animals.'

Moth is totally opposed to killing animals. 'It's a male thing. We exploit animals the way women say they were exploited. For every goat or cow that gives us milk, its male offspring have to be slaughtered. Do we have the right to rape dairy livestock for milk and to steal their offspring? How can you respect your own rights if you are denying others their rights whilst exploiting them? We have the ability and the intelligence to survive without causing the death, suffering or exploitation of any other animal and to realise that they have feelings and respectable social structures.'

(*Dorothy writes:* I find Moth's arguments appealing but I wish he did not say them so angrily.)

A clear vision of a hard-working and well-scrubbed Keveral Farm comes from Gina, a beautiful, dark-skinned woman with luxurious black hair. She is thirty-four. Gina speaks quietly, with great conviction, as she tells her story.

'My mother was flamboyant and exotic, so I reacted at sixteen, and soon married a conventional man with a job. It didn't last. Four years of that and I was climbing up the wall. The whole of society seemed to me oppressive: it was always "never enough". So I went back to education and did a three-year Arts course and found myself back in the same trap — just as conventional and constricting.'

She spent years searching, taking drugs and sleeping rough. 'I came into a personal crisis because I could not make sense of the world from a spiritual point of view. I got involved in opposition to the Gulf War and the poll tax. Being in the middle of Trafalgar Square when riot police were coming at you was a crisis point for me: I realised that direct action was not achieving enough. There has to be a way of changing attitudes and society.' She joined a religious community where she learnt to meditate, but she found the place too authoritarian and left. She has been at Keveral for almost a year. Her relationship with one of the members has just ended and now she is starting another with Bill the Engineer, whom we met at Pure Genius in London (Chapter 3), who was about to move from that community to this. They'd met at a recent permaculture course held at Keveral

Farm which impressed them both; they intend to apply its principles here.

In her mission statement, Gina relates that the religious group she had lived among kept their house spotlessly clean. 'I am not suggesting we have to go to such extremes, but I think you will get the drift. I am aware that some people here have rotaphobia, and I can understand that, but surely as a group we can come up with some way to ensure that the place is at least clean. Also from a spiritual point of view, the act of cleansing, if done with the right attitude, is like opening the windows and blowing away all the cobwebs of tensions, emotions etc. Basically it makes you feel good and instils automatic respect for that space, especially if everyone is involved. And I feel the whole of Keveral needs the same treatment. Like the house, I see the cleaning, re-organising and throwing away of any unnecessary junk as very relevant and symbolic of clearing away the past and making space for the future.'

Next to Keveral Farm a gigantic field is put down to wheat — twenty hectares without a tree, without a flower. The wheat has been combine-harvested and the straw rolled into enormous bales waiting for a twenty-tonner to trundle down the rutted lane and remove them. The field has been so well dosed with chemicals that no weed is daring enough to show a leaf on what is in effect a factory floor. Misty, late summer morning air, with its hint of ozone from the nearby sea, wafts over the sterilised field.

It is easy to criticise Keveral Farm's haphazard efforts at organic farming, the lack of a master plan and the absence of a common will to work. Yet amongst the luxuriant hedges of the property, the whole of which would fit into this monster field with space to spare, we saw the wild flowers of late summer, the bees, butterflies and insects. Does farming have to present the mechanical horror of the shorn wheat field or the stressful chaos of the far more environmentally friendly Keveral? The real problem at Keveral seems to be the lack of a firm ideology. Anarchy, attractive as it may seem to people who feel oppressed, doesn't butter any parsnips. The unsolved problem, more troubling than the dispute about veganism, was: who should work, when and how? Some members were quite happy to subsist on benefit; others needed moral and physical independence.

In the end we felt Keveral Farm's problems were soluble because enough influential members were determined that it should be a place of work, order and reasonable cleanliness, and because the culture of endless Benefit payments for anyone who wants them was being killed off by a Conservative government, soon to be followed by a Labour government determined to finish that job.

Organic farmers, organic consumers

Organic vegetables are grown in the countryside while consumers live in towns; in a Living Lightly culture, the two must be linked. Without a steady urban market, organic growers cannot survive. Supermarkets have been trying for a decade or so to supply organic food, but they are an imperfect medium for this trade. Natural farming is less predictable than factory farming; its produce is less uniform, less suitable for bulk buying. Supermarkets operate by placing very large orders for an array of uniform produce — orders which they must feel free to cancel at short notice if the product doesn't sell as well as another.

A more flexible system is needed. In the US, farmers' markets have become popular and numbers are increasing — there is a lively and successful one twice a week in the heart of Manhattan. Many organic farmers sell by mail order. In Britain the most successful method of distribution has been the box scheme — in which vegetables are packed into standard boxes and delivered to the customer. Britain's largest co-operative box scheme, Organic Roundabout in Birmingham, takes weekly deliveries from a rural co-operative which trucks the vegetables into town. All these co-operatives — and the two co-operatives involved in Keveral Farm as well — are funded through Radical Routes, a 'co-operative of co-operatives' which plays a key part in organising finance for sustainable living in Britain.

The young people in Birmingham who distribute the boxes are radical seekers for new lifestyles, anarchists although they rarely use the word, living, working and reflecting in a paradigm of natural food, local economy and co-operative living. The farmers who supply them with organic food, on the other hand, are conventional people, 'growers' as they call themselves to distinguish them from market gardeners, who are simply filling a market niche.

British food and drink imports exceed exports by £5.87 billion. Yet a significant amount of the food imported could be produced or processed locally. Why import lettuces, spinach and apples in autumn and summer when they can be grown equally well locally? Why import so many apples from France when they could be grown here and when we are grubbing up orchards at an increasing rate? Why eat so much Danish bacon, when domestic pig producers could easily (and would like to) expand production? Why bring asparagus all the way from Spain for sale in English supermarkets in June, at the highest of the English asparagus season? Why demand that shops have strawberries all the year round, when the traditional availability of strawberries from May to July partially defines for most people the meaning of summer?
· Jules Pretty, *The Living Land*.

How strange that supermarket food, with so much that is exotic, treated, doctored and elaborately packaged, is considered 'mainstream', while the organic food that is natural, local and fresh, should seem alternative and eccentric!

Sustainable meat production

Organic growing is not all vegetarian, as we saw in the last chapter. The jury is still out on how much meat should be produced and consumed. Many growers consider livestock an essential part of a farm for the sake of the manure; some argue that milk production necessarily involves the birth of heifers, others like eating good-quality meat from a healthy animal that has been reared humanely. And this can be done. Helen Browning's 530-hectare mixed farm (dairy, pig and grain) near Swindon, on the Oxfordshire-Wiltshire border, is one of the larger organic farms in Britain, and one of the most successful, with a million-pound turnover on the farm and another million on its meat business. Helen says that after the BSE and other health scares the organic market had become so bullish that one farm in five could profitably convert right now, even though government support is minimal. In spite of growing public support for organic food, only 800 of Britain's 100,000 farmers are organic, farming only 0.3 percent of the farming area.

Helen believes that most farmers in Britain are too old to convert. She herself was twenty-five when she took over the tenancy of Eastbrook Farm from her non-organic father in 1986 — 'still young enough to make these quite substantial changes. It's much more difficult in your fifties.' She started with small-scale trials. It took seven years and only finished two years ago: a difficult time. 'We couldn't have done it in one go without heavy support because you have nothing to sell while converting.' To get an organic certificate from the Soil Association, every acre must be managed organically for at least two years.

At the beginning, Helen's main interest was the health of the soil and the animals. Ten years later she's more interested in the health of humans. 'At first I wasn't convinced that organic food was actually good for us. My views have completely changed and it began with the conversion of our livestock. I've *seen* the difference it makes. Changing cows' feed from commercial composites to organic pasture and forage and giving up systematic use of antibiotics changed their appearance from the first year. The look of the coat, the eyes, the shine, the general vitality of the herd just improved enormously.' It worked for people too. 'My diet has changed over the years. I'm not perfect and don't eat organic all the time but I feel much better and I've brought up my daughter that way. She's six. She has tremendous vitality and doesn't get colds and

In Western Europe the area devoted to organic agriculture has increased tenfold from 120,000 hectares in 1985 to 1.2 million hectares in 1996. The most rapid expansion was in Austria where organic farming now covers about seven percent of all farmland. The principal reason is the high level of funding and support from national policies and the public at large. Organic agriculture in Austria has become mainstream, with organic produce no longer selling at a premium but now a staple for many. In some locations whole villages have shifted into organic production, using box schemes for direct marketing. Labour use is ten to fifteen percent higher on organic farms, and so this agriculture is helping to keep communities economically viable.
· Jules Pretty, *The Living Land.*

coughs and it's been fascinating.'

And profitable. Milk from the farm goes through an organic co-operative and earns a premium of four pence a litre. Meat has been good news, too, especially since the BSE crisis which was 'a pretty crucial warning to the world. It produced a rise in all organic sales because people have realised that you can't just forget about where food comes from.' Organic dairy herds have had no BSE cases since 1986 with home bred animals. The couple of cases they did have were from calves brought in from non-organic farms.

Helen says the organic movement has a vegetarian image because its first successful products in the UK were fruits and vegetables. Now most organic farms are mixed. 'I think we do eat too much meat in our diet; if we had a wholesale shift towards organic agriculture we would see a reduction. Meat should be a treat, with some respect for where it comes from.'

Conversion to organic farming is expensive and risky, and many organic farmers are bitter that big subsidies go to chemical farming, leaving them with next to nothing. British farmers converting to organic methods get the equivalent of 82 ECUs per hectare (about £79 or $127) in government aid in the first two years for all categories of farming. The EU average payments are 190 ECUs for cereals (Austria, at the top of the league, pays 335 ECUs), 210 for grassland, 280 for vegetables and 540 for fruit trees.

Organic growers need a certificate from the Soil Association, Organic Farmers and Growers Ltd or the Biodynamic Farmers Association. The Soil Association, largest of the three, was founded fifty years ago by Lady Eve Balfour who had noticed in India that good husbandry results in healthy farms and people. Her observations are still being confirmed as recent tests show that children fed from Green Revolution crops, which require fertilisers, pesticides and irrigation, show mineral deficiencies, particularly zinc, and perform poorly in IQ tests. Such deficiencies are especially serious in the South, where people are more dependant on staple crops and enjoy less variety. The Soil Association campaigns for healthier food and a reform in European agricultural policies to reduce subsidies for industrial farming and increase help for farmers converting to organic. Few organic farmers want their produce to be subsidised: they want official help in converting their farms, and an end to the enormous subsidies for industrial agriculture, including the invisible subsidies inherent in the absence of penalties for the pollution caused by excessive transportation of industrial food.

Seeds

In North and South (see Chapter 9) people are making efforts to preserve traditional seeds. A British organisation promoting good gardening and farming is the Henry Doubleday Research Association, which offers advice, conducts research and runs a prestigious display centre at Ryton, near Coventry. This is one of those organisations that enables people who don't want to make enormous steps in changing their mainstream lifestyles to take small, progressive steps. The HDRA has a Heritage Seed Library which gives its members packets of seeds, in more than 800 varieties, that have not been recognised by the European Union and cannot legally be sold. Many such varieties, like the crimson-flowered broad bean, were once commercial favourites but have been dropped from the national list, so it is illegal to sell them. Each December, members get a Seed Library catalogue, from which they choose up to seven varieties for the coming season. HDRA reaches out to the South in its Tropical Organic Agriculture Project with help and advice to farmers. The association's Tropical Tree Seed Distribution Service has sent fourteen million tree seeds to over 400 groups in Africa and Asia.

When food is grown organically and distributed in its local bioregion, the problems of modern agriculture — food miles, poor quality food and soil degradation — will be solved. Organic agriculture *can* feed us all if we in the North are prepared to pay its higher cost and to lessen or eliminate our consumption of animal protein. Paying more for healthier food will save us money in the long run.

6

Farming with a face

●●

A **New England autumn** is one of those sights that you have heard about,
feel sceptical, and then find reality exceeds any expectation — like the
Taj Mahal by moonlight or King's College Choir, Cambridge, in full choral
voice. We were driving from Pennsylvania to New Hampshire, through woods
in their fall colours, from purple across the spectrum of reds and golden
yellows. In the last century there would have been far fewer trees. Most of
these glowing oaks and beeches are self-regenerated woodland since farmers
have stopped working the land. It is unusual in the modern world to find farmland returning to forest; we are tourist beneficiaries of the decline in local
agriculture.

Eighty-five percent of New England was once farmed — now barely five
percent. Nine-tenths of this region's food is imported from all over the US
depending on the season. Secluded and mostly affluent homes have replaced
small farms and the tree cover has returned. Foliage time in New England
creates a mini tourist boom; guest-houses were full and prices up.

We have come to New England because we want to see community
supported agriculture in action. CSA is an innovative way of keeping small
farms viable as part of the community they serve. These intensive organic
farms do not need a lot of land and are never likely to be a threat to the
woods.

Our hosts in the university town of Durham are John Carroll and his wife
Diana, who are younger than us by a good decade (nearly everyone is, since
we aren't researching in senior citizens' homes.) John is Professor of
Environmental Studies at the University of New Hampshire. He subjects his
students to the concepts of farming sustainably and living lightly, which, he
says, are so unfamiliar and disturbing to some of them that they get
depressed. John's friends include all the CSA farmers of New England. So he
is a good contact for us as well as a good friend and host.

The Carrolls have remained in the same house and the same marriage for
over twenty years, an uncommon statistic in American academia. Because

there is no perceived need to save money and energy by grouping dwellings together, houses here do not line the edge of the road but stand solidly, unfenced behind their tree screens. Diana shows us around. House style for her means a level of comfort and ease, a matching of fitments and linens, a lavish use of wood panelling and a choosing of objects for both utility and beauty. The house is carefully, not ostentatiously, luxurious in every detail. Two teenage daughters are away at school; the elder at a prestigious New England college, the younger on a wilderness training programme in Mexico.

Diana is deeply concerned for the state of the environment. The values of a working class Catholic upbringing taught her 'that certain things mattered — they still do.' Conscious of the energy demands that their way of life entails — the high-ceilinged living room, electric cooker and washing appliances — the Carrolls, like so many of us, feel trapped in the world as they find it. And in their America of affluence and wide spaces the unease can be sharper.

'Our efforts to reduce energy,' says Diana in her diffident manner, 'are only a drop in the bucket.' Their light bulbs are low-energy; their clothes dryer stays unplugged until the winter and a wood-burning stove in the sitting room keeps the oil-fired central heating low. Although the Carrolls could afford a second car, they persist, in spite of their daughters' complaints, in owning only one — the sole one-car family in the block. At the nearby high school the parking lot is filled with the students' cars, not to speak of the much larger one at the university.

Can all the world ever live like this? The uncomfortable statistic bandied around the Carrolls' living room at a Sunday brunch is one we know all too well: with less than a twentieth of the world's population, the US emits nearly a quarter of CO_2 emissions.

This is the country with the worst environmental record and the most audacious thinking on the alternatives. Gasoline costs less than bottled water and homes and offices are still as overheated in winter and overcooled in summer as they were before the days of environmental awareness. In 1997, lobbying by a consortium of energy corporations was able to defeat the President's minimalist proposals for cutting greenhouse gas emissions. New England is the cradle of American environmentalism, where the first pilgrims settled, prospered and named their towns after English ones. Today the United States, main home of the corporations which rule the world, is also the home of the most advanced planning to circumvent the corporations' power. Thousands of Internet sites and hundreds of specialist forums and chat-lines are devoted to this cause and explore the theory and practice. The science of ecology is well served in this country with writers and scientists like John Muir and Aldo Leopold. The early protest against greed and waste was etched into the literary tradition when Henry Thoreau, in 1865, briefly abandoned his bourgeois lifestyle for his sustainable sojourn in the woods around Walden pond. Today, the sharpest edge of environmental research and technological achievement is found in the US — in Amory and Hunter Lovins' futuristic eco-home and laboratory, which grows bananas with solar energy in the Rocky Mountains, or in fields of perennial wheat and rice with which Wes Jackson hopes to replace agriculture in the next century, or in John Todd's Living Machine which can turn a whole town's sewage into compost by natural processes, or in high-tech solar homes, some made of old tyres, called Earth Ships, in the Arizona desert.

Community supported agriculture is a simple idea: a farmer invites a group of local people to share the costs of each year's production in return for a weekly box of fresh, organic produce. The members give the farmer interest-free operating capital and share the risks as well as the produce of each harvest. Marketing is taken care of in advance: there is no middleman and the farmer does not need to sell to supermarkets more interested in cosmetic uniformity than taste. There are over 650 CSA schemes in North America, numbers are growing and arrangements becoming more sophisticated, as CSA farms have begun to include foods from neighbouring farmers to increase variety.

John Carroll suggested we visit Sam and Elizabeth Smith at Caretaker Farm — one of the earliest and one of the most successful CSA farms in New England.

Caretaker Farm

The farm sits in the extreme north-east corner of Massachusetts on sixteen hectares of some of its poorest soil. On prepared vegetable beds of around two hectares, it produces organic vegetables for 250 adults and children living in and around Williamstown. Each shareholder pays a lump sum at the start of the season. In return they collect their vegetables twice a week, pick their own soft fruit and herbs, let their children see and touch real farm animals and, if they wish, help out from time to time. The cost of a share, fixed every year in advance at a meeting, is currently $620 for a family of two or more: $310 for single membership.

Both sides in this bargain are happy. The shareholders think of their membership as a privilege and they say it has revived their community. The Smiths can grow organic food, which is their passion and which is tricky to sell through mainstream channels, and still make a living.

Sam says his son-in-law criticises him for his sloppy fences and his sloppy appearance: we saw him wearing a worsted waistcoat buttoned to the neck

If there is a standard model or average CSA in the United States, it would probably serve sixty to seventy families using approximately three acres of farmland, excluding grazing or feed crops. Its annual budget would range somewhere between $50,000 and $75,000, with a share costing $400 per year. An overwhelming majority of customers are white professionals living in urban areas who want a deeper connection to their food source. They're also willing to support farmers who can guarantee a steady supply of 'clean' food for their families. These households can afford to pay for their food months in advance, a privilege people living from pay-cheque to pay-cheque can't consider. A number of CSAs have tried to address this issue by accepting labour and food stamps in return for shares. Interestingly enough, members who invest in a CSA pay slightly less for what they receive than they would if they purchased organic produce on the commercial market.
· Daniel Imhoff in *The Case Against the Global Economy.*

over a battered check shirt, and a baseball cap. A lanky figure at sixty-three with a weathered, sunburnt face, he speaks in measured, ringing tones suitable for a pulpit; a favourite subject is radical theology.

We arrived to find Sam in the fields with Stephanie, the current apprentice, covering raised beds with straw to keep them warm enough for early spring planting. We were allowed to help but Sam bellowed at us in his sonorous voice when, to get hold of a new load of straw, we stepped *onto* the bed. 'Never across the bed! Take the long way round.' We had transgressed the morality which enjoins that soil must never be compacted, even by human weight, and raised beds must be cosseted. Most organic farmers find that raised beds produce higher yields than flat beds.

When we explained we'd driven from Maine with the help of a computer-printed itinerary, Sam shuddered and said he was a Luddite — identifying himself with Kirkpatrick Sale, Satish Kumar and others in the Living Lightly movement who are hostile to computers because they serve the interests of the corporate as opposed to the convivial society. Straddling lifestyles and attitudes, the Smiths' farm has solar panels for hot water on the bakehouse roof, but also a heavy-duty tractor (working between the raised beds, not on them, of course) a car, mains electricity, mains water. Although there's no dishwasher, the Smiths have allowed themselves a floor-to-ceiling refrigerator and washing machine. Sam often asks the time, explaining that his own life needs no watch but he has to ask out of consideration for other people.

The stone farmhouse dates from 1810 and the Smiths have been able to refurbish it with their steady income from the shareholders. The house's timbered walls and low ceilings provide a warm and intimate feel: wood has ousted plastic: wood floors, wooden cupboards, wooden cereal bowls on the

Sam Smith at Caretaker Farm.

table. An ancient apple tree dominates the garden and further on is a magnificent, golden-skirted willow. From the kitchen sink you look down past the
raised beds, and up again through woods to a ridge in the Brodie mountains.
A shoulder of Mount Greylock, the highest in Massachusetts at 2,000 metres,
closes the view to the left.

Sam and Elizabeth, both slow speakers, don't mind being interrupted, especially by each other. Their marriage, like that of their friends the Carrolls, is of
a rare longevity in America, having started in 1959 and still continuing. They
squabble and contradict one another with the ease of long practice. Elizabeth
has a perfectly proportioned face with one thick pigtail hanging over a shoulder.

Neither of the Smiths had a farming background, having come into agriculture through the route of social protest, and now they grow food as an act

of right livelihood. 'For me it goes back a long way,' Elizabeth said. 'When I went to college the civil rights movement had begun.' Studying art at Yale, she met another anti-Vietnam war student, they fell in love and married. 'People would call us hippies but that was not how we saw ourselves. We both became teachers.' Sam is a freethinking Protestant who says he'd be perfectly at home being a Jew because his moral inspiration comes from the Torah. 'My reading of Genesis is that humans are on earth to work and look after the land.'

Elizabeth adds, 'With the oil crisis of 1974 came a mood of people wanting to be more independent. We began a food co-operative in Vermont, associating with certain people who felt like us. We were among the founders of NOFA (North-eastern Organic Farmers Association); it was a people's movement. Pure logic: without any oil this country could become victim of a food crisis unless we are self-reliant. A whole group of farmers were out to prove that you could grow food here.' This is the catastrophe theory we hear over and over again in the Living Lightly movement. Its acceptance by the Smiths has reinforced their wish to farm oganically.

Sam resigned as a teacher. They bought Caretaker Farm from their savings and a parental loan. When they started farming they took odd jobs in winter to eke out revenue. They sold vegetables to restaurants and opened a farm shop and bakery.

Over the farm shop they hung a sign: Come and See the Farm. 'We wanted to educate people about farming, show them how important agriculture is in care of the land. The message was not getting through. Tourists came to the shop who'd go home and never be changed by the experience. We were providing a form of entertainment. And the locals thought we were gentlemen farmers. CSA gave us a way out.'

When they started their CSA: 'We were very idealistic. We expected to revolutionise people, now we respect where they are and try to accommodate them. At first the share price was $450 with people taking all they wanted. That was too idealistic. People didn't like it. They signed up but didn't understand it. Some said: This is America, we don't want communism. Later it went to $300 per adult and limited quantities to be taken in small baskets which can contain any mix that people want.'

'This is the Kingdom,' Sam said as we came back in from his fields for breakfast of corn pancakes, maple syrup and yoghurt. Harvesting leeks while discussing radical theology under an autumn sun before breakfast had been a pleasure that amounted to a sort of paradise. Elizabeth accepted our compliments on her pancakes.

She pointed to Hereford cows grazing in a neighbouring field, and her eyes filled with tears as she said the farmer could no longer get enough for his milk to keep his dairy viable, because another supermarket had opened. In 1969, when the Smiths bought Caretaker Farm, there were fifteen dairy farms in the region. Now there are three, and one soon to close. Along their road four poultry farmers used to sell eggs and other food; none are left.

In contrast, the CSA enables the Smiths to live adequately in return for very hard work. The shareholders provide them with a wage of $14,000 a year each — equivalent to what they used to earn from the market stall and restaurant they owned. They are now much better off: in addition to their income the CSA arrangement provides them with $3000 for their health insurance and another $2000 for their pension contributions — and now they have no more marketing costs. 'We live at a standard slightly below an average two-adult family but we're doing what we want,' Elizabeth said. The farm's total annual budget is $72,000.

> If society values the lowest possible food prices and the highest possible wages, then the family farm will not survive. But other values are both possible and more appropriate. We need a food system that is efficient not just at turning labour into cheap food, but that is efficient at turning energy into food.
> · Paul Fieldhouse in *Agriculture and Human Values Journal*, Summer 1996.

The shareholders in the CSA come from an educated, white middle class, interested in alternative ideas. The social aspect of the CSA is what draws many of them. Most of the shareholders call to collect vegetables, help out, or bring children for an outing. 'It's a pity that more people are not into all this,' said Margery, a teacher. 'You need a certain amount of education to see that the less than perfect vegetables that I get from the Smiths are so much tastier and healthier than the globular tomatoes from the supermarket.'

Ray was bringing his compost, a plastic bucket of vegetable and kitchen scraps. All shareholders are encouraged to do this and many do. Ray doubts if he could get his vegetables cheaper elsewhere, but his main interest in the farm is not the food. 'We need to support small farms. We're fortunate that a CSA can exist in this small town. Maybe the presence of a college helps, bringing in the kind of people who care about this.' (The Smiths' CSA members amount to barely three percent of the Williamstown area's population of 8500.) What really attracts Ray and his wife are the side benefits. 'It's the flowers and herbs we can pick. The people we meet. When my wife comes here and picks strawberries she feels happy.'

For Beverly, going to the farm has become a highlight of her week. 'I love the food and also it's a connection to the land which recalls an earlier, less complex time in my life. The farm rejuvenates our spirit. We can't wait to see how the peas are doing, or if the basil is plentiful.'

The Smiths don't complain about their work load: they thrive on it. Nobody at Caretaker Farm comments on the fact that there is too much work. Elizabeth carries out one farm job after another, ending at 10 p.m. when she takes the swill bucket out to the pigs. Sam is always out longer than he intended, mulching, shifting straw bales with his tractor, lifting leeks, moving harvested cabbages, mending the deer fence. Yet there is order: the mulching of the beds and the last of the leek harvest can still be done before winter, in spite of the frosts that have already set in. There is no panic. Winter will be more restful.

We are shown with pride the root cellar stacked with potatoes, leeks, cabbages, squash and root vegetables — enough for their shareholders throughout the cold season. Practically everything has been grown with no outside inputs. A few hundred bales of straw were bought for mulch and animal bedding.

Sam throws straw bales about as effortlessly as he manhandles the boxes we have packed with leeks, which are even heavier. The modern generation will not work that hard, Sam says. The Smiths doubt whether either of their daughters or their son will take over their farm. Their daughter lives on the farm in another house, a pragmatic choice (both partners work locally) rather than a return to the extended family.

'There's an aversion to work in our culture,' Sam says. 'But if people have ownership, and something to gain and a decent incentive, I think many would be willing to work. After all, think of city people with two jobs: they work abominably hard and have no ownership and no real security.'

The Smiths' attitude to animal husbandry is similar to Helen Browning's (Chapter 6). They don't object to mixed farming provided the animals have a reasonable quality of life. Since the apprentices are usually vegetarian, they only eat their home-produced lamb or beef when the apprentices are absent.

Sam and Elizabeth run a practical, successful farm with an underlying spiritual element. Neither Sam nor Elizabeth admit to what seems to us a profound love for what they are doing; when you talk to them you are aware of the spaces between the words. Conventional farmers can be heard laughing at organic farmers dabbling in 'muck and magic'. It is true that many organic farmers subscribe to a mystical approach they call biodynamic. The Smiths spoke with respect of biodynamic methods but a more thoroughgoing practitioner is Trauger Groh, whose farm in New Hampshire we visited next.

Trauger Groh at Temple-Wilton Farm, New Hampshire.

Trauger Groh

Trauger grew up in an anthroposophic family devoted to Rudolf Steiner's biodynamic principles of farming which he describes as 'a spiritual idea that is not an economic idea.' In this method a farm is self-sustaining, producing its own organic inputs and recycling its own wastes, and plant growth is managed in accordance with the magnetic effect of the stars and planets as well as the moon.

Trauger inherited a farm that was eventually expropriated by the German Air Force which gave him enough compensation for a new venture. 'So when I was thirty-five I had to decide: do I want to stay in farming? I had this friend with 200 acres near Hamburg and he could not make a living. He could hardly support his family. He asked me to join him and I had to tell him that as long as we privately own that place we could never really manage. With owning land come the problems with mortgages and so on. A farmer may *think* he owns his land but he doesn't; he has a mortgage and he has to grow what will pay the mortgage, not what he wants. We wanted to co-operate more with people than with banks. So my friend decided to donate his farm to a non-profit land-owning company. We wanted to separate the farm operations from the property.'

This is no solution for traditional farmers who, in any case, are dying out, but can serve newcomers coming into farming who have neither land nor capital. They need to be connected to people who inherit land and want it to serve a social purpose. Trauger contributed his own capital to the trust, a CSA scheme was formed and works well to this day. He had introduced a new dimension to community-farming: that a farmer should be relieved of the burdens, not only of the operating costs but also the ownership of land.

Trauger withdrew from the German project, came to the US, re-married

Land cannot be used as a commodity. The history of farm mortgage and property taxes is the history of farm crisis, the depletion of land, of deforestation, of erosion. Whether the farm has a good year or bad, whether there is drought, or hail, or general crop failure, both mortgage and tax payments become due. This again forces farmers into growing market crops that promise a short-term profit. Local land suitable for agriculture must be gradually protected by land trusts. To do this, every piece of farmland has to be purchased for the last time and then, out of the free initiative of local people, be placed into forms of trust that will protect it from ever again being mortgaged or sold for the sake of private profit. Non-profit land trusts must then make the land available to qualified people who want to take it into ecologically sound uses. Such arrangements will give the right of land use to individuals or growers, either for the time they are willing or capable of using it, or in a lifelong contract that could include the right to find one's successors.

· Trauger Groh, *Farms of Tomorrow.*

and set up a new CSA farm at Temple-Wilton. Both the German and his American farms are biodynamic.

After forty years of farming, he has the authority of a man who has reached his own conclusions through his own experience; he is a hands-on philosopher with no New Age talk of 'energy' or 'vibes' . He manages to make the moon-talk and star-talk that goes with biodynamics sound like common-sense.

As a farm, the thirty hectares at Temple are not highly productive: the soil is poor and a much wider variety of vegetables needs to be grown on it than it can easily bear. But the CSA works. Every Tuesday and Thursday throughout the year the 105 shareholders (sixty-three families) can take as much seasonal farm produce as they wish. Trauger took us into the distribution shed, where vegetables are neither weighed nor washed. How did this help-yourself-at-will policy work? It hadn't worked at Caretaker Farm. 'At the beginning we had problems persuading people to take enough. There were a few cases where people grabbed, but that was the certain exception.'

When the scheme began in 1986, Trauger pooled the farm's resources with two others and invited local families to give land for the joint farm; people without land could contribute money instead.

Fertility and productivity in nature arise out of diversity, not out of specialisation or monoculture. The author counted up to seventy plant species in use on one of the biodynamic farms he served, including six grains, eight leguminous fodder plants, twelve grasses, numerous brassicas, vegetables and herbs. By contrast, a modern dairy farm in New England cultivates, beyond its hayfields, usually only one species: corn.

· Trauger Groh, *Farms of Tomorrow.*

The farm employs three workers and two apprentices. Today's shareholders pay whatever they feel they can afford in support of the farm's annual operating budget of $109,000. The better-off subsidise the others. The altruism of those who pay more is perhaps helped through the influence of Rudolf Steiner's anthroposophy; many Steiner devotees live in this area.

There are many unconventional features on this farm. Trauger does not believe that pasteurising is essential with milk from healthy cows. Selling unpasteurised milk does not break New Hampshire law because shareholders are legally farmers and can consume their own produce. The members have their own milk bottles ranged on shelves and they are responsible for washing them.

The store also has items for sale: bread, organic meat from the farm, pastas, soaps and cheese from neighbouring farms. Trauger's principle is: 'We share the costs of the farming with our members but if they want us to process something then they have to pay.'

Healthy food could be puzzling to some new members: 'One of our new customers called frantically after she had cracked the first of our eggs. She thought that we'd want to know that the yolk was "terribly orangish". She had never before seen a healthy egg.'

Would such an integrated farm be possible without animals? Trauger insists that it would not. 'The danger is that CSA becomes just a special way of marketing. We want a new idea of farming in which *people* participate. We can save the world only if every farm in itself is sustainable. If the American prairie is exploited that is no good for organic farming. Here we don't import

---

In the biodynamic approach, the farm is seen as an organism; the function of each part is essential to the existence of the whole, and also to each of the other parts. An organism has its own inner life and circulation that is different from its surroundings... The organism of the farm is created by the domestic animals. Inside the farm's legal boundaries the farmer established a herd or various herds. Ideally they feed from the vegetation inside the farm, summer and winter, without anything brought in from other farms. The animals respond with a manure that is formed exclusively by the flora of the farm organism. This manure is collected, and when properly treated comes back to the plants of this place, stimulating them. In this process of correspondence between farm animal and farm vegetation, the farm develops and becomes more and more individualised. Over time the animals adapt and become rooted to their place. This is reflected in better health of the animals and in a better performance. The inner health of the animals radiates back through the manure into the plant world. An organism is born and develops in time. As with any organism, the farm organism needs a stronger inner circulation of substance.

· Trauger Groh, *Farms of Tomorrow.*

anything. We work with local forces of nature and with local skills.' Trauger is convinced, and convincing, that properly managed organic farming can provide enough food for local populations.

We put to Trauger the argument of vegetarians and vegans that animals consume too much grain — desperately needed by humans — to be a sustainable part of human diet if future famines are to be avoided. They argue that animal manure is not needed: clover and green manures are enough to produce healthy crops.

Trauger replies that he does not feed grain to his animals, a rare, hardy breed descended from original stock brought by English settlers. His cows are fed on pasture and hay and produce a satisfactory amount of milk. Ruminants, according to biodynamic principles, are not supposed to eat grain which weakens them but to consume large amounts of forage. 'One of my cows can easily have fifteen calves — the average is 2.3 in Germany and three in America. I tell vegetarians that I would keep cows even if nobody ate meat because I want the highest possible

> The moon influence is easy to test. If you plant in the waning moon then the germination is much slower and you get more weeds to fight. Close to full moon you have an immediate germination. We have in the zodiac four basic influences: water, earth, air and fire. So if you want good root crops, better plant when the moon is in an earth sign. Virgo is an earth sign. If you harvest in a watery sign, things don't keep well. The roots rot. It's not moon phases this time, but the position of the moon in the zodiac. It goes through the zodiac in twenty-eight days. All you need is Maria Thun's plant calendar which comes out every year in twelve languages. Most organic farmers use it. This is a new science which will develop, like chaos theory.
> · Trauger Groh (interview with the authors).

quality in vegetables and for that I need dung. The cow is an animal that in certain cultures has been kept holy. The people don't know why themselves. They don't eat the cow but still need her. The digestion of the cow is an enormous process that really brings cosmic forces into the substance. And since they are not conscious like we are they cannot abuse this. They give something in the manure which we could never make for ourselves. Our thinking processes and our consciousness degrades our excrement.' At this point, Trauger lost us a bit.

In its self-sufficiency, biodynamic farming shares some basic principles with permaculture. After harvest the ground is not ploughed for the next sowing because aerating the soil is good but turning it is bad. 'The modern plough came into use in 1830 or thereabouts and since then the fertility of our soil has been going down. People have to throw more and more lime.'

We suggested to Trauger that biodynamic farming, especially its connection to the heavens, was a part of New Age superstition, on a par with astrology. He was neither offended nor ruffled.

'You see, the plant is totally an object of its environment. It has no self-being. What influences it? Everyone respects a major cosmic influence like the season, which is the sun and moon, the light and so on. People have forgotten other constellations have an influence too, especially the distant planets. It's not just in ancient Greece and Rome that they did things by the stars. In a scientific way, it has been shown that if you repeatedly let copper chloride crystallise, under different constellations, you get measurements of the influence of the constellations on matter.' We were glad to have these esoteric matters explained, but remained agnostic.

Biodynamic farming includes spraying crops with diluted compost preparations. Trauger used two sprays and five medicinal plant composts. Stinging nettles were very important: 'We harvest them when about to bloom, dig a hole and bury the greens for a year: then we have a blackish, decomposed matter which is the preparation. We have two field sprays. Ground silica crystal we put into a cowhorn which stays in the earth from the end of September to Easter, then we stir that for a whole hour and then we spray it. We also fill the horn with cow manure. One cowhorn is enough for one acre. That degree of dilution is mysterious to some people but one has to get a better feeling for the polarity of manure and the silicon. Silicon can carry cosmic forces. It has many sides to it. Cow manure is very earthy. We spray the horn manure preparation on the soil, the silica on the leaf. Silica is not soluble in water: the tiny crystals are intact in the water, but the force of the silicon has been taken on by the water. Silica has to be there. Some people think they can achieve the same results with meditation, as they do at Findhorn. This is something I cannot follow.' Nor could we.

Robyn van En[1]

For a less mystical view of farming we went to Robyn at her Indian Line Farm — the first CSA in Massachusetts. Her scheme collapsed after disagreements with her shareholders and she is now a full-time organiser, a director of CSA of North America. Robyn is an evangelist, a one-issue person, restless and fast-talking, driven by her vision of a nationwide partnership between people who grow food and people who eat it.

'I'm an organiser person; I'm ego-endowed I guess. CSA gets me out of bed in the morning, this is some of the best news I've ever heard and given what a crazy world it is, and it looks like they're getting worse and worse, the potential is tremendous.'

Robyn is in dispute with the biodynamic part of the CSA movement which she sees as splitting the organisation. 'Biodynamics is brilliant and anthroposophy is wonderful, but it doesn't really get through to most people in CSA. I had a connection with the larger community. People are barely ready for organic; we have to take this a step at a time. Organic is a universal concept which anyone can be part of; we can't have any sectarian aspects to it. We tend to be a very ego-endowed group and sometimes we get aggressive.'

She sees the potential of CSA as applicable to a wider cottage industry movement. She is impressed with Japanese co-operatives where people began with vegetables and moved into household goods in general. (See Chapter 12.) 'If you can keep an honest community scale and really local economics and the well-being that comes from that, then you start to question how many things we are importing and why. Massachusetts imports 85 percent of its food to the tune of four billion dollars a year when it's been determined that we can produce at least thirty-five percent of our food, putting another billion dollars in the Massachusetts economy as well as employing local people, enhancing agricultural integrity and preserving open space. One dollar spent within a community is worth three dollars after the spin-off effects.'

'Many farmers are afraid to open their doors to a CSA because they don't want the people coming to their farm. But they don't have to: all they need to do is network with others who don't mind, who love it. With this flexibility, farmers of every kind can draw up their budget, claim a share of their production costs and link up with a CSA that has 200 families. And that arrangement can include spring water, or wine, cheese, candles and soap and so on. In Washington State they have fishing shares on the CSA principle: everyone pays their share of costs and gets their share of fish in the season.'

Robyn is working to make CSA link town and country. She put eight farmers in touch with 350 New York city families comprising 1000 people;

The easygoing inefficient farmers are mostly all gone now. Every acre a tractor won't fall off is operated by a gung-ho farmer-tiger with a banker on his tail, in front of whom he must take his yearly oath of obeisance. 'I do hereby solemnly promise to do everything in my power to raise more corn and soybeans than I did last year, no matter how much it costs me, so that I might enrich my bankers, my agribusiness suppliers, my government advisors, my farm magazines, and hopefully, myself, while I claw my neighbour's eyes out'. Priding himself on his businesslike attitude, he then goes forth to do what no businessperson would dare contemplate: to produce for a market, heedless of what that market needs.

· Gene Logsdon, *At Nature's Pace.*

those families now get their deliveries and come out occasionally to the farms for a spring planting 'pot-luck' or a fall harvest festival. Their share price includes delivery to the city to a drop point, a day care centre and a food kitchen.

Liberating land for small-scale farming is another top priority for Robyn, who works closely with local land trusts. Landowners who join such a trust are offered money for giving up development rights on their land. Such land can never be built on in the future but it can be farmed, and is more likely to retain its value if it is. The scheme enables farmers to lease land. The land trust derives income from donations by people interested in protecting land for farming and for conservation, and from renting houses already on the land. Many of these sites are beautiful but only because they are farmed. When you preserve such a property for non-development all the adjoining properties become that much more valuable because of the open space. In Massachusetts, weekenders from New York are catching on. A community land site is held in perpetuity but it has houses on it and the sale or leasing of those raises the money needed to preserve the land. A farmer in this scheme also leases his land; if he leaves, the land is reserved for another farmer who will also have priority for a house.

The idea of land trusts has come from South to North. In rural India the Gramdan movement persuaded owners to give some of their land to community organisations for landless peasants. People cannot simply and easily return to the land; it is too expensive. In Britain a few land trusts administer properties which are farmed for the sake of conservation. Land trusts will be needed if large amounts of land are ever to be farmed intensively and with conservation practices.

CSA farms grow food organically, following traditional methods. Some adopt biodynamic or ermaculture methods, or sometimes a combination. We found at Caretaker Farm and also talking to other organic growers that they sought and found values apart from the profit and loss of commercial farming. This was never more evident than at Genesis Farm, New Jersey.

> Environmentalism is the new religion of our age, but it is only a Sunday morning religion because we still reserve the right to sell the land we own and care for to the highest bidder. We have yet to fully imagine and embrace a culture in which land use is allocated by social and environmental contract rather than by chequebook.
> · Robert Swann, President of the Schumacher Society, USA.

Genesis Farm

Down the hill you come to a handsome, timbered farmhouse. This is where the three Dominican sisters live and work, with helpers and volunteers. The farm centres around a big shed, the distribution centre. The Earth Literacy classes happen somewhere quite of out sight, in another handsome old house called Bread and Roses, behind a wood on another hill.

We were received with warmth and herbal tea, accepted as fellow travellers in a global culture which recognises its own. Marylin Ferguson has named it in her book, The Aquarian Conspiracy. You can move round in this fraternity, like monks of old, and find recognition and acceptance, an openness to the stranger that grows rarer in our society.

Sister Miriam MacGillis said right away the place was not religious, you could be anything or nothing and even use bad language if that helps you out. Our friend Satish Kumar, editor of *Resurgence* magazine in the UK, had claimed she was remarkable. You only have to spend five minutes with her to feel the unqualified commitment, the humility, attention to detail and determination to live as she preaches, that make her so. She and the other two sisters wear sweaters and miniskirts.

The house and land were given to the sisters for farming and contemplation and gradually the idea of a teaching centre and a community garden developed. The teaching is based on the conviction of Thomas Berry, priest and writer, that a new paradigm has dawned, replacing the narrow 'scientism' and dualism of the Enlightenment with a holistic and spiritual interpretation of the cosmos. The teachers are convinced the paradigm has arrived because it had to arrive, since the old paradigm has failed. The evolution of the universe is a spiritual unfolding in which a new point of consciousness has been reached. Human beings are that consciousness which must now bring the universe into a new harmony.

The purpose of Genesis Farm is to grow food, distribute it and eat it as a spiritual experience. This non-religious spirituality runs through the Living Lightly culture. Religion 'proper' is too man-centred: open-ness to nature doesn't go with the closed systems of religious dogma. So nuns and priests in the movement tend to be the rebels like Berry, sometimes, tragically, the outcasts of their Church like Matthew Fox. We do not yet know what sort of rebel or spiritual adventurer Sister Miriam is.

We have planned to stay a week, work on the farm, attend the courses and learn from Sister Miriam. Soon after we arrived it was supper time. Whoever has cooked the meal introduces and briefly describes each dish. Then a circle is formed and everyone gives thanks for something good that happened during their day. And the vegetarian food was good, if a little bland for our taste after all those years in India. Our first meal was cooked by students at the cookery class which is held in the farmhouse.

Seventy shareholders come once a week to collect the fruit and vegetables produced on Genesis Farm's 2.4 hectares of garden and ten hectares of orchard, The average share is 5.8 kg for a family of four. Some members have only a summer share, others only a winter share. A capital fund included in each year's share price, with gifts and interest-free loans, has helped to pay for development on the farm, including a root cellar and three greenhouses.

The shareholders are the outer layer of this farm, like lay supporters of a monastery. They want tastier and safer food and they want to help grow it; several come every week to join in the packing, others act as unpaid distributors in their own areas. The toddlers tumble under their mothers' feet, while older children pick berries

On our first morning, an early frost delayed spinach-picking to an hour uncomfortably close to noon, when the shareholders were expected. It was a crisis and the farm staff worked extra hard, braced by the abrupt arrival of cold weather in early autumn. We felt at ease working among them. The garden workers care for their earth as if they were monks, taking care not to step on it, leaving the spinach roots in the ground to nourish the soil, and harvesting the herbs so as to allow maximum regeneration. They earn only seven dollars an hour. Even on low wages, they don't complain often and talk of their work as a privilege.

> It has become clear to me that the concept of food itself is the key to the transformation of our ecological crisis. Unless our human species can open itself to the concept of food as a holy mystery through which we eat ourselves into existence, then the meaning of existence will continue to elude us... When we understand that food is not a metaphor for spiritual nourishment, but is itself spiritual, then we eat food with a spiritual attitude and taste and are nourished by the Divine directly.
> · Miriam McGillis (interview with the authors).

One of the gardeners is Matt Pearson, almost thirty, a biologist who has conducted research on whales, dolphins and fish. He hated the 'politics' of universities and 'sucking up to people to get grants,' and decided 'to learn how to grow my own food.' That choice he describes as 'a selfish thing — it was what I wanted for myself.' None of the gardeners has been trained in biodynamics, although a few of the shareholders are keen on it and the sisters prefer it. 'We're going to have to attend courses on it,' Matt said. 'Basically, this is an organic farm: biodynamics is added.'

Sister Miriam was forty when the direction of her life as a nun was changed by Thomas Berry, a Passionist priest who is President of the American

Teilhard Association. (Teilhard de Chardin was the great Catholic philosopher who tried to combine faith and scientific traditions in an integrated world
view culminating in the idea of human perfectibility through accelerated
evolution.) She was teaching social justice when they met. 'None of us had
heard of him. I didn't know what he was talking about but I was dazzled.' In
the intervening years, she has become a leading exponent of Berry's
cosmology.

We objected mildly to the belief that humans represent the consciousness
of the universe. How does that fit in with the probability that life exists on other
planets? Sister Miriam replied: 'Consciousness is a dimension of the universe
and we participate in our own way, but that doesn't mean that consciousness
is limited to human beings. Our little tiny earth community's self-reflected
consciousness is a unique capacity of the human but that doesn't mean it's
different from the universe as a whole. Our planet goes back five billion years.
The earth is now capable of thinking about itself and that is the human — the
being in whom the earth has become spiritually aware, awakened into
consciousness. In the human the earth begins to reflect on itself. Humans are
the earth, conscious. Yet the human species is very young and very primitive.'

When we asked if this cosmology made her move away from Christian
orthodoxy, she replied indirectly, with tact, in the affirmative. 'These are issues
of cosmology, not religion. When you change the cosmology then you have
to reflect theology in a different way. That's why my approach is never to
come in with religion: first reflect on the universe. You never learn that from
theology.'

Sister Miriam is proud of the way Genesis Farm has developed. 'We sisters
and the first volunteers had no money; all of us had to have other jobs. There
was no space here: just a tractor shed; no kitchen or other facilities. A
Benedictine monk nearby did beekeeping and he employed me in the winter-
time. He came one day and said we had valuable trees for lumber and could
probably raise several thousand dollars. We made $13,000. It was mixed
wood. That was the break that opened it up. We understood that the land itself
would support the mission. So I built on the kitchen. Then a wonderful
cooking school. I had become a lecturer supporting myself. I wasn't focused
on support from the local area at that time, but that lecturing was creating a
network of interested people.'

The arrival of Heinz Thomet, a Swiss volunteer, brought in a new profes-
sionalism and introduced biodynamic farming. 'At first the local farmers
laughed at us. They certainly should have laughed at me because I was ignorant; when Heinz came they knew they were talking to someone properly
grounded.'

Biodynamic gardening provided a new challenge. 'We had no background in anthroposophy and he had no background in the new cosmology, so there was a tension, a lack of understanding on either part. Sacred agriculture is really what we both believed in.'

The community garden at Genesis barely pays it way. Extra income comes from Earth Literacy courses, cookery courses and Sister Miriam's lectures. She is in wide demand both in America and abroad; cassette tapes of her lectures sell in thousands.

The Earth Literacy courses began when she invited people interested in Berry's teaching to discuss how it could be taught more formally and become part of academia. St Thomas University in Miami offered to award undergraduate and graduate credits for courses at Genesis Farm. Jean and Larry Edwards were brought in as supervisors, and the Dominican order agreed to extend the property by acquiring the house called Bread and Roses.

Larry and Jean began their programme in 1993 — a two-week course plus another ten weeks for students who stay on. Their brochure promised they would 'teach a new story based on science and spirituality. Physicists are the new Mystics.' The course is divided into modules: Exploring the sacred universe; Story and culture, Wisdom traditions and Bioregionalism. The two-week course costs $650, the 12-week course is $4600, plus more for graduate and undergraduate credits.

Larry was a chemist, Jean a teacher. Deeply involved in the Green and anti-nuclear movements, they had established what they called 'a learning centre of like-minded people' in Washington, when they heard one of Sister Miriam's lecture tapes and read Berry's book, *Dream of the Earth*. Jean told us: 'We already understood the need for a myth, and now here was Berry saying that scientists have given us the myth: the flaring forth of the universe in its psychic as well as physical dimensions. Everything that goes on can seem sacred.'

Sampling the course for short periods during a week, we found it rarely dull though hardly rigorous. The students are not encouraged to be critical. There is much interpersonal and self-analysis.

Saturday morning. Jean's weekly recall session. Susan, Peter, Mary, Eileen are present — and the two of us. Jean is cross-legged on a chair, inviting comments on the week's reading. She uses a jargon of familiar words and phrases in comment on everything: connectedness, gift, redefining power; 'We need to be storytellers'; 'I'd just like to affirm you, Mary, in taking that step...'

Peter teaches at a local school and is planning on giving that up to manage the local watershed. The week's study has given him a stiff neck and a rash: now he's better and 'no longer racing inside. I'm reading things for the first time — *Plain* magazine and *Utne Reader*.

Mary weeps as she quotes Sister Miriam as saying we have to own the grief and despair but not let it paralyse us. 'How can I step into action?'

Susan is older, an experienced seeker. She gave up her job as a journalist seven years ago. She doesn't know what next but wants 'to live as neighbours in a bioregion, looking to create something apart from the global system.'

Eileen, in her early fifties, has come from Florida where she was working in a women's healing centre. Her brother sent a newspaper clipping about Genesis Farm and its Earth Literacy course. She put the dog and two cats into her van and arrived. Now, still living in the van, she wants to stay until next spring. What she loves about the course is the connection with the earth, the rituals, the visits, the books. Eileen, in a quavering voice, reads aloud her statement which we thought expressed deep feeling that it is not easy to speak of aloud:

'In reviewing this week's reading I am moved by many things. I have learned in greater depth that the destruction of our earth home brought on by industrialisation is vast, and it continues seemingly unabated. There is lots and lots of work to be done. It's not yet clear to me exactly what I will be doing in the great work. I am confident that it will unfold as long as I remain a seeker. There are many who have already begun this pioneering work. Why was not my voice heard sooner? I was caught up like others in the almost all consuming distraction of materialism, individualism and mobility — upward, outward and all around. Travelling and living in different countries I gave little thought to the idea, let alone the importance, of community or roots and definitely I had no sense of place, no sense of belonging to any particular place. If you don't stay long enough anywhere you don't have to deal with anything seriously, and so the truth of real happenings in a place remains hidden.'

These questions are deep, too deep perhaps for Jean's elementary-school approach with responses like: 'That was *great*, Peter' — even if Peter had said something quite off the point. At the start of the Saturday recall class Jean played a tape of Australian birds intertwined with sickly, sentimental music. It made Mary cry and as a result Mary was unable to produce a composition of her thoughts for the week. 'That's *quite* all right, Mary.' We might have been back in childhood at a particularly nice primary school or holiday camp, sure of a gentle, encouraging reception by people who always say Yes.

We spent some quiet hours in the October sunshine in the meditation garden, or following the special trail. The sisters and helpers have set aside a wooded hill for the purpose, and laid a trail with pauses. At each pause you find some artefact or natural object, a pile of stones, a sculpture, an arch of roses. The experience expresses the spirit of Genesis for us more clearly than any words.

It isn't a perfect place — where is one? There is not much energy efficiency:

the electricity and water are on the mains and the whole place is centrally heated. There are plenty of cars. But life is lived lightly and with deep gratitude. Genesis Farm, like the best monasteries of old, is a centre of excellence, of good food reverently grown and eaten, of faith in spiritual and human values, of extraordinary kindness to one another. Its influence radiates out into the countryside as a model of right livelihood.

The Animal Blessing

While we were at Genesis the annual Animal Blessing took place at St John's Cathedral in New York, just two hours away. Larry and Jean loaded up their car with anyone who wanted to go.

After the eucharist and the post-communion prayer the cathedral doors swung open and an elephant decorated with garlands was led right up through the congregation to the sanctuary, closely followed by a camel, a pair of llamas, a priest in white robes carrying two parrots on his shoulders, another cradling a chimpanzee, yet another with a falcon on his shoulder, and another with a boa constrictor wrapped round his shoulders, its head up as if piloting their passage up the aisle.

This was the annual Feast of St Francis at the Cathedral Church of St John the Divine. The cathedral was packed: people had queued for hours, filled the side aisles and perched precariously on the base of pillars. They brought their dogs, cats, hamsters and parrots — all of whom were better behaved throughout the three-hour service than small children in church usually are.

The long cathedral, receding through sombre walls and columns to a sanctuary with scarlet spaces between pillars, formed a perfect theatre. The sound was awesome; howling and roaring filled the cathedral to its roof, and then African drums, even louder, joined in with cymbals and castanets. Above it floated the clear and plaintive voice of a soprano saxophone. Some of the children looked apprehensive as wolves howled and dogs barked.

In his sermon Dean James Morton spoke of St Francis as the first modern man, the first planetary citizen and the first global ambassador. He commended the saint's deathbed hymn to Brother Sun, Mother Earth, Sister Moon, Brother Wind, and Sister Water. He said: 'We are all stardust from the original star.' He suggested that what Francis meant by poverty was openness and availability. The saint had called it Lady Poverty. He explained how poverty dovetailed with communion, compassion and joy in a way that could put human beings once more — using a deliberately modern expression — in sync.

The old dean's sermon was more eloquent than a score of Green books about the link between Living Lightly and caring for the poor, the animals and the earth. Here was the Church doing its job — and people came crowding in with their children and their pets.

Paul Winter, the darling musician of New York's Green culture, had composed this music and played soprano sax supported by his eight-person ensemble and a strong choir and soloists. Winter's music in a concert hall can be sickly and repetitive. Here, with that space and resonance and that animal enthusiasm, it was tremendous — lucid, devout and compelling.

We spend a lot of time wondering if there can be a new consciousness, a transition to new values, a new world myth. Here suddenly it had come to be! This was the new cosmology of Thomas Berry and Genesis Farm, the spiritual corollary of quantum physics, relativity and chaos theory, the end of dualism and dry, detached rationalism. If only this service could be done in every church. If only archbishops did not have to ape prime ministers in applauding economic growth lest they be marginalised as mavericks. Only adventurers like Dean Morton, or our British David Jenkins when he was Bishop of Durham, or the egregious Donald Reeves, Rector of St James's, Piccadilly, can put on a show which puts religion back in touch with reality, which is not prayer or ritual or good deeds or an afterlife, simply people and animals and the earth and the stars and the sun and the moon. In this cathedral today, to their great credit, were several bishops with mitres, strolling relaxed and smiling down the aisle to pat the heads of children, and rabbis and Muslim and Hindu clerics as well.

Some communicants took the bread and water cradling their cats or small dogs or carrying a cage with their hamster. After the service, out in the cathedral garden, they queued with their pets to have them blessed. A woman priest sat on a stone bench and fondled dog after dog, cat after cat, before moving her hand in blessing. On another bench, a black bishop in red robes blessed a white rabbit.

The symbolism and the philosophy behind this event were so powerful and so clear in their meaning that every child could understand and be enthralled. The final procession had not only elephants and giraffes, it included a glass jar filled with algae, and a wheelbarrow full of earthworms. One priest carried a squealing piglet decorated with a garland of fir twigs. Here was Creation as it needs to be worshipped.

Note

1   We are sad to write that Robyn van En died in the spring of 1997, a few months after we met her.

7
Designing a village?

●●

Think of a cottage in a village: a weekend retreat with roses round the door — or a wooden shack surrounded by eroded fields? In the Living Lightly movement, we dream of eco-villages — planned communities where self-reliant villagers return as much fertility to the soil as they take out. Villages existed like that for thousands of years. Today, many villages in North and South are impoverished and depopulated, their inhabitants forced off the land. Yet visions — of the village as a proper place to live a sane life — persist. Like this one:

'People go about their business of stewarding the land to produce all manner of goods that are consumed at Crystal Waters Village or transported to other markets in the bioregion. A productive landscape of apparent chaos is given order and a sense of comfort and stability by strips of lawn and groundcover along roadsides and near homes, walkways that have mixed plantings of ornamentals and fruit and nut trees, meandering hedges and trellises that line some of the orchards, timber lots and vegetable growing areas, rows of fodder trees sweeping over slopes and ridges and the formal entrances to houses dotted over the ridges, and many majestic trees that line the roadways. On the morning walk to the village, the long way round, the path passes animals grazing, some horses and riders just setting off on an early morning ride, cows content after milking and a few sheep growing next year's woollen jumpers.'[1]

Although Max Lindegger's vision has not become reality, his village exists. Crystal Waters, fifteen kilometres from Maleny in south-east Queensland, has an unique reputation as the world's first *designed* permaculture village.

Isn't a village something that has grown up across time, haphazardly fitting its houses to the bends of the road and its fields to the contours of the land? Can you actually design a village? Yes and no. You can design a physical living space; the difficulty is to design a social space. The planned village is vulnerable simply because its designers try to *anticipate* its needs rather than accept realities that have been taken for granted for generations. In the modern world we can find man-made environments designed at any level from the grandiloquence of Chandigarh, Punjab's le Corbusier capital, to the mistaken notions of high-rise, low-cost housing in London, later demolished because living there caused so many social problems. Planned villages and small towns in Britain — like Welwyn Garden City or Hampstead Garden Suburb — have had only a limited success.

The designers of Crystal Waters wanted a settlement in which energy demands would be low, most inhabitants could work in and around the village and the land would produce much, if not most, of its own food using permaculture methods. Given the living standard that most Australians would consider minimal, this was not a realisable goal. Even to approach self-sufficiency would entail a subsistence standard of life that wouldn't be acceptable.

Crystal Waters was designed as a permaculture village, adapted, of necessity, to the unique requirements of the site. permaculture (*perma*nent agri-*culture*) a word coined in the early seventies by Bill Mollison and David Holmgren, is defined as 'the harmonious integration of landscape and people,

> The core of permaculture is design. Design is a connection between things. It's not water, or a chicken, or the tree. It's how the water, the chicken and the tree are connected. It's the very opposite of what we are taught in school. Education takes everything and pulls it apart and makes no connections at all. permaculture makes the connection, because as soon as you've got the connection you can feed the chicken from the tree.
> · Bill Mollison with Reny Mia Slay in *Introduction to Permaculture.*

providing their food, energy, shelter and other material and non-material needs in a sustainable way.' It's not a catchy word but a better hasn't yet arisen. The village traces its roots, like many other communities we visited, to the back-to-the-land movement which spread across the industrial world during the seventies. Crystal Waters began as a hippie commune. It became available for permaculture through the action of a single individual, Bob Sample, who doesn't advertise himself as a benefactor though that is what he is.

Bob's background is similar to many of the innovators that we met on our travels — a comfortable, middle-class family whose values he rejected. He ran a successful dairying business until his mid-thirties. He felt a 'call' for the land of Crystal Waters, which lies in a boomerang-shaped valley between a lazy river and the hills — 'sacred' land which had been used by Aboriginal women for initiation rites. Finding the 260-hectare plot for sale, Bob bought it.

'I'd read New Age books, talked to a medium. I read *The Magic of Findhorn* and met Eileen and Peter Caddy (see Chapter 14). Eileen Caddy's

BASIC STEPS TO PERMACULTURE DESIGN

There are two basic steps to PC design. The first (a) deals with laws and principles that can be adapted to any climatic and cultural condition, while the second (b) is more closely associated with practical techniques, which change from one climate and culture to another. Principles under (a) are:

·   Relative location; every element (such as house, pond, road, etc.) is placed in relationship to another so that they assist each other.

·   Each element performs many functions.

·   Efficient energy planning for house and settlement (zones and sectors).

·   Emphasis on the use of biological resources over fossil fuel resources.

·   Energy recycling on site (fuel and human energy).

·   Using and accelerating natural plant succession to establish favourable sites and soils.

·   Polyculture and diversity of beneficial species for a productive, interactive system.

·   Use of edge and natural patterns for best effect.

Bill Mollison with Reny Mia Slay in *Introduction to Permaculture*

presence worked changes in me on an energy level. I discovered an inner voice answering questions.' Bob claims that through a channelling group he learnt that people were needed to understand his land and that they would come to care for it.

Up to eighty people lived in the new community but it lasted only five years. 'I was seen as powerful and there was resentment against me,' Bob says. By 1984 the place was in crisis: 'Many people did nothing and the rest were resentful. People left. We were back to four or five.' The story Bob told was similar to that of many seventies' communities. They start with a strong leader, resent him and gradually disintegrate. With Crystal Waters, Bob did not give up, he turned in another direction. 'I heard of Max Lindegger. We had no cash, so were interested in proposals for the land. Max had a proposal I liked.'

Max and three co-designers were interested in developing the site on permaculture principles. A design was drawn up with eighty percent of the area reserved for common use, to be developed later on permaculture lines. 'A wonderful design, it went through the local council's planning procedures without opposition,' Bob says. Instead of fees, each designer received his expenses and one of the blocs.

Once the permaculture people became active Bob effectively withdrew. 'I'm not a permaculturist — I have a lot of trouble with the mechanistic approach of some of their design: it doesn't flow enough. Yet I feel good about the way it's going.' Whether he regrets his dream of a commune, he won't say.

Permaculture design is modelled on natural ecosystems, so we were expecting to find Crystal Waters a jungly paradise on the wet, sub-tropical Queensland soil which can turn a gum sapling into a gum tree in a couple of summers. We were puzzled to be driving into what seemed a manicured garden suburb. Mares with foals grazed in a low-lying paddock by a steamy river. A lack of trees along the roads made driving hot and dusty. The road, skirting tall grassland and the banks of artificial lakes, snaked and divided without signposts, except a sign saying 'Residents Only' and another saying 'Visitors Report to the Office'. With no obvious village centre, houses nestled anonymously behind lawns and trees. The architecture was astonishing with houses built of pisé, pole frame and mud-brick, their shapes round, square, many-sided, domed and geodesic. Each house was clearly designed with care to sit harmoniously within its site. The site looked so prosperous, so comfortable. Would this turn out to be little more than an original hideaway for the sixties baby-boomers who had flirted with the Age of Aquarius?

At Max's guest chalet

We arrive at a sturdy Queensland-style farmhouse on stilts, on a steep site belonging to Max Lindegger, our host. Permaculture principles are on show. On the slope behind the house, which runs down to a man-made dam, comfrey has been planted as a ground cover between young fruit trees. The terraced vegetable garden provides much of the food Max and his wife Trudy need, as well as providing food for students on permaculture courses. Max's living lawnmower — a friendly ewe — has to be parked in the shade to work efficiently.

Max — with ginger beard, piercing eyes, gaunt features and authoritative manner, one of the four designers of Crystal Waters and serious guardian of permaculture orthodoxy in the village, is referred to by critics as a tall poppy, an Australian expression meaning someone who needs to be cut down. We were to stay in his guest cabin as WWOOFers — Willing Workers on Organic Farms, an arrangement by which people work for their keep on farms in USA, Britain and many other countries. On our first night a misty rain shrouded the hills. At first light, four wallabies were grazing on the rough grass underneath the veranda. The dam smelled like a sewer. It wasn't sewage, Trudy said, merely vegetation swept down after the rain. She must have been right because the smell went away in a day.

However far you travel you can't leave your cultural baggage behind. Max's all-wooden cabin is the nearest thing to a Swiss mountain chalet you'll find in Queensland (creaky floor, gingham checked curtains): it was perfect. We found a Downmus toilet installed (see Chapter 11). Everything Dean Cameron had said about it was true: no smell, easy to use. Dot writes: once I got over initial squeamishness, watching the tiger worms at work through the porthole used to post kitchen waste and paper scraps fascinated me. With a compost toilet like this, you have so much less rubbish to dispose of.

Crystal Waters excites both WWOOFers and permaculture students; they want to transfer and adapt the principles for their home regions. Permaculture courses attract students from all over the world — North and South. (And everywhere we travel we come across American and Japanese young people in revolt against the current mainstream.) Ten thousand people worldwide have graduated from permaculture design courses and numbers are increasing.

We agreed to work a modest two hours a day for Max in return for lodging. The first morning's work was a fiasco. Following Max's instructions, we arrived at 6.30 a.m. at his citrus orchard — a hectare and a half which he leases on the communal land. We were supposed to clear undergrowth from a wire fence and repair the holes so that ducks could forage in safety amongst the trees. After half an hour of clipping short lengths of wire and twisting them together to repair mysterious holes in the fence (who made them — a goanna or a monitor lizard?) we were scratched, bitten by insects, sweat-stained and discouraged. Whatever animal made the holes once will surely make them again. We were supposed to mend the fence with chicken mesh, the thinnest of wires, and the undergrowth was too thick and thorny to be cut with the clippers we'd been given. After an hour, whacked by the early morning heat at the end of summer in January, we admitted defeat and clambered back to the cabin for showers. Next day, Max put us on onto weeding and mulching in his vegetable patch beside the house, a task more suited to our ageing abilities. Every morning by breakfast time, our chores finished, we set about meeting Crystal Waters residents.

Permaculturists young and old

Barry Goodman is one of the elders. No-one enjoys his plot more: he calls it, 'a typical permaculture garden where you can literally graze or browse about the place and expect to find food. You can pick strawberries wherever I planted them, bananas are growing here there and everywhere.' Grizzled, beetle-browed, bushy-haired and *very* naked, Barry is considered a grand old man of permaculture. We'd been warned that he never wears clothes. 'To start with, it cuts my washing down to almost zero. What's the point, in this climate here, of clothes?' We're invited to disrobe and refuse the offer; it's raining, and slightly chilly inside Barry's house.

Barry had been a chemical engineer — loved gardening and hankered for freedom from the supermarket. 'I'm old enough to be a product of the Great Depression and of course so much self-sufficiency came out in those days.' This was a repeated theme from older people, who remember both the Depression and the Second World War when frugality and self-reliance were desirable social goals.

None of Barry's seven children have followed his example in either nudism or permaculture. 'All conventional business types,' he says with a sigh.

His house is designed for minimal environmental impact, mainly of wood and sited for winter sun and summer cool, using as much renewable energy as possible within the framework of what is affordable. The cost of using alternatives is often greater than buying mainstream electricity.

When we next met Barry, driving in his small car, he was wearing a mini-sarong which he kept on when we asked him to our cabin for coffee. In a climate as hot as Queensland's, his nakedness isn't as dotty as it seems at first. The Aborigines who lived on this site long before Bob Sample wore no clothes for thousands of years.

Jane, James (and baby Ash).

Jane and James, with baby Ash, have come from England. Attracted by the promise of permaculture, they have bought a steeply sloping, north-facing field, where they'll live in two caravans for a year while they plan their design. A good permaculture design is closely allied to an intimate knowledge of the site — every advantage and drawback of situation and soil — and many practitioners camp on their sites for up to a year. 'We're really excited by the shape of this sloping land — like an amphitheatre, it has scope for anything,' James said. They plan to share their site with another couple, in the belief that they can grow enough food to meet the basic needs of two families.

Jane is a nurse; James studied construction engineering. They saw Bill Mollison's video, *Visionaries*, and it fitted in with the way James had been thinking about design, housing and sustainable living. He read the *Permaculture Designers' Manual*. Then he read about Crystal Waters. They bought the land in November, 1995. Prices had already nearly doubled since the village started. It cost A\$45,000[2] — almost every cent they had — for a little more than half a hectare.

Money is tight. Jane works part-time in the village shop, James does road works and weed control management in return for A\$12 plus three *bunyas* an hour on the Local Exchange Trading System. 'We'll build the house with uncoarsed earth, mud and straw — second-hand materials we've already begun to collect. We'll have to earn as we go to get the materials. We expect to do it all ourselves, employing only an electrician which we have to do by law.'

Jane was critical of the Crystal Waters design as 'too spaced out — you need motor transport to get around. But one day when the walkways and clusters are done, and we have a better centre, this will really be a village.' James' ultimate ambition is: 'to be free to live our own lives and not the lives expected of us in the system.' Jane added: 'My father was a doctor who died of overwork at forty-nine. I want to avoid that. We want a home where housework takes ten minutes.'

No dogs or cats

This land was degraded cattle country from which wildlife had long disappeared. It has been transformed. Fifty thousand trees have been planted; kangaroos and wallabies graze in gardens and fields. Within the limits of the by-laws, the 250 members are free to behave as they wish on their own plots. Crystal Waters has no gurus or hierarchy. A full-time ranger is supposed to enforce the by-laws.

To become a member you buy your plot and agree to obey the Body Corporate By-laws, especially 'To care for the earth with all its flora and fauna.' No dogs or cats, no chemicals on the land except those accepted in the land use policy, no fishing, no firearms, no nuisance to neighbours, etc. Most of the by-laws are little different from those in any rural suburb except the ban on dogs and cats. Domestic pets gone feral, especially cats, decimate Australian native fauna which has no inbuilt defences against them.

The designers of the 260-hectare site were Max Lindegger, Robert Tap, Geoff Young and Barry Goodman, permaculture experts with previous careers in engineering, surveying, town planning and industry. The design provided a framework in which eighty-three plots, each around half a hectare, were for sale where occupants *could* practice permaculture. No mechanism was envisaged to *make* them do it. However, most of the site is common land which can be used as the residents may decide, leaving open the possibility of a more integrated permaculture system in the future. Common property includes a village kitchen and shop, a space for common meals and another for lectures and courses, and a camping area for visitors. Only a minority of residents use these common facilities regularly.

Water — always a central feature in a permaculture design — is drawn from two rivers by underground pumps into a network of fifteen dams. Although many houses have solar power systems, the water pumps and most domestic appliances run on mains electricity, so Crystal Waters cannot claim to be self-sufficient in energy. Robert Tap explained: 'The whole village is a design in the making. permaculture design means you go on designing as you go. This is nowhere near the end product. Yes, we use mains electricity. If we used hydraulic pumps to lift water we'd have had to import very expensive machinery. Solar energy isn't always economic or even environmentally friendly — solar cells and aluminium parts are manufactured in polluting techniques. Batteries are outdated. Taking a 200-year view — in the present state of technology mains electricity is justified; later we can move on, maybe to high-temperature steam or solar-based heat storage.'

Crystal Waters people fret and often argue about the unsustainability of much of their practices — like using petrol for mowing the grass verges. Some would like sheep or cows to eat the grass, which would be true to permaculture principles — but there is not enough time, expertise or money to look after animals and there are no fences.

The community is designed to pay its way by using its common land for enterprises. About a third of the common land is now used commercially: horses — a left-over from the hippie commune and not the kind of animal normally included in a permaculture design — occupy twenty hectares; other sites include a lotus-root enterprise (of which more later), two forestry plots, a Bush Tucker business (see Chapter 11) and pecan nut and citrus plantations like Max's where we tried our fence-mending skills and failed.

Each plot is well set back from the road on the east or west arm of this boomerang-shaped site. The main through-road is four and a half kilometres long. Some residents complain about the long and straggly layout with distances between houses and communal areas being too long to walk comfortably,

We were disappointed that out of eighty-three plots with over sixty occupied, barely a dozen practise permaculture. But these practitioners include some of the finest examples in the world. Frances Lang, who teaches the methods both internationally and with Max at Crystal Waters has a garden that could illustrate a permaculture text-book.

Frances Lang's garden

Frances has taken advantage of Queensland's sub-tropical climate to produce a luxuriance of annual and perennial vegetation in only four months; her first attempt had been burned down in a bush fire. Frances, her American-born partner Jeff and two children live in a spacious modern bungalow on a lofty ridge with views from picture windows and a veranda. She and Jeff run a mail-order firm supplying seeds for trees and green manure. In her garden, with the temperature at nearly thirty-five degrees centigrade by 10 a.m., two British work-exchange volunteers, Brice and Jenny, red-faced and straw-hatted, are weeding and mulching. Frances pays them enough to pay off the balance of their design course fees.

Frances, we aren't surprised to learn, has been gardening since she was five. She left Sydney as soon as she could and in her twenties became involved in the back-to-the land movement in Tasmania as 'an old-style hippie in a remote mud-brick house on the only land we could afford. We were growing food on land that the farmer said couldn't run a wallaby. I probably had three hundred sorts of herbs at one stage.' There she learned about permaculture. 'It was fascinating to see how you could design a whole system, integrating animals and plants.'

Land was too dear around Sydney and she didn't want to live in another commune, so she bought her acre at Crystal Waters for A$22,000 — a tenth of the cost in the big city area.

Frances and Jeff have built themselves a passive solar house which traps the sun's heat in winter. The garden, a little more than half a hectare, feeds the family and provides for the commercial nursery. When the students attend courses, Frances grows the major part of their food.

Near the road are windbreak trees — native legumes, acacias and some larger trees to help shade people walking along the road in front of the garden. permaculture design pays close attention to the perimeter which should be productive like everything else — offering shade or food or both. Inside the treeline are rows of plants grown mainly for mulch — pigeon peas (a legume), and canaregulous (arrowroot).

Frances has made her garden as diverse as possible — another permaculture feature. 'We try to not have large areas of one crop, in an attempt to confuse pests, so it's different vegetables in relatively small patches. Some plants are in there purely to enhance pest control, particularly ones that flower and are attractive to predatory insects like hover-flies or the parasitic wasp: we call those insectory plants.'

Permaculture favours perennial plants over annuals, to save labour, and plants are often grown just to improve the soil. Frances' perennial vegetables includes cassava/tapioca, Jerusalem artichoke, sweet potatoes, a large bed of jakon (Peruvian ground apple) which grows two metres high and has five or six large kilo-sized tubers. She has an edible hibiscus hedge with a dark reddish stem, and dries the harvested fruit for tea and for making jam.

Taro (Tahitian spinach) is grown as a vegetable in the wet season. At the other end of the garden a different type of Taro is grown as a root vegetable, and beyond that, on a trellis, is a hiccama (climbing yam bean) which produces large tubers for use in a stir-fry, or salad. Small ponds are filled with Chinese water chestnuts and duck potatoes, a native American Indian food. The beds of lemon grass are used as a mulch and to make dried herb tea: a third use is in its pest repellent properties. Frances tries to have each plant fulfilling at least three uses.

'Everything that we need *for* the garden we try to have *in* the garden: plants to fix nitrogen as fertiliser, plants that we cut as mulch, plants that enhance pest control and lots of food to eat, so we try to combine it all together. It's very low in inputs. Besides water, which is essential here in summer, I garden with virtually no inputs from outside.' She uses no commercial sprays — not even organic ones. She does use additives like chicken manure, blood and bone during initial planting, to build up her poor quality granite soil.

A dozen Rhode Island Red chickens and some bantams scratch at our feet: 'So we never have to buy eggs and they're also my daughters' pets. They're in a moveable hutch and we only let them out when we're around the garden, and that's not just to stop them destroying the garden, it's also because our main predator is a hawk. Their little hutch is built like Fort Knox because our other predators include large pythons which we call carpet snakes: they can eat a substantial-sized hen.' A smaller wheeled hutch houses guinea pigs. 'A sort of mobile lawn mower; we just roll the little hutch along and the guinea pigs keep the grass short and they're pets as well.'

Frances only grows temperate vegetables like potatoes, onions, beans and cabbages in winter because in summer they get too many diseases. 'People do grow them in summer, and then they're using fungicides which I don't use. In summer I prefer Madagascar beans, snake beans, and wing beans, and French beans in the Spring.' This is the hot, wet season and there is no need for irrigation. Through the dry season Frances has to water regularly, using the village's private system — a series of large tanks gravity-fed from nearby streams with water which is pumped up at night with electric power to the tops of hills and gravity-fed to the individual lots. 'We use electrical power because we don't have sufficient wind for a windmill and the streams are too distant to use water to lift it as well. In the future we might be able to switch to a solar pump as they become more efficient.'

Frances reckons her garden will be mature in three years. 'Then I expect, apart from the nursery area for the business, I'll maintain the garden in about two hours a week. It will provide all our vegetables and all our fruit.'

She is optimistic that permaculture will blossom and mature at Crystal Waters. 'So far most people have been too busy building their houses, and then their own gardens, to bother about the common land.' She aims to finish her own garden this year, as well as those of her mother and sister who have moved down to Crystal Waters too. Then, as all good permaculture gardens do, it will largely look after itself. 'Then at last I'll do something on the common land if I can get the funds from the Body Corporate. I'd like to work on creating wildlife habitats and corridors, and tree shading for pathways to encourage walking and sociability. Eventually we should put a nut plantation where the horses are.'

The permaculture gardens that we saw show the system producing an astonishingly large quantity of food on a very small area, using non-chemical means, expending little energy and labour, and enriching the soil year by year. This is in contrast to industrial farming, which is sustained by the myth that a monocrop planted over a huge area and sustained with chemical treatment will produce the highest yields. Estimates vary but an intensively gardened area can easily produce between three and four times as much food as an equivalent industrially farmed area.

The lotus pond and other controversies

As the days pass, some with rain but most hot and sunny, we begin to glimpse strains beneath the sunny surface. We sense the perennial problem with communal living; the individual will pitted against the collective. Barry Goodman complains that there is a lack of entrepreneurial spirit in many community members, but the spirit of enterprise can sometimes cause conflict — as in the lotus root controversy.

Regina, an opponent of the scheme, took us to see the lotus pond which has caused a serious rift between the pro and anti factions. To the untutored eye the pond was a peaceful sight, a man-made dam covered with the flat leaves and waxy flowers, growing so thickly intertwined that it was impossible to enter the water. The roots fetch good money in Chinese restaurants, the leaves are edible, the flower pods used by florists. The whole enterprise appeared practical, profitable and useful — until the lotus roots colonised the pond and some people feared their escape into the Mary River would cause havoc, choking the river as they have choked the dam.

Nonsense, say the lotus promoters, the lotus will adapt and prove harmless. Regina, who sits on the Body Corporate, insists the lotus pond has taken away the neighbours' amenities. 'They used to swim and have a small canoe on that dam: now look at it!'

To make matters worse, Hans, who planted the lotus with his partners, has also planted bamboo as a commercial crop. That displeases Regina who favours reforestation with local trees. 'To harvest and use bamboo you need lots and lots of cheap labour which we don't have here. You will never have a market for bamboo in this country.' And she adds: 'The people doing this are just romantics. They don't seriously harvest the bamboo or the lotus. Hopefully they will see reason and get rid of both.'

Management of Crystal Waters has run into other difficulties too. A levy on all members is supposed to pay for common services like fencing and road-side trees. The trouble is that many members are cash-poor, quite a few live on the dole, and they always oppose such levies. There is a shortage of ambitious projects because of the law which says that all communal ventures must be agreed unanimously. Would-be entrepreneurs find it hard to get loans for commercial ventures with so shaky a legal title. Lawyers are trying to change the village status from 'group title' to 'community title' to solve this problem. Crystal Waters allows common land to be used for individual enterprise, but Queensland law says that any use for land must be decided unanimously at the annual village meeting. It is a Catch 22 situation.

A more fundamental question: is Crystal Waters succeeding as a community? Some members find the long, boomerang-shaped layout unsociable because there is no natural centre. Other critics find fault with the design itself, complaining that permaculture theorists have been insensitive to community needs.

Skye (that is his first, last and only name) is one of the critics. At forty-six, he is a figure in the Aquarian mould — flowing silver hair, necklace on a black string, black and red tee shirt with solar design. He teaches three permaculture courses a year with his former partner, Robin Clayfield.

These two became dissatisfied with Max's and Frances' teaching methods and set up an alternative based on game playing and role playing. These rival design certificate courses are advertised on the notice board in the communal kitchen as promising 'to put the emphasis on creativity and interaction and the social aspect.' Skye does not see permaculture as 'permanent *agriculture*' but as 'permanence *in culture*', that is, sustainability in culture. 'In the early days permaculture was essentially landscape design. I see it as more of a change in headspace, a change in paradigm.'

This approach leads Skye to criticise the design of Crystal Waters as not sociable enough. 'Why is there no system for decision-making? I don't think planting trees is that important: if we left them alone they'd grow by themselves. Our environmental problem is in fact a social problem. In this we are at an early stage and don't have any answers yet.' Skye wants the lay-out adapted to provide an intensive central area, with three-storey buildings for shops and other amenities, a living centre surrounded by half hectare (one-acre) lots, small orchards and intensive gardens. Further out: two-hectare farms.

'A very simple life'

Meanwhile, Crystal Waters offers a home for those who are not here for permaculture but want to live lightly in a community. Of these, few are as contented as an ex-Liverpudlian living in a forest clearing in a ramshackle wooden hut with a wide, creeper-covered veranda.

'I'm a city girl. I had to give up my dog and cat because they aren't allowed here, never mind, it's worth it. I live in almost Third World conditions but nobody turns their nose up at me. There's no housework; it's a dream. It's a very simple life, we re-use things and make them work.' After twenty years in Oz, Patria Cardle's Liverpool accent still rings clear.

Since coming to Crystal Waters six years ago, she discovered hidden talents. She learned to play the humerimba, a wooden xylophone with the resonator made from recycled plastic supermarket bags. She belongs to a group of eighteen who play regularly at festivals dressed up in their purple and green costumes. 'I didn't know that I was a clown until I did a clowning workshop and since then I've done street theatre. To me this is so exciting, a woman in her fifties doing things like that ... why wasn't I doing this twenty years ago?' While Patria showed us how to play the humerimba, a king parrot with orange head and green body perched on a branch to peck seeds from a bean plant, undisturbed by the music.

Sunday brunch at the village hall in Crystal Waters.

Patria arrived with Eric and soon after, they split up. So, we noticed, did a lot of other couples in Crystal Waters, and other communities we visited. Everywhere we noticed a high turnover in relationships. Patria's explanation was: 'Being here gives you a chance to experiment sexually; it can't be hidden under the carpet. No, not a lot of sleeping around; it's people getting to know other people really well. You're in each other's company much more than you would be in the city where one partner goes out to work. And then the stress of not having enough money to manage, or one partner feeling frustrated because they're not pursuing a career. A man might feel passionately about his career — this is true of at least half a dozen people in this community — his wife may have had a good career for a woman: she comes here and she's got nothing to do, can't get the same sort of job, so she becomes a housewife and gets restless. In my case, Eric wanted to explore other relationships and I wasn't prepared to live in a triangular situation, so we split up but we stayed very good friends, we're still a family.'

Patria believes her taste for simple living owes something to her early Liverpool childhood during and just after the Second World War: 'I don't use a scrubbing board like my granny but I do go to the local well as I call it — our community washing machine. That's a place for meeting other people so I take my washing there, we'll get talking, share information, we'll network. Once you get your own washing machine you don't leave the house.'

By drawing A$310 a fortnight in dole benefit, Patria can just afford to run her old van. 'I have no qualms even though no member of my family has ever been on the dole. I regard it as an early pension after working for twenty-six years — like a rural subsidy; the Government is paying for people to live where they do less damage and use less resources than in a city.' We heard this attitude repeated many times: that modern society is so warped that anyone willing to try to live differently is owed some sort of a living. And besides, Patria says, people living in a community on the dole are putting their money back into the local economy.

While we are drinking coffee, a goanna (a lizard-like creature nearly a metre long plus tail) waddles across the mown grass. Says Patria, 'That's Wartiback. He and I have a running battle. I object to feeding my chooks for him to eat the eggs. The climate is very difficult to deal with, the humidity and heat. We move very slowly here.'

And that is perhaps her secret. She has learnt to move slowly and live fully in the present. She is aware that two strands of opinion co-exist at Crystal Waters; those who want to concentrate on the permaculture part, and those who are more interested in the social experiment. If the village is ever to become a viable community, these strands will have to mesh together.

Meanwhile, women form a close, feminist group that acts as a counter-weight to the sterner theoreticians and practitioners of permaculture. At river bank picnics, everyone swims naked and in the broiling sun of a Queensland January the clear water is cool. Annie said she'd been having a good DM with one of her mates. DM? — Deep Meaningful Conversation.

The nearest thing to a village centre is the hall and shop, where Sunday morning brunch is a tradition. The villagers who attend belong to the clique that wants more social activity. It's a convivial occasion with out-of-towners driving over from Maleny and groups forming and reforming.

For a resident like Steward, over seventy and seriously crippled with a bone disease, it's the one occasion in the week where he meets friends and can be sure of company. Steward, an idealist like Bob Sample, gave away a fortune of a quarter of a million Australian dollars to set up a trust fund to manage a forty-hectare wood for public use. As everyone sits under the wide overhang, chatting and drinking in bright sunshine, it's hard not to idealise this set-up. But still there are grouses. Denise Sawyer, who lives in a converted railway carriage and grows most of her food, says, 'Max goes around the world extolling Crystal Waters and people come here to visit and find that reality is far different. Economic problems hurt: there are no jobs here.'

Phil and his partner Annie, residents left over from the commune days, attend brunch most Sundays. 'I suppose I'm an old-style hippie,' Annie says. 'I didn't want all this development.' They feel pushed out by the influx of well-heeled settlers and by the bewildering mixture of motivations. For the last few years at the annual meeting Phil has suggested they drop permaculture from the village title, to reflect its mixed character. Phil says: 'We'd have preferred an arrangement that didn't allow just anyone to come. For any design to work the social design must come first. Crystal Waters was designed by people with an engineering-type background.' But Phil adds: 'What's happened has made me grow. I wouldn't have missed it.'

Max replies to the critics

Feeling like ambassadors bearing grievances, we pass on the criticism we have heard. Max admits to no regrets and insists, as do the other designers, that his project is on the rails: it is a potentially viable village settlement with people of all ages and many professions. He dismisses complaints that Crystal Waters could look to the casual observer like a retirement village for the well-off.

'That's ridiculous. The average age is probably under forty. There are people retired; that to me is an important element of a village. It's the problem with many of our suburbs that there are no retired people, we put them into retirement homes. Here we have a mix of people: we've got them from yet-to-be-born to ninety-three; we range from Bahais to Pentecostal Christians to agnostics, from the very poor to the very well-off.' He is proud of the number of people at Crystal Waters who earn their living on the site. 'Most of the work is done here at home, which is very important in a village. You can't do that in a town legally. A small number leave the village to work. We're much closer to the ideal of being able to live and work and play and grow our food and retire in the same place.'

Would children want to stay on here? It was too early to say. 'The difficult time is for adolescents: we probably lack tolerance to them. There was an application for a shooting range; it was totally safe with adult supervision but it was thrown out twice. It's true many kids waste their time. Most of the youngsters have contributed to tree planting, though maybe sometimes under some pressure.'

Max sees the next most important step in making Crystal Waters a real community as 'the cluster idea' — his plan to transform the settlement into a series of intimate hamlets in which homes are linked by walkways shaded with trees. The idea was designed into the initial project, but there has been insufficient time and money to realise it. The cluster idea is part of a wider dream, shared by everyone in permaculture, of making rural environments attractive again, to stem the migration to cities. 'The village should be a place of culture, social life, personal growth,' Max says with fervour.

Why did Crystal Waters' layout place the communal area right at one end, with a result so different from most people's idea of a village? Max insisted that the communal area was in the middle, if you think of the stringy, boomerang layout as two welcoming arms. 'People from the UK come asking why houses and communal units are so far apart. Most Australians want five acres for their homes: who wants to live in a rural environment and be forced to live on top of each other?'

Why does a permaculture village use energy to slash the grass in its communal areas? Max has a solution. 'I'm starting a flock of sheep and I've got thirteen geese and thirty-eight ducks. You have to remember that all animals are selective grazers, they don't necessarily eat what we want them to eat. What's left behind we still have to cut. And that really tough bladey grass needs cutting. We are trying to establish softer grasses. In parts of Europe you see sheep being herded along roads. Over here, to slash a few times a year costs a couple of thousand dollars; to have somebody herding sheep is just not affordable. I know Skye wants to use cows. They are a danger to themselves and to others, at night you don't see them. You need to feed them all the year round. Come winter there could be a shortage of animal feed. You'd need rangers or a herder. It's not easy to find the right solution. All this has come from Skye who has no knowledge of animals.'

Max accepted the criticism that he, and some others, took little part in social life. 'I guess my social needs are satisfied by the stream of visitors we get. There is not a day when we don't get people. I was overseas last year for fifteen weeks. It's true I'm not clubbable: if I've had a busy day I quite like to go down the river with a fishing rod. I think it would be wrong if people feel obliged to turn up at communal meals.'

We asked Max whether Crystal Waters had fulfilled its promise and he said it would be like asking if a four-year-old child has succeeded as a person. You can see how the constant sniping wearies him. 'We made a design which makes permaculture possible: we cannot *force* people to do it. A dozen or so have made a good start, but we have all been too busy designing and building our houses and getting together our livelihoods. If some people are disappointed here, they have perfect freedom to sell up and go and start something else. We can plan a design; people have to find happiness for themselves.'

We left Crystal Waters conscious that to call it a permaculture village you must be generous in your definition. It is a settlement with a strong bias towards permaculture. The design did not *prevent* a greater sense of community although it hardly facilitated it. Problems boiled down more to money (lack of) and conflicting aims amongst the residents. We were more convinced than ever that permaculture is an extraordinarily useful design tool. It is easier to practise on an individual holding than in a communal one. As the ideology stands at present, it addresses more completely the physical environment than the social.

David Holmgren

To widen our perspective, we visited David Holmgren, co-inventor of permaculture with Bill Mollison. He lives at Hepburn, near Melbourne, which has a more temperate climate than Queensland, conducting design courses and putting his concepts into practice.

His plot is slightly more than one hectare. The intensive use of every centimetre reminds you of Japanese and Chinese horticulture. David hasn't bought vegetables for eight years now; he produces most of the food for himself, his partner, his son and twenty students at a time in his summer courses. He speaks with the quiet authority of someone who practises a theory with visible success.

David began as Bill Mollison's pupil and became his co-designer. When he first met Bill he identified him as: 'The first person who met my criteria of what an ecologist was. I was studying environmental design and now I wanted to re-structure my whole education.' In the early seventies David went to live in Bill's house in Hobart, Tasmania, and together they developed the garden from which the permaculture idea emerged. Then, while Bill became a worldwide permaculture guru, David re-made his own lifestyle in the image of his new teaching. 'We can't be just teachers; we have to develop some natural authority by our practice, re-thinking the issues of career and status in society, changing to a low energy lifestyle, using less money.'

David sees himself as Bill's 'practical and rock-solid' alter ego, but he, too, is a visionary of a world in which gardening, as distinct from farming, becomes the norm. He has devoted his life to proving that gardening can dramatically reduce the resources currently devoted to the production and distribution of food.

He points out that a sophisticated garden-based cuisine using in-season, fresh produce with minimal processing, involves very different domestic habits and skills to the fridge-based, year-round food culture common in Australia and other rich countries. 'The idea involved re-designing our culture. We already have cultural disintegration, so redesign is already happening because there is no choice.'

Critics say that permaculture could never feed enough of the world to make it useful on a wide scale. David replies that gardens are the most energy and resource-efficient forms of agriculture, particularly in the production of perishable food. 'Gardening is democratic and easily available to large numbers of people.'

The first Mollison-Holmgren book, *Permaculture One*, sold 40,000 in Australia in its first edition and appeared in six languages. 'Many seeds fell on barren ground or grew and then died. In the eighties the interest in sustainable alternatives dropped off. Then, in the late eighties, a TV programme by Bill Mollison, and his new *Designers Manual,* set off an absolute flood of interest. All the small permaculture groups couldn't handle it, there were very few places they could direct people to.'

David's handsome, single-story house is low-energy, low-cost. In a climate which goes over thirty degrees in summer for days at a time, he needs no air-conditioning. A system of vents cools the rooms, and the house is built to gain advantage of winter sunshine. The same vent system provides a cool room for the storage of fresh food. David's vine shades his veranda. His flowers protect his vegetables from insects. Each corner of the site provides both usefulness and beauty. 'We have a policy of selective disconnection from mainstream society: our son was born at home and has been educated at home. We live frugally but not from a sense of denial; that's the way we want to live.' Our lunch with David may have been frugal by his standards, we found it outstanding: home-baked bread, fresh-culled salad, home-made goat's cheese and fresh fruits.

Australia: a flawed paradise

It is difficult to imagine Crystal Waters anywhere else than Australia, where there is enough land, wealth, sunshine, communitarian spirit and ecological awareness. To become a member you need enough money to buy one of the plots. It is no accident that permaculture should have attracted so many Australians. Their country is still only just finding a mature identity and part of this is an acute awareness of the fragility of its ecosystems, the part played by thoughtless 'development' and reckless imports of flora and fauna in bringing about ecological disasters like soil erosion and salinity and the looming shortage of water.

The ozone hole and global warming and the sudden realisation that this could affect Australians themselves moved environmental consciousness sharply forward. Skin cancer, crop damage, species endangerment, soil degradation have arrived. Poor land management robbed land of its ability to cope with drought and nearly every summer in South Australia the wind carries clouds of topsoil from the north to the south. Great initiatives were taken: a Trees for Life fund, a Men of the Trees campaign, a plan for a billion trees in ten years, people in cities growing seedlings to take to farmers for planting out.

The Green viewpoint features prominently in the media: it was a major election issue when we were there. Almost everybody has heard of permaculture, organic food is increasingly available in the cities; parks and reserves enjoy careful preservation with painstaking emphasis on the native flora and fauna. Modern flush loos in Australia give you the choice of a half-flush to save water. Recycling is far better developed than in most other rich countries. The Aboriginals had been given historic land rights three years before we visited — which is philosophically and ecologically a major advance in perception. In the affluent Dandenong hill stations outside Melbourne we saw a multiplicity of Green adverts on the notice boards for alternative therapies, permaculture courses and people living in tipis seeking land. The fate of the Aborigines provides a sombre and sad chorus for much Australian life. You hear it in the place names; you see it in the vast distances.

At the same time Australia has a ruthlessly expansionist economy and is still cutting down vastly more trees than it plants, subdividing more and more agricultural land for far-flung and extravagant human settlements, constantly increasing its car pool while shamefully neglecting public transport. Its social security bill is becoming unaffordable just like everywhere else, while its city dwellers are as subject to stress, overwork and over-consumption. Its CO_2 emissions are among the highest in the world.

But there are encouraging signs: a third of Australian farmers are members of one of the 2000 Land Care groups, dealing with degradation, salinity, etc.; a highly effective dry-area irrigation system known as Keyline Farming is featured prominently in permaculture manuals and has been adopted by mainstream Australian agriculture. Australia's harsh environment and the disasters of modern agriculture (salination and damage to soil structure) have encouraged the development of more sustainable methods. In Europe and the US, agriculture hasn't faced that challenge because the land is more resilient.

Permaculture for us?

Permaculture tantalises with the possibility of manipulating our space until it becomes permanently benign, not through duress but because everything is in its natural place and activity. We have this from Bill Mollison's mordant certainty, from his earthy knowledge that efficiency is simple and simplicity is efficient, from his cruel humour about the vanity of mowed lawns, imported yoghurt, pet dogs and regimented rows of plants. The sight of Bill, an uncouth and sardonic Australian, sweeping aside the inept contradictions of a doomed culture with the assurance of Christ pushing money-changers out of the temple, liberates us.

How can we practise permaculture, where can we see it done? In Britain the permaculturists are earnest visionaries with dirty fingernails, meeting at courses and conferences where they talk about swales and inter-cropping, mulching, terracing, reed beds for purifying sewage, and solar panels. What have they to show for it? Eighty-six sites are listed in the 1997 edition of The Permaculture Plot, the official guide. But many of these are still in an embryonic stage. Meanwhile, the permaculturists are busy with their courses and conferences. Permaculture only becomes self-seeding, self-mulching and self-watering when it is mature.

Walter writes: Representative of how the ideas are percolating, if not into the mainstream at least into the alternative stream, was the annual general meeting of the British Permaculture Society. If there is a Green new culture it was here in the cluttered courtyards and unruly spaces of Wheatstone, the housing co-operative at Leintwardine in Herefordshire, known to locals as the Travellers Camping Ground, where practitioners, teachers and affectionate admirers of that esoteric science met for a weekend of camping, workshops, networking, drumming and singing into the night.

Most of the people are pointedly unkempt with straggly knotted hair, torn jeans and floppy, unwashed sweatshirts. A closer look shows there is a wide range here, familiar at such gatherings — academics in their oldest sweaters, people in woolly hats, vegans with intense eyes and thin bones, eco-tourists who turn up everywhere, true pundits who have come to teach, true disciples who have come to learn, fundamentalist feminists artfully dressed to repel men, earnest suburban folk who want fresh wisdom for their gardens and their lives — and of course the quiet organisers who have made it happen with too little money, and remain at hand to make sure people get fed and find their way to their workshops but don't put up their tents in the hostile farmer's field or leave without paying.

Permaculture has become an international *lingua franca* among Green people, a faith that binds and creates fellowship, a doctrine rich and loose and resonant enough to unite the idealists and the cynics, the urbans and the rurals, the theorists and the practitioners. Rachel Banks, one of the quiet organisers of the association's meeting, said the numbers of UK members had gone up twenty-five percent to over 1000 since last year.

The seven workshops were held in bare rooms in the ramshackle farmhouse, under a marquee or in tented domes with people sitting on straw bales or on the grass. They were about nascent permaculture sites in cities — Bradford's Springfield Community Garden had support from the city government's Agenda 21 staff — or rural organic farms like Ragman's Lane in Gloucestershire or the Dyfed permaculture Trust in Wales, where an old-established farm has been given over to the new structure.

On the last morning Rob Hopkins, sitting on a chair, appeared before his judges, who sat on the floor, as candidate for his permaculture accreditation diploma. Andy Langford and three other top designers listened to Rob's proposed design for Bossington Place in Somerset, a stately home whose owners wanted to run an organic veggie box scheme.

Young Rob illustrated his own permaculture activities with homemade cartoons. Speaking with plenty of earthy humour, he told of permaculture groups in Bristol who exist only to hold meetings 'for people who like meetings so they can disagree and hold more meetings.' He was frank about his disappointments when re-visiting the site of his careful design and finding everything gone wrong and much of his advice ignored. Too frank. He was sent outside for half an hour while the jury deliberated: they gave him his accreditation with a rider that he should 'pay more attention to the subtleties of client relationships.'

These are designs for a hoped-for future. Meanwhile you can visit Robert Hart, now well into his seventies. His tiny forest garden in Shropshire can feed four people all the year round without their doing any weeding because the forest garden gardens itself. It is self-mulching and self-watering thanks to the stream and a system of canals and pumps. Robert's garden is magnificent but it is too specialised in rare and costly trees to enable many of us to imitate it.

We host a course

What can permaculture offer the rest of us? You don't have to change your whole life and become a self-sufficient peasant. Why not convert half the lawn to vegetables? Don't dig it up: just put down an old carpet or a few layers of newspaper in the autumn, cover with thirty centimetres of manure, and your soil will be ready in the Spring. You will have practised a permaculture technique. We, before we set out to travel for this book, have tried it. It works.

We offered to host an advanced permaculture Designers Course at home. We feared that the association, which plans designs for any size of property, would turn us down because our middle class house, set in three hectares of rural Essex, has what we thought were the ultimate permaculture sins: a paddock for horses, a lawn, and a plastic-lined swimming pool inherited from previous owners. No problem, they said. Twelve students and three teachers agreed to come in return for four days food and lodging.

They divided into four groups, one for the garden, one for the paddock, another for the energy use in the house, one for the swimming pool. For four days people kept asking us, and the children: 'Which part of the lawn do you use when you play football?' 'When you're swimming, would you object to fish?' 'How often do you use the spare room?' The final report recommended a mixture of the practical, the far-fetched and the far-out. One idea was to install a small community of permaculture people in our meadow and convert the house and the grounds into a productive and sustainable unit. Seven families would live in capsules (low-impact dwellings shaped like tunnels) in the paddock. Horses could stay, provided we could protect the newly planted fruiting hedges from them, and install drinking water from a new pond. Poultry, of course. Hydroponics could be practised in the loft. The swimming pool could stay if we stopped using chlorine, filled the pool with fish and surrounded it with plants.

To our regret, very little of the proposal has been put into practice. Our field still lacks human habitation (would we have got planning permission, anyway, for capsules — and who would have lived there — friends or family or strangers? How would they have supported themselves?) There are no hydroponics (yet?) in the attic (we don't think the ceilings would have held); no swales (ditches to collect water for a clay dam) have been dug (we never found the time: we were too busy researching and writing this book). However, two permaculture plots have been prepared and have provided us with a good crop of staples like potatoes, onions, salads and peas. We have a long way to go.

Notes

1   Crystal Waters Conceptual permaculture Report by Max Lindegger and Robert Tap, Nascimanere Pty. Ltd.

2   A$1.00=£0.40=US$0.64

Part 3 : Some answers to globalisation

8

Nowhere left to hide

● ●

We were international and cosmopolitan and we always thought the global village would be fun. We were both predisposed to like the global economy. We lived in Africa, Israel, India and France. Our third daughter, Zoe, was born in New Delhi, our last child, Zachary, in Compiègne. We believed in free trade and the European Union and looked forward to the Channel Tunnel.

It *is* fun. Travel is easier, the Chunnel is open, Europe has become a single market, unlimited quantities of French wine and cheese can be brought in at Dover. The global market appears profitable, too, giving us an astonishing variety of food at the super-market and consumer goods in the High Street. It is hard to imagine life without the global economy, and it is becoming ever more seductive. And the joy does not end in rich coun-tries like ours. We can imagine that the global economy bene-fits the whole world because the South exports its produce to the North and imports know-how without restriction, giving poorer countries the chance to develop. So eventually the fun will be shared by all.

> The average American can choose from 25,000 supermarket items, spends six hours a week on shopping and is subject to some 300 messages every day telling him to consume more. Tomatoes and green peppers that last a week are sold in foam containers that last a century.
> · Alan Durning, *How Much is Enough?*

Why, then, is the world so cruel? Why have homeless people and beggars reappeared on our affluent streets? Why, after half a century of aid, 'devel-opment' and unparalleled economic expansion, are 800 million people still classed by the UN as malnourished, of whom 400 million are officially 'chronically undernourished?'[1] In North and South, for every plus there is more than a minus. We in the North, who are given the luck of the draw, can buy a wider variety of goods and luxuries — but our cities are intolerably polluted by traffic, our unspoiled countryside shrinks year by year and the whole world's environment deteriorates to a point where even sunbathing involves the risk of skin cancer because of damage to the ozone layer. The gaps between rich and poor are getting wider all the time. Thousands of new millionaires and scores of billionaires have appeared in the last decades, while one American child in seven lives below the poverty line.[2] In rich countries as well as poor, public services from schools to hospitals are deteriorating to the point of disintegration through lack of public money.

Why? The reason seems obvious to the people we have visited in writing this book. They are in revolt against the emerging global economy and want to set up viable local alternatives. We now agree with them. We have become convinced that the world's economic system is flawed: many of its rewards are illusory, effectively diminishing instead of enhancing our well-being; others are unhealthy; all are unsustainable. The globalisation process has more victims than victors. In 'rich' countries, a permanent underclass of the unemployed and the low paid has re-appeared — a class currently quantified in Britain at thirty percent of the population. In the South, globalisation has widened gaps in wealth, destroyed cultures and despoiled, denuded and polluted the environment to the point where it threatens the survival of the poorest people who depend on natural resources like trees, clean rivers and plentiful fish. The 'cheap' food we enjoy in our supermarket is not cheap when we count the exploitation and impoverishment of people in the South involved in its production, or the pollution costs involved in the packaging and transport of the goods. The average item of food sold in the US has travelled 2080 km.

Did we speak of fun, of comfort and convenience? It does not seem so to anyone living near a main road in Europe, where, every decade, the Single Market doubles the distances travelled by lorries criss-crossing the continent with food, consumer goods and materials for industry. The average-sized diesel lorry pumps a quarter of a kilogram of deadly particulates into the air for every 160 kilometres of urban road it travels.[3] The links between respiratory diseases and this pollution are well known; a British Government report

---

Globalisation operates by standards-lowering competition to bid down wages, to externalise environmental costs, and reduce social overhead expenses for public goods. But it is far worse than an unrealistic public dream — it actively undercuts the ability of nations to continue dealing with their own problems. Globalisation requires that for a nation to be rich, the majority of its citizens must be poor, increase in number and live in a deteriorating environment.'
· Professor Herman Daly speaking at the Right Livelihood Award ceremony in Stockholm, 1997.

says that traffic fumes hasten the death of 24,000 people a year in the UK and put a similar number in hospital.[4] Almost thirty percent of British children now suffer from asthma at some stage during their childhood.[5] And yet, most items transported back and forth could easily be produced in the regions where they are consumed.

That is only one example of how the global economy robs us even as it seems to reward us. In this chapter we look at four principal reasons for disenchantment:

* Globalisation lowers the quality of life for most people — even for many of those whose standard of living it enhances.
* Its effects are unjust, tending to enrich the few and impoverish the many.
* Globalisation is unsustainable. Several planets the size of Earth would be needed to realise its promise.
* Globalisation destroys cultures, gradually reducing all values to those of a global hamburger/Coca-Cola society.

We will end the chapter with a look at some remedies.

Higher living standards for some, lower quality of life for almost everybody

Everybody experiences the deterioration in their own way. When we were young — in the UK in the fifties and sixties — with a good education we felt assured of a job. If we liked our job we could expect to stay in it for a long time, and to enjoy our leisure as well, and if we didn't like the job we could find another. One good job was usually enough to support a family. Today our children have to struggle to find work, struggle to keep it, and struggle to manage on the money. Most families need both parents' incomes to manage. As large companies reduce their workforce in order to compete with workers in countries with lower wages, those remaining at work are required to work harder. Affluent society seems to be divided between people who work too hard for a decent quality of life, people who earn too little for a decent standard of life, and people who have no work at all.

Deterioration happens gradually and often goes unnoticed for a long time, like the number of diesel lorries passing by our house, or local shops going out of business, or the deteriorating services offered by cash-starved schools and hospitals. In our childhood we could buy organic vegetables and fruit from our greengrocer and fresh local bread from our baker. Today organic produce is available only in favoured areas and at a premium: it has been replaced by homogenised, chemically grown food which is often flown in from a different continent.

(Sometimes there is a jolt. Until recently I, Dorothy, had my stories published in such literary magazines as *Panurge*, *Writing Women*, *Raconteur*,

In 1960, the income distribution ratio of the world's richest twenty percent and the poorest twenty percent was 30:1. Today (1995) the ratio is 60:1.
· *Development*, Journal of the Society for International Development, 1995:3.

Between 1979 and 1992 the Fortune 500 companies (the world's top 500) abolished 4.4 million jobs to improve their efficiency and competitiveness. Over a quarter of the thirty million unemployed in the developed countries have been out of work for more than two years
· *Development*, 1995:3.

Tees Valley Writer and *Iron*. During the single year of 1996, all five of these journals closed down. The world economy gallops ahead and gives us more to buy but our lives are impoverished and retrenched. Public services in every country, rich or poor, have come to be seen as an unjustified drain on economic resources and therefore a threat to global competitivity.)

We can now measure this decline in the quality of life, thanks to a movement of new-style economists, in revolt against the obsession with the use of economic growth and Gross National Product (GNP) as the sole yardsticks of progress, who have devised better indicators. Clifford Cobb and Ted Halstead invented a Genuine Progress Indicator and found that in the US the GPI grew, along with the GNP, up to the year 1968 and began to decline in the 1970s, falling over forty percent by 1992.[6] Similar calculations in other industrialised countries, including Britain and Germany, show even sharper declines in 'welfare indices,' leading the economist Richard Douthwaite to conclude that 'the world economic system is now running backwards, and although it is producing more goods and services each year, all the increase and some more on top is required to keep the system functioning and to compensate for the damage it does.'[7]

A nation can get richer without making its people better off. In Britain

Over the last decade, of forty-six countries with economic growth, only twenty-seven saw employment grow too. Nineteen, or more than forty per cent, experienced 'jobless growth', including India, Pakistan, and Zimbabwe. In the industrial world unemployment now affects thirty-five million people, with another four million too discouraged to seek work. The proportion of unemployed people in the workforce ranges from 2.5 per cent in Japan to twenty-three per cent in Spain. In Eastern Europe and the former Soviet Union countries, unemployment has gone from near zero before 1990 to double digits in some countries: nineteen per cent in Albania and seventeen per cent in Bulgaria and Poland, with the members of the former Soviet Union still counting.
· United Nations Development Program Report, 1996.

GNP grew by fifty percent between 1972 and 1997. During the same period violent crime quadrupled, the incidence of asthma tripled, the number of workless households tripled, car traffic almost doubled and the number of climate-changing gases in the atmosphere grew to perilous levels.[8] The New Economics Foundation in London has an Index of Sustainable Economic Welfare. The ISEW starts out with the conventional Gross Domestic Product (GDP), based on consumer expenditure, and then adjusts it to account for social and environmental costs — including car accidents, water and air pollution, loss of habitat, loss of farmlands, depletion of non-renewable resources, long-term environmental damage, and the money we all have to spend to fight and control pollution. The ISEW grew by almost three percent a year during the 1970s but has since been in persistent decline, reflecting a marked downward trend in the quality of life. Since 1980, according to the ISEW, real well-being has fallen by over twenty percent.

A welfare index on a world scale, used by the UN Development Program and known as the Capability Poverty Measure, reflects the proportion of children under five who are underweight, the proportion of births unattended by trained health personnel and the rate of female illiteracy. Using this index, the UNDP estimates that countries like Cote d'Ivoire, which has been moving backwards in education, may require sixty-five years to reach the amenity levels of industrial countries, and that those further behind, such as Mozambique and Niger, will take more than two centuries, without changes in policy and much more help from outside.[9]

Economic growth does not necessarily create jobs; indeed in rich and poor countries alike, growth and globalisation have fostered unemployment. Britain, which had had a trade surplus in manufactured goods in every peacetime year for more than a century and in 1972 had exported goods worth fifty-five percent more than those it imported, went in 1982 into what became a chronic trade deficit, which by 1993 amounted to £13.4 billion. Richard Douthwaite calculates that if the goods that sum represented had been made at home, a million extra jobs could have been created, halving the unemployment figure.[10]

The global economy, often associated with progress and higher living standards, is widely assumed to be good for health. In fact, there has been a decline in many departments of health in both the North and the South. A Harvard Working Group on new and resurgent diseases blames the major economic strategies of globalisation — privatisation, export agriculture, deregulation, rapid growth and free trade — for the spread of disease in many new ways.[11]

In rich countries, health is undermined by stress, overwork, chemicals in food, unhealthy lifestyles and pollution. In both North and South, malnutrition becomes more widespread as the gap between rich and poor widens. Publicly provided health care is in decline in both North and South as national budgets shrink to fit the harsh criteria imposed by global competition.

In the US, tuberculosis, after steady decline since 1882, rose by eighteen percent between 1985 and 1992. TB, which the World Health Organisation describes as 'out of control in many parts of the world', affects mainly poor inner city communities. Worldwide there were eight million new cases of tuberculosis in 1991 and one third of the world's population is now estimated to be carrying the infection. Diphtheria is back as a major killer of adults in Russia, plague has resurfaced in India, malaria returned to regions once eliminated. The first ever epidemics of dengue fever transmitted by mosquitoes occurred in Venezuela, Brazil, India and Australia. Cholera for the first time in almost a century has re-emerged as a major killer in Latin America and yellow fever re-emerged in Kenya.[12]

Nor should we take progress in nutritional standards for granted. One of the showpieces of the advanced global economy was the Green Revolution, which introduced high-yielding grain seeds and Western agricultural techniques to Asia and parts of Africa and South America. Between 1955 and 1985, the revolution lifted world grain production from 273 to 343 kg per person; India's production trebled over that same period. But the 'miracle seeds' need fertiliser, pesticide and irrigation, all of which are affordable only by relatively rich landlords and are damaging to the ecological balance of the affected area. Poor farmers and landless farm workers are forced off the land and become economic refugees in city slums. Over-use of chemicals causes salination and erosion of the soil — with the result that still more chemicals need to be applied. So much irrigation water is pumped up from wells that the water table is lowered and village wells run dry. Worst of all, the high yields are now diminishing and no longer respond to increased inputs of chemicals and irrigation.

As if this were not enough, the high-yield rice, wheat and maize varieties that the Green Revolution introduced are lower in minerals and vitamins than

Provisional figures suggest that 83,664 people in England and Wales felt ill enough last year to see a doctor over food-poisoning, in almost every case as a direct result of intensive meat farming — a revolution that scientists and farmers have long urged is safe... What is remarkable is that we can poison ourselves so casually, so frequently and not think it unusual; that millions of us accept that we should have to boil water before drinking it. Or wash fruit before eating or not swim in the sea, or sniff too deeply the roses that we have bought. And not feel angry.
· John Vidal, in *The Guardian*, 7 March 1997.

the traditional varieties of fruits, vegetables and legumes that they have displaced. As a result, the diet of many people in the South is now dangerously low in iron, zinc, vitamin A and other micronutrients, resulting in an increase in incapacitating mineral deficiencies 'which is threatening to lock parts of the Third World into an endless cycle of ill-health, low productivity and underdevelopment,' according to a report in the *New Scientist*.[13]

Globalisation enriches the few and impoverishes the many

A new class of global super-capitalists has acquired fabulous wealth and successful financiers, entrepreneurs and most skilled employees have prospered. The rest of us are generally excluded from winning the globalisation game. In rich and poor countries alike, smaller businesses disappear, farmers and peasants producing food for themselves and for local people are displaced by more profitable firms growing crops for export, or by industrial projects which can profit better from the global economy. The liberation of capital and currency movements throughout the world has made money itself the world's most profitable commodity, creating fabulous wealth for financiers who produce nothing.

Why have these problems become so acute? Piecemeal globalisation has been with us for millennia — ever since people began venturing forth on foot, on horseback or in small boats from their native regions. However, in the last three decades globalisation has acquired the scale and momentum of an entirely new phenomenon because for the first time there is nowhere left to hide from the torrent of goods, capital, mass entertainment and commercial propaganda, as the last barriers are systematically removed. The process has been hailed as a victory for the free market. But this new world market is not free. The dominant role is reserved for a handful of transnational corporations based in rich

---

The assets of the world's 358 dollar billionaires exceed the combined annual incomes of all the countries in which nearly half (forty-five per cent) of all the people in the world live. Eighty-nine countries were economically worse off in 1995 than they had been ten years earlier, and some were worse off than thirty years earlier. Despite a dramatic surge in economic growth in fifteen countries over the past three decades, 1.6 billion people were left behind and are worse off than they were fifteen years ago. In seventy developing countries, today's levels of income are less than those reached in the 1960s or the 1970s. And in nineteen of the countries, including not only war-torn Haiti, Liberia, Nicaragua, Rwanda and Sudan, but also such countries as Ghana and Venezuela, per capita income today is less than the level of 1960 or before.
· UNDP Human Development Report, 1996.

countries whose wealth protects them from democratic control. The global system enables, indeed compels these corporations to relocate their plants where labour is cheaper, forcing local workers to choose between unemployment and low wages.

As a result, Britain, among other countries, has become a low-wage economy. British pay rates were the same as Italy's in 1980 but had fallen twenty-five percent lower in 1990.[14] In France unemployment climbed from 420,000 to 5.1 million during a period in which the economy, measured in terms of the GDP, grew by eighty percent. In the US, the Clinton administration in the nineties was boasting of 'growth' creating jobs, but many if not most new jobs are dead-end, or temporary, or low-paid and without security.

The South fares much worse. The UN Development Programme's 1996 report found that economic growth had failed to improve the lot of more than a quarter of the world's people in over 100 countries (most, but not all of them, in the South). The report predicted that if current global trends continued, polarisation would increase within countries and between countries, between workers who had secure and well-paying jobs and those who did not, between countries that were growing fast and whose people were climbing the skill and wage ladder, and those that were left out of the global competition.

> Thirty percent of the Philippines' cultivated land including the most fertile areas is given over to cash-crop production for export by multinationals exporting bananas, pineapples and sugar cane, even matchsticks. Coercive measures to edge out peasants stubbornly clinging to precious parcels of land include burning of homes, strafing and executing local residents who actively oppose the entry of agribusiness corporations.
>
> · The Ecologist, *Whose Common Future?*

Perhaps the most damaging human consequence of globalisation in the South is that farmers have been replaced by entrepreneurs growing crops for export. The land has now become unavailable to the poor to grow the staples they require to meet their own basic needs. In the logic of the global market, this development makes sense, as it earns foreign exchange which, in theory, pays for imported food from countries like the US where it is produced more efficiently. In human terms it is a disaster. Displaced farmers have no other livelihood. The new arrangement is grossly unfair, because 'cheap' food from the US or the European Union is subsidised at home. The result is a tragic transfer of resources from poor to rich. Much of the grain that many southern countries import from the North in exchange for their own food exports is used as feedstocks to produce meat for upper-income urban consumers.

> The great, centralised economic entities of our time do not come into rural places in order to improve them by 'creating jobs'. They come to take as much of value as they can take as cheaply and as quickly as they can take it. They are interested in 'job creation' only as long as the jobs can be done more cheaply by humans than by machines. They are not interested in the good health — economic, natural or human — of any place on this earth. If you should undertake to appeal or complain to one of these great corporations on behalf of your community, you would discover something most remarkable: these organisations are organised expressly for the evasion of responsibility. They are structures in which, as my brother says, 'the buck never stops.' The buck is processed up the hierarchy until finally it is passed to 'the shareholders,' who characteristically are too widely dispersed, too poorly informed, and too unconcerned to be responsible for anything.
> · Wendell Berry in *The Case Against the Global Economy*.

The impoverishment of the poor is tragically evident in the stream of economic or environmental refugees, estimated at twenty-five million at any one time, who are forced to leave lands so degraded and denuded by the direct or indirect effects of economic 'development' that they cannot subsist there any longer.[15] In India, large-scale development projects have displaced well over twenty million people over a forty-year period. In Brazil 28.4 million people were displaced between 1960 and 1980 by the systematic conversion of agriculture from the old system of smallholders producing food to capital-intensive production for export.[16]

One effect of the unfairness in the world's economic system is the chronic and crippling debts imposed on governments in the South. When repayments falter, the International Monetary Fund (IMF) and the World Bank force 'structural adjustment' on debtor nations as a condition of further loans. This is designed to force sluggish converts to the global system to hurry along. A typical victim was Costa Rica, which is traditionally a more egalitarian society than its neighbours, with a strong base of small farmers and few large landholdings. Consistent with orthodox practice, the IMF imposed policies that deliberately removed economic incentives from small farmers producing food for local consumption, and transferred them to large estates producing for export. As a result, thousands of small farmers were displaced. Costa Rica's income gap between rich and poor has become as wide as it is in the rest of Latin America, and a sharp increase in crime and violence has required corresponding increases in expenditure on police and security. The country now depends on imports to meet basic food requirements — and the foreign debt that structural adjustment was supposed to reduce has doubled. The IMF and World Bank nevertheless point to Costa Rica as a structural adjustment success story because economic growth has increased and the country is now able to meet its growing debt service repayments.[17]

It is argued that the relative prosperity of the 'tiger' economies of Southeast Asia shows that nations of the South can emerge from poverty by performing well in the global economy. If Taiwan and South Korea can do it, why not everybody else? In fact, these countries had exceptional advantages which cannot be reproduced elsewhere: their relatively small populations (except Indonesia), substantial aid from the superpowers during the Cold War, and subsidies from the state to help and protect local industry. Moreover, these economies were not soundly based, as the South Korean and Indonesian crashes of 1997-98 showed. Even before that, the 'miracle' in these economies was coming to an end because their workers demanded higher rewards and these countries' economic advantages were beginning to pass to still cheaper labour markets elsewhere.

Supporters of the global economy argue that the world's population explosion makes such arrangements inevitable, because only industrial agriculture, traded on a world scale, can feed the hungry. Unfortunately, the poor do not have enough money to buy the food. This, perhaps, is the underlying tragedy of the global economy: it has turned goods and services — which previously were produced by the poor for their own consumption or exchanged according to custom and local obligation — into commodities which only money can buy. This process is not an accident but deliberate. The General Agreement on Tariffs and Trade (GATT) and its new executive body, the World Trade Organisation, are designed expressly for that.

Far from feeding the hungry, the global economy is terribly wasteful of resources, diverting essential raw materials and food from the poor who need it to the rich who do not. We have seen that the Green Revolution, which has replaced peasant farmers by industrial farming, has effectively run out of steam. In the decade from 1985 to 1995, global grain harvests rose by only two percent,

---

Seventy percent of world trade is controlled by 500 corporations, which also control eighty percent of foreign investment and thirty percent of world GDP. Almost forty percent of world trade is carried out within these multinationals. The top five companies have seventy-seven percent of the world cereal trade; three banana companies share eighty percent of the world banana trade; three cocoa companies have eighty-three percent of the world's cocoa trade; three tea companies have eighty-five percent of the world's tea trade. Shell Oil's 1990 gross income of $132 billion was more than the total GDP of Tanzania, Ethiopia, Nepal, Bangladesh, Zaire, Uganda, Nigeria, Kenya and Pakistan combined.

· *Whose Common Future?* (The Ecologist).

while the population rose by 19.5 percent, which is a per-capita decline of four-teen percent. The rich minority consume more and more while the poor majority get less, and for them the decline is far greater than fourteen percent. Meat eating, mostly a privilege of the better-off countries, diverts thirty-eight percent of the world's grain to feeding livestock, enough to take care of the basic grain needs of 3.3 billion of the world's 5.8 billion people. Meat-eating is an inefficient and luxurious way of using resources. Producing one kilogram of industrially-raised poultry or fish needs two kilograms of grain; one kg of pork needs four kg of grain; one kg of beef (the preferred meat) needs seven kg of grain.[18]

The global economy is unsustainable

Since 1950 the world economy has nearly quintupled. In that half-century humans have consumed more natural resources, and generated more waste and pollution, than in all previous human history.[19] Consumption of grain, beef, mutton and water has tripled, fossil fuel use and carbon dioxide emissions (which are the main cause of global warming) have quadrupled.[20]

Most of this expansion has benefited the richest one-fifth of the world's population, which doubled its per-capita consumption of energy, meat, timber, steel and copper since 1950, quadrupled car ownership and quintupled use of plastics. The poorest one fifth barely increased its per-capita consumption.[21] Now another 750 million people are hoping to enter the consumer world —

> Since 1950, industrial logging has cleared nearly half of tropical rain forests and more than half of temperate forests. Forests have all but disappeared in Nigeria, Benin, Côte d'Ivoire, Togo, El Salvador, western Ecuador, Ghana and Haiti. Most forests now occur in fragments surrounded by degraded land and cannot sustain viable populations of wildlife. Wetlands, essential for regulating water flows, removing sediments and pollution, habitats for waterfowl, fish etc., are threatened all over the world by drainage for industrial agriculture or urban expansion. In Australia, New Zealand and California ninety percent of the wetlands are gone.
> · *State of the World 1997.*

350 million in China, eighty million in India, plus others in scores of countries. This is about the same as the number of long-established consumers in the rich countries.[22]

Most people in the South hope that their societies will 'catch up' with the living standards of industrialised nations, but the hope is shattered by the calculation that, on average, a citizen of an affluent nation needs four to six hectares of productive land to sustain his or her lifestyle — while the amount of such land worldwide is only 1.7 hectares per person If everyone on earth were to consume at the rate of affluent nations, we would need an extra three planets like Earth.[23] William Rees at the University of British Columbia, Canada, has developed the concept of an ecological footprint. How much are you using of the world's resources? Rees points to the obvious fact that in a finite world not every region or country can be a net importer of biophysical goods and services. He concludes that if the earth's sustainable natural output were shared equally among the present world population, the needs of all could be met — but not at North American or European or Japanese levels, which must be halved, at least, as the world population doubles.

The global economy has been compared to an aeroplane which has to go on flying in order not to crash. This economy only works if the amount of economic activity — which is today practically synonymous with industrial activity since farming has become an industry too — constantly increases throughout the world. Since the world itself does not expand, this cannot last. The current official yardstick of economic success is *increase* in the GDP of a nation, which must mean a *decrease* in reserves of fossil fuels, water, forests, topsoil and clean air. The statistics of depletion and devastation fill libraries of books, reports and specialist periodicals. The Internet has tens of thousands of websites telling the same story, belonging to American universities, government research institutions such as NASA, environmental pressure groups like Greenpeace and Friends of the Earth, and a surprisingly large number of local enthusiasts trying to keep track of their own watersheds, wetlands, forests, flora and fauna. A convenient overview of this information, with expert commentaries, appears in the annual State of the World report of the Worldwatch Institute in New York.

Excessive economic activity threatens the earth's life support systems. The emission of chlorofluorocarbons and other chemicals into the atmosphere destroyed five percent of the protective ozone layer over North America, and probably globally, between 1980 and 1990. Destruction of this thin, vital vein in the stratosphere above the earth exposes light-skinned people, especially children, to higher risks of skin cancer when they are in sunlight. A UN study speaks of 'conclusive evidence' that the hole in the ozone layer harms plankton, which is essential for marine life, and that the increased ultraviolet radiation has damaged fish, shrimp, crab, amphibians and other marine animals.[24]

Much of the damage to the earth's soil and atmosphere is caused by industrial agriculture, with its high reliance on chemical fertilisers and pesticides. A fifth of the world's topsoil and nearly a third of croplands have been lost through erosion and oxidation in the last forty years, leading to a net decline in percapita croplands from 1986 onwards.[25] Carbon dioxide emissions resulting mainly from farming and industrial activity increased by twenty-five

Since 1903, the US has lost most of its 20,000 varieties of agricultural plants. China had 10,000 strains of wheat in production in 1949, but only 1000 in the 70s. More than eighty countries reported to the UN Food and Agriculture Organisation that a wide range of locally grown varieties are being replaced by a few profitable alternatives from abroad. Seed banks around the world attempt to hold diversified stocks for future use but their facilities are so inadequate that more than half the world's 1300 stores are perhaps incapable at present of performing the basic conservation role of a gene bank
· Rob Edwards, in *New Scientist*, 17 August 1996.

percent in the last 100 years, with the result that global warming is now recognised by world leaders as a deadly potential threat to food supplies. Yet the same leaders press on with the growth-based global consumer economy that causes the problem. It is a schizophrenic attitude, a world gone mad.

Year on year expansion of economic activity results in year on year diminution of the natural world. Edward O. Wilson, a Harvard biologist, estimates that 50,000 invertebrate species a year — nearly 140 a day — are condemned to extinction by the destruction of their tropical rainforest habitat. The loss of species is a threat not only to our natural inheritance and our pleasure in living on this earth, but also to our future health and food supplies. The UN Food and Agriculture Organisation has identified 30,000 edible plants in the world, of which 7000 have been grown or gathered for food. But today ninety-five percent of our protein and calories comes from only thirty crops. More than half our energy intake from plants comes from wheat, rice and maize. US main crops depend on fewer than nine varieties. European barley could be wiped out in a single evolutionary step because it depends on one gene.

After its worldwide industrialisation, agriculture is now on the threshold of an even more thoroughgoing revolution: the introduction of genetically modified plants and animals. Genetic engineering is being justified as a breakthrough in providing more, better and ultimately cheaper food for an exploding world population. In reality the over-riding aim is to make hitherto undreamed of profits for the giant multinational corporations which will hold the patents — especially Monsanto which dominates the field. Scientists in several fields have expressed grave misgivings, complaining that much of the technology is insufficiently tested, and that its results are so unpredictable that it could cause an agricultural, ecological and health catastrophe. A genetically altered species such as the soya bean, bred to be immune to Monsanto's own herbicide Roundup, could breed with its wild relatives and produce 'superweeds' immune to Roundup or indeed any herbicide. Or the new hybrid could itself become a strongly growing weed and drive out fragile and rare plants from its habitats.

Genetic engineering is based on the premise that a gene performing a useful function in one species can safely be moved to another species. However, David Ehrenfeld, biology professor at Rutgens University, among many others, points out that genes can change their behaviour when they are put into a different environment, perhaps with disastrous effects.[26] From that fundamental uncertainty, others derive. For example, the proposed transfer of insecticidal genes to corn or cotton will make the emergence of genetic resistance among pests 'almost a certainty', according to Ehrenfeld. Monsanto's bovine growth hormone, designed to boost milk yields in a country which already has a huge surplus of milk, carries the danger, according to the company's own package instructions, of numerous serious diseases. Because cows treated with this hormone need more protein, their diet has to be supplemented with ground-up animal meat — a practice which has already resulted in the 'mad cow' syndrome and its horrific human analogue — Creutzfeld Jakob disease.

The introduction of patents on genes, plants, animals and parts of human bodies gives a startling new dimension to the globalisation of the economy. Legitimised 'bio-piracy' will allow a handful of corporations to appropriate the benefits of traditional knowledge in seeds and natural medicines. A massive surcharge on medicinal products that have been patented could throttle any research that is independent of the corporations. The new regime is a serious

---

Genetic engineering recombines genetic material in the laboratory between species that do not interbreed in nature. While conventional breeding methods shuffle different forms (alletes) of the same genes, genetic engineering enables completely new (exotic) species to be introduced with unpredictable effects on the physiology and biochemistry of the resultant transgenic organism.

Gene multiplications and a high proportion of gene transfers are mediated by vectors which have the following undesirable characteristics:

a.   Many are derived from disease-causing viruses, plasmids and mobile, genetic elements — parasitic DNA that have the ability to invade cells and insert themselves into the cell's genome causing genetic damage.

b.   They are designed to break down species barriers so that they can shuttle genes between a wide range of species. The wide host range means that they can infect many animals and plants, and in the process pick up genes from viruses of all these species to create new pathogens.

c.   They routinely carry genes for antibiotic resistance, which is already a big health problem.

d.   They are increasingly constructed to overcome the recipient's species defence mechanisms that break down or inactivate DNA.

· Mae-Wan Ho in *The Ecologist*, July/August 1997.

new threat to biodiversity: patented plants have to be uniform, distinct and stable, which will force food corporations to introduce monocultures to the international seed markets, replacing diverse varieties.

Food miles

Some of the more obvious absurdities of the global market are at last becoming recognised and reported in the media. In a British television programme, *Keep on Trucking*,[27] road tankers were shown carrying milk 3200 kilometres from Bavaria, Germany, to a yoghurt factory in Greece, before shipping the yoghurt all the way back to its markets — although the same type of 'Greek' yoghurt is made in every European country. Other trucks were carrying bits of white cotton and lace for knickers, cut out in a Swiss factory, all the way to Portugal, 2000 kilometres miles away, where four seams are sown in a twenty-second operation by workers earning a third of Swiss wages. The knickers are then trucked back to Switzerland to be finished, and then trucked out again to the various countries of their sale. No European country to our knowledge is incapable of making knickers, but this trucking arrangement halves the Swiss factory's production costs despite the transport costs involved. Freight companies pay neither the environmental nor the health costs which have to be met by society as a whole. Whether we buy apples or knickers, butter or trainers, we, the consumers, believe that we benefit from this convoluted system because we pay only the market price for our goods, not the pollution costs the goods have incurred in transit. However, we, as citizens, do pay those costs.

None of the appetites of a voracious global economy looks more insatiable than the demand for water. Human use of fresh water doubled during the period 1940-80, largely because industrial agriculture needs so much, and is expected to double again by 2000. Already the world uses fifty-four percent of available freshwater runoff, an amount projected to rise to seventy-five percent by the year 2025 through population growth alone, without allowing for any increase in per capita consumption. The total of water-short people today, 550 million, could soar to three billion by the year 2025,[28] when water may well have replaced oil as a major cause of war.

What will happen if the global economy marches on unchecked? In the next generation there could be twice as many people, seeking three times as much food and fibre, consuming four times as much energy, and engaging in five to ten times as much economic activity (the latter merely to enable the developing-world majority of humankind to climb out of its poverty). In a grim summary, the British environmentalist Norman Myers concludes that since per capita consumption worldwide has increased by three percent per year during the past quarter century, it is reasonable to suppose that people in future will want it to increase by at least two percent per year, if that should prove sustainable. 'Per capita consumption would then double in thirty-five years, quadruple in seventy years, and increase eightfold by 2100 (no more than the USA has achieved during this century, albeit starting from a much lower base).' Myers concludes: 'It is not that consumption levels, and hence resource exploitation, *should* go down among affluent communities. They *will* go down if only because Earth cannot indefinitely support our present consumption loading, let alone future loading.'[29]

Globalisation undermines cultures

The ethos of economic development is one of individual striving and success. It is an ethos at odds with many traditional societies which are calibrated on communal values and a smoother, more stable continuum. Faced with this onslaught, a traditional culture develops an over-riding shame; those who resist the new culture and try to retain their old values against enormous odds become a sub-class. One result of uncontrolled economic development has been the bastardisation of cultures that were not built around a non-stop drive to accumulate. The fundamental change from a traditional society to an economic one is that goods and services which were exchanged, or provided gratis, become monetised. Any culture built on mutual obligation and service is destroyed.

In a high Himalayan mountain village in Nepal, not accustomed yet to either tourists or developers, a couple of children in knitted hats, holding hands, offered us a handful of apricots and smiled. In a similar Indian village down in the plain, the kids circled us screaming for rupees or when they were not forthcoming, 'gimme pen.' And when that was not forthcoming, threw clods of earth. The latter children were already habituated to want, the former still accustomed to share. The South is accepting modernisation as a creed, leaving itself no escape from the hegemony of the North's cultural values.

To equate the degree of civilisation with the level of production constitutes one of the most potent myths of our time: from it flows the fallacy that the less you produce and own, the more you need to be helped, exploited or pitied. Helena Norberg-Hodge, a development economist whose special study is Ladakh, tells a story of a young man showing her around his village which is poor in consumer goods and rich in space and beauty, and has enjoyed a sustainable way of life for many centuries. He was proud of everything in his village, from the hand-carved balconies to the apricots drying on the roofs. When Helena asked to see some poor people, the young man said nobody was poor in Ladakh. Some years later, she found the same young man in the same village. He was apologising for its 'poverty'.[30]

A single global market threatens ultimately to create a single global consumer society with a single set of values. Ostensibly these will be liberal values, favouring personal freedom, democracy and competition. In practice, this new system destroys the social cohesion of societies, devalues the skills of artists and craftspeople, undermines local systems of care for the old, the young and the disadvantaged — and, in many countries, props up unsavoury dictatorships.

Remedies

The Living Lightly people in this book, in flight from the global economy, are themselves the remedy. They invite modern people to return to the values of co-operation, love, simple living, respect for nature and openness to transcendent realities. Living in this way in the context of the global economy is an uphill struggle, but it must not be shirked. The ideological void that has followed the collapse of socialism and communism leaves the search for a communitarian economy as the only radicalism left. Since these new radicals are unlikely to win over the corporate powers and their affluent defenders, they can only hope to prevail through their own example and the gradual erosion of the dominant system through local initiatives that exchange high living standards for a high quality of life.

However, creative minds within this movement have devised ways in which these ideals might be transferred, piece by piece, into mainstream society so as eventually to transform it. First, there has to be to be a shift in consumption patterns among affluent people in order to move towards global sustainability and set a better example in the rest of the world. Norman Myers says such a shift would mark 'one of the greatest revolutions in human behaviour' but adds hopefully that such revolutions can occur, citing the fact that fifty-five million Americans gave up smoking in the eighties.[31]

A new school of economists have, as we have seen, invented alternative indicators to measure real progress and real well-being rather than economic growth. The most radical of these want to abolish the objective of economic growth, arguing that a 'steady-state' economy is essential for

> For developed-world people the age-old priorities of getting supper on the table is history. This means there is scope to reflect that the good life may not consist in piling up ever more goodies — and that nobody says on their death-bed that they wish they had done more consuming.
>
> · Norman Myers in an unpublished thesis.

sustainability and would be quite feasible. Herman Daly, a reformed World Bank economist, has argued that a steady-state economy 'can develop qualitatively, but does not grow in quantitative scale, just as the planet earth, of which the economy is a sub-system, develops without growing.'[32] Failing such radical reform, the economists who criticise slavish adherence to growth insist that prices should reflect real costs — which in economic jargon means to 'internalise externalities' by including hidden environmental and resource costs in the price. Such measures would compel Americans to pay the 'real price' — about six times the present price — for their gasoline. Politically driven subsidies on resource-extracting industries like fishing would have to be abolished. We would need to calculate our 'ecological footprint' and begin to match what we use with what is available to all. We would promote efficiency and sufficiency, eliminate excess packaging and direct official propaganda towards promoting sustainable values instead of consumerism.

Leading writers on these matters have offered their own wish list. Helena Norberg-Hodge wishes that we:

- Shift massive transport infrastructure investment to local and public transport — and bike paths etc.
- Phase out subsidies for big energy plants.
- Shift agricultural subsidies from agribusiness to small farmers.
- Shift money for supermarket infrastructure to public markets and farmers' markets.
- Aid local entertainment facilities.
- Shift money from huge urban hospitals to small clinics.
- Improve spaces for public meetings.
- Curb corporations by using tariffs to regulate imports. Tax big business, not small; tax energy used in production; lend to small businesses.
- Use land trusts etc. to save land from development.
- Change urban zoning to allow small shops and artisan business near homes.
- In the South — shift from large dams to local projects; shift agriculture back to diversified local production for local needs; let countries protect their natural resources and businesses; end promotion of Western style monocultural education; decentralise health facilities; use counterdevelopment messages in the media and schools to boost the image of primary producers; encourage community banks, Buy Local campaigns, Farmers Markets and Ecovillages.[33]

David Korten, whose writings expose the harmful role of corporations, offers a list which includes a ban on international arms sales; a fifty percent tax on advertising in the rich countries; economic accounting to reflect performance 'on the basis of human needs met and the enhancement or depletion of a country's human, social and natural stock'; anti-trust laws to break corporations into local enterprises serving local markets; land reform for family farms; repudiation of ninety percent of Third World debts.[34]

Can the juggernaut of global trading, pushed ever further forward under the awesome authority of the World Trading Organisation, ever be checked? The traditional opposite of free trade is protectionism — a historically unpopular option associated with the protection of privilege, inefficient agriculture and industry and high prices. Two British researchers and campaigners, Tim Lang and Colin Hines, published *The New Protectionism* in 1993. They urged curbs on international trade designed to protect majorities, not minorities as in the old version of protectionism — not by means of crude tariffs alone but as part of a wider effort at national or regional self-reliance.[35] They want to make regions the centre of economic activity. 'Every effort should be made to meet requirements from local sources first, then nationally, then regionally, and only after that internationally.' Lang and Hines offer a Green vision of revitalised local economies that would get many more people to work, spread wealth more evenly, and give us tastier, if simpler, food. To pay for it — that is, to compensate for lost revenue — they propose 'Green' taxes on energy and pollution, and even on foreign exchange to curb cross-national investment. Under the new protectionism, tariffs would be placed not on goods but on their environmental impact: they would become eco-taxes.

Most Green reformers agree that some form of protection for local agriculture and industry, and Green taxes levied on pollution and resource use, will be needed if economies are to be shifted towards equitable and sustainable practices. The Worldwatch Institute argues that if governments phase in environmental tax codes and eliminate subsidies for destructive activities such as mining, overfishing, and fossil fuel burning, they can cut annual personal and corporate income taxes by $1 trillion — one seventh of the global tally for all taxes.[36] Companies which damage the environment should be forced to include the costs in their balance sheet, the Institute says, adding that in the US the unpaid costs to society of driving cars — ranging from lung disease to noise pollution — are estimated at $218 billion per year.

Some eco-taxes already work well. In the Netherlands, taxes on industrial emissions of heavy metals have led to a reduction in the leakage of cadmium, copper, lead, mercury, and zinc into canals and lakes by 86-97 percent since 1976 and made the country a global leader in water pollution technologies. Australia, Denmark and the US used taxes on CFCs to help phase out these chemicals, as required under the 1987 Montreal Protocol, the treaty to protect the ozone layer, in less than a decade. The US tax has raised $4.1 billion.

HERE LIES THE GROWTH ECONOMY

Died: Late 20th Century, after long and painful illness; once adored by all, eventually despised for breaking so many promises. Flourished in days of greed, status and power, but withered when sense prevailed. Was driven to mental depression, fits and starts: when depressed was prone to trample farms, workers and whole regions.

Fatal illness: gluttony. Daily consumption reached 50 million barrels of oil, 9000 tonnes of copper, 13 million tonnes of soil, 20,000 Third World children, $2 billion worth of arms, 100,000 acres of rainforest.

Symptoms: waste, pollution, urban decay, selfishness, apathy, war, underdevelopment of property and repression.

Finally choked to death unable to consume all it produced or reduce consumption to sensible levels.

Mourned by few (the few who owned all the capital).

RIP (Really Inadequate Performance)

· Ted Trainer, *The Conserver Society.*

Most discussion on environmental futures is inevitably joined sooner or later by 'techno-fixers' — people who believe that technology will eventually solve environmental problems. New energy, new materials and new techniques can, they claim, counteract most or all of the ill effects of global economic growth. The most serious such attempt so far is made jointly by Ernest von Weizsaecker, President of the Wuppertal Institute in Germany, and Amory and Hunter Lovins, whose Rocky Mountain Institute in Colorado, US, makes and promotes many of the latest techniques in environmental efficiency. In their book *Factor Four — Doubling Wealth and Halving Resources,* the authors argue that the amount of wealth extracted from one unit of natural resources can be quadrupled by the use of more efficient technology; this can enable us to live twice as well while using half as much in resources. They claim in addition that 'doing more with less is not the same as doing less, doing worse or doing without. Efficiency does not mean curtailment, discomfort or privation.'

These writers cite amazing figures to show how much energy and raw materials are needlessly wasted, especially in the US, and

In 1991, Sweden cut personal income taxes by four percent while offsetting this with environmental taxes on emissions of sulphur dioxide and carbon dioxide. These taxes in Sweden reduced acid rain by 30 percent between 1989 and 1995, switched power stations over to burning coppiced wood instead of fossil fuels and installing desulphurisation equipment.

· *State of the World 1996.*

describe gadgets ranging from hyper-cars that cross the continent on one tank of fuel, futuristic houses and electronic books, to 'low-energy beef' and other more productive forms of agriculture, including perennial grain crops grown in a polyculture. That last experiment, carried out in Wes Jackson's famous Land Institute at Salinas, Texas, shares many ideas with oermaculture. (See Chapters 5 and 7.)

However, these prophets are forced to admit that if exponential economic growth goes on at its present rate, the Factor Four efficiency revolution — even if it happens — would be swallowed up. There is, after all, no substitute for a change of values with a new emphasis on sufficiency, equity and quality of life. These authors' solutions are seductive but unhelpful because they provide an alibi, an excuse for not addressing the profounder issues of values and lifestyles.

Pioneers of lighter living hope, instead, for a transitional world economy in which a co-operative, sustainable sector could co-exist with the 'official' globalised sector, in much the same way as the 'black' economy co-exists with the mainstream. This alternative economy and society will be localised — small in its unit size, vast in its aggregate size. The Dutch economist Willem Hoogendijk hopes that an alternative sector of this kind, centred on organic farming and affiliated trades, 'will be a true people's economy, region-orientated and based on its own production of food and energy, on repair and re-use, on its own education and care, and on its own money, i.e. the circulation of money which remains in the region or country.'[37]

We, the authors of this book, and most of the people we write about, believe that the spread of the global consumer economy into every corner of the world is sustained by vested interests more powerful than any that human history has ever known. We hope for a return to viable national and regional economies, equipped to supply basic needs and many luxuries before venturing abroad to buy imports. We believe local economies can offer a more satisfying life, even if we have to make do with fewer brands of shampoo or if we have to buy vegetables, or yoghurt, or trousers made in our own country instead of the other side of Europe or the world.

The spread of a global economy has been made possible by a faith — the irrational belief that an endlessly increasing standard of living will produce a better quality of life. This modern faith has spread throughout the world in an evangelical success unmatched by Islam or Christianity in their heyday. The faith has enjoyed a fresh boost since the collapse of communism and the triumph of capitalism at the end of the 1980s. Market capitalism is now unchallenged as the victorious ideology; there is little public debate about its triumph because the political Left and Right throughout the world accept it as the true faith. However, the fact that a faith has spread, helped assiduously by those who profit from it, does not prove that it is true. In India, where the ill effects of globalisation are severe, we found a different view of progress working at the grassroots and providing local solutions, which we explore in the next chapter.

Notes

1   Development Report (UNDP 1996).
2   Development Report (UNDP 1996).
3   *Keep on Trucking* (British ITV World in Action programme produced by Kate Middleton, January 1997).
4   *The Guardian,* 14 January 1998.
5   Richard Douthwaite, *The Growth Illusion.*
6   *The Case Against the Global Economy,* Jerry Mander and Edward Goldsmith (eds.).
7   Richard Douthwaite, *Short Circuit.*
8   *More Isn't Always Better,* New Economics Foundation, London 1997.
9   UNDP Human Development Report (UNDP 1966).
10 *The Growth Illusion,* (op. cit.).
11 *The Case Against the Global Economy* (op. cit.).
12 World Health Organisation, quoted by Harvard Working Group on New and Resurgent Diseases.
13 'Hungry for a New Revolution', in *New Scientist,* 30 March 1996.
14 *The Growth Illusion* (op. cit.).
15 Norman Myers reporting to the Climate Institute, New York, 1966.
16 Bruce Rich, *Mortgaging the Earth.*
17 Alicia Korten, in *Multinational Monitor* (July/August 1993).
18 Norman Myers, 'Consumption in Relation to Population, Environment and Development', in *The Environmentalist* No 17, 1997.
19 J. E. Cohen, *How Many People can the Earth Support?* W. W. Norton, New York 1995.
20 Lester Brown, in *State of the World 1996.*
21 Lester Brown, in *State of the World 1995,* and *UN Development Program Report,* 1995.
22 *Foreign Policy,* Issue 101, (1995).
23 Alan Durning, *This Place on Earth: Home and the Practice of Permanence,* Sasquatch Books, Seattle, 1997.
24 United Nations Environmental Program Report: *Environmental Effects of Ozone Depletion:* 1994 assessment (Nairobi 1994).
25 United Nations Environmental Program Report: *Environmental Effects of*

Ozone Depletion: 1994 assessment , Nairobi, 1994.

26 In *Resurgence*, January/February 1998.

27 *Keep on Trucking,* (op. cit.).

28 R. Engleman R. and P. LeRoy, *Sustaining Water, an Update*, Population Action International, 1995.

29 Unpublished thesis.

30 Helena Norberg-Hodge, *Ancient Futures.*

31 Unpublished thesis.

32 The Other Economic Summit, 1984, quoted in *The Living Economy*, ed. Paul Ekins, Routledge, 1986.

33 *The Case Against the Global Economy* (op. cit.).

34 *When Corporations Rule the World* (op. cit.).

35 *The New Protectionism*, Earthscan, 1993.

36 *Getting the Signals Right: Tax Reform to Protect the Environment and the Economy*, Worldwatch Institute, 1997.

37 In *Development*, 1995:3 (published by the Society for International Development, Rome).

9

Cures for economic development

• •

Returning to India twenty years after we had lived there, the over-whelming sense is of exploding numbers and bustling enterprise — so many more people, shops and roadside stalls, lorries, buses, cars, scooters, bicycles, rickshaws. If people are poor, they look too busy to feel it, jostling for a place in the scrum that develops wherever they buy or sell, or board a bus, or cross a road. Along the highways, where rickety snack stalls used to sell chai, there are neon-lit tourist motels with new cars parked outside. Although beggars still solicit you in Bombay, the city breathes a new confidence in which foreigners are less respected, less noticed.

This change of look and of mood has a political reason; it results from the policy of liberalisation — the government's decision in the early nineties that India should no longer hide behind the walls of its planned economy and must play the global game like everybody else. The old system is now contemptuously remembered as the 'permit Raj' in which you needed a licence, and often a bribe, for dealings with 'abroad'.

Who shares in this spirit of enterprise? Who benefits? Who suffers? A highly visible yuppie class has emerged, as foreign and Indian firms look for eager youngsters to work in the new spirit of enterprise. On a train from Pune to Bombay we met Sanjay, a young executive in a cordless telephone company, who'd just been offered a job in Pune to head the local sales force of a leading American Corporation at fifty thousand rupees a month — a princely sum, as he acknowledged. Sanjay was excited, bursting to tell his father and sad, too, because he loves Bombay, the centre of all the fun and action he has seen in his life.

Our train broke down twenty-five kilometres outside the city and rather than wait for what the tannoy announced at half-hourly intervals as coming-some-time-soon for the replacement engine, the three of us shared a scooter rickshaw into town. We rattled past kilometre after kilometre of shanty towns.

The overwhelming majority of our population is poor and unable to participate in the market. To hope that the forces of demand and supply in an open economy will operate in our society to bring about balanced growth is sheer folly... Manufacturing consumer goods on the basis of centralised and mechanised production based on the economics of scale, as is the objective of reform economics, will not help provide productive employment to the vast population in rural areas. The direct impact of the current reform strategy will be large-scale migration from rural areas to urban pockets, bringing in their wake the resultant economic and social evils. Gandhian economics of decentralised production of at least consumer goods has never been more relevant. Gandhian moral philosophy must prevail over amoral market ideology.
· Vasant Sathe, in *Indian Express*, 15 February 1994.

What did Sanjay think of them? 'These people haven't a care in the world, nothing to lose, nothing to look after. You see a man aged fifty and not a white hair on his head. Many of them work in the city, and inside some of the huts you'll find a colour television.' Sanjay didn't want us to argue against his optimistic view of industrialisation.

Yuppies aren't all as energetic, or as thoughtful, as Sanjay. They include idle sons of the new rich who cannot find jobs or do not need them, driving Dad's car and causing trouble. In his book, *Butter Chicken in Ludhiana,* Pankaj Mishra observes these bright new people at the Delhi bus station, standing out amid the squalor and rush in their Hawaiian shirts, stone-washed jeans and pseudo-Italian shoes, with diamond rings, gold chains and fake Ray-Bans. Among such new Indians, Mishra finds a taste for strident politics, violent films, lewd music, rumour-mongering newspapers, plenty of consumerist passions, no civic sense and a generalised cynicism. This comment is typical of the regret expressed in rich and poor countries alike. But such critics rarely reach the roots of the problem or offer any feasible alternative.

How many Indians are upwardly mobile in this liberalised economy? Estimates we heard range from eight percent to twenty-five percent. There are so many different ways of calculating gains and losses. After that first impression of bustling enterprise, we soon saw that in the old India of parched and stagnant villages and in the slums and shanty towns, conditions have worsened for the poorest. Rural and urban tragedies of impoverishment are linked, of course, because millions have fled their hopeless villages for the hope deferred of towns.

India is not alone in suffering traumas of modernisation. Returning after a long absence to Nigeria, or Malaysia, or Mexico, travellers find the same urban squalor and rural hopelessness, the same stampede into a largely illusory consumer market. In every country, the policy of trade liberalisation has its critics. Vocal and politically effective opposition often comes from nationalists and fundamentalists. In India, the Hindu-nationalist BJP party and its allies, who have become strong in federal, state and municipal politics, criticise and sometimes, when in office, delay the introduction of foreign-financed enterprises. But these Hindu nationalists have not made any determined retreat from the global market. The retaliatory power of the World Trade Organisation, combined with the strength of the business lobby at home, are too awesome to resist. Throughout the world, Left and Right support the global economy. Radicals who challenge this consensus must find a different political home, in Green pressure groups in the North and in grassroots activism in the South.

Happily, India has a sturdy tradition of concern for ordinary people's quality of life. Gandhi, who saw dangers in globalised industrialism long before there was a Green movement, posthumously inspires much of this tradition. He wanted development to be village-based, offering people the means and skills to satisfy their own needs instead of buying them from outside. His vision of a free India was not that of a nation state; he worked for a confederation of people, self-governing, self-reliant, self-employed, living in villages. The Gandhian ideal with its mistrust of consumer culture is derided by his critics as puritanical and impossible to achieve. However his ideals are probably still held by millions of Indians. After Gandhi's death his solutions lost the political argument and Nehru came to power with plans to industrialise India. However, the Gandhi tradition remains alive in spiritually-based reform movements for fostering deeper communal values than those of the market place, like Vinoba Bhave's *gramdam* campaign for transferring land from the rich to the poor through gifts, and the *sarvodaya* movement for community action. Today the need for local self-help at grassroots level motivates thousands of environmental movements and NGOs throughout India and other countries in the South.

Most Indian intellectuals, professional and business people of the older generation rejected Gandhi and opted for Nehru — and remain convinced that rapid industrialisation in the mainstream of the global economy is the correct course. Green ideas coming from the industrialised North strike them as a new form of colonialism — seeking to prevent the South from acquiring the wealth and influence that industrialisation brought to the North. This line is taken, for example, by our oldest Indian friend, Abu Abraham, the cartoonist. He lives in semi-retirement in Trivandrum, Kerala, still publishing his views in a popular newspaper column.

Walter writes: I stayed with Abu while I was writing about the protest against the gigantic Narmada Dam which threatens to displace 200,000

THE NARMADA DAM PROTEST

The marchers set up a camp at the border and refused to move, in a bizarre confrontation between two opposing concepts of progress: industrial mega-development versus more decentralised, smaller-scale and sustainable methods. The Gujarat state government assembled groups of women and children to chant slogans in support of the dams, and put up huge posters proclaiming the benefits: 'Irrigation and drinking water to prospective populations of nearly forty million', and 'India must be self-sufficient in food to avoid going round the world with a begging bowl.' The Government says its scheme breaks with past precedent in having generous rehabilitation written into its structure, including a promise of at least five acres of fertile, irrigated land for every male adult oustee, whether or not he owned land previously. It points to state-of-the-art safeguards against waterlogging, siltation, earthquakes and other ailments that have marred the big dams of the past. It promises to plant twice as many trees as it fells. But opponents see this as mere window-dressing for a scheme that will benefit politicians, engineers, contractors, foreign suppliers and the local rich farmers at the expense of the poor and the environment. They claim the Narmada's waters are better harnessed by small dams, earth barriers and tanks — traditional methods that are back in use all over the world after big-dam disappointments and disasters.

· Walter Schwarz, in *The Guardian*, 25 January 1991.

---

people to provide power and water, mainly to the already rich. Abu was convinced that the dam was justified and we had heated arguments. With his artist's eye, Abu is keenly aware of the degradation in India's rural and urban environment but he believes it is a price that has to be paid and, meanwhile, he loves looking after the goats, ducks, hens and fish that occupy all the space around his house. In space-hungry Trivandrum his garden is only a few hundred square metres.

Nationalists like Abu argue that India's industrial revolution is only going through the traumas that the North experienced in its day — poor people uprooted from villages and herded into cruel cities. From that beginning, the first industrialised countries grew rich, and the descendants of factory-working children live today in affluence. Nobody should stop India following that route. Abu is a patriot of life-long left-wing convictions whose cartoons in British and Indian broadsheets have devastated imperialists and other villains. He could not agree with me that the global economy was driven by a *new* imperialism and that India's industrialisation, in its present *laissez-faire* mode, was both victim and perpetrator of that new imperialism. Where I saw destruction, he saw progress.

Abu's daughters Ayisha, also an artist, and Janaki, an anthropologist, take a different view. They and many of their friends doubt the justice and utility of giant dams; they doubt the morality of an industrial system that enriches the already rich. Whoever is right, India's industrial revolution cannot follow the English pattern because India has neither an empire nor the abundant reserves of fossil fuel needed for classic industrialisation on the nineteenth-century pattern. The work of her brilliant scientists and technicians is being matched by other countries in the South who want their share of the rewards and won't be content to be India's market or supply India with cheap raw materials. Time is running out for easily earned bourgeois affluence, which was always the product of privilege, imperialism and exploitation, and still is.

And yet India does have a vast and lucrative 'empire' inside its own borders: the poor peasants displaced by industrialised agriculture who are forced into the cities, the remaining small farmers whose food is bought cheaply to feed those cities, and the pre-Hindus known as 'tribals' whose forests, fields and water sources can be confiscated in the interests of industrial 'progress'. These exploited people have been voiceless. Now, an embryonic national liberation movement against the new imperialism has arisen. The anti-Narmada Dam movement — India's first nationwide environmental protest — brought together campaigners for peasants' rights, fishermen and the urban poor from all India. Their leaders formed a National Alliance of Peoples Movements which includes groups of small farmers in Karnataka who are in revolt against industrial agriculture based on imported seeds and chemicals, fishermen in Kerala fighting for their marine preserves and reefs against the depredations of foreign trawlers, and women from the Chipko 'tree-hugging' movement whose militancy has saved some of the Himalayan forests.

Less visible than hunger strikers and marchers is a movement of grassroots action to promote village-based development. Thousands of non-government organisations are involved, some government-funded, some foreign-funded, while a few manage on their own or through charity. Some, but not all, of these village groups are radical movements, disenchanted with the official 'development' process and determined to draw on local, indigenous and sustainable resources. The most radical of these movements have been joined by young graduates who have given up career prospects and city life because they want to help. Most of the couple of months we spent in India researching for this book was spent meeting these people and the following pages tell you some of their stories.

Datye's story

K. R. Datye — water engineer, activist, patriot and philosopher — lives in Bombay where he's at the hub of a network of alternative development workers. The alternative works. Datye has designed a small people's dam as a defiant grassroots answer to the gigantic Narmada. Water collected in such dams is shared equally by every household in a group of villages for use in organic, low-cost agriculture that generates its own energy and conserves its resources. The result is sustainable agriculture in an Indian context. Nobody knows how many people's dams have been built. Datye's is part of a growing movement for village-based development.

At almost seventy Datye has the enthusiasm of a young activist. His wife's ninety-year-old mother lives with him so he excuses his wife from meeting with us — she is occupied with taking care of the old lady. She herself is a Sanskrit scholar, Datye says with pride.

Mr Datye (we never discovered his first name, which friends don't use) lives in Ville-Parle, a once genteel and spacious suburb in north Bombay, not far from the airport, which has now become a teeming, overcrowded city in itself. He received us with absent-minded courtesy and when he found we shared his hopes for a more humane form of development, he talked unstoppably about his dam, his career of critical participation in building up a modern India, his philosophy and the many friends and colleagues who were helping him in his village projects.

In his youth he was both a Marxist and a Gandhian, 'buffeted between the two.' We found the same complication among several of his younger associates, and many other volunteers in alternative development. He concludes from his hybrid ideology: 'There is no conflict between growth and fairness as long as growth begins at home where the people are: we need growth in food, fodder and vegetation.' He insists that these villagers cannot aspire to the consumer lifestyle of the North. When a rich Northerner says this it smacks of hypocrisy; when Datye says it, it resounds with common-sense.

> I believe, and hope, that the current dominant system will collapse like the Roman Empire. Replacing it, we need the kind of science that developed windmills in Holland and hydro-electric energy in Switzerland. Today the new frontier is the sun. • K. R. Datye (interview with the authors).

After graduating as an engineer Datye volunteered to work for two years in the *Gramdam* land-gift movement in which rich farmers were persuaded to give away land to the poor. In backward and remote villages in Orissa, Datye learned that what village people needed and wanted was far removed from what was on offer in the official development process. After India's independence in 1947 he worked as a water engineer and by 1962 he was a superintendent with a staff of 200, controlling one third of the irrigation of Maharashtra. He soon realised the drawbacks of 'development'. The water system he was working on could reach less than a quarter of the population.

'I saw that our "development" was based on an internal power game, a new imperialism in which water, energy and all the other resources were being appropriated by the rich and powerful.'

Datye, disagreeing with more conventional nationalists, is convinced that India has neither the resources nor the infrastructure for the industrial course set by Nehru at independence. 'We have 500 kg of coal-equivalent energy per capita per year, while most industrial countries have ten times that amount. There is a little coal, some oil, and there is nuclear energy with all the expensive and hazardous pitfalls attached to it. None of these is a base for an industrial revolution.'

Datye told us to: 'Go and look for sustainable development in the villages,' and sent us on our way.

The people's dam

Setting out for one of the people's dams, we first took a two-hour train ride to Pune, a city many times larger than it was when it had its colonial spelling of Poona. Here we met Datye's rural collaborator L. K. Joy, a younger man, not yet forty, who already has behind him nearly two decades of struggle for villagers' rights. He, too, is a Marxist who has learned from Gandhi.

> It's when the economy is dominated by cash that the farmers need cash, so we get farmers growing flowers for export or using high-tech systems, but we can generate cash through other means. If everyone gets his share of water he can grow some of his own food as well as cash crops. In some cases sugar cane replaces vegetables and the result is economic disaster; they tried soya beans, got a good price for three years and then it dropped. • L. K. Joy (to the authors).

Joy, a social worker by training, worked for a time in a self-help village project funded from Germany but left because, 'Foreign funds make people dependent and we don't have the freedom to work as we want and be political.'

Convinced that water was the key to survival in Maharashtra, Datye and Joy started a movement for getting the best out of the available groundwater. They promoted organic farming to ensure high quality and to save village farmers from chronic indebtedness to chemical and fertiliser companies. Working with 200,000 people in 118 villages, they collected data on local needs and drew up a land use package for small plots, instead of the large holdings required by industrial agriculture.

Datye and Joy believe that India's villagers can produce enough renewable energy and store enough water for their needs, if these needs are kept simple. 'The climate has great potential for photosynthesis and solar energy with cheap collectors, but not enough energy for roads and cars and all the paraphernalia of a Western lifestyle.' Datye adds: 'Water needs to be stored close to roots of plants: it took me twenty years to understand what villagers always knew.' This is a different development ethic, far removed from that of 'experts' telling villagers what they should have and how they must use it. Good water sharing is not enough: villagers must plan to make the best possible use of the water for biomass production, so that a village can grow not only its own food but also its fodder, firewood and materials for bio-gas energy.

'Only in this way can we avoid the disastrous effects of industrial farming: waterlogging, salination, erosion and lowering of the water table.'

> *It is possible to live even on a very low rainfall if sixty percent of the water could be stored and harvested. We were integrating what people have been doing for centuries with scientific knowledge. In the right conditions, even a quarter of an acre is enough to feed a family of five.'* • L. K. Joy *(interview with the authors).*

The people's dam villages we were to see lay a four-hour car trip from Pune, along a single-track road choked with lorry and diesel fumes which also serves as a pedestrian and bullock cart highway. Sanjay, one of Datye's field

The People's Dam at Baliraja.

workers, came along as our guide. Deeper into the Maharashtra countryside we entered a more political and more radical group. We were among Marxists who, having fought all their lives for social justice, were now concerned with ecological justice. We spent the night at Kasegaon village, ten kilometres from the dam, in Indutai Patankar's household — a long-established Communist stronghold. Portraits of Marx, the young Lenin and Mao hung garlanded with fresh marigolds. And a sad reminder of high infant mortality; Indutai's two-year-old granddaughter, dead a few years back of meningitis, shared the places of honour amongst the family's gurus. As we sat cross-legged on the floor, comrades came in and out all evening and murmured political discussions continued far into the night — talk not about the dictatorship of the proletariat but about timber houses instead of concrete, small dams instead of large, the importance of growing food and fuel crops instead of sugar cane.

Indutai, a veteran freedom fighter now in her seventies, was in the Communist Party of India most of her life, but now she complained that the Party was interested only in land reform, not water reform which was more important in this dry region. She has been a widow for nearly half a century; her husband was killed by gangsters, leaving her to raise her three children alone. Bharat, her son, and Gail Omvedt, his wife, are both intellectuals in the village reform movement: they live partly here, partly in California where Gail works as a sociologist. On the living room floor among the cushions lies Gail's book, *Dalit Visions*, in which she deals with the plight of the lowest group in the Indian caste system.

Sanjay talks with the enthusiasm of a twenty-five-year-old about the NGO he works for — People's Science Research — which promotes Datye's building techniques using timber instead of steel and concrete. He explains that casuarina and eucalyptus mature in three or four years, while steel is under the control of the industrialists and gets dearer every year (the price doubled in the last four years), and the price of cement goes up every month. Sanjay's NGO takes local workers at low cost, making their houses still more affordable and helping to employ village people.

Indutai presides over her household until everyone goes to bed at midnight. (*Dorothy writes:* getting up for a pee at two a.m. I saw Indutai writing a speech sitting cross-legged amongst the cushions of her mosquito-netted four-poster. She left the house before eight a.m. holding a black umbrella over her head, on her way to teach birth control to a women's meeting.)

Sanjay took us to the people's dam in Baliraja. On the road we passed through a time machine as bullock carts laden with sugar cane were overtaken by tractors pulling the same load. Sugar cane is the rich man's crop, a thirsty product needing constant irrigation and using up scarce water resources. Sangli district is one third highly irrigated and two thirds drought-prone. It has waterlogging and salinity problems associated with over-irrigation and chemical inputs. The cane is cut by migrant workers. The man cuts, the woman binds. During their six-month season the couples work twelve hours a day, seven days a week, cutting a ton a day and earning Rs 92 (less than £2 or $3) — Rs 60 for men, Rs 32 for women. They stay for the season in straw wigwams, a little larger than dog kennels. Seeing their toil, can anyone really argue that they would not be better off subsistence farming on a small local plot if such a plot could have enough water?

The dam is made of timber with a falling shutter-gate. It has been built with love; a decorative grove of *neem* trees surrounds a Freedom Fighters Memorial erected on a mound of silt taken from the defunct government dam. Datye's low-cost, low-energy techniques are evident. To convey the run-off, the builders have used low-density plastic pipes, reinforced by natural membranes and a system of small tanks. The ferro-cement was made in the village from the river sand.

For the first time in generations there is equitable water distribution in these villages. Datye's scheme, which cost less than half the estimate for a conventional dam, includes a detailed agricultural plan which guarantees an equal share of water for every household — irrespective of the size of its landholding — so a small farmer can sell any surplus water to a richer neighbour. The plan prescribes that each 1.5 hectare farm should devote the largest proportion of the land to growing the staple *jowar* and wheat, while the remaining plots should be devoted to vegetables, agro-forestry to produce biomass (fodder, fuel and timber), and fruit trees.

A similar scheme is in operation in the neighbouring Tandelwadi village for 100 households on 220 hectares. It is too soon to judge its success. The farmers told us they had all agreed to the uniform cropping and to refrain from planting sugar cane, but we had seen so much cane on the road that we doubted whether all planting had really stopped in this village; sceptics say you can never stop these plantings because the crop is too lucrative. Optimists told us that other villages want to follow Tandelwadi's cropping pattern, that soon there would be a second dam and that this grassroots development technique was spreading south to the states of Tamilnadu and Karnataka.

Volunteers in the villages

1. The Village Academy

Village-based initiatives for grassroots development are mostly managed by volunteers with a middle-class background coming from elsewhere. Every generation of graduates from Indian universities has its quota of concerned men and women who want to go to the villages and help. Many intend to stay for a short time and then, having discovered village life and the contribution they can make, stay on. Ulhas Gore was one. After graduating in geology he went to work in villages 'for a time' but never stopped. He is a friend and collaborator of K. R. Datye.

Ulhas wears the robust black beard that is politically correct for Indian environmentalists. Still unmarried at forty-eight, he says he couldn't expect a wife to share the discomforts and endless travel of his life. He and a group of friends founded the Academy of Development Science (ADS) in remote Maharashtra countryside to build up an integrated scheme, with a dam, a food processing unit, a school and an institute for herbal medicine. The scheme covers the fifty villages, with 60,000 people, of a 'tribal' area in Karjat district. Funding comes from charities in India and abroad for individual projects but administrative expenses have to be met from the proceeds of a village food-processing factory which turns out pickles, chutneys, candies, jams and bottles of mango squash. The aims are to improve and share out water supplies, process local fruit to enable local people to make a living, educate children in the context of their own culture and environment, and rediscover traditional forms of health care.

We arrived at a peaceful campus of yellow-washed concrete houses with steeply sloping tiled roofs. The houses contain the offices, food factory, school, refectory, staff homes and guest house. This campus has been built as an oasis of hope, but the parched red soil is crumbly and dusty, in need of knitting with vegetation. There is a lack of someone with a will to green this campus. Remnants of forest, dotted with teak, neem and other noble trees struggle to survive against the ubiquitous goats and cattle. Village goats and the occasional stray cow roam loose because there are no fences. Ulhas explains that fences would deprive people in the area of the free grazing they need for survival. This classic rural problem, the cause of so much environmental degradation all over the world, has not been solved even here on a model development site.

For three days we shared vegetarian meals with the staff and the schoolchildren, sitting cross-legged on the floor and eating with our fingers. We felt fitter and more clear-headed on this delicious diet of organic vegetables,

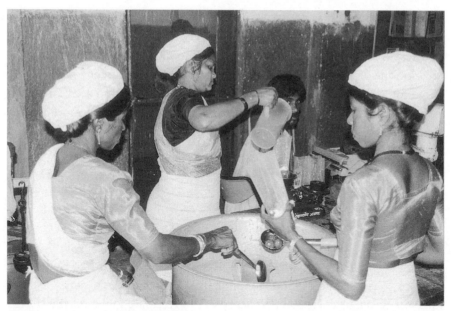

Food processing at the Village Academy.

served with lentils, rice, yoghurt and chapattis made from unbleached flour.

The primary school, with 150 pupils and fourteen teachers, is called 'experiential' and children are taught about the watershed management on which the development project is based. To our eyes lessons were extremely formal with utter silence in every classroom. The books in the small library are too precious for daily use and are kept behind locked doors.

The food processing unit works day and night in the busy season, with forty farmers supplying the fruit. We found the tribal women, wearing white aprons with their hair covered in white cloths, more giggly than the schoolchildren. Amongst the villagers there is not yet anyone sufficiently educated to manage a marketing system, so the packets of processed fruits are sold by the Academy.

The dispensary offers traditional, Ayurvedic treatment for everyday complaints including diarrhoea, dysentery, measles, scabies, skin rashes and minor gynaecological ailments. The revival of Ayurvedic medicine is a national movement, destined to play an important part in rural India's re-emerging village culture, but it has a long way to go before it can challenge the official system. The doctor in charge, who had studied Ayurvedic medicine for thirteen years, remarked sadly that the villagers preferred Western pills bought in town.

The showpiece of the Academy's efforts at rural regeneration is the herbal nursery which grows hundreds of indoor and outdoor medicinal plants on its eight hectares. Every year fifty varieties of seed are collected in this region or produced in the nursery and given to colleges whose students come here for courses. Many of the seeds are rare and only found hereabouts. The seeds are sold for one or two rupees, a nominal charge to make sure they are properly cared for. (Wherever we went in North and South we found active involved people trying to preserve the world's seed heritage.) Seven gardeners are under the management of T. K. Shrirao, a self-taught plantsman from Kerala, a former fireman with a military moustache and bearing but dressed informally in *lungi* (the Keralan cotton sarong) and shirt.

Green nets shield Mr Shrirao's test beds from the glare. His impressive display garden is arranged in fifty groups, each plant listed by its botanical name, local name, Sanskrit name, habit and use — ranging from analgesic and sedative treatment to cures for snake bite, lice infestation and indigestion. A plant labelled 'For Impotence' was bare-stemmed; Mr Shrirao said not to worry, it was in its dormant phase. One plant which makes a substance that kills rats is in particular demand because villagers have killed off the snakes which feed on rats.

Ulhas drove us out to see one of the village dams, planned by the Academy and built by the villagers, designed to allow farmers to plant a second crop in the dry season. The Academy's ambition is to enable them to remain in the villages all year round, even in the dry season.

The Ayurvedic plant nursery at the Village Academy.

Baghat Panduram, who farms 2.5 hectares, is an activist in the development plan. He told us he hopes his four sons and two daughters can eventually live in the village throughout the year without going out to look for seasonal work. He himself has not yet reaped the benefits of the improvements. Land reforms have transformed tenants into owners but conditions are no better. 'It's all right when there is a good monsoon, otherwise miserable.' He's a member of the Water Users' Association but the ponds will take two years to complete. Meanwhile he has to work as a labourer on soil conservation works and as a rice paddy worker. He has twenty goats but can farm only one crop of rice and millet — just enough for the family's needs.

For centuries these villagers have paid exorbitant rates of interest to moneylenders to finance their seed grain. Now fifty villages have put up straw silos to house a grain bank. Every spring the bank buys rice and millet from the market and distributes it to the farmers — 125 kg per family of five. In the autumn the farmers pay back the grain with twenty-five percent interest; in four years the debt is paid off. Ramnath, the man who runs the bank, told us he had had 100 percent repayment from the farmers and that all the villagers' debts to the moneylenders have been paid off. A scheme like this — locally devised and administered — enables villagers to break the cycle of poverty and debt.

But what constitutes progress? A couple of richer farmers have built one-room concrete houses with tin roofs which are hot, crowded and much admired. Traditional houses are made of dried reeds and grasses — mud-floored, roomy and cool, their roofs thatched with pigeon-pea straw.

Ulhas Gore's Academy works slowly, on a small scale, chronically short of cash. A culture gap yawns between the organisers and the tribals with the result that the volunteers appear to work *for* the people rather than *with* them or *among* them. Gore told us: 'These tribals are intelligent but need supervision. They spend any money they have, they are like children.' Perhaps a bright future can only begin in the next generation, when the villagers run their own Academy.

2. The hospital

In Bangalore, a friend suggests we visit the Vivekenanda Youth Project for tribals in the Mysore district. It started in 1984 when a group of three young doctors gave up the prospect of city jobs and started a hospital in the forest area. The project has widened its scope and now includes a school and is involved in teaching better agricultural techniques to the local people. Our guide was to be Ramuswamy (Ramu) a retired civil servant. He is our age which is enjoyable. At sixty-nine, Ramu busies himself with local NGOs.

What excites him at present is a scheme for creating full employment for

thirteen villages based on grassroots development. He acts as unpaid financial advisor in the hospital for 'tribals' we are going to visit.

The Vivekenanda Youth Project is set up in Heggadadevanakote, a forest
region eighty kilometres from Mysore. Ramu explains that development
money has been coming into this area for fifty years. 'It gets siphoned off. You
see, when the tribals are moved from the forest they are given land in compensation — but they don't get all of it; the government officers keep some of it
back for themselves.' The problems of this area are not unique — everywhere
the poor are squeezed by 'development'.

The hospital was only built because three young idealists came to the area.
Dr Balusubramaniam, who tells us to call him Balu, arrived almost as soon
as he qualified. He says, 'You must not think I'm the chief person here. I'm
only the spokesperson for the three of us. This is my career: my wife married
me because I'm doing this. When I was nineteen, in the third year of medicine, I realised the medical scene was bad, with eighty percent of doctors
concentrated in urban areas serving twenty percent of the population. The
system was still modelled on the UK. Most people simply could not afford the
allopathic medicine on offer — which is alien to this country. Unless we
empower people economically they won't be concerned about their health,
especially when belief in rebirth takes away the fear of dying.'

Balu's small, clean, white-washed hospital in a forest clearing has beds for
up to twenty in-patients. Equipment is basic but adequate. The three doctors
are excited about the recent arrival of a surgeon. The very day he arrived, a
twelve-year-old boy was brought in with a snake bite on his calf. The new
surgeon performed a skin graft. We watched the nowcured boy being sent
home in a bullock cart ambulance. 'He is lucky,' said one of the doctors. 'He
could have lost his leg.'

At first the three young doctors were given a dilapidated shed. When the
villagers saw them cleaning it out, they gradually came to help. 'Then,' says
Balu, 'we had a stroke of luck; a child fell into a water tank and we were able
to revive it.'

Balu said he was motivated by faith in the teachings of Vivekananda. 'You
have to understand that India has a faith in gurus — not gods but guides.
What's the use of wealth — you have to die anyway? Each individual must
find his own soul but also help others. By tradition, Vivekananda's devotees
move into disaster areas and offer long-term solutions.'

Ten kilometres from the hospital is a school run by the Ramakrishna movement: a tree-lined compound of eight hectares with dormitories, school halls,
classrooms and a row of single-storey guest houses. Each guest house
contains two Indian-style beds, wooden with thin mattresses, a washroom

with cold water tap and a table and chairs. There is electric light: everything you need and nothing superfluous. We are reminded of an *ayah* who said to a Belgian woman living in Auroville, 'Why do you people have so many *things?* If I had so many, I would give them away.'

The brick house where we stay is at the edge of the compound; behind its wall stretches the forest, or what is left of it, retreating yearly as logging continues. A ditch to prevent elephants coming into the compound has been dug. The schoolchildren have an experimental garden of fruits and vegetables. The cleared forest around the school compound has not been clear-felled. Single trees stand in lonely isolation like sentries.

We take a dawn walk with Ramu. He points out the tracks leading into the forest. 'This is the reserve. The tribals are forbidden to enter but they still go to collect firewood and cut bamboo for their baskets.'

The tribals, whose children are pupils in the school, have been brought out of the forest and settled nearby. They have been moved twice; first when a government dam was built, and again when a tiger reserve was put in place. These are typical victims, economically and politically weak, who lose out from modernisation. Until recently, what they have to offer in terms of sustainable living has been despised as backward and primitive. Now there is a growing realisation that their traditional knowledge ensured a way of living in the forest that was sustainable for hundreds of years.

The tribals were hunters and practised a shifting cultivation, coming out of the forest to trade honey and baskets woven from bamboo. Since they have been resettled, their traditional means of subsistence have been either eradicated or curtailed; they have been given small plots of land but they have no farming traditions.

It seems that corruption deprived them even of the limited compensation on offer. The tribals never 'owned' land — the British kept them in the forest to grow teak. They used to catch elephants. They still say: 'The rajahs were kind to us for we were the guardians of the forest where they would hunt.'

Progressive opinion in India admits that the tribals have had a shabby deal. We have niggling doubts as Balu waxes eloquent about 'my tribals'. We hold suspicious memories of District Officers in Northern Nigeria in the sixties, who'd talk about 'their' people. There is no room for paternalism in the present situation but we are perhaps unjust. Effectively there is no one to speak for them. Balu says, 'When I came they were suspicious. They only found exploitation coming from outside. Even now twenty or thirty percent of them wouldn't trust me.'

One young man who trusts Balu is Mara. He and his family were moved out of the forest when he was four years old. Now his father farms 1.2

hectares. Mara was an eighth standard drop-out from a nearby tribal village and was then persuaded to go back to full-time education. Now he is finishing a degree in history and political economy at Mysore University. The sophistication and charisma that he shows us cross the barriers of age, race, language and gender. 'In the forest you are a free man. It is not essential to learn history for survival, but whatever there is to learn I want to learn it. Then I want to come back to my people.' But he wants to develop his own initiatives. Like the doctors who run the Youth Project, Mara dreams of a better village.

Mara is an exceptional student and would be so in any environment. Will he come back after graduation? The answer, here and in so many other villages, will depend on what the village has to offer. Ramu is planning a high school to be grafted onto the present primary school. The plans are drawn up; the funds are available. It is now a matter of getting the project off the ground. He says, 'If forty students graduate from the new high school and ten come back, I'll be happy.'

'You sound optimistic.'

'Yes, I am. I'll tell you, when I ask the standard six boys what they want, they say, I want to be an engineer, a doctor. One boy says to me, I want Dr Subramaniam's job. That is what I like to hear.'

Term is almost over. The hot season is beginning and then the monsoon. The teachers are proud that nearly half the students are girls and the first girl from a tribal village has completed standard ten.

We sat under the palm thatch and passed time with a group of tribal women who had come to the school compound to hold discussions with Mamata, the social worker, about their savings. With Mamata translating, they were highly amused to talk with us. Puttana, unlike Mara, the student, says she is not sorry to have left the forest; she has no rosy recollections of the joys of primitive life: 'Now even if we have to steal bamboo to feed the children — it is better. In the forest, I could not always feed the children.' The women always talk about their children; men about themselves. Puttana's three children of fifteen, ten and seven are still at school. 'Previously, if a jeep came into the forest, our mother ran away. Now if a jeep comes, the doctor fetches us here to meet people and learn things.'

They began a loud and animated conversation with much laughter, complaining that a government official on a visit who had distributed free saris had not brought enough. Their teeth and the insides of their mouths were stained red with betel juice and their hands callused. They were small, thin-boned and dark-skinned. At over thirty every woman looks used up. Life expectancy is fifty-five years and infant mortality ten percent. Impossible to know whether Mara's rhetoric of the joys of forest life was as honest as Puttana's statement that she'd rather live in a village.

Caste and class show up even in this area of southern India. The teacher and the social worker are lighter skinned than the forest women and taller, too. Even without understanding what they were saying when Mamata was not translating, it was evident which one of the women was the boss lady. She spoke at length. The women laughed in agreement, but with nothing subservient in their responses, nor did they stop interrupting when they felt like it. They all wore glass bangles. A couple of them had tattoos on their foreheads.

Mamata said that improving the status of these women was easy because in their tribal life they are relatively free from the constraints of traditional Hindu culture. There is no dowry system in their tribal areas. Puttana is the leader of a women's group which runs a savings scheme to buy agricultural implements. They have 12,000 rupees and qualify for a matching amount from the Youth Project. There are seven self-help groups. The money is in the local branch of the Grameen Bank, an institution dedicated to low-cost credit for village people.

There was not much nostalgia in Kenchanahalli for traditional forest life. And in any case it is too late to go back. Much of the forest has gone. Of the people we spoke to the older ones regret the forest, the younger ones like the comforts of modern life. Madiya, a bearded village chief, said: 'Yes, the grandchildren will regret.'

Balu says, 'You see, that shows their confusion. They cannot go back to the forest. The solution that I am looking for is to keep their tribal values and get them the best of the modern. They had wonderful values. Just something so simple as sharing food. Basic human values. That is the school's dilemma: each passing year, new values come in and something of the old values is lost to our children. So our basic dilemma is — are we justified in doing this?'

One of the other young doctors replies, 'We can't stop it.'

Ramu says, 'The best we can do is to increase local autonomy and decrease dependence on foreign markets.' But he is aware that the work is precarious. 'These villagers feel they are underdeveloped because they do not have the things that can be bought in the town. Are we making them greedy? Are we giving them wants they did not have before?'

The tribals' way of life has lasted for many generations. It was not change-less but change was gradual and society appeared stable. Mara, the tribal student, has jumped several centuries in a few years. The villagers are marginal farmers not yet sucked into the Green Revolution. They hold four hundred hectares between them. Properly farmed, using sustainable agricultural methods, the yield could be increased fourfold and the land could feed double the number of people it does now.

The Vivekenanda Youth Project is duplicated in hundreds of similar or dissimilar projects all over the South. It is an amalgamation of government and private aid and it is carried through with the idealistic work of the doctors. What we saw was a tentative attempt at a synthesis of what had been and what is. The hope must be that the tribal people will be able to adapt into the twenty-first century with enough of their culture left intact and enough self-reliance to resist the false promises of city life.

Seeds of renewal

Vanaja Ramprasad lives with her husband in a suburban housing estate in Bangalore, with apparently nothing to distinguish their modest house and tiny garden from all the others packed into a warren of identical streets. If, however, you go out of her front door and up a narrow staircase, you reach a small office-cum-showroom which is a centre of resistance against the industrialisation of agriculture and the destruction of biodiversity. Vanaja neither demonstrates nor agitates. Her life is devoted to the collection, storage and redistribution of traditional seeds. One wall is lined with plastic packets of labelled seeds, another with photographs of native millet, herbs and scores of plants that have been developed by local farmers over millennia and now face slow extinction in an economy given over to standardised 'improved' varieties. Books about plants and seeds line another wall; a computer with a modem waits in the corner.

Vanaja is a small woman whose comfortable presence and soft voice hides the passion and ceaseless activity of her calling. She runs the regional centre of Navdanya — a voluntary organisation for researching, rescuing and distributing seeds to maintain the kind of farming that feeds people, sustains families and looks after the earth. The Navdanya organisation was started by Vandana Shiva, India's best-known ecologist, a physicist who conducts a crusade against destructive industrial farming. It has other centres in different climatic regions ranging from the

I started a program for seed conservation — a programme called Navdanya — which means nine seeds. The name came to me while travelling in a tribal area where a farmer had nine crops growing together in a field. It instantly clicked because in India at birth, at death, and at marriage we have ceremonies using nine seeds, which reflect the cosmos and planetary constellations. So the name symbolises the relationship between the cosmos, the seed, and the human situation.
· Vandana Shiva, in YES Magazine, Winter 1997.

Himalayan foothills to the wet Deccan plain. India used to have 30,000 rice varieties. The Navdanya programme has already saved up to 600 varieties of rice, 100 varieties of kidney beans, and hundreds of varieties of millet.

Like Dr Balusubramaniam in Mysore, Vanaja is motivated by her spiritual beliefs. 'Unless I change my own lifestyle and live appropriately I cannot hope to influence society,' she told us. She is a follower of the Indian philosophers Sri Aurobindo and Swami Satiananda. She showed us the *puja* (devotional) corner on her balcony where, each morning

> The damage that the Green Revolution strategy has done to the environment is only now beginning to be understood: steady depletion of micro-nutrients from the soil and utter disruption of its natural chemistry, lowering of the water table to new depths, sometimes as low as 100 or 200 feet, inadequate recharging of underground aquifers due to higher evaporation losses, destruction of the contours of the land leading to excessive water run-off and topsoil erosion, spread of salinity and waterlogging, and the poisoning of the air, water, land and vegetation by toxic agro-chemicals on an extensive scale. All this must be placed in the context of deforestation, misguided emphasis on large dams which disrupt whole watersheds, and unrelieved land and water mismanagement.
> · Praful Bidwai in *Times of India*, 20 February 1988.

and evening, she burns a piece of dried cow dung and invokes the sun during a brief meditation. 'The sun is the origin of all life. The idea behind everything that is worthwhile is to try and work with nature instead of pushing it to do more and more for us. The cow dung reminds me that cattle are vital because they represent wealth — power for ploughing and providers of compost.' (A similar idea motivates Trauger Groh's biodynamic farm in New Hampshire — see Chapter 6.)

With a master's degree in human nutrition and a PhD in commercial development, Vanaja began working with private agencies involved in conventional development, and soon she was asking fundamental questions. The spread of industrial varieties of high-yielding hybrid seeds — hailed as miracles of productivity in the Green Revolution — appeared as a disaster for the health of the land and the livelihood of small-scale farmers who cannot become entrepreneurs. The Green Revolution strategy sought to master and overpower nature and to 'emancipate' agriculture from its cycles. It consisted of promoting a handful of crops, and among them a handful of exotic varieties, uniformly across diverse agro-climatic zones, with a standardised regimen of farming practices. And it aimed to maximise grain (or oilseed or lint) yields alone, on an exclusive basis — i.e. at the expense of the rest of the plant, which is why dwarf varieties, which alone can bear the weight of the grain, became necessary. This it sought to do through reliance on high-energy, high-input, factory-made inputs whose use had to be specially 'extended' to the farmer.

Vanaja argues that these new inventions were not high-yield seeds at all, but high-response seeds: highly responsive to highly expensive fertiliser, pesticides and irrigation, highly destructive of soil fertility. 'Only one crop is grown on one field, whereas the traditional crops grow convivially amid many other plants, providing food for the whole family, medicinal herbs, and support plants that have evolved in a particular place to deter pests and preserve moisture.'

The hybrid seeds were 'a fashion and a thrill for the farmers; they enjoy going into town to buy them. Those seeds do get higher yields, but the farmers don't count the cost. And these hybrids don't yield seeds for replanting the following season, so every year you have to buy them again from the multinational companies at prices which reflect research and distribution costs. And of course these farmers don't grow food for themselves on the same fields, as they can when using traditional varieties. Their wives know all this and they're dead against hybrid seeds.'

Vanaja runs a seed plantation of 2.5 hectares just across the state border in Tamilnadu. In between her weekly visits, it is looked after by two full-time farmers. Plants are grown without irrigation and with organic manure produced on the farm. Organic rice is watered only with rainwater. Many kinds of local millet are grown and medicinal herbs. A co-operative of twenty farmers use the seeds and often exchange them among each other the following year.

Vanaja has no illusion that the high-yield cultivation can be stopped by her tiny movement. 'We must be able to offer serious alternatives that work in the field. This is slow work with no dramatic effects. We are working with seventy-five farmers on a regular basis, each with two or three acres. They are seed-keepers, looking for old seeds. These traditional seeds have many advantages. Cattle prefer the straw, diseases are fewer, the inputs are less.'

She believes that there will be two economies — 'the high-yielders who are in effect entrepreneurs, and the subsistence farmers. At the present the latter are being squeezed out and impoverished. We aim to preserve their livelihoods — and they are a vast number in India: we're talking about hundreds of millions.'

Vanaja had just held a *beej mela* — a seed fair which attracted 100 farmers including seventy-five women. This has been a drought year, farmers' reserves are low and there was demand for more Navdanya seeds than were available. Small-scale, traditional farmers volunteer to act as *Beej rakshak* — seed keepers. The *beej mela* was attended by farmers who had shifted away from traditional agriculture to try the new seeds but had been disappointed by poor results and now wanted to re-introduce diversity into their fields. They had been caught on the treadmill of increased costs and the necessity to buy new seeds each season. Vanaja said the most common reason for shifting back to traditional seeds had been the search for security and a measure of independence from the cash economy. 'Returning to use traditional seeds implies a political, social and often a spiritual commitment to sustainable production and utilisation of resources. Farmers who have tried the path of modernisation and wish to retrace their steps are among the best motivated for *in situ* seed conservation. There is a growing refusal to accept the values of modernisation.'

Vanaja Ramprasad is proud of her achievement. 'It has taken us four years to collect, multiply, grow and distribute these seeds. They can grow in mixed cropping. There are forty-five varieties of foxtail millet — mixed varieties with all the genes mixed up — thirty varieties of finger millet. We are coming to the point when the farmers take over from us. In two years hopefully, we should reach a point where the seeds are sufficiently in use for them to be safe, and where the farmers themselves organise seed banks and seed exchange.'

At that point, she plans to move from her house to live on her plantation. When she does, a new stage will have been reached; her seed project which will have become self-perpetuating. Everywhere in our Indian travels we found that the efforts of scientists, teachers and helpers were provisional, keeping an option open for the next generation. Their achievements are small-scale, partial and precarious. The people's dam and the Academy of Development Science have not yet revolutionised the lives of villagers who still depend on the vagaries of the monsoon and the favours of corrupt and lethargic officials. Ulhas Gore's campus still has the look of an outpost, infiltrated by straying cattle, still without its perimeter fence. The people's dam, the academy, the hospital and Vanaja's farm are all seeds for a slower-growing, more humane development for India. The seeds have yet to germinate and spread.

10

Acting for ourselves

● ●

Cities too large, too polluted, full of crime and social stress, are also centres of excellence, style and comfort — the zenith of our technological and cultural achievements. How can the two opposing aspects be reconciled? A compelling question because in the early twenty-first century the majority of us will be living in towns and cities. Everybody — not just Greens — recognises the problem of cities — so it is being tackled top-down as well as bottom-up at grassroots level. Enlightened and determined municipal authorities have tried to re-humanise their towns and cities. Hundreds of European cities have pedestrian zones and the worst excesses of thoughtless planning like tower blocks and inner-city by-passes are not being repeated. In the South, too, there are striking examples of best practice. In Curitiba, southern Brazil, an enlightened mayor, Jaime Lerner, has made the city convivial, convenient and fair to the poor. Curitiba went from half a square metre of green area per inhabitant to more than fifty.

Curitiba is exceptional. And even here, Lerner's reforms cannot work wonders because in his city, too, the global economy imposes lifestyles which are neither convivial, nor fair, nor healthy, nor convenient. We cannot change the global system. To live differently, we need to act for ourselves at grassroots level. There are different ways to do so. Joining an urban community is a solution for people who like communal life. In the early seventies, rebellious squatters occupied a disused army camp in the suburbs of Copenhagen and called it The Free Town of Christiana. They resisted every attempt to disband their township until, with a thousand

> No one has driven at a snail's pace through London ... without fulminating at the road system; no one has approached Caracas or Rio through the awfulness of their shanty towns without wondering why they are tolerated; or seen the street-sleepers of Calcutta — or those under Charing Cross Bridge for that matter — without being convinced that man has made his own hell.
> · Emrys Jones, *Metropolis: The World's Great Cities* (Oxford University Press, 1990).

inhabitants, they were grudgingly recognised by the city and Christiana survives as an alternative community, even though it has become more assimilated to the mainstream and has only limited success in achieving its aim of economic independence. In the UK, out of sixty-nine intentional communes and communities listed in the handbook *Diggers and Dreamers* (1996-7 edition), twenty-five are urban. These are small initiatives. Can a larger number of citizens organise themselves for living lightly, and well, and autonomously, without turning their backs on mainstream city life?

The answer depends on which city you live in. In this chapter we start in one of the cruellest, Bombay, where groups of women shanty town dwellers have been agitating to have permanent homes, and collectively they have started to save some of their meagre income to buy them. From Bombay we move to one of the richest cities, Chicago, where residents of a black ghetto act to re-humanise their suburb and earn themselves a living in the process. Neither Bombay's slums nor Chicago's ghettos are places where people aim to live lightly: on the contrary, they need more goods and services than they can presently afford. However, grassroots movements, when they are successful, give us reason for optimism. Once they have acted to achieve their immediate goals, they can act again in pursuit of more ambitious aims. Today's agitation for decent housing in Bombay or the west side of Chicago can be tomorrow's search for cleaner air and healthier food. As we shall see, Bombay or Chicago's poor may be interested only in a better standard of living, but in other cities we found luckier people in a position to go further and seek a higher quality of life. Such efforts involve the re-invention of communities. We visited people using the alternative money of Local Exchange Trading Systems, as a way of surviving when they have too little official money; many of them see this device as a step towards a more co-operative society.

Looking at still more radical solutions, we found that urban people *can* live lightly, convivially and in a culture of their own. In Utrecht, Holland, we stayed among members of the VAKgroep, a network of libertarian co-operatives. These mild-mannered Dutch anarchists take a communal approach to their housing and their livelihoods but one dimension of living lightly is missing: they are not much concerned about where their food comes from. That void is filled by the British co-operative Organic Roundabout in Birmingham, which brings fresh vegetables into town and distributes them in boxes to their customers. Elsewhere, we found that a surprisingly large amount of food can be produced inside cities: urban gardening is a growing movement which we found in every city we visited. The VAKgroep has a libertarian, anarchist tradition, although, as we shall see, they are perfectly law-abiding. Their ideology is relevant to anyone's search for a Living Lightly society, and we therefore end our chapter with a visit to the Social Ecologists.

Bombay

The wide pavement is obstructed by hawkers, parked rickshaws and assorted debris, so you step blind into the choking fumes of seamless traffic. This street is so hazardous that we have the sensation of stepping into hell. This is the new India; these dense, hurrying crowds have been encouraged or lured or forced to leave their villages for this madhouse world in return for a few — or perhaps none — of the comforts and luxuries of affluence. In Bombay, India's second largest city, more than half the population lives on pavements, in slums or in squatter settlements. They have no legal *right* to live there.

In the sprawling slum known as Byculla, the worst-off live under a sack or scrap of cardboard, with just their bundle and a rectangle of pavement. Others attach a tarpaulin or a plastic sheet to the wall of a building; some pavement dwellers have better shacks constructed like a garden shed — never larger than three by five metres, more usually three by three or four.

Laxshmi is the only Hindu among Muslim neighbours in Sophia Zuber Road. The inside of her hut is scrupulously clean with straw mats covering the pavement slabs, clothes stretched out on a line across one corner, bedding rolls along another, metal cooking pots stacked up, a calendar and family photographs nailed into the back wall of her dwelling which is the perimeter wall of a large house. The space is lit with a paraffin lamp. You can only stand upright in the centre. The roof consists of a tarpaulin supported by bamboo and scrap wood. Laxshmi fetches water from a stand-pipe and washes herself in the hut. Her still luxuriant brown hair is tied back in a bun. How does she keep it so clean? She must pay fifty *paise* (1p or 2 cents) to use a latrine nearby. Dense traffic roars by incessantly and conversation in the shelter needs to be loud. Outside, Laxshmi keeps two grey parrots in cages, their feathers bedraggled in the heavily polluted air.

Like most incomers to cities in the South, poverty drove Laxshmi to Bombay. She came alone from Orissa thirty years ago because her parents could not support her. She was just sixteen; she has been living on the pavement ever since. She is married; her married daughter lives elsewhere, her fifteen-year-old son is at school and shares the pavement space with his parents. Laxshmi is illiterate but her daughter finished standard ten and so will her son.

Laxshmi has lived in this shack for fifteen years but at last she hopes to have a proper home, because for the last ten years she has been a member of a

Laxshmi outside her pavement shack, Bombay.

women's co-operative known as Mahila Milan. In a plastic carrier bag she keeps the passbooks for 110 women in the savings scheme she has administered on her pavement since 1986. Her small stipend is earned by collecting money from the others and depositing it daily in the branch office. The savers, all illiterate, recognise their own passbooks by coloured tabs on the covers. A Mahila Milan sign hangs on Laxshmi's street door — a safeguard against harassment by police.

She talks with calm composure and fluent hand gestures. A helper from Mahila Milan translates for us. 'In 1981 this place was calm with no traffic. My shelter then was on the other side of the road, under the staircase of the house where I worked as a cleaner. When I moved over here I was staying illegally and could not put up a roof. Finally I covered it but my position was not secure until we joined Mahila Milan.' While we talk in stifling heat and dust, Laxshmi fans us hospitably with a sheet of paper.

'Five of us went to see Sheela Patel and we joined this movement.' Since joining Mahila Milan the pavement dwellers have been freer from interference by the Bombay municipality, which used to break down their hutments and move them off. Her family income varies, depending on when her husband can get work on a building site or she finds work as a cleaner in a middle-class household. She now hopes that after thirty years of pavement dwelling she will quite soon have her own house — a standard 'Mahila Milan house'. She

Traditional NGOs treat women as consumers of their services; the women have abdicated responsibility and decisions are taken by one or two men. We say: in all situations where women face deprivation they're best equipped to say what they want and to develop solutions. We asked them: what type of house do you need? How much water do you need? What institutional structures?
· Sheela Patel, SPARC (Society for Promoting Area Resource Centres).

knows where the house will be, on reclaimed land by the coast. The drawback will be travelling time for residents of the new settlements — 25 km from central Bombay.

Sheela Patel runs the Society for Promoting Area Resource Centres (SPARC) in a tiny, bustling office with a line of computers against one wall. She sits cross-legged on a chair at a tiny table, interviewing and negotiating. She has a bulging, well-thumbed Filofax, overflowing with addresses and notes — clearly a networker. Sheela read sociology at the Tata Institute — a nursery for many prophets and practitioners of grassroots development. SPARC, she says, was inspired by Marxist/Gandhian principles. She believes there is no evidence of a 'trickle-down' benefit for the poor from India's 'development' and industrialisation, but she does not see herself as pioneering a new society. 'In the first place we need to understand the system, explore what works and what doesn't. If you try to replace the

Sheela Patel at the SPARC office.

system you end up re-creating it. How far can you stretch the system before you kill it? I am in sympathy with Green alternatives but not clear how you get there.'

Mahila Milan is a network of women's collectives with an outreach of tens of thousands, operating in twenty-one cities. They build houses of a standard design and teach others to use it. Sheela said that eight years ago there was no housing finance institution for giving loans. 'It took us five years to convince agencies to provide loans.'

At the Mahila Milan office in the Byculla district of Bombay, Celine D'Cruz, the volunteer in charge, was checking through the dog-eared passbooks of the pavement-dwellers' savings accounts. Women were sitting cross-legged in a circle on the floor, chatting, Celine told us they have gradually developed trust in their passbooks. Her district has 536 account holders, with 1.8 million rupees in the kitty. The savings scheme is not a bank, Celine says, 'not just a monetary transaction: it has a human element, creating a

> People learn most effectively in a peer group through an experiential methodology. This is particularly true for women in a male-dominated society. The initial group of Mahila Milan women were able to teach other women in settlements in Bombay and later other cities. By sharing their experiences they deepened their own understanding.
> · SPARC (Society For Promoting Area Resource Centres) brochure.

system. That model suits poor people, it wouldn't suit the middle classes.'

The women have developed enough confidence for a core group of twelve to negotiate bank loans to supplement their savings. Mahila Milan negotiated for land beside the railway track — 'so we have moved on from confrontation and agitation to self-development.' Building will soon start. To avoid specu-lation, the new home-owners have to promise not to re-sell their houses for five years and the resale price is determined by the housing co-operative according to inflation, not the market: the house must first be offered to a Mahila Milan member. The houses — three metres by four — were designed with the members' co-operation; the women wanted latrine and tap outside (to save space) and a loft to double as extra rooms.

Mahila Milan members are part of a global movement of urban self-help. They have visited Northern Ireland for a meeting with Homeless International, a group based in Coventry. 'In Ireland we felt the women could be women in Bombay or South Africa: we agreed about everything, laughed about the same things. Our Mahila Milan methods are spreading. The same thing is developing in Africa, Cambodia, Vietnam, Thailand and Bangladesh.'

Celine's hope is that a global movement for the poor reaches a position of power vis-à-vis their exploiters. The self-empowerment of these very poor women and the dedication of Celine and Sheela and their volunteers to the cause was inspiring.

Chicago

West Garfield Park is a half-abandoned slum, much of it burned down in the riots after Martin Luther King's murder in 1965. Abandoned houses, still not pulled down, are used for crime and prostitution. Most shops are boarded up; drug dealers loiter all day at street corners. Twenty-eight people were murdered inside this square mile during 1995 — the highest rate in Chicago's seventy-seven community areas.

The city authorities had given up on West Garfield Park. Some people decided to act on their own. David Nelson, pastor of the Lutheran church, his sister Mary and a group of friends founded Bethel New Life (BNL). They aim to clean up the slums, take over abandoned houses, provide jobs and reclaim the streets from drug dealers. The core activity is taking houses abandoned by white absentee landlords who won't rent to poor blacks and won't even pay taxes on their useless houses. When the tax backlog is due, the landlords have to sell. BNL buys the houses, renews them in partnership with the City and charitable sources and divides them into apartments and condominiums.

BNL has set up health schemes to emphasise prevention and self-help, and waste recycling projects that clean streets and provide jobs. Reclaiming the streets, they organise fairs and fetes in streets where drug dealers have ruled

---

We had an 89-year-old on our board who was from the South, a former sharecropper. She gave us vision, she knew how people could manage on little and be positive. In the beginning we used children as the focal point: people who wouldn't help each other often agreed to do things for children. We used old people and mobilised their skills. Seniors taught history at high school using their own memories, and telling things from an Afro-American perspective. Teachers didn't object because they were too overworked and overstretched anyway.

We had kids collecting garbage and doing gardening. A group of thirteen kids who were on Crack were put to work on this. A spirit got going, at festivals the drunks would clean themselves up to come. A group of unemployed — Black Men United to Health — fixed houses and cleaned lots. We tell the group they must be sober Monday through Friday. To get more jobs, we make connections and pilot projects, start entrepreneurships, draft applications, get hospitals and schools to use more local contractors.

· Jackie Reed, Director of West Side Health Authority, Chicago (to the authors).

supreme. In its first fifteen years, BNL developed a thousand housing units and placed 4000 people in jobs through training schemes, a youth enterprise network, house refurbishing, recycling and other industries.

Bethel New Life is not unique: the urban renewal movement includes 5000 community development organisations in the US. The tradition of self-help goes back to the Industrial Areas Foundation started in 1941 by Saul Alinsky, a flamboyant Chicago trades-union organiser. Alinsky set up a stockyards community in Chicago in 1939; he organised Eastern European immigrants in Chicago's Back of the Yards neighbourhood and inner-city Black areas in various towns. He taught people to organise their communities, to target power-brokers and politically out-manoeuvre them. After his death in 1972 it was churches, not unions or political wards, who turned out to be the best building blocks for broad-based activism.

Urban regeneration often starts with Wellness Centres — a self-reliant answer to a health system based on dependency. Jackie Reed, Director of West Side Health Authority, had been a social worker for thirty years when she started a new health strategy for 250,000 people, mostly Afro-American. She told us the strategy was based on 'assets, not needs, wellness not sickness. We hired people to find assets and make a list — who can visit, who can pray, who can cook?'

We explored West Garfield Park with David Young, the overworked organiser of Bethel New Life's re-neighbouring work. He sits on school councils, runs Wellness Centres and co-ordinates liaison with police. He organises popular actions 'to reclaim the streets' from drug dealers at intersections or in parks where they operate, collecting as many people as possible including lots of children, who then set up stalls to sell hot dogs and ice cones. The street actions have had some success in discouraging drug dealers. 'At least they cost the dealers thousands of dollars each time,' David said. 'Often they come right back, but not always.'

The drug dealers are mostly young boys. We saw them waiting in clusters,

---

We base our jobs policy on the idea of people as assets. The government pays $800 a month to keep old people in institutions, we look after them at home for $271. We employ 320 people in this every day. Many never had a job before. Garbage, too, is an asset for BNL, providing 35 jobs in a business that has been sold to a recycling company: the jobs are still there. BNL bought a 9.2 acre site from a hospital, created 150 jobs in child day-care and small businesses. We work for an affordable, liveable, just community with a vision of 'wholeness' which comes out of religious faith.
· Mary Nelson, Director of Bethel New Life, Chicago (to the authors).

hunched together in the cold. Kids are used because they cannot be convicted: they get arrested and are back on the streets the same day. They are recruited at school and agree to work partly because they fear the gangs, partly by the lure of easy money. Every so often a car comes by containing the high-ups who keep an eye on the kids. The customers come in their own cars from the suburbs. A car stops, a woman steps out and pays the money, the 'rock' (of crack) or 'blow' (of heroin) is rapidly fetched from its hiding place (the young dealers never have it on them) and the car is gone within a minute. The young dealers look out for police in all directions; they have routes for instant escape. David said the kids can earn $500 a week from drugs, as against $150 for flipping burgers.

Johnny Williams, another volunteer, is more optimistic and claims that conditions are 'a thousand times better than last year. The drug scene on my streets is slowing down because of all the Watch programs and street actions and community marches.' He still complains: 'The police arrest people but they don't stay arrested.' Johnny says some young people lead double lives: they sell drugs but also help the community to plant trees, clear parks, clean neighbourhoods and organise events. 'When they come we feed them just like anyone else.' Johnny wears a BNL tee-shirt which says: TAKE BACK THE STREETS — CEASEFIRE. He says, 'This community was lazy and complacent and let the deterioration happen. Now some folks are waking up.'

The 're-neighbouring' of West Garfield Park has persuaded people to stay, and some who left are now coming back, according to Cherry Francis, Senior Vice President of BNL. Echoing a phrase we heard in Bombay, she said: 'We are giving people empowerment to make demands on authority.' We asked her if urban gardens to grow food were part of the BNL agenda. She said the churches had a strategy for city gardens but it wasn't applied here. 'People don't have the time. Besides, the rats eat almost everything and people steal the stuff that's left.'

In many cities of the developed world there are more radical groups looking for self-reliance, sharing resources in their housing and their livelihood, living in co-operation instead of competition. Many call themselves anarchists. It isn't the old-fashioned cloak and dagger business but rather a political philosophy aiming at personal and regional autonomy. 'Not to be owned' as one Vakgroep member told us. The Vereinigte Arbeits Kollektive Groep, just entering its third decade, is a network of workers' co-ops and housing co-ops in Utrecht and Nijmegen, Holland.

VAKgroep

VAKgroep people hang out at the Averechts café-bar, a centre of 'the scene' where you meet urban anarchists who live as they have chosen — an apparently carefree life which in fact is highly organised. Some people drinking here are members of worker co-ops in the VAKgroep; some live in a shared VAKgroep house. The café is not normally open until nine p.m. because the servers are volunteers after their daytime work is finished.

Arno is behind the bar, serving himself as fast as the customers with Belgian lager. A teacher for six years, he became disillusioned with 'a rigid and impersonal system.' Then he met Paul, the VAKgroep founder, discovered 'the scene' and found himself in an informal community of anarchists. Since then he has refurbished dozens of VAKgroep houses on behalf of ex-squatters who want to become co-operative owners, going about in his mini-van with the tools of his firm called Helping Hand.

The new-style anarchists of the VAKgroep are neither against the state nor have plans to overthrow it. They believe that what people organise for themselves will work better than anything authority or business firms can set up, and that the freer people are from authority the better they will behave. 'It was my personal ideal,' says Arno, 'to be in a group, to live like Paul in a small housing community with a shared garden in the middle, a stream at the end and lots of kids and animals around. We're not changing the world: all we want is to be free in our homes and our work, *not to be owned.'* Arno, a successful entrepreneur at forty-one, has a horror of becoming a capitalist. 'I just get angry at injustice and hypocrisy and when there's no sharing. I feel like Bakunin who could not be happier than the least happy person in the group.'

Nearly 200 members are directly involved in the federation of housing associations, small co-operative firms and voluntary work projects; seventy work in commercial or voluntary projects and 130 live in housing co-ops. In Lorraine, France, the VAKgroep has set up a communal goat and cheese farm in an isolated village, with a summer school for arts and co-operative skills. The web of interaction is spreading.

The VAKgroep was using the Averechts café to host its annual meeting with urban grassroots groups from other countries. Stuart and Roger have come from Radical Roots, the 'co-op of co-ops' in Birmingham, UK; other dele-

> It's an economy without interest — a model which could be useful for the whole world. My dream is that it will end up as a closed system in which you get your food from a VAKgroep store, photographs from a VAKgroep photographer and so on.
> · Nils, manager of OM, a VAKgroep graphic design company (to the authors).

gates are from a union of worker collectives in Berlin and from a group of German rural co-ops. Roger is impressed with the VAKgroep because it has survived for so long and, even more, because it is financially secure. Its central fund collects FL 150,000 a year from member firms and holds at least that amount as reserves. The lending organisation normally has a million Guilder at its disposal and is now ready to seek ethical investments from further afield for projects across Europe.

Paul Dijkstra is older than everyone else, a father-figure with a self-deprecating, jocular voice. Bald and red-cheeked, he has the self-confidence of a man who has realised his vision. As founder, chief planner and internal critic, he's the only person sitting in on all the VAKgroep's amorphous and interlocking segments. Does this make him secretive? Hard to say. He is not talkative: you have to ask relevant questions for information, and he does not object to silence. Yet he radiates bonhomie as he lights one cigarette after the other, or cooks meals, or looks after other people's dogs.

Paul takes us back to his home, which is just as Arno had described it: he shares a canal-side compound with four other members of the Rainbow housing co-op. His ground-floor flat is in the corner of a cobbled courtyard which is slowly grassing itself over. Another house, backing onto the Vecht canal, is the office of OM, a VAKgroep graphic design firm. In a wire pen in the courtyard, Paul keep chickens and a noisy duck. In the group's lifestyles, we saw this blurring of urban and rural which is so much a feature of Living-Lightly initiatives.

Paul's career was in the aid and development business, but he decided: 'There is no help for the Third World unless you start with people right here: the West is the root cause of all the problems,' so he started setting up urban co-operatives. 'This was 1968. I had a strong sense of people's rootlessness and helplessness, the absence of humanity in society, the way the police and military were used by faceless manipulators. People should be able to live a decent life and get their prosperity into their own hands.'

He organised six friends into a club for debating social-anarchistic ways of organisation, and this group began setting up housing associations and co-operative companies. A commercial and housing complex was launched and run without outside help or subsidies except routine renovation grants. Paul himself was earning a salary as a teacher at a theatre school. 'Since I had my own autonomy I could slip into things, as people did then. Most of my friends were doing all this as a hobby and they soon slipped back into their own careers. For me it wasn't a hobby.'

Paul and his friends don't expect anything from the state. 'A state today is like the Church: in a world run by corporations the state stands for values, but

No project can take any decision for any other project: all determine their own working and living arrangements as far as possible. Any surplus assets generated are used to support other projects, to work with them and thus create common responsibility for the achievements and assets of those activities. Implicit in our structures is the ideal of social anarchism, feminine socialism or whatever name one wants to give it. The basic aim is to find an alternative to a world in which people harm each other more than they help and support each other — an alternative in which the initiatives spring from the base and working together yields an added value which in turn creates space for additional projects, without the need for people to rule over others.
· VAKgroep mission statement.

we have to organise our own lives.' His own company, called Verandering, helps charities, artists and housing groups set up viable projects for living and working. Just now Verandering is setting up a firm running bicycle vans for delivering goods in city areas where cars have been banned.

The VAKgroep headquarters, behind a shopfront a few doors away from the compound where Paul lives, has no sign — a precaution against attack from fascist groups and also, Paul says, because people who need a sign don't need the VAKgroep. The open plan office looks like any other commercial premises. Instead of a sign, a few posters. Inside, pigeon holes store mail for KURF (Utrecht Committee Against Racism and Fascism), a group for supporting immigrants, a support group for Kurds in Turkey and another for East Timor.

The VAKgroep is a replicable model of urban self-help because it is relaxed, pragmatic, convivial, financially sound, democratic and self-perpetuating. But it is not Green. We asked several members if they had considered the argument that without a source of local food there can be no autonomy and no convincing resistance against the domination of the corporate global economy? Hannah, a young woman who is involved in every aspect of the 'scene', said bluntly that food wasn't a problem for her. 'I hate cooking, I don't have a garden. Autonomy is not an objective. We've gone too far for self-sufficiency in Holland.'

It's like a family: we get tensions and fractions but we overcome them as a family does because you have to. The rent we pay here is based on what we earn. We run the place ourselves, we're the landlords. This is the future. I think slowly people are starting to change and to see that growth capitalism is not the right way. The VAKgroep is a kind of bank set up for a more anarchistic way of life.
· Aron, a British member of the VAKgroep's Rainbow housing co-operative (to the authors).

Organic Roundabout

A more positive view about getting local organic food into cities prevails in Birmingham, England, at Organic Roundabout, a workers' co-operative which operates Britain's largest 'box-scheme'.

Anyone designing an ecologically sustainable city would surely have people living and working co-operatively, bringing in organic food from the countryside and distributing it. These conditions are met by Organic Roundabout which, in addition, is hardworking, businesslike and successful: its main problem when we visited was its too rapid expansion.

Organic Roundabout buys its produce from Organic Marketing Company, thirty miles away in Herefordshire, which was formed to buy from growers who had been disappointed by the unreliability of supermarkets and were going out of business. The produce goes out from the Marketing Company at 4 a.m four days a week, reaches the Birmingham packing station — a hired warehouse — at 5.30, and is packed and delivered the following day. The vegetables are boxed by members, paid staff and volunteers before being driven to the customers in two lorries, one owned and one hired. Most of the members live in housing co-operatives and, like the VAKgroep people, work for just enough money to live on.

Too businesslike for a hotbed of radicals, too informal for a business, too spartan for a home, too serious for a club: the atmosphere is unique. This is 24 South Road, a suburban terraced house in Birmingham where Organic Roundabout operates.[1] The seventeen-member co-operative is described by a local newspaper as the fastest-growing business in the West Midlands. Its delivery system of organic vegetables made it, for a time, the largest CSA (community-supported agriculture) scheme in Britain, with a turnover of half a million pounds.

A small sign labels the house simply as New Education Housing Co-operative Ltd — the residential co-op which owns it. The front room is an office overcrowded with people at makeshift tables operating telephones and a computer. This room is the headquarters for Organic Roundabout, its parent co-operative Radical Routes, its sister co-operative Astrix which does organic catering, and Carrot Computers, another co-operative which brings in cash to support the others.

People live in this house but there are few concessions to bourgeois comfort. The threadbare stair carpet is overdue for sweeping, doors are half-painted. A frugal sitting room has flaky off-colour walls and a television, the kitchen has vegan recipes on the wall and earth-covered organic vegetables in a basket. The top floor houses two families. Roger Hallam's personal upstairs

---

RADICAL ROUTES

Radical Routes is a UK wide secondary co-operative whose members are small independent workers' or housing co-ops. Each in its own way is working for a socially just and ecologically sustainable society. Our central aim is to empower people to take control and responsibility for their own lives, especially in the areas of work, housing and education ... We are a recognised Promoting Body for Housing Co-operatives and so are able to offer a relatively cheap registration service. This is handled by one of our members, Catalyst Collective Ltd., and is available to any potential co-op, not just prospective members of Radical Routes. We also operate an ethical investment scheme providing a loan fund for our members. Most commonly we make top-up loans for the purchase of property, with Triodos Bank, The Ecology Building Society or ICOF acting as the main lender. Although Radical Routes might only provide 20 to 30 percent of the purchase price, this contribution is often essential for the project to go ahead.

· Radical Routes website, www.newciv.org/GIB/BOV/

---

office is also his bedroom. He's the Organic Roundabout co-ordinator, in charge of market development, the nearest thing to a boss.

It is 10 p.m. on a hectic night before delivery day. All of the key players are still at work in various rooms. Roger makes last-minute telephone calls to clients, Sarah matches last-minute demand with supply for the weekly rounds, Sue is poring over accounts. In the afternoon all have been at the weekly business meeting focused on the problem of bad debts arising when customers don't pay on time, or ever, for their bags. Another Roger has cooked a vegan meal; people take half an hour to eat and go back to work.

Next morning at seven we go with Alex in the hired van on the Coventry-Leamington run. We service seven pick-up points — four in private houses, two in shops and one privileged old lady who has a home delivery. A man at a pick-up point asks if five pounds of his £35 takings can be paid next week. Alex, debonair and easy-going, says OK, though he knows bad debts are running at £400 a week and threaten to tip the balance between operating profit and loss.

Another headache threatening Alex's good humour is vegetable fatigue. He has brought an extra basket of decent cabbages to replace faded ones in the customers' bags at the last minute. But there are not enough to replace all those tired cabbages. So with a heavy heart Alex delivers six bags with whitening cabbages and yellowing water-cress. We are back at noon in time for lunch cooked by the Astrix people while the van is reloaded by volunteers and contract workers for its next round.

Eight-year-old Lorna, watching telly in the threadbare sitting room with walls in need of paint, has to vacate for the weekly business meeting. One member sits on her rocking horse. Roger's manner is strange: he speaks in a barely audible monotone with no facial expression. Is he running the show while straining terribly hard not to appear to do so? The main topic is the late payments for the bags and a plan to cure it, and the problem of half-rotten spring greens and onions.

Finances remain precarious and Organic Roundabout is almost always seeking fresh loans from Radical Routes, the parent 'co-op of co-ops'. Bad debts are the most immediate problem for Roger. 'We live in a supermarket culture where the consumer rules. Our customers are all pleasant middle-class people who don't try to avoid paying, but if they want to pay late we can't use a big stick. There's no simple answer to the payments problem. The freshness problem has also to be addressed. The bigger the range the more the problem arises with stock control. But we're buying a cold store which will take care of the immediate problem.'

Roger Hallam is very lean — like all the other vegans we have met — with sunken eyes, a sparse beard and swept-back hair parted in the middle and tied behind in a tiny bob. His manner is brusque, defensive, dissolving into surprising smiles. He is dressed uncaringly in a stained trainer-trousers and tee-shirt.

A hands-on manager, he telephones 450 city customers each week to make sure they are ready for their boxes. He used to do canvassing door to door to open up new areas. 'We'd sign up two or three in each street: if we could do that throughout Birmingham we'd have 30,000 customers. Right now we have 1000 in the city, another thousand outside.'

Roger's main problem is too fast growth: expenses go up as demand rises

---

TRIODOS BANK

Triodos Bank is a social bank lending only to organisations and businesses with social and environmental objectives. The bank is well known for its innovative and trans-parent approach to banking; savers know where their money is working... When money is deposited with Triodos Bank, innovative enterprises can develop, community project can be helped and environmental initiatives, like wind energy, can be funded.

Triodos Bank NV was founded in 1980 in the Netherlands and is a fully-licensed inde-pendent bank, owned by public shareholder, with offices in Belgium, the Netherlands and the United Kingdom. Triodos Bank finances exclusively the development of renew-able energy sources (solar and wind), organic agriculture, art and culture, protection of the environment and conservation of nature. Triodos Bank also plays an active role in the developing world (microcredit).

· Triodos website, www.internation.co.uk/network/

LETS SING!

Lets trade, exchange together,
Lets aid, lets work together,
Lets live, lets give, lets love.
Lets live, lets give, lets love.
Lets spend, Lets earn together,
Lets lend, Lets learn together,
Lets live, Lets give, Lets love.
You may say we're crazy, You may say we're mad, (so we're mad).
Lets eat together, Lets meet together, Lets think together.
You may say we're crazy, You may say we're mad, (so we're mad).
Lets live, lets give, lets love.

· Song by Tariq Shabeer, Bradford City Council's LETS promotion officer,
who takles his guitar to meetings.

---

while the boxes are paid for a week late. But Roger believes size is essential. 'The objective is selling organic vegetables and providing employment in a co-operative. We are growth-orientated, Our ethics are based on scale: the more of a good thing the better. If we go on growing we can have enough capital to compete with supermarkets who may try and take over the trade. We have to look for little cracks to create capital, little cracks to achieve the freedom for what we want to set up.'

Roger's ideal is to have ten growers around a town organised in a co-operative, working with a co-operative in town and selling 500-plus bags. 'What we have here is the nearest thing, and it's a big advance on most of the little schemes: an infrastructure here in the city and a rural marketing organisation in Herefordshire. This opens the possibility of providing two to three percent of the population with organic vegetables in ten to fifteen years. If we'd kept to the small-is-beautiful scenario we'd have had no incentive to grow. You have to take risks to create something interesting.'

Much of this philosophy is open to criticism by Green purists who look for small-is-beautiful operations. Organic Roundabout buys its produce centrally from a wholesale co-operative instead of direct from the farmers, and delivers its boxes as far afield as Brighton, 170 miles away, adding to atmospheric pollution and the burning of fossil fuels. Roger is impatient with 'Green idealists who go on about local economies. Most people don't have access to land, and we don't have the choice of suppliers. If we could get three or four farms ten miles outside Birmingham we could deliver food one day fresher, and cheaper. For us to join in with growers would be a ten-year project just to get it off the ground: to make it viable would take twenty years. And Brighton will one day have its own box scheme'.

Many people who are interested in a better quality of life for themselves and a higher level of community involvement find themselves half way between the mainstream and the alternative, an uneasy balancing act for which techniques need the be invented. Often the limiting factor is lack of money. So skills lie dormant, wants unfilled. And most of the money available is spent on services and goods provided by people with no stake in the community, so the money goes elsewhere. The answer is LETS. We saw Local Exchange Trading Systems working in Australia, Canada and the UK. The one we describe first, in Stroud, England, can represent the others.

LETS

Go for lunch at Mills Café, just off the High Street in Stroud, Gloucestershire. On Thursdays, Fridays and Saturdays you can pay half the cost in Strouds. 'It's good for business,' says Maggie Mills, the café's owner. Strouds are units of the Local Exchange Trading System which Mrs Mills helped found. In four years it has grown to 450 members with a turnover of 96,000 Strouds a year and is still growing.[2]

To join you pay £10 and submit a list of your skills, hobbies and anything you have to offer from organic cabbages to painting houses, baby-sitting, hairdressing, osteopathy or giving lifts in your car. You get a LETS cheque book and you can go into debt straightaway, without interest, for as much as you want, as long as you want. Newcomers to the scheme are encouraged to get into debt to start them trading.

In the official money system if you are hard up, you cannot afford to pay for skills or services that other hard up people could offer you. LETS turns the system upside down, waking dormant skills and talents and waking up local economies that have been put to sleep by high unemployment and low earnings. LETS keeps wealth in the local area instead of siphoned off through banks and supermarkets. LETS brings people together who otherwise would never meet. Running parallel with the mainstream economy, LETS is a tool for living lightly and a transition to a Living Lightly economy. You can pay with Acorns in Totnes, with Trugs in Lewes, Brads in Bradford, Links in Wiltshire, Bunyas in Maleny. With more than 1000 systems in the world, most still have less than 100 members but a few have more than 1000. In 1997 the UK had some 400, Australia had 200, France 100, New Zealand 50.

Mrs Mills spends some of her Strouds on organic vegetables from Helen Brent-Smith, a part-time clinical psychologist who accepts fifty percent in

Strouds. Ms Brent-Smith was planning to expand into apple juicing, accepting part-payment in Strouds which she would use to pay her pickers. She already pays in Strouds for music lessons, Alexander technique sessions and for buying the odd present from Sophie Hughes, the potter, who takes 100 percent Strouds for some of her wares. The potter said LETS was good for business because people who come to pay in Strouds often bring friends who pay in pounds.

This Cotswold town boasts more residents who follow a Green lifestyle than most, but the philosophy behind LETS systems is shared by Living Lightly people who want to encourage local skills and products and gets things repaired instead of replaced. And the LETS enthusiasts go further, arguing that the money system which rules our society is its most harmful feature — and LETS systems are a small but essential step to changing it.

As a way of rescuing dole-stricken communities and eventually reducing social security payments, LETS has started to interest governments, local authorities and the European Union. One in four of Britain's 400 LETS schemes has local council aid. To take LETS down-market, council staff in Bradford try to overcome the middle-class bias in which organic vegetables, shiatsu, hairdressing and car lifts have often been the biggest items traded. 'Here, what's most in demand is having someone sit in your house to stop it being burgled when you're out,' said Andy Ramsden, trainee community officer at Buttershaw.

'LETS currency is infinite, interest-free and never leaves the local community,' says an explanatory leaflet. But what interests Bradford Council more is careers. Officials' favourite success story is about the Manchester woman who made such lovely hats in exchange for Bobbins that they started selling for sterling and she has now opened a shop called Hat Trick. Runner-up is the Bradford man who cleaned windows for Brads: now he's in regular trade with a council grant for a new van and equipment.

Nighat Taimuri runs Bradford's downtown LETS, already four years old, whose 265 members have traded more than 25,000 Brads. Membership costs £2 a year for the unwaged, £5 for the waged and £10 for companies. 'In LETS, you don't talk about debt: you talk about commitment. The good people are the people who spend,' said Nighat. The Bradford LETS quarterly directory lists hundreds of offers ranging from small business computing, car maintenance and cat sitting to DIY help and 'Morning After Party clean-up and tidying'. Current requests include help with job applications, Asian cookery and Urdu translations.

LETS schemes aren't foolproof and some of them stagnate because supply and demand for services does not balance, leaving some members chronically in credit, others in debit. For David and Molly Sommerville, LETS has not been user-friendly. Both teachers, they jointly run the Bradford Traidcraft branch. They offer the goods for fifty percent Brads, but that means trading at a loss. 'If LETS really took off we'd be in difficulty.' Molly finds it difficult to spend her Brads usefully. 'People in the system are rarely professional and often not too competent. We went to a party where the cooking was done for Brads but it was so awful I'd never use those people myself. To work well, our LETS would need to be either smaller and very cosy and neighbourly, or bigger so that you might really find what you want. I believe there's a very good LETS in Hebdon Bridge, Yorkshire — a small town where the scheme is intimate and successful.'

LETS was invented in British Columbia, Canada, in the 1980s by Michael Linton, an unemployed computer programmer who saw that many people were like him — with skills but no job and not enough money to be useful. Linton called his units Green Dollars. The idea was especially welcome in Australia in the slump that followed Britain's adhesion to the European Common Market in 1992. The Australian government invited Linton to set up LETS all over the country and provided money for infrastructure, education and publicity. Thousands of members, including hundreds of businesses, soon found that LETS increased their turnover. Patricia Know wrote in *Earth Island Journal* (Winter 1995): 'If the global economy crashes, Australia would be the country most likely to survive, having developed a thriving alternative economy.' In 1994, the world's largest LETS was in the Australian Blue Mountains with more than 2000 members trading the equivalent of US$40,000 a month.

What happens to spongers who exploit the system by staying in debt? A Stroud members' meeting decided against credit limits and so far no LETS scheme to our knowledge has suffered from bad debtors. LETS transactions by businesses usually have a component in official currency to take care of overheads, labour costs and tax. If you regularly convert part of your main income to LETS, you have to declare it for taxation. Stroud members say they do, and are duly taxed on the assumption that a Stroud is a pound. They find the tax man ready to ignore the occasional Stroud earned from hobbies. In parts of Australia, more advanced in these matters, members pay tax on their LETS income in 'green money', which is then spent on local schemes in which workers are paid in the same coin.

A big brake on the system's spread in the UK is unemployed peoples' fear of losing benefit if they are seen to do 'remunerative' work more than sixteen hours a week. When we asked a social security spokesperson he blew hot and cold, beginning warmly by saying that benefits in kind are normally disregarded unless they are regular. He went on more coldly to say that those claiming unemployment benefit must be available for work, which they cannot be if they are busy earning Strouds or Brads. The situation is still not clarified, but Bradford councillor Bob Cannell has no doubt: 'Free market economies have left entire communities excluded from the economic mainstream. LETS, credit unions and things like that are seeking to create village-type economies based on barter and social interaction.'

The LETS approach is part of a wider search for solutions to a basic problem raised by the global economy: there is often not enough money to meet the simplest of community needs, even when plenty of idle people are available to do the necessary work. The Living Lightly culture has embraced quite a number of local-currency and interest-free-money solutions, some of which have a history going back centuries. Margrit Kennedy, a leading German exponent of such reforms, argues that interest acts like a cancer in our social structure because it causes money to grow exponentially, not by natural or linear growth.[3]

City gardens

Nobody living in a city can even dream of self-sufficiency, but citizens in many countries are interested in fresher and healthier food than supermarkets provide. Box schemes that bring food into the city are flourishing in the USA and starting in UK. Another solution for wholesome food is to grow it *inside* the city itself. Urban gardens are becoming popular all over the world; they grew more rapidly during the eighties than population, urbanisation or the economy. Spaces left by defunct industries, a new neediness among city dwellers buffeted by the global economy and a new ecological awareness among councils all combine to give a boost to city gardening. In the last twenty years the gardens movement has reached all American cities. In New York, 300 volunteer 'green guerrillas' distribute plants, reclaim land and teach youngsters to garden. Seattle has its Pea Patch programme, San Francisco's SLUG — League of Urban Gardens — hires ex-offenders, teenagers sentenced to community service and other unemployed people for construction and development work. According to a report by Canada's Office of Urban Agriculture, 'Millions of urban farmers may be the most powerful tool we have to close open nutrient, carbon and pollution loops.'

Women in the South prize their gardens as a source of food that is not dependent on cash incomes or fluctuating markets; in the North, city farming creates jobs for low capital investment, stimulates urban economies and gives low-income groups better access to healthy food and income. In Western

Stephen White at New Green City Garden, Philadelphia.

Europe, renewed interest in city farming has been spurred by environmental concerns. In Central and Eastern Europe it is a matter of need, because of the hardships imposed by the rapid introduction of capitalism and an increasing awareness of the effects of contaminated food. City gardeners tending their tiny plots intensively during Russia's short growing season probably produce as much as a quarter of all the country's fruit and vegetables. Russian town dwellers produce eighty-eight percent of their potatoes, forty-three percent of their meat, thirty-nine percent of their milk and twenty-eight percent of their eggs on tiny urban household plots which, together, constitute only four percent of agricultural land in Russia. Ex-communist cities are well adapted to urban farming because most buildings are high-rise mini-cities, leaving more open land near the old urban centres than in North America or Western Europe. As energy and transport costs multiply under the new capitalist economic system, urban food production offers obvious advantages.

In Philadelphia, USA, we found city gardens a blooming part of the landscape. The city's Food and Agriculture Task Force says that 501 community vegetable gardens produce two million dollars worth of fruit and vegetables every year, involving 3000 families.

'This was one of the worst drug blocks in the city; people used to look out of their windows and see the drug deals and fights. Now they see sunflowers.' Stephen White was showing us round the eight-month-old New Green City Garden between 25th Street and Spruce. Stephen is an architect who has devoted most of these eight months to organising the garden. Rows of beans and lettuce are framed by skyscrapers giving the garden a surreal look.

The City agreed to tear down six derelict houses and clear half a hectare for this finely planned garden: a double row of fruit trees, a fountain, a rose garden, cold frames and a greenhouse, a school plot, a nursery for trees, honey bees. The planting has already started. With one hundred gardeners already inscribed, there's a waiting list.

Stephen grew up on a farm and had wanted to garden for years. Now he finds the garden has brought about a greater sense of community. 'I've been living here twenty-five years and I got to know more people these last months than in all that time.' The suburb has one-third Puerto Ricans, some blacks and Koreans. The meeting to organise the garden was held in Spanish and English.

Older and more mature, and only ten minutes walk from City Hall, Schuylkill River Park Garden is grandiose and genteel with its fountain and wrought iron railings. Frank Lyons said he can get his organic vegetables at the supermarket, so he grows exotic luxuries here. Indian and Peruvian cotton with beautiful yellow flowers, wild tomatoes from Chiapas, heirloom beans, chillies from North Mexico and a grass called Job's Tears: from its seeds you make rosaries. Frank is a devout Catholic and an environmentalist, and for him the garden embodies his philosophy. ' I was brought up in the thirties when people cared about each other; today they don't. The global economy will fall apart and then God will remind people they're on the wrong track.'

Midge Fluellen, a jolly grandmother, took us in her car to see her small community garden in one of the poorer blocks. She insisted on driving us there because it wasn't a safe area to be walking. She didn't have the gate key with her but called 'Hi' to Warren who was painting out graffiti on a neighbouring wall. Warren let us in. He was spattered in paint wearing tattered overalls and baseball cap. Midge picked some bunches of collards. Did we know what they were? We didn't. 'Old folk used to cook them with pork. People aren't so fond of fat now.' The collards, a healthy crop, were a form of brassica. Why did Midge and her husband garden? Midge laughed. 'I know what I'm eating. The worst that can happen is that the birds give us a little fertiliser.' She plucked a fresh tomato and said: 'Eat it, it will remind you of Philadelphia.'

London's total footprint — that is its social, environmental and economic impact upon world resources — is more than 125 times its surface area, or nearly 20 million hectares. Home to only 12% of Britain's population, London, nevertheless requires the equivalent of all the productive land area in Great Britain to sustain itself. Sustainable agricultural production within cities and towns may be one way of solving this problem and lead to an improvement in the quality and sustainability of urban living.
· European Support Group on Urban Agriculture Internet site at www.cityfarmer.org.

There were kale, peppers, herbs and flowers on the quarter-acre plot divided into thirty small beds. Around the perimeter grew neatly tended marigolds, busy lizzies and asters. Midge said: 'A lady called Florence — she comes and does the flowers.' Warren stopped painting and came to talk to us. Have you got a job, we asked somewhat tactlessly. He laughed. 'I'm an auditor.' That put us in our place.

Warren Bell cares deeply about community gardens. He said that sixty-six percent of people in some of these blocks live below the poverty level. That day he had volunteered to paint out graffiti because he thought you should do whatever you could to improve the quality of life in your community. There was a breakdown in communities all over this nation, he said. Warren saw the garden movement as spiritual, not ecological: it had brought people together for a common cause. A young white couple were harvesting their tomatoes in this predominantly Black block. Warren said: 'This is a meeting place, a place of beauty, a place where the earth reclaims itself.'

Social ecology

Is there a theory to guide us for living lightly and justly, a credible utopia in which we can be free? In this chapter we have visited the urban idealists of Utrecht who are experts at living simply and working enjoyably together. They are anarchists because they look neither to the state nor to the global economy to solve their problems. For housing, livelihood and social needs, they look to themselves. They are not theoreticians but underlying their activities is a theory — social ecology. The basic idea is that we can never stop despoiling the earth until we dismantle the power structures involved — and replace them with small, autonomous, face-to-face communities, linked to others only through loose confederal ties.

Our research begins at a summer conference in Scotland which is to launch an International Network of Social Ecologists. We are in a stately home, busy with plans to abolish the state. On a lawn as big as a football pitch, backed by walled gardens and a lily pond with a fountain, we sit cross legged in a circle, debating our hopes for radical municipalism. We look over the Firth of Clyde across lazy waters, and we argue about popular local assemblies which will be sovereign — the only seat of political and economic power, allowing nature to blossom while the state withers. Apart from us, the participants are young.

Does it sound solemn and academic? Conspiratorial? Don't confuse the new wave of eco-anarchists with the communists, or even sixties anarchists. Social ecologists don't *have* to be anarchists but mostly are. They believe nothing can stop the destruction of the environment by a globalising market economy until the exploitation of man by man is stopped. They have their

> As an anarchist Murray Bookchin is not of the bomb-throwing kind (it is governments that throw bombs) but in the tradition of William Morris, Tolstoy, Thoreau and Kropotkin — believing in decentralisation, minimal government, self-sufficiency, mutual aid and other ideas which are as far from those of Reagan and Thatcher as they are from those of Marx, Lenin, and Mao. What he calls for instead is a 'stateless, class-less, decent, decentralised society in which the splits created by propertied society are transcended by new, unalienated relationships.' A society that is diversified, balanced and harmonious. Where human behaviour is dictated not by laws but by a basic sense of decency.
> · Richard Boston, *The Guardian*, 30 January 1986.

jargon, of course, and their big prophet — Murray Bookchin, an irascible American academic who writes difficult books and refers to Deep Ecology as 'eco-lala' — meaning bourgeois obscurantism. But unlike communists they believe that scientific objectivity is neither possible nor desirable, though they believe passionately in reason and are perfectly convinced that our present social, political and economic arrangements are not based on reason. The political order they want is municipal confederalism — a system in which every village is completely autonomous, combining with others only in a confederation for administrative, but not policy, decisions. Nobody mentions Gandhi, although his vision of a free India was for a confederation on lines similar to theirs. The social ecologists aren't always respectful of their own prophets, even of Bookchin, their erudite patron saint.

They are much more fun than communists. Dario and Roberta from Padua (actually she's an American academic but works in Italy, studying the local anarchists and trying with immense courage to help organise them) offer a double-act résumé of the *autogestione* scene in Italy over the last century — the base communities, the factories taken over and the brave local actions they see as the precursors of libertarian politics. They put it across humorously as urgent and true, but also absurd and probably hopeless.

Erik, Paul, Peter and Jan are sunburnt camping types from Social Ecology, Norway. In week-long arguments over the wording of the Declaration to launch the Network, the Norwegians are so radical they can't accept any text that doesn't explicitly condemn the market economy. Christina is more sophisticated. She is twenty-one, dark, relaxed, lively. She is helping to convert a building in central Athens, donated to the eco-anarchists, into a centre for a national network, starting with a library and a café. The movement grew out of a political void after the collapse of communism, the retreat of social democrats from radical reform and the bourgeois ineffectiveness of the Greens. Then anarchist and libertarian left groups became aware of Murray

Bookchin who gave them new perspectives.

Brix, an ex-sociology lecturer, lives in County Donegal, Ireland. He is setting up the kind of alternative café he knew in San Diego, California. He wears beads and has a caressing New World voice and New-Age manner. Sylvia and Edward, from Woodford Green in Essex, England, are jointly or singly part of every eco-protest you can name, and are here to broaden their theoretical base. The conference's top guru is Takis Fotopoulos, a former economics lecturer who edits *Society and Nature,* the biggest-selling academic journal in Greece, dedicated to critical versions of Bookchinism. Takis delivers an authoritative guide to the latest theory and practice — 'transitional strategy' as the jargon calls it.

This is a challenging background for Living Lightly people; it makes autonomous activity not just liberating and relevant, but the *only* thing to do. 'We have a choice: democracy or barbarism,' Takis said at the end of his talk. He is heavy and swarthy, in need of exercise, but has a gentle voice and soft eyes. He means *his* democracy and Bookchin's — direct decisions by popular assemblies which will form confederations and increasingly challenge the state, and local community ownership of the means of production.

Not everyone present wants all of this or thinks that much of it is remotely feasible. Yet it is increasingly apparent that every Green with a brain is a social ecologist to some extent even if she's never heard of this new orthodoxy. Even Arne Naess, the founder of Deep Ecology whom Bookchin sees as the embodiment of *eco-lala,* agrees the growth economy effectively runs the planet, deprives us all of power and autonomy and needs to be drastically curbed.

Radical municipalists cannot yet claim many success stories, which made the visit of a group from Pollock Free State all the more exciting. Here was action. The heartening thing about this veteran anti-road protest in Glasgow is that it was started by activists from elsewhere and has been joined by locals who have set up a permanent camp. Alex tells in a rich Glasgow accent how he was happily working for the Glasgow city roads department when the Pollock protest suddenly made him see that the land belongs to the people. 'The politicians aren't any use here. Even the Scottish Nationalist Party is in favour of this motorway. The best tactics are doing what you feel like.' The Pollock Free State camp is a makeshift community centre where kids can learn skills like pottery and 'anything anyone wants to teach who happens to be around. No-one decides. Everyone's equal.' Not yet a sovereign popular assembly in the making, but the beginnings of libertarian communalism.

Where then is the model? Bookchin's theory begins with the Greek city state, but the movement has become uncomfortably aware that the *polis* was based on a slave economy in which women had no civic rights, and that groups of orators often dominated the civic assembly while the majority became effectively powerless. In modern times there is little municipalism to show since the Paris commune, which effectively discredited the idea.

Some of us were doubtful about Bookchin's political programme. He envisages that each direct assembly will be part of a wider regional federation but that political power will always stay with the community assembly. Delegation is for administration only, never for political decision. But what if a community unreasonably objects to a scheme all the other communities accept? And what happens to minorities? Here Takis gave an answer reminiscent of the old communist dream that a good state will produce good citizens. He said human rights presuppose a state; the notion is meaningless in a non-statist democracy. 'There'll be a new moral code — a new meaning for life and what it means to be human.'

In the end these theoreticians struck us as too remote from the practical politics of the Green movement, which they could usefully do much to radicalise. Already, the mainstream of Green thinking, expressed by flagship organisations like Greenpeace and Friends of the Earth, has moved well beyond 'the environment' to embrace the deeper problems of power, exploitation and injustice in a global economy dominated by corporations more powerful than nation states. Social ecology can help to give Green campaigners a vision of a better world. Meanwhile, in the practical world, it is the grassroots activists who will help themselves and us to live lightly.

Notes

1   After our visit, Organic Roundabout moved to new offices. See Appendix.
2   Facts on Stroud LETS are correct for 1993 when Walter wrote about it in *The Guardian*. The scheme is still expanding as we go to press, with 600 members enrolled.
3   Margit Kennedy, *Interest and Inflation-Free Money* (New Society Publishers, 1995) can be ordered in the UK from Jon Carpenter Publishing.

11

A snake behind the stove

• •

Australia has a fragile ecology. The sharp hooves of grazing cattle destroy the topsoil; twelve rabbits introduced in 1856 had multiplied to plague proportions a century later; dogs and cats introduced by settlers eliminate the indigenous animals which have no natural defences against them. The same could be said for the indigenous inhabitants whose sustainable lifestyle had no defences against guns, whisky and Western diseases. The damage gets worse as Australia increasingly models its society on the USA, allowing commercial interests the same destructive licence. Luckily, there is a counterweight in a fierce ecological patriotism, uncompromising in its determination to save and restore the indigenous environment. Everywhere we went we found enthusiasts for wombats and wallabies, gum trees and acacias. These ecologists, amateurs and professionals, are implacable enemies of pet dogs and feral cats.

In a small town in south-east Queensland these goals are far advanced. We first heard about Maleny at an eco-villages conference at the Findhorn Foundation in Scotland, where Jill Jordan described it as a town that had become so convivial and robust in its autonomous life, so firmly anchored in its rural earth and urban spaces, that it was a model which any small town in the world could follow. Was this true, or merely Jill's propaganda? Looking for life beyond consumer culture, we wanted to find examples in towns and cities, which is where where most of us will be living from early in the new century.

Frogs Hollow

Our first morning in Maleny was far removed from town life. Jill had offered us a room in Manduka, the rural community on the outskirts of the town in which she lived. She and her friends had bought forty-eight hectares of degraded, overgrazed pasture from which dairy farmers had long departed. That was seventeen years ago. Eight women, six men and two kids now live in a co-operative in which they own their homes but share the land. Their houses are built among gum trees, ferns, palms, flowers and vegetables. They have planted thousands of trees. Birds and insects clatter, buzz and whirr throughout the twenty-four hours. The place is still known by its old local name — Frogs Hollow. In the afternoon, you have to raise your voice against the croaking.

At 5.15 we woke to a dawn chorus — the screech of parrots and the cackle of kookaburras. From our veranda, surrounded by trees in hand-shaking distance, we watched three wallabies hopping shyly into a space reclaimed for their benefit. We had just spent our first night in Jill's sister's bed-sit, a hut built on stilts beside her house, which Annie calls her 'bower'. We were on the first leg of our travels in the Living Lightly culture and already we felt we were in a kind of paradise. The inhabitants of Frog's Hollow were not wealthy. With forethought, persistence and hard work they had evolved a lifestyle which was both close to the land and attached to the town.

We arrived at Frogs Hollow in time to join in the monthly community work weekend. Everyone spends as much of the weekend as they wish working on communal projects and on Saturday afternoon they have a monthly meeting and share a meal. We went down a track to a barn where Mandy, in parti-coloured leggings and a smock, was wielding a spanner. Mandy resembles a huge orchid — a strong, flamboyant woman with an infectious grin, carrying her weight with superb aplomb. 'Bloody ute got stuck in a ditch,' she grinned, and trundled away in the communal tractor to pull it out.

The weekend's tasks were building a steam house for the winter months and weeding and mulching a plantation of young paw-paws. The steam house seemed an odd project in 32 degrees but it gets cold here in winter. While some members stayed building, we helped Jill, her sister Annie, and Jan to weed paw-paws planted in a curve beside the track and mulched with hay. The ground was soft from the rains, the weeds luxuriant — some familiar, some strange. Weeding took four of us an hour and then a tea break in Jill's house. How much pleasanter it is to work in a group than struggle on alone.

Co-ops for everything

Next day Jill drove us into Maleny, leaving Manduka's trees behind, through a countryside interspersed with remnants of rainforest with a hint of mountains in the distance.

The town shows a smiling face; single-storey shops with shady overhangs against the glaring sun line the main street where pedestrians are not outnumbered by motor cars. At first sight Maleny could be a country town anywhere in the prosperous world, except that the fierce Queensland climate has made provision of shade an imperative.

Jill does not lock her car. People come to greet her and gossip even before

Maleny: the Up Front Club co-operative.

she crosses the road. After shopping we sit outside for lunch at the Up Front Club, the food co-op's sister enterprise. Food is veggie, varied and inexpensive; the café has managed to keep its prices in line with the burger chain down the road. Customers know one another. Soon everyone knows us, too, unsurprised that their town should attract writers.

Maleny has nine thousand people, one main street, mostly single-storey houses and a few residential areas spreading out into the hills. The self-respecting country town atmosphere has not been overwhelmed by the expansion of tourism, the invasion of the corporate ethic or the spread of housing over the countryside, but we will learn that these threats are real and imminent.

As we find our way around, we see that every aspect of urban and rural activity is managed by co-operatives. People buy and sell organic food at a co-op in which they have shares; the Up Front café-club next door, with parasoled tables on the pavement, is their property too. There are co-ops for small businesses, banking (a credit union), recycling waste and caring for the environment, a co-op for the arts, another for women, a skills centre for young people, a film society, a youth magazine.

The food shop

We stroll down Main Street to Maple Street Co-op to buy provisions for our 'bower'. It's self-service like a supermarket, but the atmosphere is matey: customers who are also owners help themselves to pulses, pasta, dried fruit out of bins. Cereals are kept in bulk and oil in huge drums. Several kinds of home-baked bread, farm-made cheese, organic tofu and organic milk. We weigh out and grind our own coffee, bring our own containers and re-use our plastic bags. Maleny washing lines flutter with plastic bags. We fill ours with organic mangoes, yoghurt and cream cheese for our breakfast. Prices are higher than in the two supermarkets, yet business is brisk. We notice sadly that even in this organic food shop, produce has travelled too far — shortbread from Scotland, Chinese cosmetics and other inessential imports. It seems that no business which needs to attract enough customers to stay viable can ignore the global market entirely; at least that market can be kept in its proper place.

The first co-operative to start up was the food shop. Maleny was just a decaying little rural town like many others in the North, its pastures badly degraded and its economy depressed. The early years of the seventies saw hundreds of people across Australia move into the rural resettlement movement. Jill Jordan and a group of friends were among them.

'At that stage we were very confronting to the old farmers,' Jill said. 'We knew we were right; we knew how to do things, we knew they were degrading the country. We were horrible to them, no understanding of community building at the time. But we soon learned. We all decided to supply ourselves with bulk wholefoods and we were growing vegetables and wanted to find an outlet to sell them. We decided, quite bravely at the time, since none of us had any business skills but we were all quite bright, that we'd start a main street business and that was the first enterprise which opened its doors in 1979.'

Australia had many rural wholesale and farming co-operatives but a retail organisation was rare. The Maleny co-op started with six members and soon built up to fifty — almost all newcomers like Jill herself.

The locals joined in. 'The most beautiful thing was that we got them in through their own traditional values of recycling and resource saving. We used to recycle plastic bags and glass jars and old women came in to bring us their jars; they remembered their time in the war when jars and string and bags were valuable and that touched a cord. At first they wouldn't buy from us but brought their jars in and they'd stop to talk and they'd see that we didn't have two heads and they saw us selling fruit and vegetables on consignment for people and they'd ask, "Who are you selling for?" and we'd say anyone who grows stuff can bring it here. "If we grew stuff?" Yes, of course. Then these very conservative farmers' wives — they'd never grown vegetables on this rich alluvial soil — grew stuff for extra money. A lot of them would use non-organic fertilisers and pesticides but we never refused anything that came through the door: we just labelled it. The organic food sold better than the non-organic, so they started growing organic and their husbands joined in too.'

Now, twenty years later, the Maple Street Co-op is, if not exactly prosperous, at least keeping its own in competition with the supermarkets in town. Not everyone will shop there. You can judge a person's political views very easily in Maleny: do they shop at the Co-operative and take a jar at the Up Front café, or are they to be found in the Red Rooster Burger Bar after shopping in the supermarket?

Making a living

Without attention to jobs and businesses, Maleny could have failed as a centre for self-reliant living, as many others did. To show us how the problem was tackled, Jill took us to the old butter factory, built of brick in the middle of the last century with that familiar corrugated iron roof you see everywhere in Oz. The factory closed down when dairy farming died out here; now it is home for Maleny Enterprise Network Association (MENA), where people are trained for work or helped in starting a business. Eight young entrepreneurs run their firms in the building; unemployed young people practise their writing skills in the youth magazine; others learn skills ranging from using computers and the Internet to the design and manufacture of singing kites.

Lea Harrison, a resident of twenty years standing, remembers the first co-operative store meeting. Fifty people turned up, of whom forty-five were registered as unemployed and were drawing benefit. 'At the most recent meeting last year (1995) there were still about fifty people and none was registered as unemployed. Most considered themselves self-employed.' She says with pride: 'The unemployment rate in the region is around twelve percent, but in this specific area it's less than three percent. Community self-help programmes through the co-operatives have done that.'

The farming community was spiralling downwards, Lea points out, until people began community-based initiatives which persuaded the government to show an interest. And the downward trend was reversed.

MENA's director is Sammi Ringer, a West Coast American who came to Maleny for a short while, loved the life and stayed for good. Her favourite MENA project is the marketing of bush tucker — Aboriginal dishes based on native plants. Three years after bush tucker was 'discovered' as a gourmet food, lemon myrtle rice, quandong pie and Macadamia muffins have become favourites in Sydney restaurants. The marketing scheme works, with government help and in collaboration with the Aboriginals who have cultural copyright. Sammi enthuses over the potential for export.

When we object that exporting food increases global trade instead of local economies, Sammi isn't impressed. 'World economies aren't going to go away. Maleny's co-operatives were never set up to make us self-sufficient; each one had a different purpose. I don't feel at this stage, with the make-up of the community here, we have the resources or the will to truly become a village.'

Sammi has no choice but to be realistic. MENA, having attracted state and federal funds, is now required to pay its way. Shortage of cash is chronic and Sammi and her staff often work too hard and are not exempt from the stress that goes with competitive business.

Still, Sammi finds that the Maleny lifestyle remains humane and gentle in harsh country. 'There tends to be a lot of feminists with sensible walking shoes, and the majority of co-ops have feminist women involved. The men notice it — they're either extremely uncomfortable or they blossom and find their sensitive side. It continually amazes me how many people come up to visit and within minutes have thought about changing their lives and coming to live here. There's a vibration. Maybe it's something about the Glasshouse Mountains, a very feminine influence.'

The four wise virgins

The strongest feminist is Jill Jordan but she doesn't talk about it. Jill lives five minutes' walk away from our 'bower' in Manduka, in what is known as a cow bails — originally a cow shed. Each stall makes one tiny room with a partition you can see over. A friendly clutter of books, pictures and papers but an absence of 'things'. Today she meets us wearing a blue teeshirt and mauve cotton trousers. 'Blue is my serene colour,' she says.

Jill has no bathroom; she washes outside (no hardship in a tropical summer) from a shower attached to a water tank. Chooks scratch around the outside compost toilet; she wants to get rid of them because they scratch up the veggies. Jill is splitting up with her current partner: the chooks are his; he will remove them when he leaves. Jill is sad about the break-up. 'I love him but love means letting go.' She is too busy to brood.

In Jill's kitchen, coiled up behind the stove, sleeping because it is not warm enough to slither about, lies her carpet snake. 'She's been here for years. I'm lucky to have one. She kills all the mice.' 'How do you know it's a she?' 'I know 'cos she's had babies. They've all gone off to find their own territories. Old farming people love a carpet snake in the house.' Neither of us takes up Jill's offer to pet the large striped reptile. Before we leave the snake has gone from behind the stove; we never saw it move.

Without Jill's enthusiasm and social skills many hopes of the settlers wouldn't have been realised. Even now, few dilemmas are resolved or arguments settled without some of her input. Because she spends three days a week working in a Brisbane government office, her four days in Maleny and Manduka are crowded with meetings.

Jill was lecturing in psychology in Brisbane, but wanted to drop out from a fast, competitive and consumer-orientated life. 'In 1970 I was very married — we and another couple bought a parcel of land outside Maleny really to get away from it all. That was Manduka. In fact we plummeted right back in, there was so much to do. My marriage broke up and the other two Manduka partners went overseas.

'I had an experience where I believe the land actually talked to me. It sounds a bit weird; but it actually happened.' Jill says this apologetically. It was something we heard several times: individuals are drawn to become stewards of a particular piece of land.

Jill felt 'guided' to start a community and she did it in 1977 with three other women; they became known as the Four Wise Virgins. 'More people joined us. Two of us were psychologists, very interested in interpersonal relationships, so for the first eighteen months we did a lot of group work together.' Jill believes that what cemented the group was a fight with the local council over building a dam in the area. 'We were fortunate in having a seasoned campaigner from Tasmania who taught us how to manage non-violent action group techniques. That really heightened our feelings of togetherness and taught us about equity and decision making and conflict resolution which has stood us in good stead in the development of Manduka which is probably one of the most stable communities that I've come across and one of the happiest.'

In her view, the time is ripe for more communal living. 'The economic system isn't catering for people in the way that it did, and people see its effects in environmental degradation; they're looking for a new way. Back in the seventies only the so-called hippies tried; now a broad range of people, young and older, are involved.'

Jill thinks the world's money system could easily crash. 'Even conservative professors of economics are starting to realise there are vast cracks in the system. The alternatives we are developing now are going to cushion some of the problems that will arise out of the destabilisation when it comes. I guess we're like the women and children of the movement that averted the nuclear holocaust. That was a cry for survival from the people. We're probably the economic cry for survival of human beings.'

Paying in bunyas

Mindful of our own survival, we have been careful with our Australian dollars and we are sorry we never get a chance to pay in bunyas — the alternative currency here, named after a local nut. One person in ten is a member of the Local Exchange Trading System. This was Australia's first LETS scheme; today there are scores, and many hundreds elsewhere (see Chapter 10). About half the 900 members of the Maleny LETS are active traders.

Alternative money makes people feel richer because they can afford goods and services that are too costly in dollars. Gail Butson, assistant manager at the food co-operative, works in another shop once a week, where she is paid in bunyas. She has painted a surgery, scrubbed someone's wall and done gardening for bunyas. In return she gets regular shiatsu, and her children have drama and dancing classes — luxuries she couldn't otherwise afford.

The joining fee is A\$15 (real dollars), plus an annual A\$5. Desirée, the volunteer who keeps the accounts, is paid ten bunyas an hour for fifty hours. Sammi Ringer thinks the system works best in communities like Maleny 'with a high intellectual base and a high degree of self-induced poverty. People here can maintain things, build a retaining wall, have their windows cleaned, things like that. The system really works; currencies are interchangeable and I can go down to New South Wales and use my bunyas.'

A friendly bank

Nobody can live on bunyas alone: a sympathetic bank is needed to lend hard dollars. Maleny settlers started a credit union almost as soon as they arrived and now, for many, the CU is the most important advantage of being here. Its loans enable people to buy land, build houses and start businesses. Kinder than ordinary banks, the credit union gives people a credit rating they can later use in banks, lends to people who are on benefit, allocates five percent of its funds to community development and refuses to lend money to anything that might damage the environment.

The CU, in an old wooden house on Main Street with a deep overhanging roof, is the most friendly-seeming bank imaginable. Local artists exhibit on what were once the living room walls. A coffee machine bubbles, and business is done sitting in padded deckchairs on the shaded veranda.

Jill remembers how this movement reached Maleny. The desire for more localised banking fitted in with the seventies ethical investment movement which itself grew out of the sixties, from Ralph Nader's consumer boycott in the USA, and the discovery of consumer power. 'People in the USA realised that money is just another commodity and that just as people who bank with big corporations have a lot of power, we too can determine where institutions spend their money. We took it to a general meeting to start our own bank to stop the drain of capital out of this declining rural area. The co-op members said "great idea" so we started the CU in 1984.'

Critics called it the hippie bank when it started up. 'People wouldn't invest there, they thought we'd take their money and run away to South America.' Now, a third of all the people living in the bioregion are members — including many mainstream people as well as the active supporters of the Maleny movement.

Waste Busters

Anyone getting started in Maleny and wanting to build a house cheaply goes to Waste Busters, the recycling co-operative. People come here to drop rubbish, chat, and find what useful things they can salvage, from building materials to a paperback book or a bundle of garden poles. It's typical of how Malenyites manage civic life that visiting a rubbish dump also doubles as a fun outing.

Gaby Luft set it up. She had travelled round Australia and New Zealand to find examples worth imitating. First she takes us to the corner for collecting white office paper, cardboard and newspapers. Two compactors process plastic milk cartons. Under a lean-to, second-hand articles like furniture, clothes, shoes, toys, beds, mattresses are collected and stored. Piles of second-hand books and magazines are sold. Tins of half-used paint (take what you need for free) wait for cash-strapped decorators. Anything left over for more than a week goes to charities. A shredder turns your garden wastes into mulch for sale to nurseries and private gardeners.

On one heap people dump timber and other people rummage through and pull off usable pieces. A regular customer is Mandy from Manduka who is building her new house entirely from recycled materials. The metal pile almost topples with the weight of old washing machines, toilet bowls, car bodies and rolls of fencing wire and posts.

Gaby and two helpers are paid by the co-operative. Other helpers are volunteers: they get first choice of whatever comes into the shop, free of charge. Waste Busters' main income comes from the local council which pays the co-operative to manage this tip for three days of every week. Surplus revenue from processing glass goes into wages and into maintaining equipment. 'We are just breaking even: it's a day-to-day challenge,' Gaby says. Instead of employing two full-time workers, she prefers to create small part-time jobs. Eighteen people, including Gaby herself, earn A$30 a shift.

The site is treeless and glaring and we're glad to rest in the shade of the second-hand store where a naked doll hangs incongruously by one arm above a collection of used electrical goods.

The chief hippie-bater

The longer we stay in Maleny, the more we find the co-operative spirit under pressure; the town is too attractive for its own good. Prosperous immigrants, often without commitment to the values of the earlier settlers, are arriving from the cities seeking land, peace, clean air and the Maleny conviviality. There has been a political shift to the right. Jill Jordan was a district councillor for two years until she lost the last election. The new mood has encouraged the old guard of farmers and landowners to speak out more boldly against cultural changes brought in by 'the hippies'. These farmers have their own agenda: they want to be rewarded for looking after the unspoiled fields which make Maleny so attractive. This leaves the pioneers of Jill Jordan's generation fighting on two fronts: against those who were here before them and those who came after.

Greg Newton is a spokesman for the die-hard, right-wing malcontents. We rang him up apprehensively, expecting a brush-off, but he invited us for lunch. Greg keeps one of the few remaining dairy farms, with two hundred head of dairy cattle on 160 hectares; the paddocks stretch around his house, denuded of trees. He was born here, son of a dairy farmer, but now he feels alienated in his own town. 'It is more cosmopolitan, more mixed; you've got to be far more tolerant to live here now with these long-haired types, women walking about in bare feet without bras, the unwashed kids at school. Those sort of things get up my nose a bit. Jill Jordan's movement is a very one-eyed movement in my book: they're out to promote their own lifestyle first.'

Greg is performing: he has long been cast in the role of chief hippie-baiter and routinely attacks what he insists on calling 'alternate people'. We protest mildly that we've been staying at Manduka where most people have a job, a house which they've built and which they own, and a car, and they don't go around naked, so why call them hippies? Greg replies that he is nearly fifty: 'In my mind they're still the long-hairdo hippies that I grew up with in the sixties. I know a lot of 'em — they're intelligent people but they're very much into picking up as much free public money as they can get hold of.'

His wife, Joyce, chips in with: 'Yeah, they want the by-laws changed so they can put up a poorer style of house than this council approves of. They want school with no rules — the kids will make the rules for God's sake!' The Newtons have sent their three sons to boarding school away from such pernicious influences.

Greg's real attitude is ambiguous. He unwarily admits that hippies can be clever — even useful. 'Had to wear these damn glasses and then heard about this hippie eye doctor in Crystal Waters. She told me eyes need exercise just like any other muscle and taught me how. Now I don't need glasses at all.' And he cites with approval the example of permaculture. 'It's a brilliant thing, the way to go. The hippies have got all the lateral thinking — but it's we who are going to have to carry it out.' Greg is the first mainstream farmer we meet on our travels who will freely admit that the permaculturists (see Chapter 7) and the organic farmers (see Chapters 5 and 6) are proposing a healthier form of agriculture. But then he reverts, trotting out the argument that organic agriculture can't feed the population and that its prices are too high.

Lunch was sliced white bread, processed cheese and tinned peaches, a come-down after our breakfasts of yoghurt and organic mangoes in Manduka. Greg and Joyce posed for a photo outside their modern bungalow in front of a full-size flagpole flying the Australian flag.

The political lurch to the right becomes evident when a newspaper leaks the council's confidential plan to abolish its environment department by merging it with planning and development. The council claim the plan will save money; the environmentalists claim it is a political move to curb their influence. The plan is to come before the council on Thursday. Many protesters want to attend. Jill lends us her car and we drive fifty kilometres down to the coast to the administrative capital at Caloundra. This is the Gold Coast, expanding fast and prospering, tearing down trees for new pavements and more new concrete apartments. The main street is lined with fast-food outlets. The council building is a wedge-shaped block of concrete and plate glass painted pistachio green; no trees shade it from the glare and the interior is fully air-conditioned, although the climate is equable nine months of the year. The pro-environmentalists, about one hundred, wear green bows in their lapels. We wear one, too. Selected spokespersons are given five minutes each. Despite impassioned pleas from consumer groups, the council agrees to go ahead with its plan.

The gentle art of consensus

Back at Manduka that evening, we sat with Jill Jordan's friends round a fire, outside her cow-bails. The wine was good; Jill was philosophical. 'Politics moves in swings, there's a struggle and forces of darkness take over again. It will swing back. Most of those councillors come from the urban strip on the coast and don't realise the economic benefits that come to the region from the activities that go on up here, but the people in charge of development know. The conservative parties are basically all about control and we're all about devolution of power and people's empowerment.'

People's empowerment — it's a stirring phrase, hard to define. We understand it means having a control of your environment, striking a balance between individual freedom and the common good. People living in Manduka feel they have achieved this in their home environment, and now they are called upon to defend it.

We saw empowerment in action at Manduka, at the monthly meeting in a side room attached to the old barn. It showed us how consensus works. Decision-making by consensus instead of by a majority vote which leaves a minority disgruntled is a difficult, delicate process for any group. The practice is widely accepted and adopted in communities we visited. When it fails, it leads to enormous rifts; when it succeeds it leaves everyone feeling supported.

Battered easy chairs, a noticeboard, an old television in one corner — nine members out of a possible fourteen attend. Everyone begins by saying how they feel. Jill admits to having a difficult month, with her partner leaving. 'I've had incredible ups and downs, crying, laughing and all over the show. It's only the thirteenth of January and everything seems to be in full flight.' Her sister Annie says much the same. Annie comes face-to-face with Howard, the partner from whom she's just separated. There are no bad vibrations. Howard and Annie are both diffident about expressing emotions and apparently shy, yet they have lived together for over a dozen years and have worked out ways of consensus where an apparent simplicity conceals a complex and worked-over process.

A discussion on buying a communal washing machine. Problem: how to pay for it? Some people have more income than others. Who will pay for the electricity? They decide that Gary will make further enquiries into the detailed economics.

Bob, the oldest member, raises the question of his death. He is seventy-six and wants to be buried at Frog's Hollow. Having obtained council permission, he now suggests the members should designate a burial site. Consensus is reached immediately: Yes. Bob then makes no apology for raising something even more serious. 'Six years ago I had a heart attack at ten o'clock at night. Can I be evacuated from here in an emergency?' Everyone assures Bob that he can ring them at any hour of the day or night.

The major part of the meeting is concerned with a situation where good will and ideology cannot prevent conflict and the clash of wills. At issue is a loan that Manduka Co-operative has made to a housing trust in Maleny. The trust members living in the house want to split up but the loan has not been paid off. Manduka members discuss various solutions and permutations for two hours. The debate ebbs and flows; positions are reiterated several times. Gradually, like tide washing over sand, a consensus emerges. At the end Jill asks, 'Are you comfortable with that, Gary?' He nods.

The meeting closes with everyone knowing what they are going to do for the morrow's communal work session. It has taken four hours. The same decisions could have been taken in a quarter of that time but everyone has had their say, tempers have not risen nor have personal animosities surfaced. It wasn't at all like the committee meetings that we are familiar with, when someone, usually a male, takes up a position and holds on to it with the tenacity of a hungry rat. Afterwards Mandy remarked: 'You think that looks easy. We have worked on it for years.'

A family when you are old

After the meeting Bob Taylor asks us to his humpy (a hut in the Aboriginal style) for tea. He lives up the hill from Annie's house behind two closed gates because he keeps two retired horses in his paddocks. Bob tips ants out of the biscuit tin onto his kitchen table and offers ginger biscuits. He endures a variety of complaints including a rare cattle disease from his days as a stockman. He walks with crutches because he smashed up a knee in a motorbike accident when he was over seventy.

A self-conscious stereotype of the crusty old man, Bob hides an acute perception and deep affection for his friends. A genius with machines and engines, he's busy repairing a fifty year old water pump he found buried at one end of the property. People here take recycling seriously.

Bob has something of the Australian Wild West which suits living lightly. At eleven, he left home, worked down the mines and on odd wandering jobs, spent some of his youth 'thieving and fighting, living on one side of a tiny apple bush and a vixen was living on the other side.' In 1940 he joined the army, then went to agricultural college. Like us, he came here because he met Jill Jordan. 'I was in the Humanist Association — real people who believe in reality — and Jill came to give us a lecture on Buddhism. I've always been more than a half-Buddhist. We kept in touch. When I became too bloody ill, about 1980, I came up here.'

Kitchen chairs are stacked as a makeshift barrier across the porch, to stop the two horses barging into the kitchen for biscuits. Bob's wife lives in Brisbane where she manages a block of apartments but rarely visits because she doesn't like the country. 'I am too alone up here. It's a pity. Marriage doesn't suit a man in his full vigour but I ought to be married now.' His personal life has had more than its share of tragedy. His daughter was stabbed to death when she tried to help an old lady in a city mugging incident and one son died in a truck collision.

Two surviving children are grown up and visit as rarely as his wife. Yet Bob feels looked after at Manduka which he thinks of as a commune. 'Although they don't call it that, we are communards, a community of like-minded people. Similar to the army, certain set rules, certain social contracts. When there are jobs to do it's all sweet, no drama; we're all good mates. This is my family. There's nothing I lack for. I'm independent, I have good company, can go anywhere. Just enough money to satisfy myself. My wants are simple. Here it's a sharing organisation; we share time, tools, ideas. I am not in debt here, except that I have loyalty. I am so busy you could not believe it.'

Building her own house

Up at the highest point of Manduka, Mandy Wilson is building herself a new house. Like a stage set with three walls completed, it faces the humpy she lives in at present. A variety of trees, gums, native ginger, palms and ferns surround her dwelling with lush green; shells and stones decorate small flower beds of exotic plants. We arrived to find her asleep — she'd been dancing until five that morning.

Not until we all have mugs of tea in our hands does she explain how she fits into the Maleny and Manduka story. 'I'd say we came from a working-class Sydney background but my parents became well-to-do. They typify the Oz dream, a house, two kids, going to the beach. I'm the eldest. I left home fairly young and started college in Tasmania. Although I never finished, I made my living as a designer.' Mandy's bold and brightly coloured collages and pictures enliven her uncluttered kitchen.

Mandy moved to Maleny at the same time as Jill Jordan and they became founder members of Manduka. 'In the early days it was very utopian; you put in what you could afford, some people put in only a thousand or two, some put in ten thousand, some put in nothing. The first year I was so poor I lived on pumpkins. Four women were the original partners — Jill and Azita, Jan Tilden and me — the Four Wise Virgins. I was only twenty-two but I was ready to settle down.'

The four virgins have been unlucky and lucky. First the local authorities took away a fifth of their most precious land down by the water, flooding their swimming hole, to build a new reservoir. When the community received substantial compensation for the flooding, they were able to pay off their mortgage. It's the remainder of this money that enables the co-operative to support community projects like the housing trust that was argued about in the meeting. Mandy agrees with Jill that their fight against the dam formed the members into a team, and the solidarity has remained.

This communal lifestyle demands a massive commitment of trust, says Mandy. 'We did a lot of work consciously in the early days to bring together a group cohesion. Jill's energy was very strong. Even today some issues are still being worked out, but there is that unconditional love, that commitment to each other, to resolving things whether it takes ten years or it might just take five minutes. Now I feel that these people are my family. I don't make a decision like "I'm going to build over there." There's always that consideration of other people. It's not a burden. I don't feel I own anything here except my garden and the orchard area.'

Unlike Bob, being single doesn't bother her; she has support from the people around. She waved an arm towards a rooftop visible above a screen of trees. 'There's Gary's house. I haven't had children of my own so I feel that his girls, Zoe and Amy, are like my own. I had so much to do with them when they were growing up.'

Mandy might live here for the indefinite future, but then again, she might not. 'I don't want to be still here when we get Sunday drivers coming up. You have got to go west to meet real people. I've developed a bit of a hermit's attitude. I can live on less money out in the bush in the middle of Oz. No cheese, just garlic, onions, potatoes fish and bush tucker. Most of the day you spend getting your food and then you just sit under a tree. Great.' In the bush, Mandy would support herself as a designer and local historian of aborigines.

Mandy repairs her tractor.

At the back of her mind is the thought that society could break down in economic chaos and/or ecological disaster following global warming. 'There will be cyclones and general chaos, economic and physical breakdown, vast numbers of unemployed. Young adults in Australia have been brought up on utopian dreams: the time for that is over. They now need to be taught survival skills. It's one reason why we have to have communities: you won't be able to survive on your own.'

Up to now she has supported herself as a computer-based designer. She is a member of the major co-operatives in the town. Like others, Mandy is aware that Maleny is changing. 'When I first arrived here, I was on my motor-bike — stony-broke. An old guy selling raffle tickets said: "You look like you need some money. I'll lend you twenty dollars." He didn't know me from a bar of soap, although he knew where I was staying and who with. That's gone now.' She recognises that the influx of money from recently arrived, rich incomers, drawn here because of Maleny's beauty and the strength of its community, puts these amenities into jeopardy.

Peace of Green

We enjoyed Maleny's amenities — strolling down Main Street — taking a coffee in the Up Front café and then dropping in to Peace of Green to browse in the book and craft shop. The sort of shop which elsewhere is a commercial enterprise crammed with over-priced tacky goods, served here as a showcase for local artisans and sold its products at reasonable prices. Having no middle-man, tee-shirts hand-painted with local birds cost the same as the mass-produced article.

Jill Morris, minding the shop with nothing New Age or hippie about her, is the guiding force behind Peace of Green. She is an author, farmer, teacher and business woman, switching easily from one role to another. The co-operative unites twenty-one craftspeople, all working in different art forms — leather, a potter, a glassblower, painters. 'They share a similar outlook and push one another as artists,' Jill says. 'We aren't actually a co-op in the legal sense, really lessees in common, retaining autonomy over our businesses. We have much more freedom to fly than in normal co-ops.'

When she came to the area as a child, Jill Morris fell in love with the green hills. After a successful career in the big city she had wanted a farm life and bought thirty hectares with a rustic cabin. In addition she bought an adjoining two hectares of rainforest.

'I came here for the solitude and in one way I regret all the growth we've seen, but there you are — that's what has made Peace of Green happen. Maleny is still a very safe town. You can walk here at night. The safety is

because people care about one another. My feeling is that that attitude has been engendered by the co-operatives.'

Jill believes the traditional co-operatives have served their most useful purpose and that new, looser forms of company ownership may blend better with the future. Meanwhile, the co-operative spirit is alive in Maleny despite the influx of less committed newcomers, but hard work is involved. 'For the last year I've been saying to people: we go to meetings six nights a week. We have to because our backs are to the wall. You have to keep delivering messages to people and pulling out of the newcomers the people who are going to help. And that's paying off: among that large influx there are some absolute gems.'

A new kind of settler

One of the 'gems' is Michael Berry — the sort of downshifter we met in North America (see Chapter 1). Tall and dapper, suave and charming, he represents a type who are coming into Maleny — successful mainstream professionals moving here for a better quality of life even though, going free-lance, they may have to accept less money. It's easy to see why incomers are so attracted to the town — its green hills remind us of an exuberance of much of south-east England with remnant rainforest standing in for oak and beech.

Michael used to be a producer for Australian television, now he is president of the Maleny Residents' Association, working to preserve the district from unwholesome development. He denies having political ambitions in the council. His critics complain that he means to set up a motel on his thirty-hectare property; he says he wants to build artists' studios.

How sceptical should we be of people who oppose development once they have bought their own properties? Michael argues: 'I'm not against economic growth, it must be appropriate and in appropriate places.'

Can the co-operatives survive?

Maleny co-operatives have been through many vicissitudes. Drinking cold beer under the striped parasol outside the Up Front café, we had an ideal opportunity to discuss co-operative ideals with Dixon Hemmer. He is a young man who has bruised his ideals after serving part-time at the café during its growing pains. At twenty-three, he's become knowledgeable about right and wrong ways of co-operating.

'People who join a co-operative think that co-operation means getting your own way. They've dropped out of mainstream because they didn't want to be told what to do. From working here I could see how wars started — people full of their own righteousness. I studied Akkido which teaches that right-eousness in any form will lead to unhappiness.'

The Up Front café and club ran at a loss. Debts mounted, creditors pressed. The directors stated that the club was not viable. Dixon felt personally involved. 'I had taken on a work load way beyond my wages or my responsi-bilities or skills. The club became my baby. The staff who had kept it open were hurt but after a couple of weeks turmoil, a competent manager bull-dozed his way through the mess without much delegation. He cooked, he washed up, he laid tiles. He took on a proper role of leadership. The problem was solved in that way.'

A co-operative structure has no inherent value, Dixon concluded. 'It's no more ethical than a multinational company. The ethics comes from the people who are in it. A co-op is just an empowering opportunity.'

Co-operatives may have passed their sell-by date and new formulas may be needed. Meg Barrat, who edits the weekly newspaper, *The Range News*, has thought carefully about the future. She came here as a teacher eighteen years ago. She worked hard in the women's co-operative, now defunct. She now considers that only small residential co-ops like Manduka are likely to survive. 'The culture of the urban co-operatives is threatened, land is becoming too scarce, prices are escalating. A lot of the new people coming are just retirees with no commitment to the alternative thing. There was a time when you could walk down the main street and you would know almost everyone, which is definitely not the case any more. New people are setting up little businesses, taking advantage of the lifestyle. It's not necessarily alternative, a lifestyle of rural living and community and a safe place for children, etc. A lot of quite rich people too, buying the houses with the view over the Glasshouse Mountains. Still, the intellectual commitment to alternatives persists.

'Maleny is on the cusp — growing so quickly that suddenly you feel that influx. You feel that also in the local economy; more jobs are created by this wave of well-to-do ex-urbanites and retirees.'

The man who makes the loos of the future

And yet, we found someone who manages a prosperous business while living lightly and convivially. Dean Cameron makes a compost toilet known as a Dowmus (Domestic Organic Waste Management and Utilisation System), an advanced design which is exported throughout the world. Dean lives, like Jill Jordan, in a community within a community at the edge of town.

On a forty-hectare site six families have built their homes, created small-scale businesses and were still left with twelve hectares to set aside for conservation and recreation. The site is loud with bird song. The steel shed where Dean assembles his compost toilets and keeps a small office is almost completely overgrown by rainforest trees.

Dean Cameron and his Dowmus toilet.

Dean and his family used the credit union to finance their block of land. The site is owned by the 'body corporate' which provides the services which the council does not. Most Australian housing co-operatives are owned by this kind of body which allows each member to sell out at will.

Few features of modern living are as wasteful as our ceramic toilets flushing away 18 litres of highly purified water into a sewage system every time we have a pee. Compost which should be returned to the land is abandoned into seas and rivers. Designing a better composting loo was a hobby that turned into a life's work for Dean, its main inventor.

He has designed a single indoor system into which all the waste products go. You put food scraps, paper and lots of other intractable items into the unit. An ecosystem is contained in a tank of four cubic metres, which degrades all that material very slowly, using worms, fungi and a whole rage of organisms and microbes. The benefit is that you get very thorough breakdown and odourless operation; it's not like a septic tank and far superior to a flush toilet. The toilet sits on a flared, glazed ceramic pedestal with a wide opening. The air is drawn in and circulated by a small fan. What a user sees is the pedestal.

Dean's toilets cost A\$2705 to set up — about twenty-five percent more than a conventional system. Not a huge price for knowing that you have stopped polluting the seas, rivers and waterways of your home region. We were disappointed, however, to learn that an average family of four, after two years of putting all their non-toxic waste down the Dowmus, will be rewarded with only one or two bucketsful of rotted compost every couple of months. This is because most of the newspaper is degraded into CO_2 and water. Dean explained: 'What you're getting at the end is the resource part of the organic waste. You haven't lost any nutrients.'

Dean Cameron makes a living in an environment he and his friends have chosen. Such housing co-operatives work when they are not too large for face-to-face decision-making. Yet the co-operative method, so essential a part of Maleny's success, needs to adapt to a new world of harsher competition and greater pressure from newcomers with different lifestyles.

Saving Maleny's soul

If Maleny is to continue as a vibrant living community, a good proportion of its young people must want and be able to stay. Gary, one of the members at Manduka, told us his daughter Zoe wouldn't remain. He thought that was healthy: in a good community the members have formed a non-biological family and Zoe could go into the world and found her own. Dixon Hemmer, who was so critical of the food co-op, intends to settle in Maleny with his young wife when he has completed a degree at Brisbane University.

Meg Barrat's daughter Amy, a twenty-year-old with an infectious grin and enthusiasm to match, is studying English Literature at Brisbane University. 'Growing up here taught me about organising, and about people doing things rather than asking the government. It means you look for different ideas and methods of organising. It's true that Maleny's a really small town and you do have all this pettiness and it's a bit scary, but the co-op scene has added a lot in terms of hope, because I have more hope than lots of young people. It sounds a cliché but I feel more powerful, I can organise things happening rather than waiting for someone else to do them. I'll come back.' She intends to go part-time so that she can work in women's support groups.

If Maleny is to keep its soul, it must first be saved from take-over by developers who want to break up the remaining old farms into lots and sell them to affluent incomers from the cities. For this purpose Barbara Corbett, a feisty campaigner of many years standing, was asked to set up the Maleny Green Hills Trust Fund to stop uncontrolled subdivision of farmlands for development. The fund buys parcels of land as they become available and then decides how the land is used in a way that is most sympathetic to the preservation of the green hills. Small selected areas are made available for residential purposes, with the large balance of land remaining intact.

Barbara is in her seventies, her third husband a decade or so younger. She wears her wealth, her weight and her age lightly. The couple live in a farmhouse with a palm-lined swimming pool overlooking their grazing pastures for a hundred-strong herd of organically raised beef cattle. The 350-hectare hill behind the house is being allowed to regenerate naturally as subtropical rainforest. Scorning newcomers who want to mow acres of lawn with tractors, she says, 'You know what mows the green hills? It's cows that poo and piss and fertilise the grass.' Barbara exudes a supreme confidence that the trust will raise enough funds and the hills will not be developed.

Maleny hasn't become a permanent utopia but the co-operative life we saw there was rooted in the pioneering tradition that Australia shares with the USA. Mandy in Manduka, repairing a tractor and building her own house, Jill Jordan, a networker and social builder, both live with and on the land. This lifestyle, coming into competition and confrontation with the aggressively expansionist mainstream, appears to be holding its own.

We grew to love Maleny, where folk are open to each other and to strangers, and they're good talkers. On our second Friday evening at the weekly film club we watched the sort of art film you'd expect to have to go to Brisbane to see. Before the performance everyone had a gossipy supper in the hall. We brought in our own wine. After we'd eaten we helped remove the tables and put out the chairs for the performance.

Jill Jordan's Maleny exists: it is not a figment of her imagination. It exists in the real world, in the global economy, among red-necked farmers fearful for their futures and jealous and disapproving of newcomers and their lifestyles and their experiments. The co-operatives are impressive in their range and scope: their very success poses problems of management competition, staffing, financing, as the pressures of Australian development touch them too,. The credit union, its profit margin too small, is in danger as the big banks squeeze its business. The co-operatives may not survive in their present form. But Maleny has enough people behind its ventures, enough support that stretches far out of the town into villages and into other towns, where alternative people consider Maleny their centre, to continue along a similar route. And if the worst comes, restless rebels like Mandy will move somewhere else. Australia has the advantage over so much of the rest of the world that in spite of its fragile eco-system, it has so much space.

We have been staying in Manduka over two weeks and we have only just found the correct route through the thorn bushes to the dammed-up Platypus Pool. The old swimming hole was submerged when the Manduka people lost their appeal against the Barroom Dam. They don't like swimming in the pool because it is too sad for them. Since we have never known it before, we don't mind. Concentric rings of drowned trees stick up bare black arms. The water is warm, the silence complete. We can swim down the creek as far as the dam if we want. We swim for an hour in the flooded waterhole, hoping we might see a koala. We don't, but we hear kookaburras and cicadas. On our return to the house, Gary comes for a beer. He is late, he says, because a green tree snake was coiled around his shower head, ogling him while he showered. 'They are more aggressive than carpet snakes. They'll go for you. Just step out of the way.'

12

Living better in Japan

●●●●●●●●●●●●●●●●●●●●●●●●●●●●●●●●●●●●●●●

Japan entered the global economy later, and with even more enthusiasm, than the other big players. Only a century ago the country was cut off from the world; even fifty years ago it was still largely self-sufficient in food. Classical Japan provided a model in sustainable living because with a stable population it grew its own food and recycled its wastes. In the nineteenth century the city of Kyoto could boast over a million citizens and bring its food from the surrounding region. People lived for centuries on a healthy diet of vegetables, fish and rice, not only because they were Buddhist but also because their ecology demanded it. Soya bean, the basic ingredient of miso (soya bean paste), tofu and other staple foods provide more protein per hectare than any comparable animal-based agriculture.

After the second world war, Japan lurched willingly to the other extreme. In the last thirty years food self-sufficiency has dropped from seventy-five percent in money terms to thirty percent and today Japan's agricultural trade deficit is the highest in the world. The result was unimagined wealth. But playing the global game was not rooted in Japan's culture. There are costs attached: many people work harder, and travel longer to work, than is compatible with a good quality of life; family life has deteriorated, cities are inhumanly large, congested and polluted while villages have been depopulated. Unregulated industrialisation led to a succession of environmental and public health disasters like the poisoning of fish with mercury which caused 'Minimata disease', named after the district where it first occurred.

Now, at the turn of the new century, the continued advance of the global economy is adding new pressures and posing new questions: can Japan still afford the cosy corporate tradition which keeps almost every man (women are another matter) employed for their whole working lives? Can the economy face the rivalry of its imitators? Is the financial system sound?

We went to Japan to experience some of the grassroots reactions to its headlong economic expansion. Hundreds of protest movements on consumer and environmental problems arose and still flourish.

Our main purpose was to explore the Seikatsu Club Co-operative Union, which started as a housewives' movement in Tokyo and has become a nation-wide organisation to promote healthier food, simpler living and the empowerment of women. Visiting these idealistic and practical women led us further down the food chain to a movement for organic growers who want to revive an old system of community-supported farms, independent of the market, known as *teikei*. This journey brought us into contact with a more extreme solution to the problems of consumer capitalism — far too extreme for most of us: the Yamagishi collective farms whose members work for no money and depend on their community for all their wants from the communal crèche to collective grave. Finally we were guests in a depopulated mountain village where urban people were moving in, hoping to revive the village while returning to a more natural way of living.

Tokyo

Tokyo is cleaner, busier, uglier than London with few old buildings surviving and ranks of concrete glass-fronted monoliths. Its inhabitants are more elegant and more confident; men of all ages and occupations wear suits and ties, women office workers wear spotless white blouses and street cleaners wear white gloves. Politeness and formality remain part of daily life; people bow to one another and the depth of a bow measures the degree of deference or respect. The economic boom of the seventies has slowed but even so, society is richer than in Europe. You see no street sellers, hawkers or beggars. A handful of homeless people who congregate in the passages under Shinjuku train station live in cardboard boxes furnished with clean sleeping mats and beach-style furniture.

Yet the city is implacable in a way that London and New York are not: there seems no escape from it; there are very few green spaces, few trees and few people with time to stop; it takes hours in any direction, by any mode of terrestrial transport, to get out of the city. Even important businessmen have to use the overcrowded trains because they are faster than cars.

If the Japanese pay a price for their affluence they rarely complain. In the rush hour our train stopped on a bridge, packed with people momentarily stranded. They showed no impatience, no distress. In Tokyo, as in other mega-cities, people accept discomfort as a way of life. But here they are rich: the stalled train is air-conditioned, as are the offices the passengers are headed for, their homes are clean and cool and their refrigerators well-stocked. Against the car pollution and against excessive pollen counts many protect themselves with gauze mouth and nose masks.

Japan has pulled ahead of Europe in its shiny modernisation and its acceptance of global trends and consumer values. Every district has its *pachinko* parlours with their fruit machines and they are always busy with eager gamblers. The business culture is alive and well. Most students we spoke to gave as their ambition to land a corporation job. The idea of working for the same company all your life is still current, although it is a luxury in the global economy and is therefore under threat.

Civic values have not been extinguished in Japan: the streets are cleaner and safer than ours. We saw kids aged six wearing peaked caps and military-style school uniforms with braided epaulettes, train-travelling to and from school unaccompanied, their satchels on their backs, their hands folded in their laps. Even in the overcrowded city trains people do not jostle you. Domestic life still has attention to detail and a delicate sense of ceremony in which the visitor is taken up into a complex web of human and family ties.

However, hidden under Tokyo's prosperity lie many social and environmental stresses. It is not uncommon for the wage earner — a man nearly always — to leave home soon after dawn and return in the dark. Tokyo is indeed endless: twenty-seven cities in 5700 square kilometres in a vast heavily polluted urban plain of 44,000 square kilometres. Economic growth has been bought at a price that a sizeable minority of Japanese are acutely aware of. There are 1500 citizen groups ranging in size from a few dozen members to tens of thousands. They are interested in safer food, safeguards for the environment, preservation of community values, revitalising depopulated villages. It was with these concerned citizens that we spent our month in Japan. Without the warm hospitality of our Japanese hosts we couldn't have managed the stay there; the yen is so strong that prices are astronomical for foreigners.

Seikatsu means 'way of living'

In Japan's full-scale rush into the global economy during the sixties, trainloads of farmers were leaving the land to find city jobs. The food they had grown was being replaced by imports — and quality often suffered. To bolster suppliers' profits, milk was mixed with dehydrated foreign additives, without precise labelling.

Four women in the Setagaya district decided to take action against the costly, adulterated milk. They formed a group to buy pure milk at fair prices. The idea caught on. Soon 200 families were involved and in 1968 they founded a consumers' co-operative with 1000 members. The women branched out from milk into vegetables, fruit, meat and natural soap, free of artificial detergents. They bought produce directly from farmers to bypass a cumbersome distribution system they felt was exploiting them. The women

PRINCIPLES OF THE SEIKATSU CLUB CO-OPERATIVE

·   Create autonomous communities for collective purchase, to escape control by the state or by commercial corporations.

·   Create a new life-style to protect health and the environment, replacing passive and resource-wasteful life-styles based on commercialism.

·   Encourage fair trade because prosperity based on the sacrifice of other people, in and outside of the country, is unacceptable.

·   Create viable alternatives to enable women, who are the majority of members, to win independence and rise above the subordinate positions to which our industrialised society relegates them.

visited farms, discussed what they wanted grown, assured farmers of a secure market and agreed prices — an arrangement which evolved into the *teikei* system which we describe later. That was the start of the Seikatsu Consumers' Club Co-operative, which has become a formidable commercial and political enterprise serving over 230,000 households with reliable food. In 1986 the club launched a campaign aimed at the whole of Japan, with the slogan 'From Collective Buying to All of Life'.

Seikatsu means 'way of living' or 'lifestyle,' and the club promotes healthier food, simpler living and self-help groups. When buying its produce, the club demands guarantees that minimal use is made of chemical fertilisers and insecticides — its rice suppliers can apply pesticide three times in a season instead of the customary thirty. In its most radical step, the club has organised worker collectives enabling women to work autonomously, part-time and near their homes, in occupations they regard as socially useful. The collectives operate restaurants, bakeries, delivery systems, care for the elderly, tailoring and recycling services.

Seikatsu Club women

Only five of the 270 worker collectives include men. Much of Seikatsu Club success is due to the role it has provided for its women members, an achievement remarkable in Japan, which has triumphantly accepted the values of the global economy, while at the same time keeping women in subservient roles.

We were invited to stay with Mitsuko Matsushima, who lives in Setagaya district and has been a member for twenty years. Even when our interpreters were not with us we communicated with Mitsuko with the aid of sketch pad and dictionary, and we formed what we hope will become a lasting friendship.

In her home she combines Westernization with a traditional Japanese lifestyle. The house is full of gadgets like an electrically warmed toilet seat with a built-in spray that washes your bum; the living area has Western-style furniture but the delicious meals are wholly Japanese and the sleeping rooms bare of furniture. (We slept on futons which are rolled up and put in a cupboard in the daytime.)

Mitsuko, in her late fifties, is leader of her local *han*. A *han* is the basic unit of Seikatsu Club organisation, with six to twelve members. Throughout our visit Mitsuko's friends dropped in or telephoned on club business; for her the club recreated a sense of community, the sort of community she grew up in. Once a month she gathers the eleven members of her *han* to plan their orders for the month ahead. The club's business is a social network of mutual aid and friendship, particularly valuable for the members whose husbands are absent all day and most of the evening.

> In the early days we would ask the farmers to plant radishes, promising to buy the lot. Two hundred radishes a day arrived at the delivery centres — Japanese radishes up to a half a metre long. We had to make people eat them. We had radishes coming out of our ears! We called it the radish wars. It took years to organise computerised monthly orders from every han.
> · Mitsuko Matsushima, han organiser.

For her household of three, Mitsuko buys eighty percent of her food from the Club. Twice a week she takes deliveries of groceries produced, selected and packed by the co-operative. Fleets of vans distribute the goods among the *han* members.

The women refer to themselves as *seikatsu-sha* — autonomously-living people — but Mitsuko admits she could not spend so much time on her club activities if her husband didn't work so hard. The *han* is her major interest now that her children are grown. Like many members she is both graduate and housewife. In Mitsuko's generation less than one percent of girls graduated, and usually, on marriage or after the first child, they left any job they may have had. This has created a pool of educated women, ready for co-operative action.

'For me, Seikatsu Club activities didn't begin with any great social ideas — but simply with soap,' Mitsuko said. 'My son Nobu had come up in rashes. Lots of other children had the same thing.' Impressed by the Seikatsu Club's campaign for natural soap, she joined.

Her husband Akihiro was sceptical. In the end the flavour of the pork won him round. Seikatsu Club's meat, eggs and poultry, although not in general fully organic, are reared in selected and supervised conditions. 'His stomach

---

THE GROWTH OF SEIKATSU CLUB

1965   *Tokyo housewives organise 200 women to buy milk. The Seikatsu Club makes its first collective purchase.*

1968   *Consumers' co-operative founded with 1,000 members. Han unit system adopted.*

1971   *First direct contract with a producer for eggs from a poultry farm in Kanagawa.*

1973   *Oil crisis causes goods shortage. Seikatsu Club develops its own brand products.*

1978   *Seikatsu Club expands to five prefectures. Central office in Tokyo.*

1979   *First Seikatsu Club member elected to local government.*

1985   *Seikatsu Club established in eight prefectures.*

1986   *Mutual Benefit Fund established.*

1990   *Seikatsu Club Co-operative Union established.*

1991   *143 Seikatsu Club Co-op Societies operating.*

1993   *218,256 Seikatsu Club members; 75 Seikatsu Club members in local government; 150 Workers Collectives.*

1996   *234,368 households in Seikatsu Club.*

---

persuaded him first and when he changed to our natural soap shampoo and his dandruff stopped, that settled it,' Mitsuko said.

Akihiro remains unconvinced about the Seikatsu Club's wider ambitions to effect change through participation in local politics. When Seikatsu Club business was discussed over dinner on the rare days when he was home for that meal, we found him adopting an attitude of benign neutrality. He works for a pharmaceutical firm in a typically Japanese routine — leaving before 7 a.m. and rarely getting back before 10 or 11 at night.

The Seikatsu Club has grown strong because it represents the values of women who have hitherto had no common voice. Kyoko Miyagi, a member of the board, said: 'The problem for men is that corporations have a strong grip on their minds. Women are able to think more freely, to discuss with each other without worrying if the wrong person hears. At home, women can talk and reach consensus, and it's from that impulse that Seikatsu was created.'

The pressures on women are shown in Tomoko Masunaga's story. Tomoko is a freelance translator and interpreter. When she joined the club ten years ago, her husband objected to her absence from home on Seikatsu Club business. A crisis came when she accompanied the club delegation to Sweden to receive the Right Livelihood Award — better known as the Alternative Nobel

Prize. 'There I met Swedish women working happily while men were looking after their kids. I learned something.'

Her marriage broke up. 'When I looked for a new home, I noticed a Seikatsu Club crate in the lobby of an apartment block, so I knew that was the place for me.' She now lives in one of Tokyo's new towns, greener and better planned, a ninety-minute ride into the city centre. She would like to see more men joining the club and absorbing its values. 'This country has made amazing progress in material things; now we need a spiritual element in our lives.'

Visiting Seikatsu Club enterprises in and around Tokyo we found a cheerful, energetic atmosphere amid a lot of hard work. A camaraderie has developed amongst these women. At Hoya City on Tokyo's outskirts, a women's collective operates a bakery — the sort of friendly small shop you dream of when you're pushing the trolley around the supermarket. It smells of the bread being baked in the kitchen behind. Although bread isn't traditional in Japan, its use has spread widely, especially for breakfast. The bread and cakes are made with artisanal methods, using natural yeast and flour produced without additives. They looked delicious and tasted so. Fortunately for the Japanese, British factory-produced bakery skills haven't been imported yet but there is a niche in the market if any enterprising entrepreneur wants to produce Bakewell tarts or iced buns.

The tax and pension schemes encourage women to work part-time or,

The women's collective bakery at Hoya City.

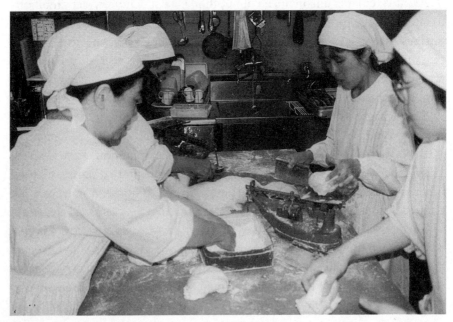

better still, stay at home. If a woman earns more than one million yen (£4700) a year, her husband's tax exemption for dependants ceases and both pay taxes without special allowances. Hence the attraction of part-time work. The women working in the bakery live locally and can earn a million yen a year working 1000 hours. All get the same pay. They started in 1987 with a thirteen million yen loan from the National Loan Company, paid it off and last year took another loan of five million yen for a new oven.

Shigeko Katoh, the bakery's 'representative' (their word for manager), told us the group agrees everything by consensus. At nearly sixty, she is thirty years older than her three co-workers. 'The younger women like this work; it's near their homes and has flexible hours which fit in with looking after children.' The bakery fell into financial difficulties a couple of years ago. Why? Because she took the staff for a holiday in Kyoto and they spent all the profits.

At Kashiwa city, just outside greater Tokyo, we visited a Seikatsu Club collective which operates a wholefood shop — another obvious success. Meat produced without hormones or antibiotics is for sale; tomatoes, mushrooms, shallots, lotus roots and dried radishes are all produced with little or no inorganic chemicals — and are cheaper than the local supermarket. Labels on each item show the name of the farmer who grew it and how it was grown and harvested. Junko Nakamuro, the assistant manager, told us that customers read these labels carefully because there has been so much negative publicity on chemically produced food.

The natural soap factory

Public unease about the abuse of chemicals — which has been responsible for some well-publicised health disasters — underlies much of Japan's environmental movement and its successes with projects like the natural soap movement. Synthetic detergents have been widely blamed for serious skin complaints and for polluting rivers and lakes.

A small soap factory in Chiba prefecture is operated by another workers collective. Tomoe Nakaoka, the manager, served us rice and fish in the main office, and the entire staff of eight joined us in a more informal and familiar atmosphere than is usual in Japan. One of the workers, a burly young man in his twenties, has graduated from a school for the mentally handicapped. Every carton of soap powder is decorated with his bright designs.

Tomoe's group had started by collecting spent oil from homes and public institutions and recycling it into soap. After three years of campaigning, volunteers had collected enough money to start the factory — which looks recycled itself, consisting of several sheds with corrugated iron roofs connected with walkways. Volunteers collect the spent oil in recycled hospital jerrycans, from households, restaurants, hospitals, shops and factories. For twenty litres of used oil, they pay 600 grams of natural soap. The factory adds caustic soda and soda ash to used oil to make a white powder soap which is sold in packages to co-operative and natural food shops. The product does have a lingering smell of old chips but we were assured its washing properties were splendid. The technical manager, tossing his gleaming locks, said he used natural soap on his head every day.

Accounting for ten percent of the market, natural soap is the most successful ecological story in Japan. The Seikatsu Club has its own factory in Saitama prefecture making both solid soap and shampoo. Portable mini-plants, which can make soap anywhere in a few hours, are used at 200 places in Japan and in Malaysia, the Philippines and Mongolia. Here in Chiba, the factory has official support. The prefecture pays a subsidy amounting to one third of costs and distributes the product to schools. Small packets of natural soap are given out by the municipality to young mothers.

Chiba is one of the many sprawling dormitory towns of greater Tokyo, an hour of train travel from downtown. It is greener than Tokyo but still heavily polluted by vehicles and factories. The district was developed in the sixties. New housing estates with insufficient drainage released sewage containing synthetic detergent into Teganuma Lake, which was once an inspiration for poets and painters, surrounded by woods, with gushing water from the mountains. Tomoe remembers swimming in it, but no children have splashed in its polluted waters for over thirty years. Tomoe took us to the polluted lake. On the shore, a concerned city council has built a smart information centre about the ecology of the lake. A pity the billions of yen were not used to clean up the water instead. You can watch videos and slides in air-conditioned comfort and never venture onto the narrow, degraded foreshore. Outside, a few metres from the bank, a pump sends a pretty spray over a group of bronze dancers in a miniature fountain — a symbolic attempt at purification.

Relax and enjoy

Seikatsu Club, in line with its motto 'all of life', has branched out from food distribution into welfare services that are neglected by society. The members are not priggish, or do-gooders, but they believe in co-operative values. At Hoya city, above a Seikatsu Club dry goods delivery centre, volunteers and paid staff run Japan's first day-care centre for old people. The you-you ('relax and enjoy') scheme's start-up costs were raised by Tokyo's 56,000 Seikatsu Club members through recycling and other fund raising, and each *You-You* centre has an operational grant from central and local government. The bulk of the caring at the Hoya centre is done by Seikatsu Club volunteers.

Japan, with the highest life expectancy in the world, (83.3 years for women and 77 for men) is worried about its ageing population. By the year 2020 more people will be retired than working. When we were in the rural areas we met old people still living with their families but city apartments have little space for grandma or grandpa. This social change shows up in Japanese films and TV programmes.

You-you centres cater for old folk who manage to live at home, on their own or with relatives. Its most popular facility is a traditional Japanese bathroom with a big wooden tub and helpers to assist. After their bath the old people sit round a long table singing nursery rhymes printed in little books, each book shared between two people, with an enthusiastic cheer leader urging them on. We saw some of the old people relaxing and enjoying, others looked bored.

A worker's collective called Youme ('Dream'), in the same building, provides a beautifully prepared vegetarian lunch. Eiko Hotta, the director, pointed out several chattering tables of town hall clerks. They have their own municipal canteen but 'our food is so much tastier,' she said.

Vote Seikatsu Club

The Seikatsu Club aims to be a political force in a land with many Green movements but little effective Green politics. Official Green parties have been dormant lately and in some areas the Seikatsu Club is the nearest thing to a substitute.

A municipal election is in progress. In Setagaya ward, Mrs Masako Ohkawara, the Seikatsu-sha Network candidate, is speaking in the rain at the railway junction. A helper holds an umbrella over her head. No crowd collects. Commuters coming off the trains don't stop to listen. A woman pushing a pram waves aside a leaflet. Masako speaks on cheerfully, regardless. She wears a pink suit and her face is made up brightly like an actress.

Masako has been a councillor for four years — one of three women network members among 128 — nearly all men — in the metropolitan government. For this election in Setagaya ward there are fifteen candidates for eight seats. The election will take place in July. Back at her campaign HQ, a rented shop in the district's main shopping centre, tea and cakes are served and the women volunteers bustle in and out in an atmosphere of great optimism, considering the poor turn-out at the meeting. Masako says people are disillusioned by politicians. 'The other parties are financed by the big corporations; we pay our own way. Our advantage is that we can argue from the experience and example of the Seikatsu Club: our practices like standardised bottles for easy re-use prove that sustainable practices work and can make money. The trouble is, people think we're communists.'

The network has been responsible for the introduction of a food safety budget and a labelling system for organic produce. Now it is agitating for more green spaces for growing vegetables in the city, with soakaway systems around buildings to collect and conserve rainwater. 'We want the city's temperature back to normal: it's risen two degrees centigrade in a century,' Masako says.

After we returned home from Japan, Kumiko Goto, who had interpreted for us, came to visit us and brought the news. Masako had lost! No one had expected it. Kumiko thought that the Seikatsu-sha Network had been so confident of her success that they had put more efforts into other candidates in other wards. 'The Green influence hasn't spread in this election,' she said. 'Pensions, corruption, medical insurance were the issues people cared about. Turnout was low because people are tired of party politics. A lot of people want a new political party but they are not yet ready for the network's ideas. We will win next time.'

Lifestyles are changing again

Changing lifestyles in the sixties created problems which suggested the Seikatsu Club solution. Now lifestyles are changing again, and the club must adapt to survive. That is the challenge facing Nobuhiko Orito, president and founder member, who works from the Seikatsu Club Co-operative Union's headquarters in the heart of Tokyo's Shinjuku business district. Orito is more philosopher than tycoon. He speaks softly, wears no tie; his buttoned-up shirtfront is a Japanese equivalent of the Nehru jacket. He told us that he was elected president in 1981 'because I was the most feminine man.'

He is fifty-eight. He never went to college and worked on the Japanese railway during the booming sixties when workers came flooding in from the countryside. 'We were lost and helpless, without grassroots organisations. Our unions were of little use because they were organised by the employers. We looked for other ways of enhancing our knowledge, skills and morale.'

Orito was influenced by Antonio Gramsci, the Italian Marxist philosopher, when he decided that the consumer movement must be organised in co-operative communities. 'So we started collective purchase. We had no capital, no labour and no premises. Looking around for ways to start, we opted for a British model, the co-operative system invented in Rochdale, Lancashire in the last century. We collect weekly contributions from the members and rent a warehouse. We started with 300 yen a month per household — now it's 1000.'

Orito said that women were active from the start but the theory and the early organisation was provided by men — young labourers who studied

Marxism. 'We thought: if we can get the housewives we can change society. We wanted to make them into a political power, teaching them economics and so forth. Soon I saw it was a mistake. The economy is not in a book, it is in Seikatsu Club: it exists in our daily food.'

Times are harder for Seikatsu Club now. Membership growth has almost stopped: for every ten who join, nine leave. As the global economy becomes more pervasive, supermarkets offer cheaper, better, and sometimes organic food — often in response to the co-operative example. More women are working and can no longer afford the time to run the *hans*, Orito said. 'An ageing population doesn't eat as much, and supermarkets are more persuasive, with cheaper, attractive imports, especially beef, orange juice, cookies, chocolate, tea, coffee.' In response, Seikatsu Club products now come in smaller packages and people can order deliveries by computer. The club has opened an Internet home page in Japanese.

> Societies rise, prosper, then decline and fall. One thing in common to them all is that agriculturally they have exploited and eroded the surface soil. The year 2000 is drawing near, and some people say that Japan, which has sacrificed its agriculture to industrial development, will be the next civilised country to decline and fall.
> · Yoshinori Kaneko in *A Farm with a Future*.

Orito regrets these concessions to individualism and he firmly resists the contemporary trend of amalgamating businesses into ever larger units. 'We're going the other way, breaking up regional offices into smaller units that people can identity with.' He remains sure that one day an unsustainable global economy will recede, and Seikatsu Club values and expertise will come into their own.

Other managers are also thinking ahead. 'More and more women are going out for work, so we will get fewer *han* members and more individual members — a weakening of our social ideals,' said Tadashi Haga. He is manager of the workers' collective which distributes Seikatsu Club produce for the whole of Tokyo. 'We'll need to go from two-litre to one-litre soya bottles. Another thing: supermarkets do direct purchase as well now, so the co-operative will have to find new ways to keep up its membership.'

The Seikatsu Club is under further pressure from rival co-operatives, several of which are much larger. The largest and oldest, Kobe, has over a million members. The rivals place the Seikatsu Club in a dilemma. The club is a big business, with a turnover of 76 billion yen (£360 million), nearly 1000 full-time staff and 28,000 local *han*. Can it survive without expansion? The delivery centres stock only 400 basic items — a deliberate choice to combat excessive consumerism and enable strict quality controls to be kept. Standardised, re-usable bottles and jars for everything from milk to soya sauce avoid waste and duplication. Instead of paper egg-boxes, the Seikatsu Club has re-usable plastic trays. These practices are labour-intensive and the club's managers report that volunteers are less willing to put in long hours than before.

Kunihiko Morita, a retired banker and economist who has devoted much of his life to researching co-operative movements, agreed that Seikatsu Club's prominence was fading because ordinary shops and supermarkets had caught up. 'Nearly twenty million Japanese belong to a consumer co-operative; most are housewives with no interest in radical ideas. However, Seikatsu Club remains a beacon for everybody by setting higher standards. It was important in the past and could be so again. The economic system we have cannot last, we will one day have to put our lands back into production — and the Seikatsu Club is preparing the way or at least keeping open the options.' Like so many of the people we talked to, from Bangalore to San Francisco, Morita is sure that the global economy isn't sustainable and more locally based economies will re-assert themselves. 'The time for the Seikatsu Club's new relevance is not yet ripe.'

Teikei: farmers and consumers in one family

Japanese farmers are amongst the highest users of chemicals in the world — spending ten times as much per hectare as American and European farmers. Just as contaminated milk led to the Seikatsu Club, so food scares led to the teikei system of consumer-supported agriculture — an attempt by consumers to buy safe food directly from the farmer at prices fixed by mutual agreement. Hundreds of Teikei consumer groups operate, with membership ranging from ten families to more than 5000.

The food scare most directly responsible for the creation of teikei was baby milk poisoned with arsenic. After pressure in the US to dispose of its dairy surpluses, powdered milk formula was aggressively marketed in Japan from the early 1950s. With the full backing of government and the medical profession, women were encouraged to bottle feed. To prevent the formula from putrefying, sodium phosphate was added to the milk product. From April to July in 1955, the Morinaga Milk Factory, Japan's largest supplier, used industrial grade soda, which was one third the price of that designed for human consumption. Unfortunately it also happened to contain arsenic and as a consequence over 12,000 babies were poisoned, 600 people died and 6,000 more were permanently impaired. [1]

To make matters worse, the mothers' own milk was often contaminated

TEN PRINCIPLES OF TEIKEI

1. Personal relationship between farmers and consumers based on friendship, not business.

2. Production plan agreed between farmers and consumers.

3. Consumers accept all produce harvested.

4. Mutual agreement on prices fair to both parties.

5. Exchange of information and communication.

6. Distribution of produce by farmers or consumers.

7. Democratic group activities.

8. Education programs.

9. Group size small enough for face-to-face interaction.

10. Aim constantly at an ecologically sound life through organic agriculture.

· Japan Organic Agriculture Association.

with agricultural pollutants. Among the developed countries, Japanese women have the highest concentration of dioxin in their milk. Since neither government nor business seemed interested in addressing the problem, mothers acted co-operatively in search of safe, wholesome food. Their wishes coincided with those of organic farmers and the result was the teikei system of community-supported organic farms. From the seventies the Japan Organic Agriculture Association (JOAA), which has 4,000 members, made teikei its priority. The aim was an alternative distribution system, independent of the conventional market.

The JOAA wants Japan to return to food self-sufficiency, a dream shared by many other critics of Japan's industrialisation. Katsushige Murayama, director of JOAA's International Division, told us he believes that teikei is 'not just organic agriculture. It is a way of making a better world. We could do it. We'd have to cut down on meat and wheat, which we import heavily, and live mainly on rice, vegetables and fish as we always have done. Of course we'd have to bring our multitude of golf courses back into cultivation.'

Different forms of teikei have existed for centuries. The contemporary system is a return to traditional attitudes to food, not as a commodity but as the product of a community for its own use. Consumers have a share in the farm, they may help in its working and they manage the distribution system. Supermarket uniformity of vegetables is no longer considered essential; knobbly cucumbers are in order, and potatoes need not have the mud washed off.

Like the CSA farms in America (see Chapter 6) consumers are required to buy all of the farm produce when it is in season, which can leads to healthier eating habits and save money on superfluous eating. A teikei motto is to 'eat from root to leaf'.

The JOAA estimates there are about 600 organic farmers in Japan, but continued growth of the Teikei system faces some of the same obstacles as those that confront the Seikatsu Club. The people who had the enthusiasm and drive twenty years ago are growing older and it is hard to find young people to replace them. Housewives who have done most of the distribution of produce are now more likely to be looking for jobs. This is a classic dilemma of industrial life: a housewife looks for a job to attain the standard of living she and her family desire, but her job can deprive the household of its quality of life.

Meanwhile, Japanese organic farmers face the problems of their own success: increasing demand has lured the supermarkets and speciality stores into the organic market, and much of what they offer is imported. However, teikei farmers believe that in the end the industrial system will collapse, or shrink, and their way of locally-produced wholesome food will become the norm.

Kaneko's farm

The 150-year-old farmhouse in Saitama prefecture has an iron roof — the tiles have gone — and in the porch is a very un-Japanese clutter of gumboots and umbrellas. In the family room a multi-dish lunch is being served for the family, ourselves, the apprentices and other local organic farmers. Everyone sits on floor cushions and our feet are kept warm by portable stoves placed in a hole beneath the low tables. Although it is midsummer, the start of the rainy season has brought a sharp drop in temperature.

Our hosts, Yoshinori and Tomoko Kaneko, are among the best known organic farmers in Japan. They sell their produce through the teikei system. The couple run their two hectares with the help of apprentices from Japan and abroad. Kaneko says that prices for his produce are fifty percent higher

Many farmers are not proud of their occupation and their traditional lifestyle now, and they have difficulty having a hopeful vision. The younger generation is not willing to take over and there were only 1,800 graduates from agricultural schools who dared start farming last year. On the other hand, you find some young people quitting their jobs and getting into the world of organic agriculture in search of a brighter future.
· Japan Organic Agriculture Association.

My father has been devoted to dairy farming. I remember buying ice cream or bottles of milk from our village shop, full of expectation thinking that there was some of our milk in them. I was disillusioned when I found the milk watery and flavourless, like powdered milk and with a taste of medicine about it. The reasons for my suspicions became clear as I learned about dairy farming at my agricultural high school. It dawned on me that milk from our cows was rarely used for the milk or ice cream on the market. That was twenty years ago, when non-fat powdered milk and saltless butter were imported at low prices and made into what appeared to be milk. This early experience taught me that all foods were not what they seemed to be.
· Yoshinori Kaneko in *A Farm with a Future.*

and he reckons his yield is twenty percent less than that of chemically farmed produce. His enthusiasm for organic farming increases the longer he stays at it. He's always ready to try a new project: his three cows produce enough methane in a biogas converter for ninety percent of his cooking needs. Every item we eat is produced on the farm or by Kaneko's customers who are also his friends. The strawberry cake was made by one, who was helping to eat it. The organic Japanese farmers, working against the mainstream, have a conviction and an enthusiasm that permeates their lives. Kaneko's mother, nearly eighty, lives with the family and tells us proudly she still goes weeding.

Kaneko's vegetable beds are a picture of happy plants; his three compost heaps would be the envy of any organic farmer anywhere. He doesn't want official standards of organic certification imposed on his produce. He shares the suspicion of other JOAA members that national or international standards could be set too leniently so as to enable the big traders to profit from pseudo-organic produce. 'My customers know what I grow, how I grow it and how I treat my livestock and they are happy'.

Organic farmers in Japan are small in numbers (out of 1400 farmers in Kaneko's region only twelve are organic) and aware they are going against the mainstream. But they are confident that the mainstream economy and food system are both running into difficulties, and more and more people will eventually support them.

The Yamagishi utopia

Where is the ideal rural community — sustainable and convivial, living lightly and free from money worries? It is in Japan, we were assured — in the forty Yamagishi villages around the country, communities where money was not used, everyone worked because they wanted to, and all work was in harmony with nature.

This claim was made by Dr Takashi Iwami, an agricultural economist who has devoted his retirement to advocating what he calls 'a new renaissance' for Japan. He offered to take us to a Yamagishi community in Mie prefecture. Other Japanese friends and advisors were doubtful, suggesting that the Yamagishi experience might not be suitable for our purpose, without specifying their reservations. The affable inscrutability of the Japanese makes them reluctant to criticise anything directly, especially when someone else has recommended it. However, the opportunity to visit a truly communist group led us to discount these reservations.

So we met Dr Iwami at Tokyo station and the three of us took the north-bound express. He was wearing a rucksack over his suit and tie. He is agile for his seventy-two years and was an attentive guide. He bought us all sandwiches for the journey, and ate his own with chopsticks, which we found harder than eating rice and sushi.

We were met at Tsu City station by a friendly young interpreter who spoke excellent English learnt in Brighton Polytechnic. She drove us to the Toyosato community of 800 adults and 900 children on the outskirts of the town. We were expecting a village — and found rows of three-storey apartment blocks, set in formal gardens with waterfalls among rocks and maples. All of Japan is extremely clean and litter-free by most European standards but here we found a perfection of order that seemed almost sinister.

Our room was in Japanese style — no chairs, no bed. A tatami floor (thick straw mats) and a low table at which we sat on flat cushions. At night, futons were unrolled and pillows, stuffed with dried beans, were brought out. A TV sat on a shelf next to a vase arranged with three blooms.

Next morning, beginning our tour of the community, we were taken to a shop where all goods on display are free of charge. We watched two women take a roll of toilet paper and a couple of light bulbs, write down their acquisitions in a ledger and walk out. Display shelves held used household goods, toys and furniture. When you join this community, you give all

---

Yasuo Yamada, aged 44, and his wife Miyoko, aged 39, closed up their barber shop 'Smile', joined the Toyosato community last summer and restarted their own job at the hairdressing department. Yasuo says: 'When I was keeping my own barber shop, I was very strict in the job lest the customer should complain — especially when a customer ordered a very difficult hairstyle, which sometimes didn't become him. But I was bound by money. Now living in the community I'd like to do a better job all the more because it is free. I don't want people to think that I do a halfway job because there is no charge.

· Article in Yamagishi's Kensan Newsletter.

> Modern education has placed an inordinate weight upon intellectual knowledge, so many children 'fall behind', creating a grave social problem. Such children have been cheated out of their childhood and have become indifferent to life and society. Yamagishi has provided an environment for children to grow in a truly child-like way in its Children's Paradise Village programs. The Yamagishism Academy, established nine years ago, is raising children who can truly become the successors to the future of humanity.
> · Article in Yamagishi website (www.yamagishi.or.jp)

your possessions. These donated goods are available here: crockery, toys, ornaments, all the ephemera of modern living.

In the clothing store, the items are available on indefinite loan — racks of suits and dresses, blouses and shirts — good quality, serviceable rather than smart. Only the cases of costume jewellery were locked for security. Members own no private clothes but they sew name tapes in their daily clothes, so they can be returned by the communal laundry. When anyone wants to go to town, or to a wedding or on an excursion, they borrow the appropriate outfit.

At dinner, everyone sat at tables for twelve. A meal of *teriyaki* was cooked at each table. Most of the vegetables were locally grown on the Yamagishi fields and were delicious: good communal food is a priority in Yamagishi communities.

Each couple has a one-room apartment — pictures of their kids on the walls, calendars, a low table and cushions and plenty of electronic hardware. The Yamagishi community is well-off. Much of its income — 20 billion yen a year — comes from a profitable egg business and from the dairying and food production, performed efficiently, all day and every day without wages, at each of their communities.

New recruits give up all their money as well as their possessions. The gift is not returnable on leaving. 'That must make you rich,' we ventured. Kitaoji Yorinoby, who was showing us round, laughed at our naiveté. 'Sometimes people bring their debts with them and we have to pay.'

As in the more idealistic early *kibbutzim* in Israel, children are raised in common, in their age groups, to keep them away from the pressure of the nuclear family which the Yamagishi believe encourages individual competitiveness. From the age of five the children live in these special houses, looked after by trained teachers.

Five-year-olds in the kindergarten were having lunch — a beautifully prepared, well-balanced vegetarian meal. The room was bright and sunny, the children eager and amused to see the foreigners.

The dairy herd was living in conditions as highly organised as the kindergarten and as spotless. The specially bred Holsteins are raised on an American intensive indoor plan. Three times a day the animals walk out of their raised straw pens and find their way unsupervised to the milking parlour. The sheds are open-walled, the bedding immaculate. Hens are barn-raised with five hundred to each barn. The Yamagishi are immensely proud of their farming. To us it was industrial farming with a benevolent face.

The wageless working hours are up to twelve a day. A former engineer who is now a potter works seven days a week. 'I don't see it as work. Every day is like a Sunday for me.' He had spent two years as an engineer in the UK. 'I hated the stress. Here I am relaxed.'

When the teenagers finish their lessons they go out to work in the fields and packing sheds. We saw a line of twenty youngsters grading spring onions, working so fast we thought they were in a competition. No, they weren't, they always work that fast. When they finish they go to their boarding houses to eat and sleep. They visit their parents once a month.

A twenty-three-year-old, born and brought up in Toyosato, works as a wood cutter. He said: 'When we see young people on the outside, we are so sorry for them. They spend all their time hanging around bars. We're working for our future.' A young woman said wistfully: 'I wish I could tell you. There is so much here. But it's not possible to explain. You have to live it.' She is twenty-six, married with a small son who stays in the crèche while she works. She is a monitor for the adolescents who live together in one of the blocks. In Japan women find child care as hard as in other developed countries; a problem which doesn't exist in the Yamagishi communities.

There was no apparent restriction of our visit. We could go where we wished, talk to whom we pleased through our interpreters. Everyone gave us the same polite smile. In the old people's house, one of the first Yamagishi members spread her palms to show the comfort and ease of her home. From what we could see, the community worked, yet even on this superficial observation a few discordancies appear. In the women's bath house (Dot writes) I asked the interpreter what my neighbours were talking about. 'She is asking about her daughter who is sixteen and has been sent to live in another village. She would prefer her to stay.'

Dr Iwami visits this community twice a year. He wants to see the further spread of the movement in which he appreciates the old communist aspiration: 'To each according to his needs, from each according to his ability.' He did not share some of the reservations of other Japanese friends who were worried that Yamagishism could degenerate into cult behaviour. For us, after two days, we felt something stifling, dispiriting, regimented, in the atmosphere. When we asked if there were human problems we were told: 'Anger and resentment are human. We study it.'

The movement began in 1953 in response to the ideas of the late Miyozo Yamagishi. There is no living guru, no obvious leader. Authority is spread amongst various groups. Some people are satisfied to exchange their will for peace and security. We met no malcontents but felt they must exist. And when they leave, they must forgo all the money they have brought with them.

The movement has gained foreign support: there are Yamagishi communities in the US, Australia, Germany, Korea, Switzerland, Brazil and Thailand. Japanese applicants have to attend a week-long initiation course. Ashes of every dead member are stored in a monumental vault in another Yamagishi village in Mie prefecture. There is room for another century or so of new corpses.

In 1995 there were 4,675 people living in these communities in Japan. The movement claims that 150 new members join every year and only 15 leave. We could not see what the recruitment is like, but a teacher in Tokyo told us he had attended a Yamagishi indoctrination and recruitment session. 'First they took our shoes away, so we could not just slip out,' he said. 'Then we had sessions lasting far into the night, with the group leader shouting questions at us. It was straightforward brainwashing.' Apparently successful: of the twenty-seven members of that session, twenty-three agreed to join.

Repopulating Oshika

High in the mountains in Nagano prefecture, overlooked by the snow-capped Mount Akaishi, the people of Oshika live in several centuries at once. The village consists of a string of hamlets spread across a steeply walled valley. The 1600 inhabitants — all that remain from 5000 in the 1940s — can take nearly an hour to drive from one end of the village to the other, but mostly they don't drive: they hardly ever need to shop because the village co-operative brings food round twice a week. Mostly they stay home. They are old and they farm their plots until they die. Their children return from the cities for holidays. Oshika is a case study of rural decline. The largest age group is sixty to seventy-five; almost forty percent are over sixty-five.

The back-to-the-land movement did not affect Japan in the seventies as it affected Australia and the US, although a few hippies tried farming or living in communities. In the seventies the movement was the other way — Japanese farmers flocking into the cities for well-paid jobs, as they had done

Simon Piggott at work ...

for two decades. Now a new disillusionment with city life has arisen, as jobs for life are threatened and prosperity cannot always compensate for stress, pollution and congestion. So there is a trickle back to the villages. A few have come back to Oshika.

The village has not stagnated. A new hydro-electric plant blots the landscape and the valleys are lapped by a sprawling new reservoir. On the 'improved' banks of the reservoir, old trees have been sacrificed and the fish have not survived the dam; up on the peaks a new tourist road threatens the habitat of crested eagles.

Yet Oshika is still a haven, a place of natural beauty and a remnant of traditional living. The village has attracted some 200 incomers, including musicians, farmers, builders, an artist, a potter. The result is a singular mixture of old and new. Oshika still keeps up its 200-year-old *kabuki* (folk opera) tradition in which local people love taking part. Some traditions have been modernised, like the electronic public address system, booming across the valley, which wakes everyone at 5.45 a.m. with a reminder of the day's events: a funeral, a tree ceremony, or a recycling expedition. To be sure of waking us, the loudspeaker booms out a culture shock: part of Beethoven's *Ode to Joy*, played on deafening synthesisers.

The incomers include Simon Piggott from Britain, his Japanese wife Masako and their three girls. The view from their wooden farmhouse is framed by sheer slopes of mountain forest, their air is sharp and clear. A metallic-grey pylon with six sagging wires occupies the centre of the view but the Piggotts see neither pylon nor wires. Simon has the use of half a hectare, split up in separate plots, where he grows most of his vegetables and keeps poultry.

Few of the incomers are New Age: they are conservatives trying to conform to the old ways. They take part with enthusiasm in the administration of each hamlet, in the seasonal routines and rituals including the care of fifty shrines and, above all, in continuous mutual aid which is all needed more and more as old people get still older.

This used to be a food producing area. Walking with Simon up a forest track to a high clearing where he keeps a store of logs, we passed overgrown patches which had been levelled for rice. Japan had a comfortable rice surplus until the global economy made it preferable to buy cheap food from abroad: the government for the past thirty years has been paying farmers *not* to grow rice. Those abandoned rice fields, now returned to secondary forest, were some of the highest in Japan.

Simon is an enthusiastic village incomer. He has become so Japanese that he says frequently: 'How would you say?' as if English had become a foreign language. He grew up with a relish for community, in a Northamptonshire village where his father was the headmaster. A romantic interest in the orient brought Simon to an English-teaching job in Tokyo. Fascinated by Japanese culture he has lived here for eight years as a part-time freelance translator working from his rented wooden farmhouse.

... and at rest.

When the Piggotts arrived the landlord took them on probation, insisting that they uphold the local traditions which the previous tenant, branded as 'a hippie', had neglected. 'It was an adventure, going back to the sort of village characters I'd known at home. I was part of history here: I could do what I liked with the house.' He replaced paper doors with windows and put in a new bathroom and stove. The neighbours, both old timers and incomers, helped.

Simon's closest neighbour, in the next house down the slope, is a woman of seventy-one who keeps her vegetable and flower garden without a single weed. 'She's neighbourly but proud: if I give her anything she always gives a gift in return.' This neighbour sends vegetables to her sons in Tokyo. Other vegetables are bought in by the village co-operative, which provides the villagers with gardening equipment, seeds and saplings.

Everyone is a member of the co-operative, paying dues and shopping there; it is active in village agriculture, encouraging new lines like silk worms, rabbits, and sheep. It acts as a bank, giving out loans. However, its mobile shop isn't organic enough for the Piggotts: the manager says he's 'not into fads'. Looking beyond the village for their supplies, the Piggotts belong to the Seikyo consumer co-operative, one of the biggest in Japan. At one time Masako ran a Seikatsu Club *han,* but there was too little money among the incomers to keep it going.

Half way between traditional farming and the new methods, the villagers use nitrogen but no pesticides. Most live without a car and exchange free services with each other. The incomers, lacking that tradition of sharing, tend to use their cars.

Simon has served for a year as chairman of his hamlet council. Attendance at weekly meetings is compulsory, on pain of a 50 yen fine in the absence of a valid excuse. Now Simon is on the traffic safety committee. We all joined in the weekly recycling effort for bringing the village's accumulated waste of cartons, plastic, bottles, etc. into the school for disposal; the children helped too.

Another 'returned' villager is Toshio Kobayashi, who has given up a job as a city electrician and come back to the family farm. He has started a lucrative cheesemaking business but his aim, he says, is a self-sufficient life. He has three hectares of agricultural land and twenty hectares of mountain forest — an enormous amount in a country where the average farm size is a little more than one hectare. He keeps three productive cows and two calves.

Kobayashi is working to rebuild Oshika's autonomy. You could call him a modernising traditionalist. When the hundred-year-old school house in the centre of Oshika was being torn down to be replaced by a concrete structure, he bought the timbers, and is re-erecting them on his land with paid and voluntary help as a conservation training centre. He was hoping to have the first group of students and visitors in autumn 1997.

He regrets that the new dams have killed off the fish in the river and now he fears an influx of tourism. 'In the old days there was less money but life was more abundant,' he says. 'Within the global economy we can still develop the local, otherwise we lose our humanity and individuality'. He feels the local co-operative does the opposite of promoting the local economy — 'they are nothing more than agents of the Japanese Co-operative Association which makes everywhere the same.'

Japan's industrial miracle was made possible only because farming has been sacrificed — and that makes Kobayashi angry. Even now he is convinced that fields could be reclaimed from the newly planted forests. 'It is ridiculous: our supermarkets are setting up their own farms overseas: why not here?' He acknowledges that although the incomers get the land they want, they can't make a living out of agriculture because prices are kept too low by the constant competition of cheap imports. People need to find a way of establishing roots outside the industrial system, as in the *teikei*.

Meanwhile this cheesemaker, for all his insistence on tradition, makes his living from producing a luxury item — organic Dutch-type cheese. He sells every kilogram he produces. It is creamy and delicious but not a staple food. There is an irony in the fact that both he and the rug weaver in the next village have returned to the countryside but need a luxury trade to make a living.

Unlike these conservatives, some of the incomers belong to a Green counter-culture. *Anaishi Gondwana* means mountain tribe. The group with that name has only five people in a rented village house, but they plan to be about fifty, and live in Oshika doing handicrafts and arts. Suitsu, a young man from Osaka, has rented a wooden house and plans to stay for a couple of years. He gave up his economic studies and is trying to become a farmer. Compared to his neighbours' plots, his vegetables are meagre, the young carrots wobble across their bed and weeds are more prolific than lettuces.

Visiting the nascent commune gave us our first sight of a Japanese not taking off his shoes in his house. The household has the atmosphere of a seventies-style hippie commune — welcoming and chaotic at the same time. Its kitchen has the unscrubbed air of communes everywhere, with an indoor cold tap and outside compost privy — amenities adequate for some. There were no women. 'It's still too primitive for them,' said Jugon, who was frying chapattis. (He'd run an Indian restaurant in Tokyo for thirteen years.)

Sawa, the oldest member of the group, describes himself as 'that rare bird

— a Japanese environmentalist.' He lives in Tokyo with a wife and small children but dreams of establishing himself in Oshika which he visits as often as he can. He is convinced that the village will accept the idea of a commune. We were less sure.

The mayor of Oshika welcomes the influx of newcomers from the city. He wants more artists and scholars to come. 'Such people need a quiet environment and we can provide it.' Whether or not the village will stay as quiet if he gets his wish for tourists, is another matter.

When the bottom line is drawn Oshika is hardly viable. It is heavily subsidised. Sixty percent of its income is from the national government, ten percent from the prefecture and only thirty percent generated locally. And, as incomers arrive, villagers still leave. We watched a video of a coming-of-age ceremony of twenty youngsters: only one of them plans to stay in Oshika. Can the incomers reverse this trend? They cannot bring a dying community back to life. Only if there is a change of priorities in Japan, involving renewed support for sustainable agriculture, can villages like this come into their own again.

There is another precondition. Newcomers in an old village cannot resuscitate a dying community. They need to create a new one. Can it be done? In the next chapters we look at three 'intentional' communities — one mainly secular and two predominantly spiritual.

Notes

1   Conference paper by Helen Kavanagh, The Asian Studies Department, University of Adelaide. 1993.

Part 4 : Living in community

13

Growing up in another culture

• •

The USA's wealth and cultural freedom allows for social experiments of every conceivable sort — from the religious to the libertarian. Communities are founded, flourish and decay with lifespans ranging from a few months to a few decades. The Farm has a special place among the 500 settlements listed by the Fellowship for Intentional Communities (FIC) in the United States. Its origins lie in the hippie movement arising out of the 'baby boom' of Americans born between 1947 and 1962 — who grew up lapped in prosperity and undermined by crises: the Cold War, the Korean war, Vietnam, the Civil Rights Movement and the Kennedy assassination. Out of a generation which seemed to have 'never had it so good' came many who rejected the values they had been taught.

The Farm's story began with an exodus of biblical resonance by 270 hippie students travelling out of San Francisco in a ragged convoy of decrepit buses and trailers known as the Caravan in search of the promised land. A pied piper led them out — Stephen Gaskin, their charismatic, New Age, LSD-tripping philosophy lecturer whose 'sermons' preached revolt against authority, against war, against violence and for love. And for going back to the land and for hard work! That was the revolution: hippies who wanted to work, live frugally and renounce hard drugs, drink, meat and even coffee. Gaskin gave up LSD at the start of the trek. The Caravan was on the road for a year; it had grown to a hundred vehicles when it reached New York's Bronx district where the hippies lectured and ministered to the poor before starting the long journey back. Gaskin imposed a strict morality, including a rule that 'if you're sleeping together you're considered engaged and if you're pregnant you're considered married.' He told his people to come off welfare and work for their living. After seven months and three and a half thousand kilometres, the caravan returned to San Francisco.

Gaskin didn't want to stay home. The Caravan set off again in search of

Stephen Gaskin taught religions, magic and parapsychology with lectures on such subjects as Einstein and God, and North American White Witchcraft. Soon he and his followers were asked to leave college and began meeting outside — in a church basement, then a theatre and finally at the huge Family Dog rock hall near the beach. The meetings, known as Monday Night Class, soon attracted more than 1000. Gaskin became his public's 'spiritual teacher' (his own term), basing himself on a 'knowledge of how the Universe works.' He said these were essentially old ideas, implicit in major religions: in particular the notion of the fundamental unity of nature (We Are All One), and the belief that people need to learn techniques and practices to get in touch with their Higher Self. Making love and psychedelics were among the techniques used in what became one big church in which 'your membership is your belly-button' and 'telling the truth' was the cardinal requisite for spiritual integrity. The new ideology denounced war, injustice, racism and violence in all their current forms.
· Michael Traugot in an unpublished history of The Farm.

affordable land, finishing up in the remotest and poorest part of Tennessee. Once settled on The Farm, they invented a model of alternative living, loving, giving birth, growing food, and helping other people. Without dole payments or other outside help, the 320 settlers survived by back-breaking work, technical inventiveness and a determination to guide the world by their example of liberated communal living. Within four years The Farm had gained self-sufficiency in food and established a construction company with eighty skilled craftsmen. The settlers, now numbering over a thousand, set up a school, greenhouses, a publishing company, dry goods and grocery stores and automotive, welding, woodworking and machine shops. Within five years The Farm had an infirmary, a laboratory, a dispensary and a neo-natal intensive care unit.

Farm people took a 'vow of poverty' to live on one dollar a day. They farmed their land, started small industries, invented gadgets, started overseas aid projects. Communal houses were homes to twenty or thirty, sometimes as many as sixty with shared cooking and laundering. The old buses, vans and cabins served as extra bedrooms. For years there was no running water. With neither electricity nor TV, direct social life flourished, with plenty of music, and the children felt part of a larger family. On 'all-farm days', everyone available turned up to work in the fields.

Mechanical birth control was discouraged. Sex wasn't just for reproduction, but was for 'meditation and ecstasy, the achievement of a state of openness and grace'. Nearly all the children born on The Farm were born at home without anaesthetic, breast-fed and raised vegetarian. Food, bought and grown, was distributed equally. The Farm published books and tapes, broadcast its message on the radio and the Internet and set up a natural birth maternity unit open to non-residents. In 1974, a good year for The Farm's economy, Plenty was founded as an aid organisation soliciting volunteers and raising funds in the developing world.

The first generation of Farm children grew up like an extended family in a commune with a highly developed world view. One student reported being taken aside by his sociology professor and asked, 'What is it about you? You are from a different culture.'

The Farm attracted 10,000 visitors a day during the mid-seventies, ten times its average population. Visitors were told they would be tested and could stay for two days — or the rest of their lives if they worked. Hundreds of women came to have their babies rather than abort, with the offer that The Farm would adopt the babies if required. Many of the women stayed on.

The 1976 earthquake in Guatemala took Plenty over there on a big scale, financed by Canadian aid, with up to 100 volunteers supplying building expertise. A rapport was made between Tennessee hippies and Mayan peasants, some of whom came to the Farm for courses. The Farm people had to leave Guatemala in 1980 because of repression that threatened all who associated with Plenty. A soya dairy project survived.

By 1983 The Farm's numbers had grown to 1500. That was the year of the debacle. Debts could no longer be paid. What happened is still argued about. Was it financial incompetence? Overstretching of resources by taking on too many people, too many hangers-on? Was it the recession? Or had the FBI, under Reagan, acted behind the scenes to frighten off the bankers and force foreclosure on loans?

At The Farm's stormiest meeting it was decided that only people who could support themselves could stay. This cataclysmic event is still referred to as The Changeover. Henceforth everyone was to earn their own keep, paying dues to The Farm for use of the land and basic services. More than half the members left immediately, soon only a third remained.

We were two hundred and seventy folks who had tripped together, meditated together, taken acid together, many of us had been lovers, we were a bunch of people who knew each other well over a long time. The second wave of people who came were people who'd heard about the nice community but the first wave — we were really revolutionary. Even though we took such a hit in '83, we were not in any danger of quitting or losing it, and right now we're having a kind of renaissance as our kids get old enough to start holding the grownups' feet to the fire about the original ideals.'
· Stephen Gaskin (interview with the authors).

The Changeover made people who had worked for the community jobless. These included the clinic personnel, midwives, teachers, storekeepers, gate personnel and promotion crews. Those who wanted to stay had to earn a living in a depressed rural economy. Michael Traugot, one of the old-timers and Farm historian, said this was the period 'when there was the most bitterness, the most anguish for many community members. People daily departed from the place where they had invested a significant portion of their lives, taking with them their experiences, but no material wealth.'

Today the Farm survives with its core ideas intact: rejection of mainstream values and a wish to live simply in a community. The adventure has been tamed, the old magic has faded: instead of living communally on a dollar day under a vow of poverty, the surviving members, now mostly middle-aged, earn their living in jobs and businesses, pay rent to the community and have trouble with rebellious teenage children. But it remains The Farm: Gaskin is still there, aged sixty-three, no longer leader but still custodian of idealism and teacher in The Farm School. Some of the children who left with their parents during the upheaval have come back as teenagers to the home they grew up in, asking to be allowed to live communally just like the old days. Thirty of the present 220 members, not satisfied with living in a market economy, have formed The Second Foundation in which their incomes are pooled. The Farm today is a part of a global eco-village network on the Internet and runs an eco-village training centre for courses in sustainable living. Twenty-five years after

The original caravan buses decay alongside the new homes on The Farm.

their exodus, the surviving Farm people have not returned to Egypt; they remain anchored in the Living Lightly culture.

The Farm today

You pass through a gate with a watcher behind a window in a guardhouse. Only with the appropriate electronic gadget in your car can you pass freely, otherwise you have to explain yourself to the Gate People, just as you always did. This is the famous Gate where thousands of visitors a day

An intentional community is a group of people who have chosen to live together with a common purpose, working co-operatively to create a lifestyle that reflects their shared core values. They may live together on a piece of rural land, in a suburban home, or in an urban neighbourhood, and they may share a single residence or live in a cluster of dwellings. Today there are literally thousands of groups, with hundreds of thousands of members, in intentional communities and extended families based on something other than blood ties. This type of living has been around for thousands of years, not just decades.
· Geoph Kozeny in *Communities Directory*.

reported on arrival. In those days the Gate People mattered: Stephen Gaskin himself took turns there. Now just one person sits behind the window and nobody comes for hours.

Our first impression — an oasis of space and peace, only 220 people on 900 hectares, but no luxury. The oak forest is bedraggled: the trees, interspersed with spindly weaklings and fallen timber debris, barely prosper. Most houses are large shacks made of recycled planks. The original caravans, with peeling slogans (Out to Save the World) are immobile and rusting with potted flowers on the bonnets, some used as bedrooms by young people and visitors. The tarmac road leads past the high school, innovative with its saw-toothed roof over a passive solar brick building, and a well-built brick community centre bright with flower beds. The road turns to a clearing reserved for the eco-village. This is a village-to-be: there is only a residence, known as The Inn, two yurts, a straw bale house, an enclosed plot labelled Organic Garden (not yet planted), and tin huts containing solar heated showers.

We had arranged to stay at The Inn and work as WWOOFers for a couple of hours a day for our accommodation, buying our food at the Farm shop. Nobody took much notice of our arrival. It's the same for everyone: if you're a stranger you're on your own: nobody knows you, nobody takes you in charge. This is a paradox in a community built on love. Farm members are people of action, individualists. Someone explained to us that this goes back to Gaskin himself. The day he announced to his huge class of students that he was going off in an old school bus, they were dismayed and many asked

Albert Bates, The Farm's eco-village director, at The Inn.

— could they come along? Gaskin strode off, turning his head to say: 'Get yourself a bus.' The spirit was already set: join us but look after yourself. This is a *yang* place (hard, masculine), not a *yin* place like Findhorn (gentle, nurturing — see Chapter 14).

The eco-village training centre is designed to be sustainable. The Inn, a typical, high-energy, wooden American house, has been retrofitted with solar and gas showers and low-energy fridges and all new buildings will be low impact, low energy. The two solar powered cars, invented on The Farm, don't run. The straw bale house is only a demonstration model as yet. The centre still subsists on outside grants but intends to pay for itself once its courses and workshops in sustainable lifestyles are well established.

Albert Bates, instigator of the centre and The Farm's chief spokesman, was too busy to help us and hinted he was too busy even to talk. He was wary of bothersome new strangers. After half a day he was talking and advising us, charming us and no longer acting busy, although he was.

Albert arrived at The Farm not quite with the Hippie Caravan but shortly afterwards, on foot from New York across the mountains. He was a well qualified young lawyer but the idea of a New York law practice held no appeal. Like many of his generation he was touched by Buddhism and other Eastern ideas in what later came to be called holism. He took a four-month hike along the Appalachian trail. After sixteen hundred kilometres, instead of continuing into Georgia, he decided to cross Tennessee and visit the most famous of communes. It was 1972; The Farm was one year old. Albert has lived here ever since.

For Albert it was like arriving in an advanced civilisation with its own dialect and subtle sciences. 'I was captivated by shorthand terms like "figure-ground" (not seeing larger concepts because of attachment to detail), "self-other" (placing too much importance on individuality), and "into the juice" (misfocusing and squandering group attention on selfish interests).'

Like other old-timers, Albert is nostalgic. 'We worked for the common good; we were saving the world. We did not mind putting up with shit. The early Farm kept going on raw faith — not just Stephen's faith and not just Haight Ashbury: it came out of the whole era, the civil rights movement successes with Martin Luther King, Bob Dylan's lyrics, the whole thing, the culture; there was a sense of courage, a sense that you can do everything. You can't discount that motivation, but it faded in the early eighties. Television came onto The Farm, a Republican government. With the paving of our main road, The Farm has become increasingly difficult to distinguish from a planned community enclave for fixed income retirees.'

Albert now lives in a yurt pitched next to The Inn. It is beautiful, as yurts are: something about the circular form, the domed roof that creates peace. He was watching CNN news on TV and drinking Bourbon. The early Farm prohibitions of alcohol and coffee have long since gone. The yurt was freezing. Why not install a woodburning stove? Albert said he would try.

Albert has his own views about the causes of The Changeover. He dismisses a conspiracy theory: 'It wasn't the FBI and it wasn't financial stupidity and it wasn't being over-extended because we had always been over-extended. It was a loss of nerve — a sudden realisation that we were up in the air without a parachute.' He is convinced that if that loss of confidence had not occurred the original commune could have survived.

> We had excellent doctors and lawyers but no accountants. We sent people off to learn accounts; they never came back. We started businesses on a whim. We started a restaurant in California and kept it going on money sent from the Farm. Lots and lots of businesses. Very few succeeded. Those that did make profits used the money to plug our sinkholes. The debt never went down, always went up. People brought in their savings and lost them. That couldn't keep up. • Albert Bates (interview with the authors).

We all agreed that lifestyle innovation was not a prime moving force in the nineties, but shared Albert's hope that an enlarged Living Lightly culture in an ailing consumer society would bring it back. Meanwhile, we were struck how capitalist in its economics The Farm had become, even if it was capitalism with a benevolent face.

Entrepreneurs

The leading personalities at The Farm today are the entrepreneurs, who have adapted best to the Changeover. Some profited from the change, others, like Frank Michael, the mushroom manager, decided to pool their earnings in the Second Foundation.

The mushroom people live among the trees at the top of the forest, where Frank runs the business from a wooden house in a clearing. Any lingering rustic atmosphere is dispelled by computers which relay information to customers around the world, and a row of clocks for different time zones. Frank, with flowing beard and white hair kept in a pigtail, still has his Spanish accent after a youth spent in Mexico. He assured us that none of the mushroom spawn he sells is psychedelic; that would be illegal. The shiitake, maitake, oyster, reishi and the other species grow from half-rotted oak logs stacked outside. The business is justified as sustainable because it offers an alternative to logging in The Farm's 800 hectares of oak woods. After they are spent the logs are used as compost. A former potato barn houses a freezing plant and an air-conditioned storage area. The mushroom company provides money for the Second Foundation, which owns it, and jobs for two full-time and three part-time workers.

Frank and his first wife came to The Farm in its second year — 1973 — and he has affectionate memories of life in what he calls 'the puritan wing of the hippies — a sub-sect.' In those early days he learned plumbing, carpentry and solar energy design, took part in the regular 'farming days' and took turns at the Gate. He, his wife and their son and two daughters had all become vegetarian. Then came the Changeover.

'It was a tragedy. I voted against it but it was carried and it changed everything. Most people left. But now we're starting to grow again. The worse the economy outside gets the more will come back.' Frank's marriage did not survive the upheaval: 'The children blamed our divorce on everything that had gone wrong at The Farm and my wife encouraged them; they have never come back.'

Now Frank has a new wife, Annie, and a new contentment at fifty-eight. He still lives simply in a converted trailer. His household earns $1500 a month — below the official poverty level but he finds it adequate at The Farm. He would like to build a small straw bale house with a big attached greenhouse of his own revolutionary design, but lacks the cash. Frank is an old, proud hippie who has not allowed the Changeover to change him.

Just along the forest road we find Total Video, a more aggressively capitalist enterprise, which makes money for its owners and staff. Doug Stevenson owns the firm; Phil Schweitzer is executive producer. Phil is a member of the Second

Foundation, but Doug will not join because the firm would then belong to the Foundation. The firm makes commercials for anyone — including car firms, a local gun firm, lots of banks and even the Republican Party.

Phil arrived with The Caravan. Twelve years later he was one of the few who did well out of the Changeover and he is happy with the way The Farm continues to evolve. 'It's true many young people left for other communities, but they found the same problems over there. Now there is a return to the ideals that we had: our own kids are more idealistic than the adults.'

Phil defends his firm's consumerist contracts though he had reservations about the Republican Party contract. 'We feel it's important for us to stay in business so that we can support more important work. We've made videos on spiritual midwifery, on Albert Bates and the Gaia eco-village network, and we'd like to do The Farm story in video.'

Doug Stevenson, the firm's owner, a slim, restless-looking man with burning, searching eyes and a vigorous black beard, is old hippie and new businessman combined. His studio in an air-conditioned prefabricated hut has the latest digital editing equipment. He was already running this business before the Changeover when The Farm owned it. 'I took it over, debts as well as assets and debts were the larger part. I worked for years to pay them off.' He says Phil is technically an employee 'but on the astral plane we're more or less equal.'

Doug came to The Farm in 1973, a nineteen-year-old high school hippie. 'I'd lived through the various phases — the progression from LSD to spiritual living and then to going back to the land. I and my partner — she was seventeen — went out West in a VW van looking for land — but we knew we'd have to go back to the city to earn the money to realise our dream. Then we read about The Farm in *Mother Earth News*, went to a concert given by folks from The Farm, finally went on a visit and we were convinced: we liked The Farm's strong political consciousness — changing the world and society — vegetarian diet and progressive midwifery. Now we could go back to the land right away.

'When we arrived they were still in buses, just moving into army tents. I joined a ham radio crew and acquired a lot more skills. I started fund raising with Plenty, then joined a new electronics company making Geiger counters, trying to help the antinuclear movement, but they didn't sell. We moved to more successful lines: a CB radio guidebook, a satellite TV guidebook. We marketed a satellite dish and were in business.'

His business is now in the mainstream. 'I rationalise what we're doing because the more information society has, the more liberal it gets — like the Discovery Channel or CNN news.' Although Doug benefited by the Changeover he was broken-hearted when the communal ideal was abandoned. He worked hard to survive in the new order. 'This firm was heavily in debt and facing collapse; I worked eighteen hours a day, commuting ninety miles to Nashville for ten years. My business was over there, but I wouldn't give up my base here and I never will: I like the community and the rural lifestyle.'

Doug maintains that The Farm is an eco-village — 'though we don't narrowly define it. We're surrounded by an economic system and have to live in harmony with it. We have to see where the compromises are. The Changeover gave us greater freedom. I'm with the general Farm philosophy: I believe in a Life Force, and in the importance of the sacraments of birth, death, marriage, healing.'

Another thrusting new businessman on The Farm who has adapted to the new arrangements is Steve Skinner who owns an electronics firm which gives him a profitable and pleasant life. Skinner wins his contracts by being cheaper. The cost of living is lower here, his prefabricated buildings were cheaper and he pays a low rent to the community. His bestselling product is a Geiger counter: it was called Nukebuster in the early days when it was intended for sale to antinuclear movements; the antinukes didn't buy it so now its main customers are laboratories and the nuclear industry itself and it's been renamed Monitor Four.

The Changeover neither surprised nor dismayed Steve, who was one of the clear winners. He had been earning good money for The Farm, installing wind generators for the Tennessee Valley Authority — 'and now that money went to me personally. But it was hard at first. The Farm's Laundromat service stopped operating because it was not profitable, and we had no plumbing for a washing machine. So I had to buy a car to take the nappies to the launderette.'

Steve's children are sixteen and twelve; the elder goes to The Farm School. They took the Changeover badly, as most of the kids did, but neither want to leave. The family live in half of a long cabin they share with Doug Stevenson's family in a co-housing arrangement. We suggested that he leads a fairly regular American life. 'Yes, but with important differences. When the kids come home from school we don't have to worry about them. We work flexible hours, a quarter-mile from where we live with time for hobbies.'

Kids

Will the kids stay on? It is the crucial question in any lifestyle experiment but it cannot be answered precisely. Teenagers go away to study, find a job, find themselves. Most Farm kids left with their parents at the Changeover. Some have come back because they missed their native home or because they found life outside to be harsh.

Melina came back. She was born on The Farm twenty years ago, left with her parents at the Changeover and now has a job as domestic manager at The Inn. She has to keep a rambling thirty-bed house in some state of order and organise the 'interns' (young voluntary helpers). The Inn belongs to the eco-village training centre where half a dozen farm kids work for five dollars an hour.

She isn't often here before mid-morning because she likes to meditate in the old bus she lives in, parked nearby. One morning she told us gently we were not doing enough work since our rent-free arrangement obliged us to do four hours between us. So we stepped up our bathroom cleaning, leaf sweeping and carpet sweeping until Melina was satisfied. For us this experience was both humbling and instructive. (*Dorothy writes:* For Wal first of all, because after decades of being treated like an important journalist he arrives some-where and finds he's just another visitor. For me — I was taking orders from Melina who was young enough to be my granddaughter and knew a great deal less then I did about cleaning bathrooms. But we both set to work with a will and enjoyed ourselves.)

In the living room at The Inn, on battered easy chairs amid psychedelic posters, the youngsters spend hours sitting around listening to CDs. We never saw anyone smoke or light up a joint, although kids here smoke hash when they're out of sight, just like anywhere else. One evening we got a group talking.

Melina: The Farm was great in the old days when our parents were the age we are now: to live like that you've got to like each other.

Kevin: Love each other.

Mortimer : About a thousand people left, including my parents. The ones who stayed didn't know each other that much, it wasn't the best of friends who stayed. The big meeting we had this weekend was the first major step taken here since 1983. I was so gung-ho, wanting the place to be well again. Can people still live at that high level?

Kevin: I think the kids do. I got kicked out of my house by my Mum; it was kinda mutual. (Kevin is sixteen.) I guess I'll move in with my Dad and his

I rejected and rebelled against what the Farm stood for. I played violent video games and ate unhealthy food whenever I could. I did not want to 'save the world' through conservation and love; I was not interested in organisations assisting impoverished nations. But despite my feelings, the commune that I lived on for eleven years taught me the spirit of co-operation and industriousness. Well before I recognised those values, I used them to bring success to my sports team and to get along with others.

· Jason, ex-Farm kid, in his college admissions application.

girl friend. I have lots of energy to put into The Farm, gardening especially, but not for school and that bothers my Mum.

Melina: I got pissed off at the Farm School. It was conventional really. We had to rebel: look, this is not alternative. We all ran away from school. Two teachers quit on us. Then we made 'em change things around. Our science teacher started taking us down to the creek to do real-life things; our maths teacher started letting kids do things at their own pace.

Kevin: I'm paying for my schooling.

Melina: I'm paying for half of it.

Kevin: I don't want to drop out.

Melina: Since I left I got a more positive attitude.

Kevin: Maybe we're just getting sick of being a pain in each other's butt. I used to break into people's houses just because I knew I could do it. Now I want to keep classes and just get the credits to graduate. Then maybe I'll stay on here till I'm eighteen or nineteen, doing gardening, then I'll go travelling with my band, maybe play in other communities. I definitely feel that if I'm ever going to have kids I'll come back here. It's really a good place for kids.

Mortimer: After the Changeover I went to public school and I felt a hundred percent different. They treated us like Blacks. There are no Blacks around here — this is Bible belt.

Melina: A black woman once told me why she wouldn't want to live on The Farm. 'We want all the good things of America, the cars and all. We don't want the vow of poverty.'

David : It's not like that now. The Farm is a just co-operative community that holds the land in common, has agreed to non-violence and to be vegetarian. Most people are living off their own small businesses.

Melina: That's bullshit.

David: Well, I know I'll always return to The Farm. This is where I want to bring up my children. I want them to have the same freedoms that I had. When we were growing up there was more community. I don't think Stephen influences me directly but he influenced all our parents. He was their teacher and in that way he influences the younger generation.

Kevin: Most of the kids love living here.

David: We are in the countryside not the city. I really appreciate that aspect. Like going down the creek to swim. But we're in this band and out here we're unconnected to the music scene. We need to let people hear our message. Spread the Love.

They now want more communal living; they regret the passing of the old ways. They share a common emotional frequency. Kevin told us how he and his friends all cried together the previous evening. 'The second that I hugged her, she cried. Heavy emotion last night, man. A lot of people coming into their power.'

The Farm kids think of themselves as part of a counter-culture and for this they have made sacrifices: they are isolated and poor. The band members work part-time on The Farm and on nearby farms to make a living. Their plan is to take the band on the road this winter but the old school bus they own isn't in working order and they haven't enough money to repair it. One of the kids says his mother lives on The Farm but for him her lifestyle is conventional with TV, supermarket shopping and a nine to five job. 'My life is different. In our house — I share with three other band members — there's no TV. Sure we have a stereo to listen to CDs. Most of our energies are in the band. People here are motivated. If they smoke pot it's as well as living their life not instead of. It's more of a sacrament, a coming together. I meditate every day — in the morning fifteen minutes to an hour.'

There are five all-youth households on The Farm which want to combine together to form a youth village, sustained by cottage industries, including the band, in which they can welcome young people from elsewhere. For months the teenagers have been meeting weekly over 'pot-luck' parties to discuss their plan. Another Melina, who is twenty-one, is behind the project. She wears a Farm-made tee-shirt with a bull charging a nuclear power station. She has been away for three years and her experiences outside 'let me see the potential and the importance to me that this really was my home.'

Melina complained of adults' lack of support: 'They've gone through it all. Now we want our space — a non-compromising lifestyle with solar energy, our own garden, a kitchen, office and meeting place and concert place in one building and cabins around to live in and for visitors. Students could come and maybe earn credits: it could be a youth branch of the eco-village training centre.'

Someone objected that inviting the whole world to The Farm could attract 'a whole lot of jerks.' Melina replied: 'There's just thousands of really juicy people out there. I can run the risk of anyone who wants to like screw me over.' Of the Changeover, Melina said it was a natural and necessary revolution. 'Since then, some of those folks went to the other extreme, protecting their property and getting really possessive. I feel compassion for them. But now we want to see some co-operative and communal patches on our land. We don't all have to be doing the same thing.'

These young people have grown up poor in terms of objects, and most of them still are, but they show little desire for material possessions. And they have a gentleness about them and a friendliness that warmed us.

Stephen Gaskin as an old man

He is growing old with grace, no longer the leader, as relaxed as ever and reconciled to The Farm's new personality. Still surrounded by young people — he teaches creative writing once a week at the Farm school — he is busy most days on Rocinante, a project to bring old people into a new retirement community on land adjacent to The Farm's. He helps with publicity work for Ina May, his wife who has become internationally known through her advocacy of home birth and her work as a midwife.

Their wooden home sprawls at the edge of a field, encircled with a collection of decrepit Volvo cars: Stephen explains that he collects them to cannibalise spare parts to keep one vehicle on the road. In the living area teenagers are washing up to the sound of reggae. Ina May leads us into the bedroom where Stephen is lying on their capacious double bed. Their son, working a computer in the corner, goes out to make room for us. Ina May sits by the bed. Books spill over every conceivable space; the wall is filled with Mayan hangings. The framed Right Livelihood Award given to Stephen Gaskin, and to the charity Plenty that he started, hangs among the family photographs.

Stephen, polite and hospitable, looks older than his sixty-three years and his discourse rambles. Is it the years of psychedelics? Hard to imagine him keeping an audience of 1000 spellbound every Monday evening in San Francisco and every Sunday morning on The Farm.

What does he do these days? He hesitates a second before replying: 'I work on the computer, writing newsletters for Rocinante, I drive tractors and build roads, and I go on the road and lecture and I write and publish and help the midwives whenever they need help. I'm pledged to the midwives like a medieval monk' (throaty laugh). We start to feel Stephen's charisma.

Rocinante is building its fourth house. A retired nurse lives in one; another nurse and a homeless old man plan to come. 'This is the way for old people who depend mainly on social security; collectivity is a way for them to survive,' Gaskin said: 'When a person dies his house will revert to the project.' Stephen thinks that Rocinante will complete his life's work. 'When we came from San Francisco, collectivity was strong, but then when people get into their good earning years they want to keep their money. That had something to do with the changes we made in 1983. We had got real good with babies and with kids but we didn't have a chance to be good with old people.'

Stephen Gaskin denies that financial failures caused the Changeover. He favours the conspiracy theory. 'The FBI came and spoke to our bankers and scared them all, and we were forced to refinance and in the refinancing our debt went from $800,000 to $1,600,000.'

However, good came out of evil. 'We bought 680 more acres last year — we're up to 4.2 square miles now and only about 500 acres is cleared. The rest is trees we're saving. The Farm has created a place for the midwife crew which has become internationally famous because they have this base to work from.'

Stephen is convinced The Farm has been a success in establishing a permanent community which has influenced American culture, even though that culture is still getting worse. 'When we were at our biggest no governor or senatorial candidate would risk leaving us out, they all came to see us. And we have established ourselves here permanently, with excellent relationships with our neighbours. I don't believe we failed. In Europe to have this kind of land you've got to be the Graf this or Lord that. The American Indians came to us and said we read about you in magazine articles and you guys are expressing sovereignty and we've come to study it with you. And we taught them midwifery. We have projects with them.'

He accepts the new dispensation : 'We now have people who do not want to be collective apart from owning the land together. The First Foundation was an extended partnership like a monastery. Now we have the Second Foundation, named after Asimov of course: we took the idea from him.

Of his own five children by his various wives, one had died, one son is in the navy and two sons live on The Farm. Floyd, the youngest at fifteen, is at the Farm school. 'I teach in the school to defray his tuition.'

Stephen told us he plans to run for president on a ticket of decriminalising marijuana. The project seems to us far-fetched. His pride in Ina May's achievement as a midwife is better grounded in reality.

Spiritual midwifery

Midwifery began in the Caravan long before it reached The Farm. In a parking lot near Chicago, a woman was about to give birth in one of the buses. Stephen was about to make a speech; nobody had any training in delivering babies, but Ina May and a few other women volunteered to help. They delivered a healthy boy. Eleven more babies were born on the Caravan. The travellers could not afford doctors and had renounced welfare payments, so when they got to The Farm, Ina May and a group of women set up a birth clinic. With a sympathetic local doctor, they taught themselves. They transformed one of the buses into a pre-natal clinic and the public health department brought boxes of vitamins, stacks of birth certificates and a tacit agreement to let them deliver their own babies. 'The entire system was based on fellowship and love,' said Pamela, one of the early midwives who is still in practice. 'We learned over and over again that birth was a spiritual event, different with every mother and baby.' In The Farm's heyday during the late

1970s, the midwives helped birth two dozen babies a month.

One of the mothers remembers: 'We were all young, all idealistic and all having babies at the same time. We had so much fun at the clinic. We gave each other a lot of confidence. We had a cultural belief that natural childbirth worked.'

Since then Ina May Gaskin has done as much as any woman in America to bring back the mysterious, personal and spiritual element to childbirth, treating each birth as unique, each baby a universe in itself. This mystery does not thrive, is almost stifled, in the technical setting of a modern hospital, yet even there it occurs. The Farm midwives returned to ancient traditions of women giving birth surrounded and helped by other women. 'A woman is not a faulty machine,' Ina May said. 'For a hospital birth you need machines, you need men, you need stirrups; you have to be flat on your back and tied down and they have to cut you and stitch you and all those things have to happen to get a baby out.'

> *If a woman doesn't look wildly beautiful when she is giving birth, then someone's probably not treating her right. We discovered that when you put enough women together and the men behave in a supportive fashion you create a very beautiful situation. Women want to be treated like goddesses when they're having babies and then they'll have the most amazing powers. I think that these powers are coming back to women.*
> • *Ina May Gaskin, to the authors.*

She still delivers half a dozen babies a month, teaches midwifery, edits her quarterly journal, *The Birth Gazette*, and campaigns for a national certification program for lay midwives. Her video showing how she delivers breech babies without large episiotomies or forceps is a widely used teaching aid. Her book *Spiritual Midwifery*, still in print after twenty years, has made her a household name in home-birth and midwifery circles.

In the birth clinic the waiting room is clean, without fuss or frills except that the midwives' offices have their walls plastered with mother and baby photographs. The clinic serves as a health centre for Farm people. The birthing house attached to the clinic, for mothers who come to The Farm to give birth, is a cosy, one-up-one-down cabin, bright with braided rugs and

---

THE FARM MIDWIFERY STATISTICS, 1994

1917 women gave birth. 803 were Farm residents, 952 were non-Farm residents, 163 were Amish. 35 had caesareans. Twelve sets of twins were born. 60 babies were breech deliveries. The caesarean percentage was 1.8 compared to a national average of slightly less than 25 percent.

check curtains, although oxygen tanks and incubators are concealed in a cupboard, an atmosphere light years away from the stainless steel glare of labour rooms most women know.

Now that there are only 200 people living on The Farm there are fewer births — five to ten a month; the local Summertown women still prefer hi-tech hospital births. A group of women who do however want to birth at home are the Amish. The Amish still pray in Old German, still wear their traditional black clothes with hats for men and bonnets for women, and still refuse the petrol engine. The local supermarket has hitching rails for Amish buggies. They eschew electricity and television and they prefer not to give birth in hospital. Although these women are considered 'high risk', since multiple pregnancies are the rule, The Farm's midwives nevertheless continue their extremely low rate of intervention. In modern obstetric practice it is common once the first baby is delivered by caesarean to continue subsequent deliveries by the same method. One of Ina May's patients, an Amish woman, is proud of having sixteen normal vaginal births following her first caesarean. It makes for a strange alliance, midwives evolved from the flower children and mothers adhering to a strict religious sect.

Ina May challenges a birth culture in which most of the advertising is for pain relief medication. 'That passes into attitudes towards childbirth; women are scared, and caesarean sections are sold as a way of getting an unmarked baby. If a woman chooses an epidural, she increases the risk of a caesarean. Of course, forceps can be helpful: (she smiles) we have used them twice for two thousand births.' Farm midwives don't speak of 'pains' or 'contractions', they talk of 'rushes'.

Spiritual and sexual — two words not often coupled — meet during Farm births because Ina May encourages contact between mother and father during labour. She remembers a woman whose cervix was fully open but she had no urge to push and the midwives were becoming uneasy. 'Knowing that stimulation of the breasts can encourage the flow of oxytocin into the woman's bloodstream, thereby stimulating uterine contractions, I asked the husband whether he would squeeze his wife's breasts. He was somewhat self-conscious I suspect, doing this in front of us, and only used one hand. After one rush in this lop-sided condition, the wife leaned over and whispered in his ear, "Squeeze the other one, too." Not more than five seconds after he had both breasts in his hands she had an enormous urge to push, and the baby's head was visible.'[1]

Ina May overturned the conventional wisdom that women shouldn't eat or sleep during labour. She says that women's knowledge about childbirth has been discredited. 'A lot of people don't know — if you take a woman who's

Although many contemporary community visions emphasise the creation of neigh-bourhood and/or extended family ties, their philosophic roots are amazingly diverse. The range includes Christians, Quakers, and followers of Eastern religions, to '60s drop-outs, anarchists, psychologists, artists, back-to-the-land survivalists — and the list goes on. The scope of their primary values is equally broad, including ecology, equality, appropriate technology, self-sufficiency, right livelihood, humanist psychology, creativity, spirituality, meditation, yoga, and the pursuit of global peace.
· Geoph Kozeny in *Communities Directory.*

having a lot of pain, and you get hold of her bottom, or the large muscles of her thighs and you just shake them, it makes her feel good and she'll relax, thereby stimulating uterine contractions.'

Ina May worked with midwives in Guatemala. 'I learnt something so simple: if the baby's shoulders are too big — put the woman on hands and knees and generally the baby will fall out. So I've taught that technique. We have never had an injury or an episiotomy from that condition. I thought that I had discovered techniques that later I read about in old books from the 1800s.'

She has none of a guru's arrogance. As she sits at her computer working on her records, or planning a new book, she plays Bach or Indian chants. Tragedy has strengthened her. Her second baby was stillborn and her grown daughter died of cancer. She has three surviving children. Of her husband's role she says, 'He taught me not to be afraid. That is part of his attraction.'

The Intentional Communities conference

We timed our visit to The Farm to coincide with a meeting of the Federation of Intentional Communities (FIC). Their directory lists 500, but the Federation estimates at least 2000 intentional communities in the USA. Some, like The Farm, have seen their income-sharing evolve into separate households; others have continued as communes, sharing a common purse.

'Hello, my name's Tree,' said a lively, frank-faced young woman who explained that at Acorn, her community in Virginia, people change their names frequently. She used to be Beth, had a spell as Ivy, settled for Tree. Now she's twenty-six she says she won't change her name again until she's at least fifty.

Tree works for an FIC-affiliated organisation, the Federation of Egalitarian Communities. She joined Acorn two years ago, after a year on the road. Her family values, secular Jewish, had been formed in civic action and the peace movement; her father is active in New Jersey local politics. Ironically, her father now criticises her lifestyle for 'running away from society's problems' while her mother is sympathetic.

'Of course I'm not dropping out but helping to create a new civilisation by living out the alternative. The majority of human history has always been community living. What we have now is a passing blip. This society is not working. A lot of people are miserable. Most intentional communities just now are growing.'

When Twin Oaks outgrew its space, with a long waiting list, Acorn was founded. Tree arrived at Acorn with a partner but they're no longer together. 'We're still friends. Community life is such an intense environment — you run through all the stages very fast. My real orientation is poly-amorous — several adults in an open-group marriage. It's been done here and there. I've not had a monogamous relationship since high school.'

Tree says that consensus really works at Acorn, which has twenty people including three children. Life is freer than at Twin Oaks. People can hold on to their pre-existing assets but can't spend them in the community. When members work they earn credits, as at Twin Oaks, but people can contract for individual full-time jobs. Tree said there were procedures for checking that such jobs are done conscientiously. She may stay — she may not, and doesn't worry about the idea of moving around which she sees as part of alternative culture. We, more staid and middle-aged, are looking for stable communities. We found one among some of the old-timers on The Farm.

Exercise class

Dorothy writes: Kathy, the director of The Farm School, lives with her married sister Pat in a house near the swimming hole. Pat and her family left at the Changeover and went to California; there they earned enough money

---

For all our obvious and troublesome differences, there is nevertheless a New Age cultural ambience at Twin Oaks. For instance, we eat a lot of beans, rice and tofu. We have 20 kinds of herb tea in the snack kitchen. We subscribe to 10 or 15 radical Leftist magazines. We wear used clothing made of natural fibres, and we don't throw it out when it becomes stained. When we buy new shoes, they are likely to be Birkenstocks. We have built geodesic domes, enjoy a rustic cabin and a tipi, and one of these days will probably get around to making a yurt. We depend on wood heat and cut our own firewood. We go in for underwater births, mud pits, nude swimming, sweat huts and pagan rituals. We think seriously about animal rights. Some people won't even kill flies.

But more than half of us do several of the following: eat meat, drink coffee, read Newsweek, go to regular AMA physicians, wear clean, neat clothing, ignore the tipi, take rituals with a grain of salt, and kill flies with a clean conscience.

· Pat Kinkade in *Is It Utopia Yet? An Insider's View of Twin Oaks.*

to come back and build their house. It is a simple single-storey house, not ecological. Pat would have liked to use solar energy but said the technology was too expensive. The regenerating forest comes within yards of the patio.

Three times a week, the open plan living room hosts Pat's friends, five women who have doing aerobics together for ten years. They are all long-time settlers on The Farm, in their mid-forties to fifties. If ever you wanted proof of the benefits of sustained exercise all you would need to do would be to watch them carrying out their programme to a flickering almost worn-out video. They invited me to join them but prudence prevailed and while they went through an amazingly tough workout I did gentle stretching alongside. Mary, Margaret and I stayed on for supper. With five women chopping the vegetables, the meal took twenty minutes to prepare.

They look back on the early days with nostalgia. 'When we were young, we had a huge base of support. Someone at home watching the kids while we were working. Living in rural Tennessee we were able to create cottage industries. Nobody had to come out with a lot of money. We were well educated; we were vegan; no-one was hyper-tense; we had this culture of empowerment.'

These women, from middle-class backgrounds, had been rebels of the sixties and seventies. Kathy said when she was young she was mesmerised by Stephen Gaskin. 'I used to think he could read my thoughts.' Her elder sister Pat was more sceptical. 'I remember when he married us, he couldn't remember my name.' Pat said that Stephen's influence waned in a natural manner. 'We all grew up.'

To earn even a modest living, most of these women work off The Farm. Mary teaches in a public school, Pat and Margaret are nurses. Now they worry about the future of the young people who want to return to the Farm. How much should be done for them? Pat has a son living on the West Coast. She says: 'You just can't live in rural Tennessee. That's reality.'

The others disagree. Kathy says: 'It's nice to think that we can create cottage industries so that more people can live here. It sounds harsh to say you were born and raised here but you can't live here. You shouldn't force the kids to go away.

Pat: 'To live here you have to think seriously about your education. You have to learn some skills. A lot of them don't think about what they should do. Why should we create jobs for them? I think the kids should get away. They shouldn't come back and expect us to figure out their lives.'

The others don't agree but these are very old friends who disagree with affection. Margaret tells me: 'On The Farm you'll find as many opinions as there are people.'

Promised land?

At the edge of the forest, Jerry and Catherine Hutchins live in a wooden house with a shingled roof. Like most of The Farm dwellings, the house appears to have grown where it stands. The open plan living room feels friendly with tie-dye hangings and cosy rugs, wood walls and a guitar on the floor and folk music playing on the hi-fi. This is home for them and their children Turner (17) and Faith (9). They came to The Farm in 1976 and lived first in two buses parked together. One of the buses still stands outside the Hutchins' home, its California number plates covered in rust.

'We're still hippies and still living here and still working hard,' Catherine said. 'The Changeover was good — being hooked up to electricity after all those years of hassle with spirit lamps, and telephones that work. We could go solar but that is too costly and anyway there isn't that much sun here.'

Catherine thinks that Stephen Gaskin, today, is an embarrassment: he should not have decided to stand for president. 'We're integrated into the community here, if we're associated with drugs again people won't talk to our kids.'

She is active on the inter-generation committee: 'There's a bumper crop of young people now and we have to help them. There are very few jobs outside The Farm — this is an area of over fifteen percent unemployment — and we need to get a cottage industry going, like the hammocks they do in Twin Oaks, or we could look at mail-order crafts, jewellery, beads.'

Michael Amundson, one of the original caravan people, holds similar views. He lives in a house shaped like a tall barrel in the wood; nearby is his carpenter's workshop. For him The Farm has moved away from its days of glory and has become a backwater. 'Originally a huge amount of energy reached critical mass in San Francisco and led to what one visitor called the exodus. There was nothing when we got here; everything had to be created anew and so many people came to experience this: so much energy from all over. Later we reached a stage where some of the young people had to be pushed out for violent and anti-social behaviour. Now we have to start anew and give responsibility to the youth: otherwise we'll end up like the Shakers — with just one or two old people left.'

Some members at The Farm want to re-incorporate young people who return, others remain suspicious of the youth. Phil Schweitzer's daughter Sarah Jane, born on the Caravan, is twenty-five. The Changeover for her was 'the saddest time in my life. If I don't see The Farm change in a positive way, I want to move to a more progressive community, more ecologically sound, not quite as money-driven. I haven't really checked any of them out. I'll maybe start one with my friends. This place is getting like the US government, so bureaucratic. My boyfriend and I wanted to start a coffee house in a decrepit building to get people together more. We said: this is a money system, why not a café? We appealed to adults with authority. They said No.'

But Sarah Jane has supporters. Just before our visit, a plenary meeting had listened to young people's views with sympathy. Later, we attended a meeting of the old-timers who serve on The Farm's strategic planning committee. Phil Schweitzer was upbeat because he thought the plenary had inspired young people to stay on. 'It was a leap forward. Only last year we were debating about whether to call the police on our young people; now there's a different atmosphere. There's a re-creation of this community and a coming out of our cocoon.'

The mission statement proposed by the old-timers was anodyne — 'to provide a secure, ecologically healthy, commonly-held land base in which the members and succeeding generations can relate to each other and their natural environment in a sustainable way...' In sharp contrast, sixteen-year-old Kevin had submitted his own draft: 'Make a circle and hold hands, focus our energy rather than having it scattered with everybody doing their own thing, in order to create a centre of love with such a kind vibe that other people will want to come and experience it, and take it with them to help transform the world'.

We left The Farm before a decision was made on which draft would win. Although Stephen Gaskin's exodus had reached the promised land, the milk and honey had stopped flowing within a decade. It took the Changeover, with most people leaving, for the remaining members even to attempt a viable economic community. To survive, The Farm has adopted a mainstream economic approach while retaining an alternative lifestyle. The future is open.

Note

1   Ina May Gaskin. *Spiritual Midwifery.*

14

The business of spirituality

●●●

To understand Findhorn we need to 'do Experience Week', the education officer told us — and sent us an application form with a blank space to explain our motives. We chewed the end of our biros and wrote piously that we wanted to go to Findhorn 'properly', to communicate with the place, the people and our inner selves. Findhorn is a New Age community where people talk with God, angels and nature spirits they call 'devas'.

This community on the north-east coast of Scotland has a global reputation among Green-alternative people, although it is sometimes criticised as a spiritual supermarket, somewhat cultish, and expensive to visit. Thirty-five years have passed since Peter and Eileen Caddy grew amazingly large vegetables (cabbages weighing-in at eighteen kilos) outside their caravan on a windy beach. Eileen talked to God, and still does. She claims that anyone can, because God is within us. Under her guidance and Peter's management the community grew. Today, 450 members and sympathisers live in the Caravan Park, in nearby centres or locally in their own homes. Ten thousand visitors, tourists and spiritual seekers come every year to the courses, conferences, workshops, treatment centres and the introductory Experience Week.

We wanted to experience the New Age, a movement which Findhorn claims to embody, if not to lead, by 'providing a model in developing new ways of living that address many of the problems facing humanity today' (Trustees' Report, 1996). Findhorn belongs to the growing Eco-Village Network, with Internet links not just to the best-known communities like Auroville in India, The Farm in the USA and Crystal Waters in Australia, but others in Germany, Russia, Israel and Hungary. Like The Farm, Findhorn was founded by a charismatic figure and began with pioneers living in caravans. Like Auroville, it is centred on a mystical message concerning human consciousness and evolution. Findhorn is called the Vatican of the New Age. We had to go.

Visitors usually fail to describe Findhorn adequately because it is a mismatch of grandeur and poverty. Fine and unusual buildings are set in a wide, secluded bay — the perfectly shaped Universal Hall, the charmingly round,

> There does indeed appear to be a magic of Findhorn. The longer one stays, the more one comes in touch with a deeper, spiritual sense of self. It is surely a sign of an enlightened mind to remain open to new senses, to new explanations and to new realities. To write off the spiritual, mystical explanation of the Findhorn story is to demonstrate a closed, rigid mind.
> · William Metcalf in *Findhorn, The Routinization of Charisma.*

timbered community centre, the stone-built meditation sanctuaries hidden among flowers, the graceful windmill out on the sand dunes, the eco-residences and homes made of recycled oak whisky barrels. Yet most Foundation members still live in caravans or mobile homes and are short of cash. The Caravan Park, still the community's main home, is set alongside an operational RAF base from which giant reconnaissance aircraft hurtle day and night to protect the skies from real or imagined enemies. Findhorn people turn these ear-splitting interruptions to good use as moments of enforced meditation.

We settled down, as so many others have done, sleeping in a caravan, eating in a community, meditating, gardening, washing up, singing and holding hands in a circle. Perplexed by the paradoxes, we were charmed by the details. Around each corner you find a curving garden of flowers, ponds and vegetable beds. Flagstoned paths wind between caravans and mobile homes. Racks of bicycles add a Green flavour; parked cars dilute it. Gardens

FINDHORN FOUNDATION
Community Centre

are well tended yet homely with the odd weed poking up among the lupins. The caravan painted pink that we're assigned for our stay is like that, too: clean, spacious and well-equipped but the lino needs renewing and the kettle has lost its whistle. We feel at home, welcomed by a vase of flowers on the table and

> The New Age is too powerful an idea to become crystallised, channelled, occultized, and thereby ridiculed and dismissed. It is an idea that is in touch with wild and primal forces of life, forces of change and growth, forces of love and sacrifice, forces of challenge and expansion. It is an idea that takes us to the boundaries and introduces us to edges where all things are made new. If you believe in the possibilities of a New Age, then you owe it to yourself to go beyond the images (or lack of them) in the media and find the elements, the people, the examples of the New Age that live up to the high possibilities within you.
> · David Spangler, *Pilgrim in Aquarius*.

a wholesome selection of breakfast foods. Our caravan is parked in a group of six behind the Community Hall, each surrounded by its own garden.

Saturday afternoon: Experience Week begins. In the sitting room of a stone house in a secluded garden, overlooking rhododendron bushes and a fern-encircled pond, our group meets for the first time. Twenty-two strangers in an apprehensive circle. We begin, as every group activity does at Findhorn, with attunement. Hold hands in our circle, left hand facing down, right hand up. Keep both thumbs pointing to the right and you can't go wrong. As the week progresses the habit loses its strangeness. We close our eyes and Fany-Lea tells us to centre our minds, first on ourselves — on our minds, then our hearts — then outwards to the group and finally to this place and the activity we are about to start. Her tranquil voice speaks of realms of separateness and of oneness and the need to unify.

Fany-Lea and Françoise are our two focalisers; their task is to channel the 'energy' of the group. A focaliser is a facilitator, manager or teacher. Fany-Lea speaks Argentinean English with verve — she's slight and fair with large, blue-grey eyes and given to rapid, delicate gestures. Françoise speaks a Belgian kind of English in a more reflective tone; at home in her lavish, well-upholstered body, she sits comfortably cross-legged in Turkish trousers. The two focalisers talk to us as equals: they are part of our group and when they ask for 'sharing' of our innermost feelings, they lead off with their own. They have not done this often before, never together. Five years ago both were beginners on the same Experience Week. Both smile often, with great warmth. Their enthusiasm makes them seem younger than they are (thirty-seven and thirty-five).

Fany-Lea lays down ground rules for the daily 'sharing'. Always speak in the first person — about yourself, not about the group or a partner or anyone else. If you reply to anyone you should first ask permission. When you finish you say: 'That's me'. The focalisers warn us all that we shall feel the strain and perhaps need to take breaks. However, we must try our best to attend every activity because our purpose is to build up a group dynamic.

Only three of us are from the UK. Ursula from Germany looks over sixty, but when she says she is fifty-nine, we know that we're the oldest.[1] The youngest is eighteen — Linda from Perth, Australia, who tells the group right off that she had to quit Australia in a rush (problems with a man). Two others speak, that first evening, of just-broken relationships. Names and countries of origin: Australia, Japan, Italy, Switzerland, Germany, Ireland, New Zealand, USA and UK. Only three men. This is usual. Findhorn staff and long-time students, we learn later, are two-thirds women.

Everyone in this first, faltering attempt at communication acts out national stereotypes: the Germans precise and down-to-earth, the Americans friendly and up-beat, the Italians smiling and gesticulating to cover a lack of English. Only the three Japanese — Takeo, Tomoko and a single woman — break the mould of inscrutable politeness as they try to communicate on an intimate level. Our three men are with partners: Takeo with Tomoko, from Japan; Malcolm with Sheila, from South Australia; and us two. Malcolm introduces himself, he is seeking spiritual reassurance after a recent trauma when he criticised the racist mayor in the municipality where he is a councillor, and found most of the town siding with the mayor. His wife says she's never heard of Findhorn — 'I leave that stuff to Malcolm' — but is game for anything.

Takeo's turn to speak. In barely comprehensible English, he appears to be telling us that his Shinto religion did not teach him to love others or even love himself, and that he hopes to find love here. The Americans have read about Findhorn and have always been meaning to come. Meryl from New Zealand, a single mum with four grown-up kids, 'simply had to be here. My friends helped me raise the fare and the fee.'

In spite of good resolutions, the two of us are the most reserved. The sharing is designed to break down barriers but, we find, the older you are, the higher the barriers.

That evening, most of our group went to watch Findhorn teenagers put on a revue. We are impressed that as many boys as girls take part, singing and dancing. The satire pokes gentle fun at Findhorn people's mannerisms. The audience of mums, dads and siblings applauds vociferously.

Zoe, one of the actors, tells us the show was put on to raise money to bring a group of orphans from a spiritual community in Russia to Findhorn. In her year out before university, Zoe is going to the US, where she will stay with

Findhorn contacts. 'I've been over there already; it really felt dangerous in an American town till I got the hang of it.' Zoe has benefited from the sophistication of growing up in the New Age Vatican and the contacts offered by a global fraternity. We feel that the kids brought up here — articulate, funny and caring — represent the best that Findhorn has to offer.

Day One

Morning. Our programme reads: Sacred Dance in the Universal Hall. This impressive building seats three hundred: its five sides allow no wasted space, the variable skylight rations the daylight and the well-sprung parquet floor is kind to bare feet. Our Sacred Dance teacher isn't a whiz at explaining the simple steps; her English is minimal. Nor do we find this dancing especially sacred: to us it's circle dancing. However, it helps to ease us all out of our self-consciousness into group awareness (already we have absorbed the jargon!).

Spirit of the Pea, Spirit of the Wind

In the afternoon we are bussed through grey-stone Forres town to Cluny Hill Hotel, Findhorn's second centre — the place where the story began. We absorb the spiritual soap opera of Peter and Eileen Caddy, played out over three decades: their rise, fall and rise again, their growing fame, their numerous friends, critics and disciples, their parting. The aftermath was tragic for Peter who died in a car accident, tranquil for Eileen who has become the spiritual 'anchor' of contemporary Findhorn.

The cast is as follows: Peter — an RAF Squadron Leader, a gifted administrator who has risen to the top of the catering division. He has left his first wife and is married to Sheena, a freelance spiritual teacher. Eileen is married to Andrew, a soldier and follower of Moral Re-Armament, the right-wing revivalist movement: they have five daughters. The action begins when Peter leaves Sheena and Eileen leaves Andrew, who takes custody of the daughters. The newly married Caddys are appointed managers of Cluny Hill Hotel. Eileen has for some years been receiving verbatim guidance from a source she

---

I attended a meeting of the Findhorn Foundation Trustees and the business managers as they looked at an annual budget of over $1.5m (US), and then later overheard one senior member telling another that the way to detoxify rat poison which had been used some years earlier was simply to conduct a 'cleansing meditation'. The juxtaposition of the rational, bureaucratic and logical with the paranormal, affective and metaphysical is an everyday occurrence at Findhorn.

· William Metcalf in *Findhorn, the Routinization of Charisma.*

calls the God within. Peter runs the hotel in obedience to this guidance, together with assiduous hospitality and business acumen, a mixture which guests enjoy. The hotel's losses turn into profit. The Caddys' fame spreads; they are joined by Dorothy Maclean, an American mystic who helps interpret Eileen's guidances, though they are simple and clear enough, and adds inspiration of her own.

In the rolling grounds of Cluny Hill Hotel, Peter has a hilltop cleared for the imminent arrival of space travellers. This is apparently too much for the hotel owners who transfer the couple to another hotel so commercially unpromising that even Eileen's guidance cannot make it profitable, so they are sacked. Peter can easily get another hotel job but, following Eileen's guidance, they tow their caravan to the Findhorn Bay Caravan Park and live there on unemployment benefit. Peter starts a vegetable garden to supplement their income.

The site is a rubbish dump surrounded by gorse and brambles on sand and gravel. Dorothy Maclean, through her meditation, can contact the archetypal formative forces of light or energy that underlie all forms in nature. These forces manifest themselves as Spirit of the Pea, Spirit of the Wind, or similar entities. Dorothy calls them 'devas' and regularly invokes them. Their garden begins producing vegetables so large that they feature in BBC gardening broadcasts, although Peter's autobiography, published posthumously, pays a good deal of attention to his assiduous collection and application of compost. Muck certainly became magic for him and provides a more mundane explanation of his harvests. Today Foundation members don't talk much about Peter's giant cabbages, but they have carefully preserved the original garden and the original caravan.

From the mid-sixties sympathisers began arriving at the Caravan Park, including R. Ogilvie Crombie, known as Roc, who enjoyed his own contacts with 'nature spirits'. Eileen now published a collection of her received messages entitled, *God Spoke to Me*. It sold out. Curious fact: the widely translated book still does best in Spain where it sells 20,000 a year.

By the end of 1967 the community had grown to twelve. Eileen had a vision of seven cedarwood bungalows surrounded by beautiful gardens. The bungalows were ordered before anyone knew how they were to be paid for. A donation arrived in the nick of time. This was to be a pattern: money arriving at the last moment to pay debts incurred by faith in 'the laws of manifestation', which is Findhorn-speak for providence. Peter's autobiography shows his supreme self-confidence. Having studied positive thinking as a Rosicrucian, he firmly believed that if you want something and have faith in God, you get it. By the end of the sixties Findhorn had grown into a substantial community and by 1972 it was stabilised as a foundation. Its stated, stirring principles:

I spent hours in the sanctuary trying to hear an inner, directive voice. I had great meditations but never heard a voice. After a while I realised that whenever I asked questions
of whatever spiritual presence I was addressing — be that God, the Angel of Findhorn
or My Higher Self — a procession of images would move across my inner screen, and
if I paid attention, they usually had relevance to what I was asking. I'd been tuning in
on the wrong wavelength!
· Mary Inglis, quoted in William Metcalf, *Shared Visions, Shared Lives.*

'God, or the source of life, is accessible to each of us at all times; nature, including the planet, has intelligence and is part of a greater plan.'

Throughout the seventies the community prospered, increasing its numbers. Gradually Peter Caddy's authoritarian governance gave way to more democratic decision making by core group members. Focalisers took over. In the seventies Findhorn was a community of its time. Everything was shared. Some of those principles remain today. Unwanted clothing is put in the boutique and people help themselves. Breakfast supplies and household items like soap and loo paper are kept in open sheds — you take what you need.

Findhorn expanded. More buildings and land were acquired, including Cluny Hill Hotel — a symbolic triumph over worldly forces. Another triumph followed when a worldwide campaign raised enough funds to buy the original Caravan Park.

Inside the old hotel, an atmosphere of faded luxury has been replaced by the vibes of an upmarket youth hostel. We assemble in a drawing room converted into a sanctuary. Full-grown trees in pots line the walls. Amid comfortable chairs and floor cushions, the focal point is a flower arrangement surrounding a candle. Sanctuaries and gardens are Findhorn's best achievements, creating an atmosphere of peace and serenity with a minimum of objects and decoration. In the 'sharing', Ursula speaks of growing inner peace — and at that moment a sunbeam strikes the clear glass dome and transfixes her in a triangle of golden light. Many in our group gasp with awe: another manifestation.

Cluny gardens have been loved for thirty years and Edward, the young man who takes us round, loves them still. He tells of sacred places, of ley lines of cosmic energy that criss-cross the site. He remarks that they are particularly strong in the laundry room. The garden is lovingly maintained, except that the hilltop lacks trees where Peter and Roc had them cut them down to make room for the spaceships.

Showing us a portion of the gardens deliberately left wild, Françoise says, 'Don't walk there, it's for the nature spirits to feel easy.' As the week progresses, we learn more Findhorn mythology. People speak of voices and spirits as everyday matters. At first it sounds silly, then it seems normal.

Eileen Caddy at home

Eileen Caddy's books are too unsophisticated for us: we find them naive and fluffy. Meeting her is different. At almost eighty, with a white quiff and bright blue eyes, she dresses in daffodil yellow, a smiley colour suiting her personality. Nothing in her looks or manner suggests anything Alternative. Her voice is soft and pretty. She is like everyone's favourite granny and radiates an affectionate and gentle calm. A few years ago the community built her a wooden house in the centre of the park, next to the original caravan and garden, and called it Cornerstone. It's a comfortable, chintzy, matching-three-piece-suite sort of house with a downstairs bedroom (white Persian cat asleep on bed) and fitted kitchen.

Eileen spoke unromantically about her seven years in the caravan with Peter and their three sons. 'We were on National Assistance, nine pounds a week, I never thought we would sink as low as we did. A difficult and wonderful time, we had all those rough edges worn smooth; through meditation and prayer we always managed to pull through.'

Anybody can have guidance, Eileen told us, if they take the time for prayer and meditation. 'Prayer is talking to God and meditation is listening. People are so busy, they don't take the time. When I sit down I still myself, and get my breath going, a rhythm, and then I become still and can pray. There are hundreds of techniques — it depends on the person. When I started I used to sit for two hours and then I could wait upon God and I would receive a message, it would just come through, and I would write it down. And that message was read in the sanctuary. That was going fine and it was going beautifully and then out of the blue I got no more guidances. Why? This was the guidance I received: You're spoonfeeding them. As long as you do that they won't stand on their own two feet. I got this very clear guidance not to give them more guidance so

In spite of the use of such terms as 'God', 'the Christ' and 'the Christ within', Findhorn is clearly not Christian. Jesus, the historical figure, is seen as one of several enlightened beings from whom we can learn. Guidance is received not from some Old Testament, personified deity, but from 'all that is.' ... Most see God as the divine spirit that lies within each and everything. It therefore follows that God is within me, and when I meditate, I may contact the God within. Similarly, through meditation, I can contact the God within another person, within an animal or even a plant.'
· Bill Metcalf in *Findhorn: the Routinization of Charisma.*

This whole community is based on the Law of Manifestation! It depends and runs on its principles. It operates in complete faith that all our needs will be perfectly met! I had asked for a year for a greenhouse; I knew we were to have a greenhouse; Eileen had received positive guidance we were to have a greenhouse, and I just couldn't understand why we didn't have a greenhouse! And then suddenly I realised what the problem was. I had been too vague. I came here, measured the space, and asked for an eight-by twelve-foot cedarwood greenhouse. It came next week!
· Peter Caddy, quoted in *The Magic of Findhorn*.

Quite what these New Agers believe is impossible to say, since they express themselves in psychobabble, but from what one can make out their beliefs are a cocktail... Eileen Caddy's background is Moral Re-Armament. Her messages don't always make a lot of sense. One of her uplifting thoughts, for example, is that 'Big doors hang on small hinges'. They don't. Big doors hang on big hinges. It's small doors that hang on small hinges.
· Richard Boston in *The Guardian*, 11 November 1992.

they could really create their own community.'

She is Christian but no longer a churchgoer. 'All I need is to be still and tap into the source. God is in everything. God is love, unconditional love. It took me five years to work that through; I had to have self-discipline and specific plans for meditation and prayer and obedience to what was pouring through. I've been living this life now for about forty-five years.'

Eileen persuades because she has suffered. 'Peter used to say to me, we are two halves of a whole and we complement each other. When he left I was absolutely devastated. And then it was an amazing revelation: you don't need anyone when you love the divinity. Peter and I were brought together to do our work. And then the time came to go our separate ways.' Peter tried to start several communities after he left. He married twice more, each time to spiritually-minded women.

Eileen now sees her role at Findhorn as 'an anchor to the spirit. I know they're mature — but still not mature enough: they're too materialistic at the moment. God has to be at the centre.' In their meditations and prayers Findhorn people speak of 'the Christ' as an enlightened man who knew how to listen. They identify Christ with the love and awareness they seek for themselves. Eileen told us: 'If I can see the Christ in myself I can see the Christ in you. That is why you have to love yourself. I said, how can I love myself knowing all my faults? And then I found myself in front of the mirror doing my hair but I didn't turn my face away and I was looking at my eyes and I realised that the eyes are the window of my soul and I was looking at the divinity within me... and then I realised, and started to love all of myself.'

'Manifestation' is an important concept within the Findhorn Foundation. People believe that material items 'float' in the universe, following the same cosmic laws that affect humans. A machine is seen to have a sort of personality. For example, the three Findhorn buses are named Heather, Henry and Francis, and the tip truck is called Tipsy, while the Cluny dishwasher is Walter, and the spin dryer in the laundry, Dervish. As I write this paper here at Findhorn, I work on a machine known as Mac, and print on Goodie Two-Shoes, who contains the advice 'Treat her with love and she will serve you well.'
· William Metcalf, *Findhorn, the Routinization of Charisma*.

Eileen's eyes have a child-like innocence. As we leave, she gives us the Findhorn hug. Her warmth remained with us for the rest of our stay.

The Angel of Healing

The focalisers want us to use the Angel Sharing method to find a special theme for our week. The angels are to make known their wishes via a board game. Fifty Angel Cards from The Game of Transformation are laid face down around the flower-decorated candle. The game (a Findhorn invention, sold here and worldwide) is for five to a hundred players and generally takes four days. The board represents each player's journey through life. It is claimed that the game offers a way of confronting some of life's key issues through a deeper self-knowledge. To play the game ourselves, we would have had to book a weekend course later in the year and pay £310. For our purpose tonight we pick a card each to identify our individual angel: Walter draws Creativity, Dorothy draws Responsibility. The gloomiest member of our group gets Joy and someone whose life is in fragments turns up Harmony. A card is picked for the whole group — Healing. Several people say they believe that something more than chance has given them an appropriate angel and Fany-Lea appears moved that our group's destiny is to be Healing.

In the evening 'sharing' Ruth, who likes to make a fable of her life, tells of the 'amazingly wonderful day' she has spent, with miraculous encounters involving coming face-to-face with a rabbit. Tomoko, Take's wife, says her life in Japan is boring because people are closed to each other and wrapped in conformity. Everybody else enthuses over their day.

That evening in our garden house, Fany-Lea reads out: Cluny dining room, Cluny kitchen, Cluny gardens, Cluny homecare, Park community centre, Park gardens, Park kitchens, Park homecare, Cullerne Gardens. We are supposed to 'attune' and meditate for guidance before choosing our work assignments for the week. With our eyes closed we raise hands to volunteer.

This routine is repeated several times before numbers work out right for each task. Fany-Lea thinks the revised choices have been guided by our Angel but in my case (Walter) I switched from the oversubscribed Cullerne Gardens to the undersubscribed Community Centre homecare just to be accommodating, as I suspect others did, too.

Day Two

We start our angel-guided work assignments.

Walter writes: Karla and I are assigned to Homecare at the Community Centre. We join the regular staff of two: Rory (American) and Chris (female, Swiss). The work session begins when we tell each other how we feel today, then hold hands around the table to attune.

Chris: 'Focus on yourself, then on our group, then on this place and the tasks ahead.'

I clean windows although they're already clean. Upstairs, in the splendid polygon meeting room with a panoramic view across the bay through stained glass, I enjoy rubbing the already clean glass. Rory has promised to find me a ladder to reach the outside, but he doesn't.

Dorothy writes: I didn't allow my angel to guide me to work anywhere else than Cullerne Gardens because I wanted to work with the head gardener, Steward, who knows a lot, and because the prospect of four mornings of housework even if upgraded with the charming title Homecare lacked appeal. The cynical would mutter that the Findhorn insistence on guests doing five morning shifts is a natty way of obtaining cheap labour. Perhaps. An often-stated principle here is: 'Love is work in action.' When I first heard it, I twitched. Auschwitz had a motto over the gate: 'Work Makes Free'. But having spent five mornings working in my group, I felt the warmth and friendliness of shared activity that our ordinary lives generally lack. Work at Findhorn goes on at a pace so leisurely it's almost catatonic. Our stint lasts a slow three hours including two attunements and a coffee break. Several people from the wider Findhorn community come to volunteer gardening work. One woman picks radishes with a baby on her back and a toddler

---

The earth yearns for, and is bringing forth, a new culture more transparently imbued with the gifts of spirit. We can't create culture as individuals; we need each other. Findhorn has already done much to help bring forth this new culture, but much remains to be done. I can't imagine anything that the world needs more from you (and from all of us!) now than to deepen your incarnation of this new culture.

· Robert Gilman in *Genesis*, June 1997.

around her feet; another has brought along home-made fruit cake to share. As in all Findhorn activities, there are more females than males.

Evening session: 'Finding the God Within' — a talk by Judith Bone. She is an American community member, plump and short, in a mauve pyjama suit with chestnut bubble cut and common-sense manner. She explains that members don't have any defined spiritual practice but simply share Eileen Caddy's belief that if you want the answer to a question you turn within and learn to be quiet. Her talk finishes with a guided meditation. On the in-breath we all say silently: 'May I have peace.' On the out-breath, we say, 'May others have peace.' (*Dorothy writes*: Amazing to see Wal, usually leery of public meditation and soul-searching of any kind, lose himself in this meditation. The magic of Findhorn seems to work.)

Day Three

Games of discovery

Afternoon: Group Discovery takes place in the dance studio beneath the auditorium. We meet here to play significant and purposeful games. Hug Tag: one person is 'it' holding a red cushion while everybody else has to flee into the safety of a hug; five seconds allowed. This game is fast and giggly, breaks the ice and really does produce a mood of intimacy. Car and Driver: you pair off into car (eyes closed) and driver (behind the car, holding car's shoulders to steer); it's meant to promote trust. Spiral: we all form a long line spiralling in on ourselves until we are a dense knot, then uncurling, a game to bond us (a dreadful activity for claustrophobics).

The games become more intimate. Blindfolded, you hold hands with an unknown partner and then relate to this person entirely through mutual touch. We are instructed to use our hands to express emotions like friendliness, curiosity, exploration and anger.

Dorothy writes: My partner's small, delicate hands took the initiative in the movements. When our eyes opened, I saw that it was Gretl. Her bossiness during the exercise confirmed my earlier impression. She led, I followed. Yet her touch was gentle and reassuring. Another game to stimulate trust. A lies curled up on a blanket in a stiffened foetal position, B has to stroke and caress A's limbs until she can be unfolded to lie on her back, stretched out, comfortable and relaxed. Then A becomes B and we start again. This game is sensuous without being sexy. Linda, who finds herself paired with Takeo, refused to do this with a man. Nothing personal. An older woman volunteers to replace her. My partner was Fany-Lea and while I stroked and gradually loosened her limbs, I felt great affection for her. In the sharing sessions other members and the focalisers use the word *love* easily. I cannot.

Back in our stone house for the evening session we sing a song: *This I know, all is well, It is safe for me to change and grow* ... repeated as a round. We enjoy this. In the evening 'sharing', everyone says the games made them 'over-whelmed', 'relaxed', 'more comfortable with myself'. (*Walter writes:* The games brought me all the way back to primary school — feeling safe in a defined space with a teacher, without knowing what's in store, ready for anything.)

Day Four

Meals at Findhorn are delicious — vegetarian self-service with lots of variety. The absence of alcohol (not even beer, but some people drink wine on Friday, the special night) did not bother us. People do drink and smoke at Findhorn but far less than in the mainstream.

Afternoon: Nature Outing. We are driven in two Foundation minibuses called Henry and Francis (Findhorn members like to give machines names) to an unspoiled forest of Scots pines carpeted with wild flowers. A turbulent river crashes past boulders, flowing red from iron deposits. Attunement in a forest glade. Growing bored with these endless attunements, we're more than faintly irritated when Françoise tells us to connect with nature, which we have been doing since before she was born without making so much fuss about it. We want to tell her this but don't.

Before the group splits up for each person's private ramble, Françoise recounts how Peter and two friends came to this river, were met by nature sprites who said they'd been expecting them, and given detailed gardening instructions. Françoise: 'I know some people find this story hard to believe. I don't know. I wasn't here when it happened but I've been told it by people I trust.'

The group appears entranced and obeys her request to walk the tracks as solitary, silent ramblers. When we are out of sight we stay together and talk (against the rules). After an hour walking in that magnificent spot, the two of us are drawn to talk together about nature, that elusive concept that has an unexplained power to awe and delight. Is there a 'spirit' in nature, a force at work — not quite God but not known to science either — which science could yet discover or may never discover? A respected school of biodynamic farmers around the world grow their plants while taking account of the phases of the moon, stars and planets and much else that is not taught in agricultural colleges.

Midsummer solstice festival on the beach.

Midsummer meditation

Every day at Findhorn, two scheduled meditations, one in the morning, one at noon, are open to everyone. Experience Week people are invited to both. Some go twice a day. (We meant to go every morning but our caravan breakfasts were too tempting and we only managed four). Experience week also includes guided meditations which you are not supposed to miss. Fany-Lea and Françoise made us all want to attend every session, although for some the emotional pressure was too high and they missed some. Meditation has a calming effect at whatever level you attempt it, but for the inexperienced the practice can be disturbing.

Midsummer day: our group has a pre-solstice meditation. The oval nature sanctuary is set in a garden, as everything at Findhorn is. At the centre of the slate floor, two halves of a stone sphere enclose a bowl of flowers and a burning candle. Concentric beams slope upwards to a circle of light. We squeeze together on the circular bench, a tight fit for twenty-four adults; a few of us sit cross-legged. As we sit with closed eyes, Fany-Lea talks about solstice mythology, the circle of light above us connecting with a higher circle. (Dot writes:) This particular meditation was the high spot of my week. Partly, because I managed to sit in Zen posture, back on my heels, for the whole hour, partly the gentle enthusiasm of Fany-Lea's invocation of heart and of light and partly the 'energy' the group generated. I have begun to think of energy in its New Age meaning of disparate individuals coming together in a common consciousness. Our separateness dropped into abeyance for those moments. We felt the energy created. I don't pretend to know how group meditation works — but it does! As we file out of the sanctuary, faces are relaxed, smiling and quiet.

Day Six

Group Project. We are bussed out to weed a field of parsnips rented by Earth Share, a daughter company of Findhorn Foundation. The parsnips have been sown too thinly; every metre or so a sad little shoot emerges from its collar of vigorous weeds and couch grass. In a light drizzle, we are set to hand weed forty rows. About a third of the field gets weeded, leaving plenty of freshly turned-up earth for the next crop of weeds. What a waste of effort, we think! Everyone enjoys singing national songs and simply being together.

Earth Share works with Cullerne Gardens in promoting organic growing in the area. *Dorothy writes:* My last work morning at Cullerne Gardens was spent packing boxes (freshly gathered spinach, herbs and courgettes) for the highly successful Community Supported Agriculture scheme that Earth Share is running, on the lines of the American CSA schemes we visited in New England (see Chapter 6). This CSA has 180 shareholders and a waiting list of twenty-four. Here Findhorn practice is at the leading edge of community farming. The gardeners want to extend their activities wider throughout the area. Problem: to obtain sufficient land and enough labour.

Our final 'sharing' came on the afternoon of midsummer night. After attunement, Fany-Lea points to a pebble resting on our group Angel card — the Angel of Healing. Whoever wants to talk picks up the pebble. Mary, an American school teacher, takes the stone first: what she will take back with her is the closeness and the astonishing way that the group became a unity for this week. In turn, several women start to cry and this is provided for; Françoise and Fany-Lea each have a box of tissues under their chairs. Three of the group are staying on for a week's workshop on Life's Purpose. A few are continuing a Scottish holiday, most are returning to mainstream lives. None of us have anything negative to say about Experience Week. People have participated on different levels of emotion but all have been moved. The box of tissues keeps circulating.

Experience Week holds a special place in Findhorn mythology. People would stop us and say, 'Oh, you're doing it. You OK? How're you feeling?' Neither of us were put in touch with our God within. Nor did we bond closely with any other group members. What we *did* experience was a jolt to our regular patterns of behaving, the pleasure of acting as a group, of sitting in a circle and talking about our feelings, about beauty and the spirit of nature and the deeper meaning behind everyday happenings.

A friend of ours who underwent Experience Week a few years ago criticised it for bringing too many emotions to the surface and having a young, inexperienced focaliser who was unable to contain them. In our group, Fany-Lea and Françoise kept a subtle guiding hand. Neither are trained therapists, yet when people expressed deep feelings, Fany-Lea always kept that edge of control which stopped the sharing spilling over into something she could not have handled.

Grown-ups hardly ever play games and our group games were a marvellous way of contacting our inner child. To let yourself be silly is fun. Nor do grown-ups often co-operate as a group as we did in our work sessions, even when these were too lackadaisical for a sense of achievement.

That evening, Craig Gibsone — he has been here longer than anyone except Eileen — took us to the midsummer solstice celebration. You did not need to find a nature spirit to believe in the magic of Findhorn. Members, visitors and people from the wider community gathered on the newly purchased dune lands. Children threw branches onto driftwood bonfires which lit up a turquoise midsummer night. Behind us the white windmill spun slowly. Drums beat out the rhythm for the Indian circle dancing led by Craig's partner May. Many folk had brought tents and intended to camp amongst the dunes. Findhorn — for all its quirkiness and flakiness and its esoteric jargon — encourages a more selfless attitude and a simpler way to enjoy the company of friends.

Does Findhorn charge too much?

We had heard criticisms of Findhorn as money-minded and costly. Course fees run from a couple of hundred pounds a week to several thousand pounds for a year's programme.

For Experience Week, the all-in fee was £280 each, but as writers we were granted a bursary reduction of £100 each. Findhorn keeps and dispenses a bursary fund to help with fees. During our week we changed our opinion: these courses are no dearer than conventional holidays and far more stimulating. Food, facilities and human care are more than adequate. The problem of Findhorn's course fees exists in the minds of customers who equate spiritual communities with monasteries or hippie communes where members live in voluntary poverty, are sustained by charity and are duly grateful when visitors leave a small donation. Findhorn is not so; it lives on its courses and conferences and does so with skill, style and warmth.

The Foundation has become a business turning over more than a million pounds each year. Can you combine spirituality with business? Yes, the Roman Catholic Church has done so successfully for centuries. In most of Findhorn's history there was no financial planning, only faith that the local angels would make dreams 'materialise'. For magnificent buildings like the Universal Hall and the community centre, faith was rewarded; donations and grants arrived just in time. The early community was open to all comers, often offering food with no checks at the canteen door. Debts reached £250,000 in 1981. 'Crazy things happened,' Craig remembers, 'like Culherne Gardens being bought after someone misheard the price thinking it was £8000 when it was £80,000. In those days we were paying £70,000 a year in rent for the Caravan Park. It took us ten years to pay off the debt. People were giving £5 or £10. An American charity gave £35,000. The seventies were a communalist utopia, the eighties a period when we had to start privatising things like Findhorn Press and the Phoenix store. The nineties will be the era of co-operatives.'

In 1996 the banks threatened to call in the debts. A Dutch business consultant attending a Findhorn conference offered to come back, free of charge, to reorganise the business. As a result there are seven new departments, each under a full-time manager: Spiritual and Personal Development; Marketing and Administration; Education; Operations and Services; Asset Management; New Findhorn Directions Ltd; and Re-Invention.

The Foundation was rationalised by hiving off its businesses — the Caravan Park, Findhorn Press, the Phoenix store, the wind park, the café, the energy company, the housing company and the computer networks — into a holding company called New Findhorn Directions. Staff were slimmed down to about ninety residents, elders and children. These staff members earn £185 a month with food and simple accommodation and no pension — but many add to their income by offering therapies, courses and writing. Another forty-

---

FINDHORN FOUNDATION 1996

Fixed assets	£2,500,000
Income	£1,200,000 (75 percent = charges to course & conference guests)
Donations	£100,000
Staff	£250,000
Conservation	£200,000
Property maintenance	£500,000
Loan liability	£900,000
The workforce:	120 staff and students
Wider Findhorn community membership: about 450	

four are contract/salaried staff, living off the site, earning £600 a month. Focalisers, who used to run everything, now run only sub-departments and activities like Experience Week. A new separation of managers and the 'work-force' is disliked as a hierarchical arrangement but accepted. Managers and workforce receive the same basic rewards.

Recipes for survival

Can a New Age community in rural Scotland survive in an unsympathetic environment? How can ordinary New Agers who are not industrialists or high earners earn enough cash to live reasonably? Many are living not far above the poverty line: some remain at Findhorn because the savings they arrived with are gone and they can't afford to leave. Fresh plans were being discussed while we were there in 1997. The current idea is that ownership of Findhorn's busi-nesses should change again — to a co-operative owned by the 450 members of the wider community.

In a first step, a £5-a-week investment would entitle members to discounts and dividends from the Phoenix community shop. Five pounds paid in for a hundred weeks (or a £500 capital investment) will provide people with a £500 tradable share in the store which gives them active participation in a local business and a share in profits if the venture succeeds. A more ambitious development could later give them a single smart card costing £10 a week as a redeemable investment — a form of savings, offering privileged terms in the shop, free entry to happenings at the Universal Hall and a range of courses and therapies. Ten pounds over a hundred weeks — a £1000 capital invest-ment — could be used to support local business initiatives, run a small community lottery and start a credit union. David Hoyle, who manages the Phoenix, sees the co-operative as a way out of the community's isolation. 'The hope for this place is in an open community, a blend of institution and sustainability, based on practical living — not talking to the inner child but learning to bake bread and build windmills. In a ten-mile radius from here there is all sorts of potential.'

David has already turned Phoenix from a modest store into a thriving wholefood and fresh vegetable centre, New Age bookstore and apothecary shop. For foodies, he stocks the best selection of organic chocolates we've seen outside of London specialist boutiques. It's cramped inside but it's one of those shops where you can browse. Shelves of books on aromatherapy, osteopathy, homeopathy, reflexology, shiatsu, Alexander technique and holo-graphic breathwork. The notice board offers: Designing Wholeness — mind, body and soulwork — Session £15–£20; Reiki, Bio-energetic massage (good for touch-resistant people); Shen Massage/polarity therapy. The wider

Findhorn community offers every alternative therapy you might want, and some you might not.

Meanwhile, in spite of financial constraints, Findhorn provides a haven for temporary or permanent refugees from the mainstream. People without savings can come here on short-term 'work exchange' which provides a room, board and pocket money. For longer stays you need money. Student programmes cost several thousand pounds, but the bursary fund will help deserving cases.

Village or eco-village?

Findhorn's new and more outgoing personality will not be secure unless it can end the long tradition of suspicion and hostility shown by locals. In the sturdy, grey stone village of Findhorn (this Findhorn was here centuries before the Foundation which has appropriated its name) and the nearby town of Forres, locals are fearful that a Foundation which has expanded in numbers and area over the years will eventually 'take over' the whole region.

A fresh wave of suspicion swept over the community in 1997 when a Foundation-affiliated company bought 120 hectares of dunelands next to the Caravan Park. Almost the same week, planning permission came through for forty-four houses in a new eco-village to be built on an adjacent site known as the Field of Dreams. To re-assure the locals, senior Foundation staff called villagers to a meeting to explain that the land had not been bought by the Foundation but by Dunelands Ltd, and that the main purpose was to preserve the area and hand over its management to a nature reserve to be run jointly with the village.

At the meeting, John Talbott, Director of Dunelands Ltd and of EcoVillage Ltd, said he hoped such an arrangement could 'heal the rift' and floated the suggestion that most of the dunelands might be re-sold at a friendly price to a village trust. An angry villager shouted 'cock's fiddle!' — as far as the village was concerned Dunelands Ltd and the Foundation were

---

The demise of traditional communities is too well-known to need much elaboration. These were communities defined principally by blood-ties, place and necessity. Looking at new-style communities, these offer an unprecedented opportunity to utilise the best qualities of traditional forms and discard most of their stifling qualities. Intentional communities are coming together formed by people who share intrinsic values rather than obligations and outside threats. Such communities whether or not the members are related are able to be flexible and encourage change and diversity. This is certainly what the people at Findhorn want — whether they will achieve it is another matter.

· Robert Gilman in *Genesis*.

the same. There was uproar when Talbott admitted that sixty additional acres — degraded woodlands and concreted runways abandoned by the RAF — had been bought and were reserved for commercial use and possible industrial development. 'So that's why you've bought it. You hive off the dunelands and you've got this precious development land for nothing!' the heckler yelled. Finally, conciliation prevailed and the villagers appointed a committee to decide how to proceed.

Findhorn's best hope for viability in the future is in the wider community of like-minded people who have settled in the area, now represented by the Findhorn Bay Community Association. Eileen Caddy's voices had predicted that the community would grow into a City of Light; only this wider community can bear such a burden. North-east Scotland is an economically depressed region and cities of light need power.

The eco-village is a Findhorn ideal but this ideal comes up against practical difficulties, here as elsewhere. The windmill provides only eight percent of the Caravan Park's energy, the Living Machine sewage disposal takes waste from much of the site but not from tourists' caravans because of noxious substances that may be present. Much of Findhorn's food comes from the organic gardens of Cullerne and Earth Share — but most is bought in, organic or not.

John Talbott, in charge of the eco-village project, wants it to be 'as sustainable as possible.' The plan is for forty-four units on thirty-three sites, allowing room for co-housing arrangements. John told us the aim was to design 'where possible' for high energy efficiency, local materials, passive solar heating and open-plan siting. The sewage will be processed by the Living Machine. John hopes for 'a culture of light car use,' although 'for now we are living in the real world and we have to cater for cars.' Critics already fear — as one of them complained to us — that John's eco-village could be 'little more than eco-friendly Wimpy homes in an eco-friendly Brookside community in a smug, New Age suburbia.'

The 'Living Machine' method of disposing of sewage, invented by Mike Todd in the US, has only twenty of its kind operational. They work like a reed bed but the process is faster and uses less land. The one at Findhorn, a thirty-metre long greenhouse at the bottom of the Caravan Park, handles sixty-five cubic metres of waste daily. Three anaerobic bioreactors buried outside the greenhouse function like septic tanks, reducing the solids in the water through the action of bacteria. The dirty water then flows into the greenhouse to be cleaned in a succession of tanks filled with rocks and plants. Each tank has its own eco-system: snails graze the surfaces and water beetles and fish complete the ecology. Findhorn's treated water, cleaner than the product of a conventional sewage treatment, flows into the river. It could equally well be used for irrigation.

Beyond the Caravan Park there are already two small groups of eco-friendly houses, including the ones that cause the most interest in residents and visitors alike. Roger Daudna bought a dozen discarded oak whisky barrels. Opened out they make extraordinarily pleasing dwellings. Craig Gibsone has put two together joined by a corridor and made a home for himself, his partner May and their two little girls.

Man of the Trees

At Findhorn you won't be laughed at if you want to set up a new form of healing, a hermitage on an island or a company to build energy saving houses. From such an atmosphere Alan Watson has drawn inspiration to set up Trees for Life, an NGO for restoring the decimated Caledonian Forest. Sadly, we never met a nature spirit at Findhorn but Alan was the nearest we got — short-legged and barrel-chested, with flowing shoulder-length hair and a silvery-grey speckled beard spreading over his chest, although he is only in his early forties.

Centuries of greed and mismanagement have reduced the once majestic Caledonian forests to a few isolated patches — less than one per cent of their original size. The forests Alan is regenerating will take two hundred years to reach maturity; he is working with his twenty-months-old son's grandchildren in mind.

Like so many others who started their careers working on conventional aid projects, Alan became a passionate opponent of 'development' when he worked among peasants in South America who had been displaced from their lands to make room for industrial export farming. They were forced onto marginal plots on hillsides where they cut down trees to survive. To express his disgust at this exploitation and destruction, Alan became a vegan, stopped drinking coffee, eating bananas — and consuming. 'I began to discover my powers as a human being, the power to make my life a statement.'

He joined the Findhorn Foundation in 1978 and worked in various departments. He started a recycling programme but even at Findhorn he found difficulties in persuading people to recycle. He set up the first ecology workshop called Living Lightly on the Earth, spent some months in Auroville and was inspired by the reforestation there: the planting of two million trees in eroded semi-desert (see Chapter 15).

'I felt the earth was calling me for help. I saw that most environmental campaigns were a damage-limitation exercise — halting the destruction, but even if that was done we'd still be left with a degraded, impoverished world. We have to bring life back and restore it. My calling is to do that here in Scotland.'

THE CALEDONIAN FOREST

Original Caledonian Forest area: 1,500,000 hectares
Present area: 12,000 hectares (0.8%)
Original wildlife — lynx, wolf beaver, boar, moose, wolf, deer etc.
Remaining wildlife — deer
Number of trees planted by Trees for Life by 10.5.97: 150,000
Number of trees protected: 108,000
Trees planted by volunteers: 1996: 22,280
                                1997: 32,500
                                1998 (estimate): 75,000

At first his movement was dismissed as cranky. 'Especially because I've got long hair and a beard — that's part of my statement about my life. I stand for things that are wild. Now there's a lot of respect and we work with government organisations.'

We joined a group of fourteen volunteers on a one-day work party to Glen Affric where the last few trees grow on steep rock faces and in river gullies — the only place where they are safe from overgrazing by deer. Four of us carried plastic sacks full of pine cones which had been collected the previous year and dried in Findhorn greenhouses. These we tossed in Biblical fashion into the scrub. We like to think our grandchildren's children could come here in 2050 and walk under new trees.

On the way our mini-bus stopped at a part of the forest fenced against the deer twenty-five years earlier and here the stately pines were surrounded by their descendants up to a few metres tall. In the unfenced sections the loss of trees continues: remaining trees are old — reaching the end of their natural life span. For over one hundred and fifty years few new trees have grown to maturity because grazing deer nip off the top shoots. The deer's natural predators, lynx, wolf and bear are long gone and the deer populations are encouraged by the landowners, mostly absentee, whose only way of making a profit from the impoverished landscape is from the 'sport' of deer hunting. Deer herds have literally been eating their own habitat out of existence.

Alan's vision is to restore the natural forest ecosystem to an area of approximately 1500 square kilometres. Instead of planting exotic and profitable species like Sitka pine which provide no habitat for wildlife and cannot co-exist with native trees, as the Forestry Commission and several other organisations are doing, Alan starts with the part of the forest most like the original ecosystem — the pinewood remnants — and allows their expansion by preventing deer grazing young trees. As a new generation of young trees begins to recreate a forest habitat, some species of plants and animals will recolonise the north-central Highlands naturally while others will have to be physically reintroduced. Over a period of decades the area can gradually be returned to something like its natural state and can offer the closest thing to a true wilderness area in Scotland. Alan intends to create forest links between glens, establishing islands of forest from which regeneration can continue naturally. Until the deer herds can be reduced, this work must proceed laboriously by building more fences. However, landowners will need a change of heart; deer hunting is highly profitable, and so is sheep farming.

Working for the last ten years on land belonging to the Forestry Commission — Trees for Life owns none of its own — volunteers protect saplings with plastic tubes and fence other areas from the grazing deer. In one enclosure near the bothy we saw last year's seedlings, a respectable thirty centimetres high.

Without enough cash to employ workers, TFL uses volunteers of all ages and backgrounds, who come in groups of fifteen to twenty, stay in tents or the bothy and plant as many or as few trees as they like. They pay £40 for their food and lodging. Our mini-bus expedition to Glen Affric was led by Sally Kendall and her husband Paul, two young graphic designers who had given up well-paid jobs in Oxford to be full-time volunteers for Trees for Life. They haven't had a day off for two weeks (the Newsletter was going to press); they live in a caravan and they are blissfully happy. Sally has been trained to focalise, Findhorn-style, volunteers who come for a week at a time to plant and fence. Our afternoon's work was only partially successful. We tubed a few dozen young aspen trees but we couldn't find a second site where twenty trees waited for plastic protection. Sally said, sadly, 'The previous group forgot to put the grid reference on the map.'

> There's a lot of people who think that spirituality is a matter of transcending the world — that the physical world is base matter and unspiritual and it's about getting away from it to get to nirvana. For me it's about bringing spirituality down and integrating it into matter because for me all of matter is spirit and my task as a human being is to help make that spirit more visible, more alive, more radiant. That is where Findhorn has some similarities with paganism in the past, because everything has spirit, even a rock, even a car. That's where Findhorn has a unique role to play. I straddle two worlds, people who are into ecology and all that, and people here at Findhorn who are into the spiritual side. I'm sort of in the middle. • Alan Watson (to the authors).

Alan's pet project is to reintroduce the wolf, but he thinks it's more likely the beaver will be allowed back first because beavers have a more cuddly image. Although the Highland Wolf Fund has disbanded, Alan is sure the wolf will come back eventually, and the moose and the bear as well, when a larger tract of natural wild forest is available. Around the restored forest Alan wants buffer zones reforested for sustainable use by the local population in small-scale, high value-added activities like making furniture from birch or firewood from thinnings. His are no misanthropic attitudes; he believes people and wilderness can exist in proximity if the right balance is kept.

Alan's work for Trees for Life is independent of Findhorn, but is nevertheless a part of its ethos. Alan and his wife Cornelia, a doctor specialising in alternative therapies, bring up their small son in a wooden house they have designed themselves near the whisky barrel houses. What are Alan's dreams for the future? He laughs. He is already in demand on the international lecture circuit. He's going to Chile to advise on regenerating the southern beech forests at Yendegaia. He hopes for global co-operation in reforestation. He demands: why can't the armies of the world stop playing war games and replant trees in the Sahara?

'In the next century the major task of humanity, once we get over our fixation with material economic growth, is going to be the healing of the earth. It will be the first shared task of humanity. I've been carrying this dream. I can't expect anyone else to make it happen if I'm not going to work on it myself.'

Deforestation is an environmental catastrophe. One individual, using Findhorn as a base, is making a small but determined impact. If you are inclined to scoff at Findhorn's New Age navel gazing, you will find in Alan Watson and his Trees for Life what it can lead to.

Note

1   Names of the Experience Week participants are altered at their request.

15

City of dawn

••

Auroville aims to become a universal city of beings so perfectly evolved that they have superseded the passions and vices of the human race. It is impossible of course, a poetic and inspiring fantasy. We do not know how many Aurovilians believe that 'supramental' beings can evolve from the ordinary state you and I are in, or that their founder, Mira Alfassa, known as Mother, actually reached such a state. This is high-flown spiritual 'stuff'. You don't need to believe all of it to live in Auroville. You need to believe, however, that living at Auroville offers a new way of being for its members, for the whole of India and eventually the world. We met members of all ages who had become passionately involved in bringing one or other aspect of Mother's vision to fruition: planting trees, growing vegetables, experimenting with sustainable technology, teaching the new values to their children and those of the surrounding Tamil villages, building more of the city, and talking endlessly about the significance of what they are doing. In the parched red earth of Tamil Nadu state in South India, over twelve hundred individuals of thirty-one nationalities interpret the vision according to their own desires and capabilities.

Aurovilians are astonishingly diverse, which is what Mother intended — a cross-section of humanity. Most live lightly — some live frugally to the point of hardship; some are well-off and leave for the Himalayan foothills or the south of France when the heat becomes unbearable. Others are part-time Aurovilians who depart at regular intervals to earn their living in San Francisco, New Delhi or London. However hard or easy it is, everyone feels privileged to be here. In much the same way as Findhorn residents might shyly allude to 'the magic of Findhorn,' at Auroville we find a sense of glamour. We use glamour in its original eighteenth century meaning as something strange, as an enchantment. Auroville casts a spell that transcends everything you think you know about human nature.

Our first home here is in the guest house at Samasti, one of the small residential communities that make up Auroville. Samasti (the Sanskrit word for

---

AUROVILLE'S CHARTER

Auroville belongs to nobody in particular. Auroville belongs to humanity as a whole. But to live in Auroville, one must be the willing servitor of the Divine Consciousness. Auroville will be the place of an unending education, of constant progress, and youth that never ages. Auroville wants to be the bridge between the past and the future. Taking advantage of all discoveries from without and from within, Auroville will boldly spring towards future realisations. Auroville will be a site of material and spiritual researches for a living embodiment of an actual Human Unity.

---

collectivity) provides an oasis of green in the dry earth: a dozen sparkling-white houses in Tamil-style, with pitch-tile overhang and deep verandas. Yellow bamboo, green neem, purple bougainvillea, jackfruit and orchids; the sound of a pianist practising Handel at breakfast time, and a peacock adding its wild shriek. It was March, the end of the visitor season, already almost too hot to sit outside and we're told that next month the heat will become infernal. The guest house provides comfort with wicker furniture, herbal insect spray and Western-style loos. Most of the other guests are on spiritual holidays; they spent their days shopping for handicrafts in Pondicherry, taking part in alternative therapies, sitting on the beach or studying the writings of Mother and her spiritual partner and mentor, Sri Aurobindo, after whom Auroville is named.

From this base, we set out to explore Auroville. But where is it? Eighty settlements are hidden away in a vast, hot plain of red earth. Dwellings range from Tamil-style 'capsules' — one-room huts on stilts with thatched roofs — to simple two-room brick houses with or without bathrooms, right up to luxurious villas with lawns and sprinklers, tended by Tamil servants. Auroville always seems to be beyond the next bend, elusive to the visitor and to Aurovilians, too, who are doomed to endless travel along the dusty red tracks in a succession of assorted two-wheelers — mopeds, scooters and motor-bikes. Whole families perch on two wheels, including European families — probably the only place in India where you can see that. It is a good way to travel. We hired two scooters for a friendly fee from Kanniappan, a Tamil Aurovilian. We would have fitted better into the scene by sharing a single scooter, but we wanted to be free for separate research. Auroville extends over twenty-five square kilometres of which nearly half the belongs to the community.

After Sri Aurobindo's death in 1950, Mother continued to run the ashram in Pondicherry, attracting a large, international New Age following. Her long-held vision of an international city in which to perfect humankind became a reality. The early years, recounted to us by old-timers, had some of the mythical, heroic quality of the pioneering days of Stephen Gaskin on The Farm (Chapter 13) — hardship, comradeship and uncompromising idealism. Soon after her death in 1971, a feud developed between the New Agers, who were digging, building and planting, and the Sri Aurobindo Society, exclusively Indian, which owned the land and claimed to be the successors of Mother and Sri Aurobindo. The Society cut off funding from the 'foreigners'. The ensuing battle went as far as the Indian Supreme Court which eventually transferred the government of Auroville to the Auroville Foundation, in which the Indian government keeps some control by appointing a senior official as Secretary.

Marti Mueller volunteered be our unofficial guide. She lives half the year in Auroville and half in Paris, where she earns a living writing and painting; in Auroville she works without payment in some of the many cultural organisations. She explained how Auroville's organisations had developed. 'First came the individualists and New Age people, children of the 1968 revolt against authority in Paris and elsewhere. Mother had this ideal of divine anarchy; an outflow of inner consciousness with no unitary form imposed on it. She envisaged that four or five people with intuitive consciousness should have authority but no such group emerged. After Mother left her body in 1973, everything was decentralised into working groups.'

Major decisions are taken at Resident Assembly meetings — if possible by consensus, but many issues remain unresolved. There are those who want to build the city of 50,000 which Mother envisaged. Others argue that this would be unsustainable because the water table is dropping alarmingly in the area, partly because of the drain from Auroville residents (some Green Aurovilians complain bitterly of watered lawns and flushed lavatories) but mainly because local farmers are growing water-hungry commercial crops like sugar cane.

The Mother's dream of a money-free economy has never been put into effect. Scores of businesses run by Aurovilians, including high-tech factories, contribute a third, sometimes a half of their income to the central fund which organises community services like health, telecommunications

What I've learnt from Mother and Sri Aurobindo's writing doesn't conflict with my scientific training. If evolution has gone on for billions of years, why should we assume it is not still going on? Auroville exists to give it a kick start.
· Michelle from Paris, aged 40, a biologist.

Maybe I didn't meet the right people. Seemed to me just a lot of rich foreigners playing at being spiritual and having nice houses and servants.
· Shelley from London, aged 20, a student.

and schools. More money comes from the worldwide network of well-wishers
— Friends of Auroville societies which are active in many countries.

To join Auroville there are no entry requirements because Mother wanted
the city to be representative of humanity. But the financial conditions make
it hard for the local Tamils to join. Auroville isn't anyone's free ride;
newcomers are obliged to pay for their own upkeep unless they qualify for a
maintenance grant for approved activities. After nine months probation,
newcomers who stay on must pay for their own house, which then belongs to
the community. Making a living is hard; there are community jobs like
teaching or healthcare; other jobs are in development projects in the
surrounding villages which are financed by grants from international aid
bodies like UNESCO, or by the Indian government.

After some days you begin to find some pattern in the settlements and the
orientation of their inhabitants. There are the Green Aurovilians, the spiritual
Aurovilians and the Tamils who either have become members or who work
in one of the settlements.

Green Auroville

As you enter the Forest Zone a sign warns: Don't Make Noise, Wild Life.
The forest zones were once eroded and almost bare; Aurovilians have
planted two million trees, bringing with them an increase in humidity and a
return of wildlife, including snakes. For us, the regenerated forest was the
most inspiring and worthwhile result of the founding of Auroville. Skidding
on our scooters through red dust, swerving down unmarked tracks, we eventually found the settlement of Fertile. Mud-brick huts hide behind palms, trees
and flowers — a set for a promotional film extolling the simple life. Fertile's
oldest tree is thirty metres high, planted by Johnny. He is from Australia, but
with his long grey beard and a white cloth wound around his head he's more
like an Old Testament prophet in shorts. His wife and children found the life
too harsh and went back home. Johnny says he will never leave.

Rainu, slender, brown-skinned, twenty-four years old, visiting from
California, had come with her husband Paco and baby Isa to help put up a
carpenter's shed. Rainu grew up in Auroville and most of her family still lives
here: her Swedish mother, her Indian father and her half-brothers and sisters.
Isa sleeps on a mat while her mum mixes cement. A group of ten are building
the shed — a corrugated iron roof supported on cement pillars. They work
as a team: two mixing; two carrying materials in shallow tin bowls; one
laying; one smoothing; one tamping. A Tamil mason corrects the surfaces
with a spirit level — the most high-tech implement in use. They will finish
within the morning; they work fast and they laugh. They are building for

Second generation Aurovilians at Fertile with a Tamil friend.

themselves and it shows. One of the cement workers, a twenty-one-year-old American ecology student on a group visit, hopes to return to Auroville and maybe stay for a year or two. 'I've never seen such spiritual energy anywhere,' he says.

The settlers in each Auroville village make a conscious choice as to what extent they will incorporate the comforts of modern living or to what extent they will imitate local Tamil society. At Fertile there are no showers, no flushing loos. Washing arrangements are a tap and a bucket in a circular brick shelter. The brick-built compost loo uses ashes — clean and odourless — and provides compost for tree seedlings. Using minimum watering techniques, young settlers manage to grow a sizeable amount of their own food. Meals are organic vegetables cooked in *chulas* (Indian-style ovens). They are delicious!

At Solitude we found another village of young settlers in an even more austere setting — five people setting up home on a bare field. They have been on the site for three months, living precariously on their savings, hoping that the Auroville farm group will subsidise their settlement. Krishna is twenty-three; he was called Duncan when he was growing up in the UK. He is building a capsule when we arrive. Three capsules are up, one still to come.

Krishna lives with Eiko from Japan, his former schoolmate at Brockwood Park, the Krishnamurti school (see Chapter 16) near Petersfield. South-west of London. 'This isn't hard living, it's easy compared to what I have done before,' Krishna says. Permaculture and reading Fukuoka's *One Straw*

Revolution have inspired him. 'I apply the no-digging, no-ploughing principle, using nitrogen-fixing plants and green manure as ground cover which is then cut down and left to die.' He is growing millet, peanuts, pulses and planting avocados, mangoes, guavas and other Indian fruits. He wants build a common kitchen garden, one communal *pukka* room and a storehouse.

As the sun went down behind the palm trees, Krishna served us a snack of freshly made peanut butter (made on a bicycle-driven press at another settlement) and wholemeal bread. Mother's teaching struck him as 'a modern thing, in keeping with scientific trends,' fitting perfectly, in his mind, with permaculture and Fukuoka's ideas. However, these young settlers' means fall short of their dreams. They have an old, crumbling well built fifty years ago by the Indian government for Tamil villagers. Their windmill was built by a fifteen-year-old village boy; one blade is missing but they cannot afford to replace it.

Krishna lights a few sticks under his clay oven to boil water for tea. We wonder how long such simplicity will last. At Auroville we found that simple living does not necessarily diminish as people get older.

Joss, from Tasmania, lives in a forest community which has set up a comprehensive sanctuary for endangered local plants. He is an old-timer: he joined the Aurobindo Ashram in 1969. Now he and eight others tend the twenty-two hectare sanctuary as part of an Ayurvedic (herbal) primary health

Second generation residents at Fertile.

care centre for the villagers. Joss's team maintain seed and gene banks and reserve areas for nutritive and curative plants. In a typically Aurovilian mix of high and low technology, the team use solar-powered computers for their research and a bullock cart to carry their manure. They have lovingly collected exhibits are a museum of traditional brooms and baskets.

Aurovilians have no common characteristics; they come from such diverse backgrounds that each time you meet another one, you have to change your mindset. With Alan Herbert we had no problem. He was the sort of British university lecturer that we were accustomed to, with an ironic turn of phrase and wry humour. He lives, as we would have expected, in Auroville's green belt with his partner, Anne-Marie.

The Samriddhi (Sanskrit for prospect) community covers twelve hectares and is run on sustainable lines using no more power or water than they find on the site. Nine people live in four houses. Their electricity is solar-powered; their water is pumped from three windmills. Alan uses propane for cooking: his neighbours use bio-gas; there are enough animals to run a small plant. The windmill which pumps domestic water was made in Auroville. Check dams along the canyon prove enough water storage in the monsoon; the lakes were excavated by the settlers themselves. 'We could be self-sufficient in water if only other Aurovilains wouldn't use water so extravagantly,' Alan said with no air of grievance. 'We don't stop people importing their lifestyles because we are pledged to admit samples of the whole world. So some people water their lawns at midday. The rest of us don't stop them: we are forced to find a truer way to govern ourselves than a mass-meeting democracy.'

Alan has noticed that new sorts of residents are coming to Auroville: 'We see more artists. And more people with money. At first people lived in thatched huts like the Tamil villagers (who were quite suspicious until they saw that the newcomers were seriously farming just like them). Now a more Westernised lifestyle has become normal.'

Alan and Anne-Marie's two-room house is spartan in its simplicity and lack of clutter. 'We built a thatched house, bought the materials, a village team put it up. We lived in it for ten years, then pulled it down.'

Alan is agnostic about the prospects of achieving the 'supramental' state.

We aim for a race without ego but I don't know when we're going to get there. Spirit and matter are not separate. Mother spoke of goodwill as belief in human unity. Something has been established here — and according to Sheldrake's principle of resonance, it can occur elsewhere. This can act to counter the vibrations of destruction.
· Roger, Auroville resident (to the authors)

'I don't know about Mother's divinity or avatar status, but clearly she was very far ahead in consciousness. I can only hope to move forward a few steps. Maybe I can see some signs already: I already feel part of a community sharing some sense of a common consciousness. Even when we quarrel we feel that underlying unity. There's no dogma here and no living guru. I meditate on my own; some do it in common in their communities.'

No distinction is recognised at Auroville between the scientific and the spiritual. At the Centre for Scientific Research, Bill Sullivan, the director, is an ex-Jesuit seminarian from California (he never took his vows). Bill told us Christianity took one evolutionary step but got stuck in the medieval system of thought. 'What happened to Mother happened to others too: gurus' bodies have not decomposed — Sai Baba, the contemporary Indian mystic, has raised people from the dead. Who knows? It's not impossible. I subscribe to Sri Aurobindo's view that all life is yoga. Evolution can proceed in quantum leaps: suddenly everything is different. These things go in circles: people knew in the past, now they're waking up again: the feeling that we have to change is becoming more and more generalised'.

The Centre is registered with UNESCO and gets a Indian Government grant for developing bio-gas and other Green technologies.

The planners

There is a master plan for Auroville designed, according to Mother's instructions, in zones: city, forest, industry, culture. In addition, an international zone will one day house pavilions from different countries. So far only the Bharat Nivas, the Indian pavilion, is in existence and the others may never be built. They may require too much money, and another problem is that some national pavilions are scheduled to be built on land where a Tamil village already exists.

Louis, one of the chief planning and architectural advisors, brushes aside these objections, as well as more profound doubts on the ecological viability of the future city. 'Now people are living in outer zones, but they will want to move into town; they will want to. We will build along the periphery of the central area where we shall allow no cars, only a service ring road. There will be a collective kitchen, an international hotel, shady streets and passages. I don't know how high the blocks will be. There will be schools, crèches, a university on the periphery. The cultural zone will have artists' villages. All that will need money, but when we are ready the money will come. Mother's sketch showed a labour colony on the outskirts. We'll have electric buses going round the ring roads and free bicycles inside the circle.'

Louis' plans are grandiose. How relevant are they to the problems of an

Indian rural locality? Does Tamil Nadu *need* a foreign-based and foreign-funded city in a water-scarce region? Auroville was set up on an eroded and denuded plain with 35,000 Tamil villagers living in its midst. Today the community provides work as ayahs, gardeners and labourers and gives the cleverer or luckier ones the possibility of acquiring marketable skills.

The Tamils

Kanniappan works in Abri settlement, where he maintains scooters and mobylettes. He was born in an illiterate farming family in one of the nearby Tamil villages. Auroville has been his home for the last twenty years. He is smiling, looks happy and is glad to share his experiences with visitors.

'I left school after Standard Three and worked for Rudolf as a garden boy. He was German. My parents were happy that he became my guardian. My father had a little land. Now he is old he has sold it to Auroville and he still works as a watchman. My mother no longer works — she is growing old.'

How did Kanniappan get his present job? 'By looking. By helping. I have learnt on the job. I also can repair four-wheelers. I have a 100 cc Honda. My wife had no schooling. She is twenty-nine, I am thirty-five. She went to Menakshe (a resident who runs schools for illiterate adults) and now she is almost literate. She has a job on the information desk in the Matrimandir shrine.' Kaniappan's family live in one of the settlements where most of the Tamil members of Auroville live. 'I like it here. It is a permanent place for me. I am a member of Auroville. When I joined it was easier for Tamils. Now it is harder. The poor people like it here. They see the Aurovilians wealthy. They want a good life. Outside they have no chance to learn. We can choose what we want to do.'

Kanniappan has ambitions for his thirteen-year-old, whom he hopes will get to college. Twice a week he takes him to Last School (so-called because Mother taught that an evolved society will not need schools) which runs evening classes in computers.

He says he doesn't know anything about Mother's teaching because he has no time for that sort of thing. 'I don't go to meetings and I am not interested in the politics of this place. I want my independence. I don't want to be a big shot. I don't see any difference here between the Tamils and the Europeans.' Then he could not talk any longer; he had a queue of scooters waiting for repairs.

Since Auroville began, 220 Tamil villagers have become members but, as Kanniappan points out, it is becoming harder for them to join. Tamils work in the different settlements as maids, nannies, gardeners or cooks. The casual visitor is often shocked to see what looks like a throw-back to a colonial past.

This is unfair; before Auroville was established most local Tamils were working without regular pay for a few big landowners, now they have a chance of a decent weekly wage.

However, the villagers are given daily examples of lifestyles they cannot aspire to. Some Aurovilian communities are as lavish in their buildings and gardens as a Western suburb, while the villages around Auroville continue to be dirty and run-down. Auroville Village Action exists to improve their condition and has provided water, drainage, health centres, schools, crèches and toilets. Villagers have started their own businesses after learning skills like making ferro-cement panels.

We found two opposing attitudes about Auroville's relationship with the surrounding villages. Some argued: Auroville is not a social service for the villagers; we came here for something else, Auroville is for the future, the villagers are a dead and dying past. The others said: Mother chose a populated area and declared that the Tamils were the first Aurovilians; we feel that India is our true home and we have learned more from the villagers than they have learned from us.

The bourgeoisie

Adherence to the ideas of Mother and Sri Aurobindo can give rise to

Aster Patel at her home.

LAMENT OF HENRI THE CHEF

So many different types here: people with an apartment in the 16th arrondissement of Paris who rent it out to pay costs in France, bring the rest of the money out here in rupees and live like kings and queens. I served dinner for some of these VIPs: soup from a silver tureen, me in my messy tee-shirt, it was like a salon in the 16th. Some people who were here from the start don't recognise the power those toffs have assumed.

I want a house with some privacy and distance from my work and from the guests. I have the money (I want to live very simply) but can't find the site. I can live a spiritual life anywhere, but Auroville is supposed to be a collective spiritual experience and that is spoiled because of the role of money and the way an elite has taken over.
· (To the authors.)

totally different lifestyles. Aster Patel, originally from Kashmir and a Sorbonne-trained philosopher, has a house in Auromodele — the upmarket end of Auroville. Roger Angier, Mother's architect for the Matrimandir shrine, designed most of these futuristic houses overlooking the distant sea, surrounded by lawns, flowers and lily ponds. Aster shows us proudly how 'very simple it is' — the simplicity of exquisite design, no angles in the rammed earth construction. 'Doesn't the shape remind you of a Henry Moore sculpture?' Yes it does. It also reminds us of exquisite villas in Provence.

Aster runs the Centre for Indian Culture in the India Pavilion at the International Centre. Over a gourmet vegetarian lunch served by an ayah in a white sari, we discuss spiritual matters. 'Mother asked us to build a township to deal with spiritual things in a material world. This place is for everyone. People have left interesting lives to come here. They lead perfectly normal lives, the life of the world. No single problem which is outside isn't here. It's tough. We could leave if we want to. We choose to be here. I have more stimulation here than in Delhi.' While we talk philosophy her husband watches cricket on the television.

Matrimandir

Mother's most tangible legacy, an immense sphere-shaped shrine, seems to hover just above the ground. Before her death she made a sketch with detailed instructions: the Matrimandir will be the soul, the cohesive force of Auroville. Still unfinished, the vast gold-plated ball supported by buttresses and set in elaborate gardens has become a show place of South India. It is paid for by charitable donations and building work frequently stops when cash runs out.

The Matrimandir.

Marti got us visitors' tickets and took us inside the sphere into a vast and austere inner room without windows. This immense space was designed by Mother to help achieve mental concentration. Absolute impenetrable whiteness, a feeling of being enveloped in white muslin shrouds, a white carpeted central space (several hundred people could fit in here with ease) empty except for twelve marble pillars. Two meditators (or are they supervisors?) sit cross-legged at the other end of the hall, a great distance away. In the ceiling four symmetrical vents for the air conditioning look like four ladders to heaven. Under a shaft of vertical light coming down unblinking from the domed ceiling, a crystal shimmers in the centre, a flawless sphere, seventy centimetres in diameter. The effect suggests, as is intended, concentration on a point. A point of energy, of truth, of divinity.

We tried to feel Mother's spiritual presence but too many years of scepticism overwhelmed our efforts. The crystal globe, struck with a beam of sunlight coming through the ceiling aperture, lost its magical glamour and started to resemble a monster gypsy crystal ball. Our experience was not typical, for most visitors to the Matrimandir report that they felt Mother's presence.

Marti took us to the Laboratory of Human Evolution, a small library of Mothernalia containing books about quantum and pseudo-quantum and post-quantum science, several copies of Rupert Sheldrake, the nine volumes of the *Agenda* (Mother's diaries) out on loan, nine tapes of Mother's edited conversations in both French and English. We did not hear of any experiments conducted in this laboratory, but Marti's fine paintings on the wall were fluid, full of warmth and strong colour.

Reading the Mother's sacred texts, we found a bewildering mixture of the sensible, the inspiring and the frankly batty:

'Do not try to be virtuous. See in what measure you are unified, ONE with everything that is anti-divine. Take up your share of the burden, accept to be yourself impure and mendacious. Thus you will be able to take the Shadow and offer it. And in the measure that you are able to take it and offer it, things will then change. Do not try to be among the pure. Accept to be with those who are in the darkness and, in a total love, offer all that.'[1]

We could respond to this advice, but the following left us highly alarmed.

'During the last war [World War II] I spent all my nights hovering above Paris (not integrally but a part of myself) so that nothing would happen to the city. Later it came out that several people had seen what seemed to be a great white force with an indistinct form hovering above Paris, so that it would, not be destroyed... Throughout the war, Sri Aurobindo and I were in such a constant tension that it completely interrupted the yoga. And that was why the war started in the first place — to stop the work.'[2]

The real Auroville?

Can anyone gain an impression of Auroville in a few weeks? Is the real Auroville at the Centre for Scientific Research which has invented new techniques of ferro-cement building and bio-gas energy? Or at the Village Action Group which co-ordinates activities in the Tamil villages? At the Last School where a dozen different nationalities strive to devise a curriculum? At Aurobrindavan, the centre for soil and water conservation which has regenerated 3000 acres of degraded village land and planted two million trees?

Aurovilians are New Agers, like the people at Findhorn, in revolt against the official rationalism of our time which they see as leading to disaster. They feel vindicated by orthodox quantum physics, which accepts that at its most basic sub-atomic level matter cannot be predicted

> Man has created a system of civilisation which has become too big for his limited mental capacity and understanding, and his still more limited spiritual and moral capacity to utilise and manage, a too dangerous servant of his blundering ego and its appetites. Reason and Science can only help by standardising, by fixing everything into an artificially arranged and mechanised unity of material life. A greater whole-being, whole-knowledge, whole-power is needed to weld all into a greater unity of whole-life.
> · Sri Aurobindo, *The Life Divine*.

because its behaviour is altered by the very fact of being observed. This scientific finding is taken by New Agers to mean that the official distinction between mind (or consciousness) and matter has been abolished. They draw support from the biologist Rupert Sheldrake, whose books speak of 'morphic resonance', a concept analogous to the notion of 'non-locality' in quantum physics. This type of reasoning makes Aurovillians believe that what happens at Auroville is vital to the consciousness of the world.

Mother amalgamates the old yoga tradition that all of life is a spiritual phenomenon with the modern quest for self-improvement and accelerated evolution, taking both to the ultimate — and ultimately absurd — conclusion that we can transcend our physical body. To us it seems silly — even blasphemous — to want to supersede the human body, when it is the mind that is so obviously the human problem. Mother's ultimate transcendence trip — a transformation of body, mind, spirit and nature itself — is grafted grotesquely onto the milder, more distinguished and, originally, more sensible body of Aurobindo's thought system which Mother, we are convinced, pushed beyond its original and legitimate scope.

Elitism lurks in the background of this bizarre world picture. Aurovilians hotly deny this, claiming just the opposite because they are universalists, out to transform the whole world through the microcosm that is Auroville. Yet Mother was making her claim to produce a race of 'supramental' beings and claimed in the end to have got so far that she did not expect her own body to die.

Worse, Mother and Sri Aurobindo believed they were *avatars* or divine saviours with supernatural powers. Can her disciples and imitators escape her hubris? Dead gurus are always present, and they can do no wrong. Almost every space within Auroville contains photographs of Aurobindo and Mother, laid out as little shrines.

A problem arises because, since Mother is dead, her vision for Auroville cannot authentically be kept up to date. She had no notion, for example, of a looming water shortage which, in the eyes of most local ecologists, rules out plans for a large city on this site. In this confusion are the seeds of the simmering three-sided conflict between the blueprinters, who want to build a city of 50,000 as Mother intended, the pragmatists, who want to adapt the ideal to the possible, and the ecologists, who want to stick to what will be sustainable. And yet, Mother was no prude and warned people against being 'virtuous'.

She cannot be judged on her writing alone. Everybody who knew her agrees she radiated wisdom, simplicity, humanity and understanding. She stood against sectarianism, extremism and bigotry. She was wise in the world, a woman who has lived. She was elegant and talented — the sketch that survives showing the future City divided into four zones, with a workers' colony at the perimeter, is from an artist's hand. She radiated love and affection. Was she an actress? The visions she had since the age of four were dismissed by her mother as histrionic fantasies, and she then kept them to herself for many decades until she found a more receptive audience. Did she crave attention and power? Did she use Sri Aurobindo, already a respected sage, and lead him into making claims he would not have made on his own?

We were not convinced that humanity is about to evolve into a race of supramental beings. Yet because of this notion — or in spite of it? — some real achievements have been made at Auroville. A forest has returned to a barren landscape and many local Tamils are being given a chance to improve their standard of living. The charge of colonialism against Auroville we found to be unjust. Auroville's claim to be universal and to belong to nobody stands up to a reasonable extent. It is open to anyone, including Tamils, who shares its ideals and are willing to share its over-intense lifestyle. When a highly spiritual, sophisticated and largely prosperous international elite descends on 30,000 Tamils, impoverished by centuries of exploitation and wrong 'development' and interacts with them, an upper-strata/lower-strata relationship is inevitable. Almost everyone has a Tamil servant or three. Aurovilian pioneers did their own rough work, but these days the cleaners and labourers are Tamil. However, these Tamils are offered jobs in better conditions than they would have found elswhere locally and with more perks, care and remuneration.

Many farmers have had their degraded lands watered and carefully regenerated by Aurovilian experts, funded in this by the Indian government's Wasteland Development Programme. Sustainable development is, however, deeply problematic in this region. Tamil agriculture is increasingly water based in an uncertain monsoon area with seriously depleted underground water reserves. A city of 50,000 could make that situation intolerable. The farmers prefer cash crops to food crops: irrigation and fertilisers and pesticides promise them more money. They get free electricity for their bore hole pumps, so draw their water recklessly. Bernard, a field worker from Belgium who works in the Tamil villages, showed us a field restored to use by his unit. He said ruefully: 'Now, because of us, chemicals are going onto these fields.' Sustainable agriculture needs to be organic and must be based on food crops. Can this happen at a later stage?

In spite of our admiration, we could not see Auroville as a self-sustaining community. It depends too much on funds from supporters, the Indian government or from rich incomers. It is not a locally based experiment. But then it was never meant to be. It is a place founded on a dream.

Notes

1   Mother's *Agenda (Agenda of the Supplemental Action upon Earth)*,1968, Vol. 9, p80 (Institut de Recherches Evolutives, Paris and Mira Aditi, Mysore).
2   Passages from Kireet Joshi, *Sri Aurobindo and The Mother*, (Institute of Research 1989) quoted from Mother's *Agenda* Vol 2, pp373-374.

Part 5 : Connections

16

Learning to connect

• •

Auroville's secondary school is called the Last School because the founder believed that an evolved community will not need schools. Children will learn (as they still do in less elaborate societies than ours) from imitating the adults around them. Many Living Lightly people agree in principle, but meanwhile, schools are necessary — and there is broad agreement among them on what a good school is like. A good school encourages co-operation instead of competition, compassion rather than ambition. The child's development as a caring, self-motivated and self-reliant person is considered more important than academic success. A good school's main function is not to 'fit' children for entrance into a competitive world, but to allow them to learn. If this sounds illusory and utopian, we did not find it so on our visits.

We don't want to suggest that all mainstream schools force children into desired models or that they are unaware of both the social and environmental context, nor that teachers in mainstream schools are never friends with their students. But it is a rarer occurrence. And they are constrained by the innate conservatism of institutions. Although teachers as a group are generally well aware of environmental issues, in conventional British schools they are constrained by legal obligations to teach the National Curriculum; to make continuous assessments according to parameters set by the Department of Education. They drown in paper; they are frustrated and unhappy. In a success-orientated culture, schools are carried along the current. To achieve 'excellence', high examination scores are required. But the rigours of the examination system do not encourage the searching spirit; they encourage the assimilation of facts. Knowledge is not understanding.

Good education in any age is not top-down but bottom-up; it is child-centred; it fits better with Piaget and Montessori than with right-wing-backlash critics who feel threatened by elements in society which they cannot control — and blame it on the schools. The backlash in this and other industrial countries takes several forms, including the agitation for the return of capital punishment, the resurgence of racism — and the fear of any education which helps people to think for themselves.

Problems of illiteracy, lawlessness, idleness and rootlessness are more intimately related to the capitalist system in its present phase than to the school system in isolation. Yet both children and teachers are blamed for problems in society that have far more to do with low income and poor housing than inadequate schooling.

A child learns because that child wants to — but what she really wants is to understand, and what she needs is to connect. You need enough facts to be able to make choices but you cannot choose if you have no confidence in your ability to make judgements. To allow autonomous and self-regulating abilities to develop you need to trust children to educate themselves, learning by example from their own school community and from the natural world beyond. And in the best of situations, there will be harmony between the school and the natural world.

In pursuing these ideals, schools in Living Lightly communities draw considerably on the experience of the already established movement of 'alternative' or 'progressive' education, but they place this education in the context of a new culture which resists apparently seductive values of the consumer economy. The progressive tradition is well known through the international movement of Steiner schools and Krishnamurti schools, through A. S. Neill's *Summerhill* in Britain, Sudbury Valley in the US.

In looking at alternative schools and colleges, what we found was not so much major differences in organisation — all schools have classrooms, timetables, teachers and pupils — but striking differences in the culture of the school. It shows another attitude towards authority that the 'Miss' or 'Sir' of mainstream state schools is replaced by the teacher's forename.

With the limitations of space we can only describe a few of the schools and institutions we visited: in Vancouver, Virtual High; in England, Brockwood Park, The Small School, and Schumacher College; and the Centre for Alternative Technology (CAT) in mid Wales.

These schools are fragile and their lifespan precarious; they are bound to be, operating in a minority environment. How can they fit into the exam system, maintain discipline, raise money, find the right kind of teachers? How do they avoid being swamped by the troubled rejects of the mainstream? Inevitably these schools fail to some extent. For example, a school might want an energy-efficient heating system but lack the money for investing in new technologies. The funding problems for alternative schools (rarely state-aided) are more serious than problems of curriculum, discipline, staff recruitment and student numbers.

Living Lightly schools might be expected to be the opposite of vocational. Interestingly, we found a different reality: these schools are actively preparing students to live practically in society, cooking their own meals, cleaning their premises, growing their food and even constructing school buildings. The students are being prepared for living in vigorous local communities where people are competent in basic life skills, not just narrow specialists and customers of goods and services.

> The way in which we experience and inter-pret the world depends very much indeed on the kind of ideas that fill our minds. If they are mainly small, weak, superficial and incoherent, life will appear insipid, uninter-esting, petty and chaotic. It is difficult to bear the resultant feeling of emptiness and the vacuum of our minds may only too easily be filled by some big fantastic notion — political or otherwise — which suddenly seems to illumine everything and to give meaning and purpose to our existence.'
> · Fritz Schumacher, *Small is Beautiful.*

Virtual High

At the Eco-Villages conference at Findhorn we met Ilana, Greg, Katherine and Jesse who had come over from Virtual High, Vancouver, to help out. They impressed everyone with their maturity and their deep awareness of the issues on the agenda. These were eco-village kids *par excellence*. They told us their all-absorbing project at Virtual High was to design an eco-village in downtown Vancouver, in which they wanted eventually to live.

They explained that VH was not a school but a learning centre. It had no teachers, only Learning Consultants whom the students hired (and fired). Instead of a syllabus, they chose their own learning projects. They were all wired up with AppleMacs and modems, which they used in designing their eco-village. Ilana said, with quiet aplomb, that the city authorities 'are consulting us about the design' and added that she hoped children in her eco-village 'will grow up together, like old times in the extended family. We need a new system for living.'

We were invited to spend a week at VH. The school premises were a two-storey villa in a residential suburb. Bedrooms had been converted to work stations where each of the thirty pupils had space for a personal computer. A small garden held a jungle gym and a slightly neglected permaculture plot. The atmosphere was like a club; students brought their food and cooked in the kitchen, there was a cleaning roster for the household and bins for sorted rubbish.

We found complete openness and friendliness from staff and students. We could wander where we liked and talk to whom we pleased, attend meetings and lessons and look over people's shoulders in computer networking. With thirty Learners in the top of the house and twenty more older students working on eco-village design down in the basement, the place was bursting at the seams.

VH claimed in its promotional literature and on the Internet that it developed students' self-awareness and ability to work in a group. We saw this during many meetings that we attended. VH is fond of meetings. At Maleny, Australia, we'd already watched consensus in action among adults who had practised the technique for years,. Now we watched young, inexperienced adolescents trying to achieve a similar result. We found the experience both humbling and exciting.

At the weekly BGM, the Big General Meeting, the agenda is set up to cover everything and anything. Attendance is compulsory for everyone and the school culture is such that everyone accepts this. The BGM had prestige amongst the students. Here is a detailed account of one meeting.

In the plant-decorated sitting room twenty-six students assemble, aged thirteen to seventeen. They make themselves comfortable. One sprawls on the wooden floor, another takes two chairs and makes a footrest; there is a fight over a sleeping bag; two girls cover themselves with a single quilt. Someone remarks with surprise that the LCs (Learning Consultants) haven't shown up.

'Let's start anyway.' So the meeting begins. We don't realise the significance of the LCs' non-show. One of the boys starts to moderate, but he doesn't hold the group's attention, especially when Kevin keeps interrupting. Kevin is the one using two chairs, although there is a shortage of chairs. After a few minutes Emma, slight, dark-haired, shy, takes over and remains as chairperson during the whole meeting, although at thirteen she's almost the youngest. She gains confidence as she goes along.

Routine items: Stephen says he is starting pre-production on his Space Opera film and asks help to move a jungle gym he has borrowed. A long acrimonious debate follows about whether Kevin has the right to stop people entering his office (workspace). Kevin is agitated, showing off, disruptive and mocking; the others slap him down — but constructively, trying to bring him into line.

Jeff says: 'Great if you're happy being silly. You don't respect people in here.'

Kevin, pushed into a corner, says, 'I understand.' But his expression is sulky. He pulls a trilby down over his face and wraps himself in a sleeping bag. Students wander in and out of the room.

Then the bombshell! Drew, their Learning Consultant, svelte in cream jeans and camel hair overcoat tossed casually over his shoulders, strides in. A long pause, then: 'Do you know why we Learning Consultants haven't come?' No one does. 'We did not choose to.'

Drew paces about dramatically as he reads a prepared statement in a strong, angry voice: 'You people made a firm and detailed commitment and you have not kept to it. That is totally unacceptable. Attendance is down to fifty percent in workshops.'

The performance is studied (Drew used to be an actor) but effective; a couple of boys grow quite white. Drew thunders on: 'I cannot and will not defend your existence in the community when I have nothing to defend it with. You have free choice and for the most part you've *chosen* to be lazy. People have not been finishing their assignments, have not been carrying out their commitments. You are not interested in educating yourselves.'

The room falls into total silence.

Michael and Jeannie, the other two LCs, arrive. Michael, short, dark, bearded and excited, underlines Drew's message. He's not prepared to ask for funding from parents or the government unless the students agree to make a higher commitment. 'We're going away and leave it up to you what you decide. Decide you'd like a nanny or an authoritarian figure, OK I'll stick around long enough for you to hire someone else. When you have reached consensus on how you want to show up here — then give us a call.'

With some dignity, the three Learning Consultants march out. We, the only adults left, are dismayed. Why are our visits always timed to find a project in some sort of crisis? Talking later about it, we agree that projects are always in crisis — if it's not people management , it's cash shortage. Virtual High is visibly suffering from both.

A long and convoluted discussion between the kids follows. Ken, who claims inside knowledge because he lives in Drew's and Jeannie's home, believes they'll come back. 'It's just that they don't want to be with us the way we are.'

Josh, who has been at VH for nearly four years, plays a moderating role. He's a boy, we have learned, who arrived overweight, asthmatic and with an eating problem. Now he's normal weight, has become a vegan and developed a passion for film making. 'We're floundering,' he says, and then waving his arms in the air, declaims: 'Do we want this to be a place where we follow our passions or do we want to listen to music in our rooms?'

Spontaneously the group start discussing Drew's ultimatum. But first they must deal with Kevin, still lounging across two chairs and interrupting with sardonic comments. Kevin has recently joined VH. He says: 'It's my gift to make fun and see you guys don't take yourselves too seriously.' His thin, pale face wears an unhappy expression.

Josh says: 'You're making a rotten job of it.'

Kevin: 'I'm not going to stop.'

Jeff : 'That's not consensus, it's disruptive to the meeting,' to which Josh adds: 'Sometimes you come across as an angry, obnoxious child.'

Kevin, at last on the defensive: 'I'm going to have to think about that one.'

Jeff insists: 'I want you to respect the meeting.'

Kevin: 'I understand what you're saying. I'll do what I'll do.' At last he stays quiet. Soon he goes out, only to reappear, wearing his trilby which he tips over his face as he continues to recline. He remains quiet now.

The meeting gets under way with individuals making personal statements, at first at random, then in turn around the room.

Guy: 'I came here to escape from public school. After a couple of months I felt I wanted to be part of something, to be a really good success. It took me a year. I wanted some support in keeping to my commitments. But I'm not into LCs as baby-sitters.'

Jeff to Guy: 'I appreciate the way you handle yourself but often you're late. It's real important to do what you say you'll do.' Jeff and Noah are passing comments on everyone in a supportive manner, as if they were LCs themselves.

Emma makes her statement in a trembly voice that gradually steadies. 'I want... I want from the community a certain amount of equality and respect. On the social level it's fine. I want the LCs to have a certain amount of authority — like in between being a teacher and a student. Those who are doing academics should actually do them.'

Reactions to Emma are favourable and she grins. Other statements are criticised. Josh reacts to one boy: 'You're part of a group but I don't know if I can trust you to turn up.' Jeff, hair dyed orange, curled up barefooted on the sofa, adds: 'It reflects poorly on what you're doing here when you're walking to the store at ten in the morning.'

The group decide: each will make a statement. Ryan writes these down verbatim at amazing speed on an Apple PowerBook.

Emma writes up on the board the questions everyone is supposed to answer. *What do you want from the community? How do you want the LCs to play a role in your education and your life? What do you want to commit to and how do you show up? Is that different from how you WANT to show up?*

Josh begins: 'I want us all to be accountable and make best of our learning experience. Keep your commitment, be respectful, show respect for the mentors. We have shown a lot of disrespect not showing up and not doing the work.'

Ken considers he has a dual personality — the outward part going into this community — 'and I have made a decision to put most of it into the community. What I want is support and people keeping their commitments. I want to be myself. The LCs are elders, basically, like the Wise Ones.'

Lisa says: 'I want people to notice me more but not to be on tiptoe around me.' We learn that Lisa was withdrawn and unco-operative when she first arrived here and has made a remarkable turnaround in a few months.

Steve says: 'I want the LCs to keep me on track but not kinda boss me around or always looking over my shoulder. I want to get the Space Opera done, mop the floor twice a week.' For his pains someone tells him: 'I think you've got a really neat sense of humour, are a good friend and a very special person.'

The seniors present, Jeff, with his golden hair and angelic face, and Josh, have no special position. However they comment with more precision and confidence than the others, most of whom are new this year so have only been at the school for three months. (Later, Jesse tells us that kids coming from public school can take up to a year to settle down and utilise the freedom.)

While Jeff and Josh and the others make the sharpest comments to one another, they also make positive ones. When Jeff praises Rachel for her co-operative support, she flushes with delight.

The statements go on. During the break we talk to Karen out in the garden. She is smoking her first cigarette this morning. She used to smoke a pack a day. She's fourteen. Made up with a heavy black lines circling her eyes, spiky hair and green fingernails. The tensions that make young people smoke are not absent here. Sadly, about a third of the kids do. As far as we know — no problem with hard drugs. Smoking is allowed only in the garden.

After the break, the room smells for the first time of school: too many young bodies packed in a space with the windows closed. These are city children, pale-faced, a couple overweight. Most of them lack the lanky grace we found at The Farm in Tennessee where wide spaces and lack of transport keep young people out of doors.

The discussion continues and gradually out of Drew's sharp criticism a self-critique emerges as kids agree to commit themselves more fully both to the community and to the subjects they have chosen. They don't spare one another.

Emma to Christina: 'At the start of the year I saw you as a super hyper asshole — now I see you as an artist using your medium. You're also kinda fun — a sort of role model. You seem so sure of yourself.'

Christina, who is having her back massaged by Donovan, acknowledges the tribute with a half-smile. Her critics use the word evil — 'she's a witch' — but someone else says: 'I find you're a pretty good person.'

Travis remarks: 'The LCs give me respect and they'll give me a hug.' The buzz word is 'respect'. Why do they all want to be respected so much? Do young people feel such a lack of it?

Everyone, except Kevin under his trilby, contributes with more or less energy. When Jonathan's turn comes round he shrugs. Josh says firmly: 'Jonathan, this is your community as well. If you don't care enough to comment — why are you here?' Gradually, with more support from others, Jonathan, his blush flaring round his cheeks and chin, makes his contribution. 'I commit to life — eventually death. I want to show up as myself.' He gets a clap.

After the lunch break, three of the students volunteered to prepare the mission statement in fifteen minutes. It took them an hour. When it finally arrived, it contained no apology for the subjects of the LCs' disapproval but an acknowledgement that more studying would be done more reliably.

The three Learning Consultants, Michael, Drew and Jeannie, filed into the room. Michael asked: 'So what changed?' A girl said: 'Most of us agreed with Drew,' and Emma added: 'When we had a crisis we dealt with it.' A boy said: 'We worked as a community — I haven't felt like that since last year.'

Emma said: 'We're not bullshitting. Look, you guys went off this morning, we had an empty house and we *didn't* party.'

Jeannie comes down from her stool and sits on the floor. 'For three weeks my personal integrity has been challenged — how could I tell your parents you're doing well? Thank you for all the work you did.' Drew: 'We acknowledge and appreciate your maturing bond as a community in a bad time. You've shown us the progress you want to achieve. We accept.'

A boy broke the tension: 'That was a serious kick in the pants.'

After a discussion about the school's money problems, Michael wanted the last word: 'I'd like to thank everyone. I love you all. I wanted to give you the gift of empowerment.' It was 3 o'clock. It had been a six-hour meeting.

Brent Cameron founded Virtual High as part of an education initiative he called Wondertree. It began as a home-learning centre when his daughter, Ilana, found her public school boring and Brent and his partner Maureen didn't like the way she was being taught. The centre became orientated towards eco-technology, using its first budget to buy computers instead of hiring more 'mentors', and developing its own software for ecological exploration. An on-line 'telecommunity' came to be known as Village Quest, simulating aspects of sustainable community life with the ultimate aim of building an eco-village in downtown Vancouver.

Village Quest has now been superseded by Insight Out, a team of former

VH students, graduates and former drop-outs in their late teens and early twenties. The group has government funding to consult local officials and business leaders and experts around the world on the design of an eco-village and a demonstration site for a city park, with an 'eco-café' and a permaculture garden. The crucial stage has been reached where the city authorities are about to consider whether the plan can be implemented.

The Insight Out team's plans are elaborate and well costed. The design won one of Canada's fifteen UNESCO 'best practice' awards. But the scheme operates in the harsh world of capitalist economics. No investment money is forthcoming as yet.

While we were at VH, Jesse Blum was delegated to look after us. Already graduated from the school, he still slept in the building as night manager, for which he was paid. With Brent, he is joint project leader of Insight Out. He is a bright-eyed, slender youth, self-possessed and articulate with hair dyed a pretty dark blue. Jesse shared Brent's cramped basement office, bristling with tangled wires attaching various machines to a Heath Robinson switchboard which worked fitfully. Overfilled bookshelves spill papers on the floor, computers blinked unceasingly.

However, the omnipresent screens hadn't stopped people talking, arguing and being friends. Jesse had adopted computers as an essential part of his life without compromising his wish for a sustainable environment. 'In a virtual scenario I can talk to people everywhere.'

VH meant more than just a school for Jesse. 'It is a concept, a hallucination by the people who invented it. This house has magic energy. I notice when people first come, a sense of being a part of something. There's a certain feeling of sacredness almost and a safe place, a place where I can just be. This is my home.'

He said he had no problem about a future career. He could see some of Insight Out's projects as eventually finding employment for some of the group at least. 'The group could well stay together.'

With Brent and the other LCs convinced that education must be self-directed, how much studying was done was left largely to the individual. Timetables were pinned up but each student had his/her own work space and was responsible for completing a personal schedule. There wasn't much of a library, a few bookshelves scattered around the work-stations. Information came, if at all, via the Internet. Brent believes that computer technology enables most students to learn in a self-directed way, getting their information from the Net. What we observed is what you might have guessed. Recently arrived kids from a conventional system tended to loaf about and relate to one another; kids who had already spent some terms at VH became engrossed in programmes they had picked for themselves and put in immense amounts of time and effort.

And always the underlying problem with this school, and with its two sister primary learning centres called Wondertree: lack of funds. Fees could not cover even the modest salaries of the Learning Consultants and although Virtual High was praised for its innovative work, it was never sure how long Department of Education funding would continue. Six months after our visit, core finding for VH was withdrawn for the 1997-8 school year and, as we write, only the primary schools of the Wondertree Foundation, and the Insight Out team, are in business. However Brent Cameron, his team and most of the parents and students remain convinced that the concept was so good, the results so promising that Virtual High will soon be reborn.

Brockwood Park

Dorothy writes: In the Universal City of Auroville in South India, Krishna and his partner Seiko were building a mud-brick house for themselves. They had been firm friends since school. Where? Brockwood Park. Later in Britain, Angela Oels, a young German environmentalist, suggested we go with her to a unique school which, she had heard, embodied her ideals: Brockwood Park. Soon afterwards, while we were at a course at Schumacher College in Devon, an Indian girl said she was staying for a year at Brockwood Park: she had been educated in Rishi Valley, another Krishnamurti school in North India, and she regarded these schools as part of a single community. Three recommendations in as many months. It seemed we had to go. Or at least one of us. They all said that Brockwood had a special atmosphere that had to be experienced.

Brockwood Park is imbued with the ideals of its founder, Krishnamurti, the Indian teacher and philosopher who died in 1984. Reading Krishnamurti I was neither enchanted nor repelled. Like most books by sages, you can't disagree with the major part of what you read, but the abstractions, the counsels on how to live the right, good life are too theoretical. This feeling was intensified when I visited Brockwood. It appeared a world apart: of what relevance was this oasis of calm, beauty, quiet and remoteness in Britain's crowded, industrialised environment?

Brockwood in its third decade (it was founded in 1969 in that flush of enthusiasm for the Age of Aquarius) is less like a boarding school than an agreeable mansion where a group of young people are living: — no familiar school smell of old socks and boiled cabbages. The wood panelling smells of linseed oil, the house plants flourish and flowers are everywhere, in pots and tubs. The library, in a series of bow-fronted rooms, boasts deep armchairs and

Brockwood Park School.

wooden bookcases. Students' belongings are stacked in open wooden compartments stuffed with clothes and CDs, books, magazines and teenage stuff. Nothing gets pinched, a student told me. 'Things go missing. They turn up again.'

The students arrange their own studies and choose from 120 courses on offer, ranging from the academic to the practical. Lessons usually have between one and eight students. Brockwood has one staff member per four or five students. A teacher friend of ours working in a comprehensive said sourly: 'With that student/staff ratio I'd expect results.'

Krishnamurti's aim was radical and hardly modest: 'To bring about a new generation of human beings who are free from self-centred action.... it is our responsibility, as educators, to bring about a mind that has no conflict within itself, and so end the struggle and conflict in the world about us.' Rather optimistically, he claimed that, 'If only twelve people saw the light, the world could change.' Like Sri Aurobindo and Mother, who based their city of Auroville on the hope that human beings could hasten their own evolution, Krishnamurti pointed to the need for 'an ever-deepening awareness of one's own mind in which the limitations of the mind could drop away.' An American admirer gave Krishnamurti the Georgian mansion and estate of Brockwood Park in Hampshire as a home; he immediately founded the school there. There are also Krishnamurti schools in the US and India.

School life contains two variations from a conventional boarding school; the morning meditation meeting and the cleaning of the premises. At ten to eight the whole school files into a circular, white-walled room with a domed wooden ceiling. When all eighty students and staff are assembled, the register is called, the door is shut and there is a ten-minute silence. I did not close my eyes but watched the others. An atmosphere of peace and tranquillity filled the room, an absence of sighs, fidgeting and coughs, an extraordinary still-ness. At eight o'clock, a student opened the door and everyone filed out. This silent communion focuses each day: you feel that the community has come together. What a contrast from the tedious, fidgety roll calls that start most school days.

The students, most between fourteen and eighteen, a few in their twenties, are from twenty nationalities, with the largest contingents from Japan, the US, France and India. In jeans and trainers they look like any group of Westernised students, but they dress a tad more soberly, no shaven heads and no body piercing.

How were the buildings and gardens kept so immaculate? After breakfast I found out. There are fifty students and thirty staff at Brockwood Park and everyone signs on for Morning Duty. This lasts for thirty minutes. Since eighty people participate, forty hours of daily cleaning ensures that the whole place is spotless. In addition, every student takes turns cooking and puts in two hours work a week on the grounds.

In the conservatory where the kids drink their tea or decaffeinated coffee, each wall is covered in plants and creepers and there is no litter. (I once tried to start a scheme for recycling cans in the local comprehensive where I worked. I couldn't involve the staff or the majority of the students: they were indifferent. Four keen Greenie girls and I emptied rubbish bins for two terms, collected the cans and eventually sold them to the recyclers, hoping this would encourage the others. The response, from the Head down to Year Seven, was zero; peer pressure to keep the environment clean is barely developed in the mainstream school environment.) Here at Brockwood care of the environ-ment is a way of life. A notice on the board reads: 'A sweet wrapper was found on the drive — was it yours?'

Staff turnover is high. Many teachers come for a few months or a year, which results in a lack of continuity both for teaching and social relations. Because of its low pay structure Brockwood Park can't attract many married teachers. Although there are some. Dave Robertson, a South African finan-cial expert, was prepared to give up a management salary to live here with his wife and child.

In spite of its enviable class size, the school is not renowned for academic excellence. Students complain that it is hard to study — social interaction takes up a lot of energy. A Japanese girl said, 'Other skills we learn are more valuable than a top grade in an exam. But we do have a few As.'

What Brockwood does do is give students possibilities of creative work unknown in more conventional establishments. Two teenage girls on a semester's exchange from their Californian Krishnamurti college were thatching a cob house. It stands in a grove of magnolias and bamboo next to a pond landscaped by another student to attract wildlife. The thatch is somewhat uneven but serves its purpose. 'Everyone said girls couldn't build a house or thatch it so we set out to prove them wrong.' The thick mud and straw walls are winter warm and summer cool. The final cost is around £400; if it is maintained the cob house will last several centuries. What had the girls learnt from their years of Krishnamurti education? Aja smiled, 'Seeing yourself clearly and honestly and being aware.'

Other students were more critical. Ed, a mature student, is spending a few months at Brockwood working in the garden. He finds life here 'too vaguely aspirational. You're trying to be a better person, but you are still yourself, young, angry or confused. And sometimes because of lack of time or high staff turnover there isn't the space for discourse.'

In a private school students are usually drawn from society's élite. This is true here, too, although forty percent of the students are on full or partial scholarships and there is a funding drive to raise half a million pounds for more scholarships. Some parents work hard to pay the fees. The school tries never to turn a student away for lack of funds but sometimes has to. Full fees are £8000 per year, which is less than most equivalent boarding schools and does not represent the full cost. The rest is taken up by Krishnamurti's charitable foundation. Staff accept lower salaries then they could earn in either state or private sectors. Everyone gets the same rate whether they are a director or a cook or a secretary. And everyone uses first names, staff and students alike.

Although the school is alternative, it is neither Green in any obvious way nor sustainable in the physical sense. The elegant eighteenth-century buildings and grounds which the school inherited are not self-supporting in energy, food or money. Efforts are made to adopt the best environmental principles in the circumstances. The staff would like to install solar heating and a reed bed sewage plant but the cost is prohibitive. Colin, the co-director, says that when the school opened in the sixties, oil was the cheapest choice for heating.

It is perhaps less excusable that although the school owns fifteen hectares (thirty-five acres) of prime land, the vegetable gardens and orchards are not fully productive and much food, albeit organic, is bought in. Brockwood food, especially for anyone who has suffered British school dinners, is totally amazing. Each meal comprises about twenty different fresh vegetables in assorted salads, several dressings and one or two choices of international vegetarian dishes. It's a low fat, low sugar diet, lacto-vegetarian or vegan, and everyone thrives on it. I've never seen a group of teenagers with fewer spots. However you can still find junk food packets in the bins of recyclable rubbish.

The ethos of Brockwood Park can make it hard for students to re-enter outside life. Shabnum Tejani wrote in the school magazine: 'The emphasis on the place of individual change at Brockwood has been tremendously important to me, but also somewhat myopic, in the sense that it didn't quite capture the profound ways in which I was, and am, socially conditioned. I realised with horror that I had turned into a puritanical, moralising, self-righteous individual who saw things in black and white, right and wrong.'

And yet Shabnum, and other graduates I spoke to, decided that what they were most grateful for was that very inability to quite 'fit' back into society. (We heard this remark often both from kids who had grown up in communities or been to schools like Summerhill.) Petra from Slovenia, aged nineteen, wants to go into politics after university. She had been a wild child, she said, but three years in the Brockwood environment had calmed her down. We were chatting in the greenhouse during the compulsory Land Care (two hours a week for everyone). We had several hundred annual flower seedlings to re-pot. Petra's gardening was more dashing than skilled. At the end of the afternoon we were both covered in damp potting compost. 'I'm still wild but now I'm paying attention to other people's needs.' One of her main problems with Brockwood is that 'sooner or later you have to go into the outside world.'

Staff and students *do* believe that an individual can improve him or herself through the application of careful, correct thinking. It gives a slightly pious air to the place, at the same time a feeling of immense peace. What they value above all at Brockwood is the lack of competitiveness and competition. It is a place where gentleness is not confused with weakness.

On my last night at Brockwood, several of the staff and students were folk dancing in the main hall. They began with simple dances and progressed until by 10 p.m. they were performing elaborate, complicated Corsican and Catalan steps. Georg, one of the educators, is Catalan. Meanwhile, in a contrast that sums up a clash of cultural values, a group of boys, mostly Japanese, were playing electric guitars and drums in a shed in the walled garden — a roomful of costly electronics and a throbbing sound across the evening air.

I have seen how hard it is to attempt to change values. Working part-time in a local comprehensive school shortly before we started travelling for this book, I set up a group of twelve-year-olds to try organic gardening on an allotment next to the school. The allotment ran for two years and we grew basketfuls of lettuce and bunches of radishes. One season our cauliflowers had superb heads; we never managed to stop pigeons eating the young cabbages. We never managed to swing official attitudes firmly in our favour. Our activities were always marginal and not considered 'serious' education. And as well, we went against current values. With immense effort, selling produce at fetes and printing a cookbook, we raised the money for a garden shed. Three times it was broken into and on the fourth occasion burnt to the ground. The kids knew who'd done it — but were too scared to say. The allotment scheme collapsed. A year later, I asked the 'GROWMORES' what the whole experience had meant to them.

Richard said: 'We learnt to work in a group and in a funny way it did bring us closer. If you had stayed at school we'd have carried on.' Nic disagreed. 'It was great to begin with but we never had enough support from school. And we never had enough time.' Robin agreed with Nic: 'I thought it was tailing off the second year. And when the shed was burnt, I lost interest.'

All the kids said that if school had encouraged them more, they would have carried on. They were disappointed when the school did nothing about the shed being burnt down. They accepted authority's attitudes. These are well-meaning kids; full of enthusiasm. But they are not offered many alternatives.

The confusion of their thinking and their double standards showed up in essays a group of twelve-year-olds wrote on 'My Life At Twenty-five'.

Katy wrote: 'I have many attitudes, one of my strongest is going to be Greenpeace and the environment.' Then she added: 'I would live in a house with ten rooms and my car would have to be either a BMW or a small blue Metro. I'd rather have a Lamborghini.'

Natasha was also going to have 'a smashing car plus a big house full of modern stuff like touch-sensor buttons. I will have trustworthy friends and be very Green.' Five of the eight children writing the essay said, without prompting, they were 'Green'. Ceri wanted to marry a car salesman to make quite sure she got a car 'which is really hi-tech and computerised'. She, too, was 'against animal cruelty' and wanted 'to live near the country which is peaceful'.

Will these students ever sort out the muddle between their awareness of environmental issues, their gut feeling that an endless proliferation of goods and traffic can't be right and the prevailing values? They were not helped by their school. In Devon, the Small School tries to inculcate different values in its students.

The Small School

In 1982 the village of Hartland, in North Devon, was due to lose its secondary school through lack of numbers. The nearest alternative was an 1800-strong comprehensive fifteen miles away at Bideford. The situation was commonplace: thousands of British village schools have been closed in recent years and after each closure children have to commute to a large and impersonal institution. The closure policy was designed to save money and was considered a better use of resources.

The difference at Hartland was that Satish Kumar lived there. The editor of *Resurgence* magazine and President of the Schumacher Society was already dedicated to the small is beautiful philosophy. Satish took this opportunity of founding a school on a human scale with holistic values, based on the principles to which his life has been devoted. Local shareholders raised the money to buy a disused church hall and small garden and hire the first teachers. The Small School was not funded by authority, yet it thrived and grew. Parents pay what they can and often contribute their skills in lieu of fees.

The children choose their own curriculum which may include practical skills learned from parents, neighbours, local farmers, craftspeople, business people or artists. Formal lessons are only held in the mornings; afternoons are devoted to creative activities like pottery, art and drama. Every day the children help cook their school dinner.

In some ways it is a school like any other; the boys aren't less macho, the girls aren't less giggly. Both Caroline Walker, the head, and Colin Hodgetts, the former head who teaches part-time, are strong personalities. However, subtle differences become apparent. First names are used. There is none of that irritability from teachers and surly defiance from pupils that we associate with big schools. A group of teenage girls gossiping by the fire doesn't start guiltily when a teacher walks through. In a community so small there is a freer contact across the age barriers.

The cooking of lunch is a big feature of the day. Every student takes a turn in helping and on Fridays the oldest students prepare the vegetarian meal by themselves. Whole-wheat rolls are baked daily and main dishes are mainly gratins, pasta, pizzas with salads, fresh fruits and yoghurts. The small number of vegans have a non-dairy dish prepared for them.

Caroline Walker came to the school after ten years working on village projects in South India. She believes that cooking fulfils pupils' need to give as well as receive. 'It's ideal for the purpose because it gets instant appreciation. It's also a basic survival skill for the modern world.' The kitchen is a place of gossip and friendliness. In class, if a kid feels out of sorts or angry, the custom is to go down to the kitchen and chill out. Caroline finds that time spent in the kitchen is a learning aid: 'Planning, implementing and evaluating a lunch for thirty has much in common with a good science experiment.'

Lunch doesn't start until the whole school is assembled. Gradually the chattering subsides; a few seconds silence before Satish's prayer for peace (he wrote it for his own family).

> Lead me from death to life, from falsehood to truth;
> Lead me from despair to hope, from fear to trust;
> Lead me from hate to love, from war to peace;
> Let peace fill our hearts, our world, our universe;
> Peace, peace, peace.

The only compulsory subjects for the thirty boys and girls are maths, English and cooking. The top group take GCSE exams. 'Some years they are more academic, other years less so. Where we stand in the league tables depends on that. Our parents are not necessarily interested in academic success.' Caroline refers to some ex-students working on nearby farms 'and earning more than I do,' and another finishing his PhD in Celtic Studies.

Caroline used to think that environmentalism was an expensive fad until she was influenced by the ideas of Robert Henry, the Swedish doctor who started The Natural Step programme in his country — a national effort at co-ordinated environmental action. Now she wants to base her teaching on environmental principles; to inculcate in her students the idea that they must strive not to take from the earth more than they put back. Caroline and her husband, Keith, like many educators we met, want to live more lightly themselves and educate both their own and other people's children to be aware of the choices between maintaining the status quo or working for a different society. And they make the financial sacrifices in accepting lower salaries. Teachers at the Small School get £9000 a year which is less than half what they could be paid in the public sector.

Small School economics are small-scale indeed; the budget totters from one year to the next. Not surprisingly, the physical conditions are not conducive to text-book environmentalism: a draughty, energy-hungry hall and a collection of village houses with electricity from the national grid and lavatories plumbed into the main drainage.

Colin Hodgetts has also down-shifted from a better paid job in London to work at the Small School. Burly, full-bearded, he wears sandals in any weather Devon can throw at him. An accomplished composer and pianist, he uses his skills in the provision of home-made entertainment to dilute the influence of pop-art and television. This simple lifestyle affects the children. 'They see that the teachers don't spend money on themselves and yet seem happy. We hardly need money for entertainment: we make our own.' But the Small School is aware of the wider world. When he was head, Colin raised enough money to take a couple of school trips to Japan where the Small School kids performed to village audiences. And every year at the annual Schumacher lectures in Bristol, the students cook a pre-packed lunch for several hundred participants.

Lack of cash, when it isn't too severe, leads to more co-operation. 'When we needed the main hall ceiling painted we all did it — parents, teachers and students erected a scaffolding together. We enjoyed ourselves,' says Colin, simply.

Satish attributes some of the school's success to changing public attitudes. 'Disillusion over the job market in general has encouraged people to look to alternatives like the Small School. If jobs aren't so likely any more, why not let children learn life skills and survival skills?'

He is content with the results: his own son Mukti learned building when he and others turned an old barn into the school workshop; Mukti later became part of the *Resurgence* production team. Satish's daughter Maya became a good cook and gardener while at school before going on to read philosophy at university. One graduate girl will take a year out teaching in an Indian village before studying architecture. Another ex-pupil has become a gardener after studying at the Royal Horticultural Society, another went into forestry, several into farming. Satish says the farmers among the ex-pupils tend to farm organically and to have an interest in maintaining variety of species.

Students adore the Small School. Chris, aged thirteen, has her blonde hair in Rasta plaits and beads. 'You can be yourself here. I can wear something weird. No one minds.'

Tell me some drawbacks, I asked a group of thirteen-year-old girls. They looked amused. One girl volunteered: 'A lack of funding — we never have enough money. We've only got word processors and we need better computers.'

I raised a common criticism of small-scale education — that it can be cramping and lacks essential facilities. Both students and staff countered that in mega-schools pupils are not encouraged enough to discover their real interests and talents. Here, the pottery class takes place in a rehabilitated stone barn, heated by a wood burning stove. At the end of the day, every pupil has to spend fifteen minutes clearing up. Small School students also take part in organised hill climbing, rambling and cycling, which need no special facilities. One group is tree planting in the area, another working on a conservation project. For team sports, the school can use Hartland village facilities in summer and Bideford Sports Centre in winter.

The idea of schools deliberately designed to be small is gaining ground in many places. In New York fifty small schools have opened since 1992, producing graduates with higher rates of success. Eleven schools in Britain are members of the Human Scale Education movement — a trend which owes much to the early example from Hartland. The Small School's survival will depend on outside economic pressures. School fees don't reflect the true cost of running the school — even allowing for the teachers' low salaries — and official funding will be the only long-term guarantee.

The alternative schools we visited do not prevent academic children pursuing their interests. But it can be harder because often there is no qualified teacher for the chosen subject. The emphasis is directed towards the whole person's development, and that showed itself in numerous friendly discussions with kids. In our subjective view, they lacked the cynicism of most mainstream-educated kids; they believed that social change was possible as well as necessary. Where will change come from? There are plenty of alternative schools and a few Green schools but no alternative-Green universities. Schumacher College is a first attempt to fill the void.

Schumacher College

Living Lightly is more than a choice of lifestyle, it is a way of thinking about the world — a movement of liberation from the economic, philosophical and scientific paradigm that has buttressed the dominant culture since the Renaissance. A new paradigm of interlinked ideas and thought systems is emerging — deep ecology, the Gaia hypothesis, morphogenic resonance, creation spirituality, permaculture. But where can the new paradigm be taught, studied and discussed? Universities are bastions of tradition, chronically afraid of losing respectability by admitting alternative systems of thought. Where they are discussed it's with a semi-apologetic tone. Pioneering writers in this movement of ideas — James Lovelock, Wendell Berry, Fritjof Capra, Hazel Henderson, James Hillman, Rupert Sheldrake, Vandana Shiva, Martin Kohr, Wolfgang Sachs and others — are known by their books but have difficulty in discussing their ideas in an institution that takes them seriously.

Satish Kumar wanted to rectify this deficiency. For him it was a logical step. He was editing *Resurgence*, the spiritual and artistic flagship of Green periodicals in Britain, he had founded the Small School in his village of Hartland, and launched a publishing company, Green Books. Now he wanted a Green University.

Universities are not easily founded and the plan proved too ambitious. Satish did achieve the next best thing — a residential college offering short courses in all these new disciplines, led by their foremost exponents, and awarding master's degree credits for students who needed them.

Courses at Schumacher College generally last three weeks. The venue is a medieval post house in the Arcadian grounds of Dartington Hall south of Dartmoor in Devon. The college has the atmosphere of a country house where students browse in an oak-timbered library and gather in a lofty hall with a wooden gallery. The oak chairs and cushions offer comfort without luxury.

The atmosphere is that of a Gandhian ashram. When they are not listening to lectures or reading books, students may meditate, dance, paint, sculpt, pray, go for country walks. Or they can do none of these. But they must, whether they like it or not, help with cooking and cleaning.

The beginning, seven years ago, was slow. Now most courses are well subscribed and well over a thousand students from all over the world have included civil servants, teachers, artists, business executives, psychologists, healers, journalists and miscellaneous seekers of many age groups.

Students and lecturers all attend the morning meeting at 8.30. Someone reads a text or leads an exercise or group activity. A staff facilitator helps shy students join in. Next, the morning chores, then the main lecture. Afternoons are for group tutorials with the scholars-in-residence, for crafts, preparing plays or shows, field trips, or private reading for Credits in the well-stocked library. After supper, an evening session is usually led by a student introducing her own activity or expertise. Satish himself leads an evening class on Mondays — also his evening for showing another of his talents: cooking a sumptuous Indian vegetarian meal.

The most popular courses have been about new approaches to economics and general science, and about the links between ecology and psychology, theology and philosophy. The more esoteric earth wisdom courses are less popular, and fading out, but staff have noticed that courses connected with personal growth therapies attract more fee-paying students than the more theoretical ones: people appear more inclined to spend their money on themselves. Master's degree credits are awarded through the University of Plymouth, 25 km away, and an additional master's degree in holistic science was due to begin in 1998 under Professor Brian Goodwin, formerly of the Open University.

We visited a full course of twelve students from eleven countries led by Vandana Shiva, on the implications for the global economy of the latest round of GATT agreements. Vandana, the Indian physicist, writer and campaigner, is a regular scholar-in-residence here. She remarks that the college had been helped by 'the dismal condition of most conventional universities, where students learn about development in terms of deficiencies as if conventional growth were the only goal. The system perpetuates the production of obsolete knowledge.'

Enthusiastic agreement from one student, Ania Mistry, who was discontented with the way she was being taught the economics of development at Cambridge. 'The course is obsessed with growth and Green Revolution and seeing traditional agriculture as a barrier to progress. How can people's livelihood and culture be a barrier?'

The limiting factor at Schumacher College, as in all the other experimental places of learning, is money. A three-week course costs £1200, but many students get bursaries to help them out, from a grant by the college's host, the Dartington Trust.

Schumacher College was founded because ecologically based alternatives to the dominant paradigm were not breaking through in universities. However, in the United States we learned that some shoots were sprouting. John Carroll, Professor of Environmental Studies at the University of New Hampshire, in Durham finds that there has been 'a softening towards alternative thinking' in some US university departments, especially in agriculture, after a series of ecological disasters. He mentions the University of Santa Cruz, University College, Santa Barbara and the University of Vermont, Burnlington, as offering similar courses to his own. Has economics softened up, too? John's friend and colleague at New Hampshire, Richard England, is Head of Economics. He is a friend and sympathiser of Herman Daly, the leading anti-growth economist. This, too, is a sign of softening, John says.

Most of what students learn in the above examples is in the realm of theory. Where is there a school for the practicalities?

Showing how it works

You can find such a school in an unlikely spot — a disused slate quarry in mid-Wales. The Centre for Alternative Technology (CAT) has evolved into a world-famous demonstration of sustainable living. We found practical, down-to-earth skills demonstrated with wit and showmanship that attracts 80,000 visitors a year, including 20,000 schoolchildren, to learn the secrets of compost loos, reed bed sewage, solar batteries and commonsense ways of keeping warm without using too much electricity. The demonstration is never daunting; its message is that weird and complicated machines are not the answer: you save the planet by homely commonsense, using less electricity and water and eating less meat and fewer products that have travelled long distances. The public can pick up the message while enjoying an entertaining day out. More serious enquirers can stay longer or take part in work and training camps held in two eco-cabins.

A passenger lift takes visitors to the demonstration site at CAT.

Ingenuity and simple invention greet the visitor at once. A passenger lift which works by gravity and recycled water took us up the eighty-metre climb to the demonstration site. Each carriage is hauled up by the weight of its descending twin plus a few thousand litres of water endlessly recycled — a technology used a century ago for bringing slate down from the quarry. At the top, you are guided through a collection of windmills, solar panels and organic gardens. When you are satiated with that you can eat at the organic restaurant or browse in a specialist bookshop, or you can call home from a telephone powered by a windmill (*and* a solar panel, just in case).

CAT is situated in sixteen hectares. The community housing and experimental energy sources are grouped together in little more than two hectares of flat land. The whole site, once degraded and abandoned, has become a mass of trees, plants and flowers. Peter Harper, who has been there since the start, says: 'Given certain very simple steps, intense human activity and diverse wildlife are not only compatible but may even be complementary.'

The buildings are nearly all based on the designs of the British architect, the late Walter Segal, for self-build timber-framed houses — a method he developed thirty years ago. The highly simplified but technically sophisticated method is based on the medieval post and frame. No trench foundations are needed and all the materials can be bought ready cut in timber yards and assembled on site. The design uses energy-saving features like thick walls, roof and floor insulation and passive solar techniques that get the maximum benefit from the sun.

CAT is a powerhouse of ideas, some so simple that we wonder why they aren't universally adopted — like the food store with a turf roof, frost free and needing no artificial heating, the solar pump driven by an array of photo-voltaic cells and the solar water heater. CAT's determination to remain relevant to urban living is shown in a tiny garden where herbs and salads grow in home-made compost instead of sterile city soil.

A problem which runs underneath the world's pollution and is capable of solution is that of sewage. Why aren't the solutions that we saw in places as varied as Kerala, India, where village effluent is cleaned in a series of lotus ponds, or at the Living Machine at Findhorn, adopted more widely? Is it just the expense of conversion or it is a squeamishness relating to bodily functions? A notice outside the lavatory reads: 'We compost all our sewage wastes and any contributions you may care to make are acknowledged with thanks'.

There are two reed bed systems. One takes the sewage from the restaurant and houses. The waste goes into four chambers. The solid waste is collected into nets and rested for three months. Then the nets are emptied and the solid waste is composted in bins for one year. The water is filtered through reed beds. It ends up clean enough to rejoin the river, having irrigated a willow plantation en route. When the filtered water rejoins the river it is cleaner than the river water itself. A reed bed system once set up is cheaper to run than a chemical sewage plant and looks far better.

CAT began in 1975 as a small commune dedicated to sustainable living, with no ambitions in direct public education. It was founded by Gerard Morgan-Grenville, an old Etonian and former industrialist who explained his motives: 'Unless we can pioneer some way in which life can be lived without using up the capital resources of planet earth, the collapse of civilisation is ultimately inevitable.' Gerard now remembers that many early volunteers were 'hopeless at any kind of practical work; they broke or lost all the tools and spent most of their energy discussing theories and abstractions far into the night.'

In those days all staff lived communally on site, but most moved out when the annual invasion of summer visitors 'made us feel as if we were in a play,' according to Peter

> The craze for self-sufficiency and small-is-beautiful has passed. Don't try and do it all yourself. Start where you are strong, not where you are weak. In a modern society you sell your marketable skills and purchase the rest: there are loads of other specialists. Don't try to make your energy: try to save your energy. Most of the action is going to be in cities, where the majority of humans will be soon be living and where, contrary to our old arcadian assumptions, sustainable modern lifestyles are more easily achieved.
> · Peter Harper, to the authors.

Harper. CAT is now a workers' co-operative of 28 members, all earning the same salary, of whom only ten live on the site. Although the commune evolved into a different arrangement, the centre has kept its ideals intact and can claim to have achieved a higher sustainability rating than most Living Lightly experiments. It generates 90 percent of its own energy in renewable form from sun, wind and water, and recovers 80 percent of its sewage nutrients in its two reed beds.

Peter Harper, who is one of the wittiest and most ironical of environmental speakers, was happy to give us a list of CAT's shortcomings:

* the community and its eco-lifestyle have declined and now only a minority of us live on the site;
* we don't do a very careful eco-audit in all activities so cannot measure eco-success;
* we run a lot of cars and use little public transport;
* maintenance is a bit scruffy — we're creators, not maintainers;
* not much integration into the local community;
* we always seem to be broke.

The plus points are much weightier. With its £1 million turnover, CAT has become a major resource for practical Living Lightly. The Centre's influence owes much to consultancy work which also brings it nearer to the cultural and economic mainstream. Customers have included two oil exploration companies which needed wind energy for North Sea drilling rigs. The evolution of CAT from an intentional community to a successful enterprise is not dissimilar to that of other communities, like The Farm in Tennessee, which have had to temper idealism with the practical realities of earning a living.

Ideas of the Living Lightly movement spread slowly and with difficulty in schools, colleges and institutions because co-operation is neither easily achieved nor valued in a competitive world. Such institutions have, here and there, become part of the movement, even if sometimes the pressures of mainstream society crush them. Virtual High has closed down for lack of funding, but Brent Cameron, its founder, is determined that in some form it will re-open. If this does not happen in Vancouver, surely it will happen elsewhere. At Brockwood Park the children may not earn quite as many academic qualifications as they could earn in a public school, but they have a generosity of spirit that will serve them better in the next century. The students who stay for ten days in the eco-cabins of CAT learn skills as valuable in cities as in hill farms. In both rich and poor countries, education must persuade students that to live co-operatively rather than competitively will increase, not diminish, their personal autonomy.

17

Connected for life

●●

How can groups of people living lightly, at peace and close to nature in their local communities, reach out to each other and put their message out to the world? Must they use the techniques and instruments of the global economy itself? They may, for a start, occasionally need cars and aeroplanes to attend meetings. And every day they may need computers, e-mail and the Internet, all of which are instruments of the devil.

Computers are the trickiest issue. These seductive machines and their on-line applications are a typical product of the global techno-consumer economy and are also the system's triumphant tool, but if we aim to challenge that world system, analyse its fallacies, demonstrate its horrors and devise alternatives, we too need such tools. Or do we? Thequestion has split the Green movement. At one extreme are self-proclaimed 'Luddites' who detest the computer culture as a lethal weapon used by the masters of a technological empire which is on the way to enslaving us. At the other extreme are computer enthusiasts who feel part of a global counter-culture which would be a shadow of itself without PCs, the Internet, and all the adjuncts from e-mail chat-lines to news groups.

The dilemma was apparent in the run-up to the summit on global warming at Kyoto in December 1997. Green campaigners wanting facts, figures and arguments needed to look no further than the Internet. Our WebFerret, which surfs the search engines, came up with 500 responses to 'global warming', including link sites that led on to hundreds more, ranging from NASA,, the United Nations Environment Programme and the Union of Concerned Scientists to networks and newsgroups devoted to the subject. Sceptics were well represented too — some genuine, others sinister — in scores of sites conveniently drawn together in a Global Warming Sceptics' Page. In most of these debunking sites, sponsorship was not stated but canny surfers could discover it by shortening the address and arriving at the host site. This simple ruse led us from the Sceptics' Page (www.carnell.com/global_warming/index.htm) to the host (www.carnell.com) who turned out to be a guy

The Internet is a tool used by the forces of economic globalisation to concentrate power and wealth in an international corporate elite. However, it's equally self-evident that the net is not owned by anyone. It can be, must be, and is also an instrument for the people, serving to network communities that treasure freedom, socio-economic justice, ecological diversity, and peace...

Annual reports of major corporations are now on-line for all to see (www.prars.com/). Sites like Corpwatch, Adbusters, and Descendants of Founders of Multinationals will rock corporate web hard. Being shamed in public, according to business critic Paul Hawken, has become the worst corporate nightmare.

· Allan Hunt-Badiner in Corporation Watch website, www.corpwatch.org/

describing himself as 'a libertarian so almost all of the stuff you'll find here is from a free market perspective'. Another sceptic site, traced to its home page, is put out by the CATO Institute: 'Twenty years of promoting public policy based on individual liberty, limited government, free markets, and peace.'

The Luddites are championed in the US by the writer Kirkpatrick Sale and by Jerry Mander, who runs the International Forum on Globalisation in San Francisco, and supported in Britain by Teddy Goldsmith, editor of *The Ecologist* and Satish Kumar, editor of *Resurgence* magazine. Sale, in his book *Rebels Against the Future* features the original Luddites who protested against the cruel excesses of the first Industrial Revolution, as the harbingers of a contemporary Luddite protest against the second industrial revolution which, after the Second World War, brought the global consumer economy into being.

Computers are polluting in their manufacture, say the Luddites. Your friendly PC is made of acrylonitrile-butadiene-styrene from Saudi Arabian oil, Wyoming coal and Texas natural gas and its glass monitor will be a hazardous waste when discarded. In their, *Stuff: The Secret Lives of Everyday*

The web has emerged as the major source of alternative media as well as an on-line college for keyboard activism. One has only to check the sites of Interactivism and fax protests right off the webpage about a host of social and ecological issues (www.inter-activism.com), or WebActive and monitor new developments in computer activism (www.webactive.com), or others who are betting their profitability on activism to grow and become a powerful sphere of public life. NGOs around the world are building databases, attracting members, developing outside links often starting with a simple exchange of messages and breaking new ground in efficient global networking.

· Allan Hunt-Badiner, article in Corporation Watch website.

Computer technology may be the single most important instrument ever invented for the acceleration of centralised power. While we sit at our PCs editing our copy, sending our e-mail and expressing our cyber freedoms, the transnational corporations are using their global networks, fed by far greater resources. They are able to achieve not only information exchange but concrete result that express themselves in downed forests, massive infrastructural development, destruction of rural and farming societies, displacement of millions of people, and domination of governments.
· Jerry Mander in *The Case Against the Global Economy*.

Things, John Ryan and Alan Durning claim that to make one computer's chips, which weigh one fiftieth of a pound, a state-of-the-art plant uses 1,400 gallons of water and generates forty pounds of waste. The circuit boards are made of copper, fibreglass and epoxy resin, plated with copper from Chile, tin from Brazil, and lead recycled from Houston's dead car batteries. The manufacturing of a 55-pound computer generates 139 pounds of waste and uses 7300 gallons of water and 2300 kilowatt-hours of energy. It will use four times as much energy again during its lifetime.

Far greater harm comes from what computers do to us, say the Luddites. C. A. Bowers, professor of education in Portland State University, claims that educating children through computers prevents them developing an entire set of ideas and experiences that had previously been the building blocks for a connection with the earth. Luddites agree that when everyone is sitting at their computer terminals all over the planet, this will be an expression of uniformity, not diversity.

The latest sinister use of computers is company generated letter writing campaigns used by corporations to lobby their case against legislation that threatens them — especially carbon-emission curbs to restrict global warming. New software enables companies to e-mail all present and past employees, send them pro-forma letters for despatch to their local representatives and newspapers — and then monitor which employees comply and which do not.

Undeterred by this menace, many Greens are Net-friendly and some are computer freaks. Many of us are ambiguous, just as we are about cars and supermarkets because we inhabit a culture which makes it difficult to do without such amenities. When we arrived at Sam Smith's community-supported farm in Massachusetts (Chapter 6) we explained we'd driven from New Hampshire using a computerised itinerary. Sam shuddered and said he was a Luddite, but he soon admitted to having a computer himself and said he would like us to show him how to get onto the Internet. During our busy days with him we never got round to that — and here lies a major obstacle for

While the Internet provides a global network of information we need an opportunity to build local community. Paidea Village is a human scale local area model for community. When you move around through the village you can visit various places and get involved in conferences, projects and discussions with other village members. There are a maximum of 1200 people that live in this village and their are an equal number of children and adults. The children work with each other and with mentors on various projects with an underlying theme that encourages strategies to live on this planet in healthier and happier and more sustainable lifestyles. You can log onto the Village as a Guest (password — guest).

· Internet project by students at Virtual High, Vancouver.

many Living Lightly people faced with computer techniques: they are too busy.

Living Lightly people are not nostalgic for a previous age but see themselves as modern, more truly in touch with important trends than people in the mainstream. This position is difficult to sustain without computers. We've already met in the last chapter the impressive students from Virtual High, who were designing their own eco-village on their Apple Mac laptops and interacting on-line with friend and foe alike. In Vancouver they were operating a global village chat programme on the Internet called Paidea.

On our own travels while writing this book, we found the Net culture beguiling and irresistible. Whatever we researched was somewhere on the Net (even community-supported agriculture has its Web-site although few of the CSA farmers are on-line) and most of the projects we studied provides e-mail contact addresses, so we could get to know people before we arrived. Some replied to our e-mails by offering accommodation for us as WWOOFers (Willing Workers on Organic Farms). As we travelled we had an exhilarating sense of being in a single global community. It would be foolish to ignore the capacity of computers to nourish and expand this community.

Even spiritual communities, including Auroville in India and Findhorn in Scotland, have their Web-pages and are on-line in the Eco-village Global Network (www.gaia.org), through which the surfer can also reach Crystal

Previous journeys through Ecobalance postings have interested and often inspired me, sometimes bored me, yet knowing there are many alternative eco-(etc.)-community minded people working at solutions and alternatives to the obvious difficulty us humans are having getting along with each other and the planet, creates a sense of community in itself.

· Neil Bryan in Canada, on Ecobalance List.

Waters in Australia, The Farm in the US, Lebensgarten in Germany, Rysovo in Russia, Gyurufu in Hungary and Kibbutz Gezer in Israel.

Green writers and campaigners can hardly be in the picture without down-loading the latest report of the United Nations Development Program or the Worldwatch Institute, or calling up www.corpwatch.org/, which enables us to monitor corpo-rate misdemeanours from deforestation to sweatshops.

> As a service to our site users, we've put in place a search engine that covers all the intentional communities on the web that we know about. Our REACHbook, an on-line forum for people looking for community, communities forming, and communities looking for people, etc., has been quite active. Since our last message the postings have included eleven Communities Forming, four Communities with Openings, and fifteen Seeking Community! We held an on-line chat meeting last week on the topic of 'Is Chat Really Useful?' Next week the topic is 'How to Find One's Intentional Community'.
> · Intentional Communities website at www.ic.org

Luddites are wrong in this respect: the big guns are not always on the enemy's side. Corporation Watch is part of the Institute for Global Communications (Igc) which is part of the Association for Progressive Communications (Apc) — and they are all goodies as far as we can tell. The corporations can hire Gnossos Software for their sinister e-mail onslaughts, but we can hire Igc, for a more modest fee, to design us an e-mail action lobbying group.

Every aspect of the Green culture and expertise — co-housing, eco-villages, progressive education, permaculture, voluntary simplicity, community living — has its major and minor Websites and dedicated chat lines. Many are technical, some are esoteric, like the one devoted to earthships — ecological buildings made of old tyres and aluminium cans (www.slip.net/~ckent/earthship/). Others are beguiling like Dreamtime (http://www.net22.com/dreamtime/) — an 'experiment in eco-village design whose mission is to create a new planetary culture' — which has a tempting array of links to other sites.

Some of these sites are very practical. People looking for a community setting up a co-housing group can find it on the Net (www.cohousing.org). Anyone looking for a community to join can try the Fellowship of Intentional Communities at www.ic.org/

E-mail lists and web-sites are widely used for mobilising activists for lobbying, demonstrations or more forceful 'direct action.' In Britain The Land is Ours website (www.envirolink.org/orgs/tlio) calls supporters to their actions. In the US, alerts are sent to e-mail subscribers when crucial legisla-tion is due, or when venerable stands of redwoods are being cut down in

Earth First! is different from other environmental groups. We believe in using all the tools in the tool box, ranging from grassroots organising and litigation to civil disobedience and monkeywrenching. There are no members of Earth First!, only Earth First!ers. It is a belief in biocentrism, or Deep Ecology, and a practice of putting our beliefs into action. While there is a broad diversity within Earth First! from animal rights vegetarians to wilderness hunting guides, from monkeywrenchers to careful followers of Gandhi, from rowdy backwoods buckaroos to thoughtful philosophers, from misanthropes to humanists. There is agreement on one thing: the need for action.
· EarthFirst! direct action website at www.telalink.net/~zoomst/earthfirst/index.html

California, by Epic Action Alert (epic@igc.org), which is run by the Environmental Protection Information Centre from a Website at www.humnat.org/epic/

Many of us belong to an e-mail chat-list to conquer our loneliness in the decentralised, televillage life that we aspire to. These are free, assuming you are already paying about £5 a month for your e-mail account. Anyone can subscribe, unsubscribe and re-subscribe at the touch of a button. We belong (on and off) to a lively, thoughtful, funny, down-to-earth List called Ecobalance, designed for people in eco-villages or thinking of joining one or setting one up. Ecobalance lets us chat to them every day and receive technical tips on recycling bathwater, preventing termites from invading rammed earth buildings and such matters. To join, e-mail: liststar@gaia.org with a message which says nothing else but: subscribe ecobalance (no full stop). A machine will put you on line.

Our Net enthusiasm should not stop us listening to the Luddites. Rachel

MORE LIVING LIGHTLY SITES:

Addresses begin with http://

Fellowship for Intentional Community Foundation — www.ic.org

Centre for Alternative Technology — www.cat.org.uk/

Greenpeace International — www.greenpeace.org/iinf.html

Anarchist links — www.antenna.nl/~assata/links.html

LETS alternative money systems — www.gmlets.u-net.com/

New Economics Foundation — www.sosig.ac.uk/neweconomics/newecon.html

Fairtrade Foundation — www.gn.apc.org/fairtrade/

New Road Map Foundation (voluntary simplicity) — www.slnet.com/cip/nrm

Adbusters — www.adbusters.org/

Freifelder wrote to the Ecobalance List from Davis, California: 'A social structure that depends on the Net's continued functioning is as unsustainable as one that depends on the continued long-distance transport of food by trucks in freeways. Better to set up your eco-village and your bioregional economy so that all your needs can be met locally in the event of a system crash, and consider long-distance trade and telecommunications to be beneficial but not essential. Besides, most of the essentials aren't telecommunicatable anyway. Virtual vegetables? Virtual bread? Virtual health care? Virtual music? I have a computer and a net connection but I'd rather be canning peaches'.

18

Back to the future

• •

Living Lightly people are found in small numbers — pockets of resistance to the prevailing ethic. For us this doesn't lessen their appeal. Someone can inspire by what she is as much as what she has, what she does or what she achieves. Living Lightly people are exciting to know because they don't accept stereotyped patterns of behaviour and have embarked on the adventure of re-making their own lifestyles. In general, they are kind people, because their primary motivation has been rejection of a competitive and individualistic society. We made friends in four continents whose values we share; many of them shared their homes with us also, as we have begun sharing ours with them.

There seems to be little in common between the idealistic youngsters at The Farm in Tennessee and young doctors working as volunteers in a remote forest village in India, or between Tokyo housewives running a food co-operative and the inhabitants of a permaculture village in Queensland. Yet there is a common thread: the determination to re-affirm the basic values of humanity, community, locality and respect for life and for nature. In spite of their diversity, Living Lightly people are linked on a psychological level by common values, on an intellectual level by an ideology expressed in a growing library of books and periodicals, on a physical level by courses and conferences, and on a virtual-reality level through e-mail and the Internet.

In Maleny, Queensland, we found ourselves in a kind of paradise — a regenerated community in a regenerated Australian forest. Here, in the residential co-operative of Manduka, was an experiment in living lightly which had succeeded on many levels.

What else do we single out? The Coopers in North Wales with the courage to retreat from the mainstream have become practically self-sufficient and are happy. On the spectrum of radicalism in lifestyles, the Coopers are at one extreme. At the other, the cohousing communities in California impressed us because people earning a comfortable living in mainstream society adopted kinder values in their domestic arrangements.

We enjoyed the exuberant company of the New England farmers practising community-supported agriculture — bursting with energy, radiating the satisfaction of growing healthy food for customers who were friends. In many places we went to, the kids enchanted us. At Findhorn, Scotland, at The Farm, Tennessee, at Virtual High, Vancouver — the youngsters are growing up dangerously in questioning conventional values, yet securely in belonging to a close community; these young people have become citizens of a new culture.

Some of the communities we visited are branded New Age and that is usually meant as a put-down. Indeed most Living Lightly practitioners attract the criticism that they are naive and irrational. Yet we found among them all a commitment to life, to nature and to humanity that is generally lacking in the mainstream.

Are these experiments successful? The criteria are complex. At least they have survived over a period of years, sometimes decades, and almost all are still in existence as this book goes to press. None has achieved the environmental sustainability of a true eco-village — more often through shortage of funds than lack of will or know-how. None has won freedom from worry about money, without which the good life is no longer possible. None can be sure that their children, when old enough to make their choices, will accept their parents' priorities. None has found a reliable solution to the strains and conflicts of human interaction (in several communities we found a turnover in sexual partnerships among members that was too high for their own comfort). Mixed in among idealists and hardworking achievers we met others, fragile and sometimes hopeless casualties of m a i n s t r e a m society who had come primarily to seek refuge. Most of the communities we saw were well able to cope with society's misfits — and found an added

Satish Kumar and his wife, June Mitchell, at home.

Stuart Field, manager of Radical Routes.

satisfaction in the knowledge that the strong were helping the weak.

Can these pioneers change the future? The lifestylers we have visited are only one fragile strand in a global movement of changing values in which the main groups are:

- agitators (propagandists, pressure groups)
- diagnosers (writers, academics)
- revolutionaries (eco-anarchists, urban squatters, road protesters)
- technicians (energy savers, recyclers, eco-city designers)
- fixers (improving the environment by working more or less within the system)
- lifestylers (doing their own thing)

Although they are the least prominent group, the lifestylers could ultimately be the most influential because they show how change can work for people. At present, the most influential are the fixers — groups like The Natural Step, operating in Sweden originally and now also in the US, UK, Canada, Australia and Holland, which confronts officials and industrialists with a consensus of scientific wisdom on the sustainable way forward. In Britain, Jonathon Porritt began as an agitator when he was director of Friends of the Earth, and has moved over to the fixers, working on two levels — the political (in a coalition called Real Word) and with corporations (in Forum for the Future). Corporations have appeared in this book as villains, yet they employ brains smart enough to see that an unsustainable future is no future. They are directed, staffed and financed by human beings who have children and grandchildren.

This new Jonathon Porritt told us that he is not prepared to wait for Nirvana. 'The job right now is persuading companies that being active in shaping a different world order is a practical aspiration and that a different world order wouldn't be that bad for them either. Five years ago the fifteen corporations we work with saw us as the enemy — much as we saw them. Now they're developing working partnerships with environmental organisations. To see World Wide Fund for Nature and Unilever sit down together and try to thrash things out is very encouraging.'

> Humanity can only have a satisfying sense of direction when it can calculate achievements with the help of an economics which is about persons as they really are, which incorporates irrational and altruistic behaviour in its computations, which does not assume that people are always and fundamentally selfish and which understands success even in the material world is not obtained by the exclusive pursuit of self-interest. This two-eyed economics is in the process of being born, as is a two-eyed politics, concerning itself not simply with giving victory to the majority, but with offering mutually acceptable alternative victories to the losers, encouraging, without jealousy, the cultivation of multiple loyalties.
> · Theodore Zeldin, *An Intimate History of Humanity.*

Wearing his political hat, Jonathon tries to help government and opposition 'wake up to the fact that instead of going on misleading people with false expectations of jobs in the global economy they'd be far better off empowering people in communities, people who accept a different, happier lifestyle which is just as engaged, just as rewarding and just as important for the well-being of the national fabric as this constant pursuit of a competitive presence in the global market.'

What will happen to the global economy? We have listened while many of our protagonists predict a collapse, either economic or environmental, or both, which will turn their own experiments into islands of refuge. We do not believe that a dramatic collapse is inevitable, or that this contingency is necessary to justify alternative living. The justification for Living Lightly is the hope that it can provide an alternative model — both for the richer North, where the whole spectrum of lifestyle models generally originates, and for the poorer South, whose popular current models are mostly imported. A change of direction can only come if it is perceived, in North and South, as progress.

Sensitivity to the fate of the natural environment has been present in popular culture for decades, from Brigitte Bardot's histrionic protests in favour of Animal Rights to the songs of Sting and many other popular entertainers. In Britain a road protester like Swampy can briefly become a celebrity and in many countries environmental concerns have broken through into radio and television sit-coms. Children and adolescents all over the world appear to be the group most affected by TV documentaries about threatened wildlife species. Here, globalisation contains its own contradictions as rebellious teenagers wearing trainers made in Asian sweatshops call for a stop to the culling of baby seals. A new awareness has begun to influence political decisions and work back again into society to modify its norms. In 1997, ahead of the Kyoto conference on global warming, the US government took the position for the first time that this problem was serious enough to necessitate economic sacrifice. True, the government's position was sabotaged by a mighty alliance of industrial interests and no big breakthrough was achieved at Kyoto, but a new reality had been recognised. In Britain a similar sea change occurred earlier. In 1995 when a Conservative government accepted that its programme for building more roads to accommodate predicted traffic growth made no sense because more roads would only encourage yet more traffic. The road building programme was curtailed and the cuts have not been restored. In Europe the human consequences of global competition are showing up in persistent long-term unemployment and that problem, in turn, is breaking through into European politics. In Asia the economic crises of 1998 have turned the thoughts of world leaders towards greater regulation of the world economy.

Reform and regulation, however well-intentioned, cannot change values. It is the shared conviction of all the people we have written about in this book that only a simpler, less intrusive lifestyle in affluent countries can safeguard the future. Meanwhile we must wait and hope for the following ideas to win public acceptance:

- that international trade is good but has become excessive, oppressive and unsustainable;
- that farming with science and technology is good but transforming agriculture into a global industry can have devastating consequences for farmers, for the land and for consumers;
- that economic development in the South is good, but only if it is consistent with the welfare of local communities.

Can we live lightly while the global economy still rules? A dual society is likely to emerge in which the official economy will continue to enrich its favourites and impoverish its victims, allowing an alternative culture to become an alternative economy. The Dutch economist Willem Hoogendijk greets this emerging reality as a blessing, with a 'Green-basic sector' in all countries, centred on organic farming and affiliated activities.[1] That is one possible scenario.

Let's imagine that the future unrolls pretty much as the recent past has been doing. The global economy tightens its grip on nations and individuals. To increase the GNP remains one of governments' main objectives and social welfare and environmental concerns are subordinate to that. You and your partner are encouraged to buy as many consumer goods as possible and these are not built to last. The goods you buy from a world market have been produced wherever labour is cheapest. To keep this lifestyle afloat, you have to work harder and harder while indigenous peoples continue to be exploited and decimated. International competition and declining social and environmental standards lead to increasing intolerance and aggression and a declining quality of life for almost everyone.

Now imagine that globalisation does *not* proceed in this fashion. You might find yourself living in a village, a small town or a city suburb which grows a proportion of its own food, in a house built of local materials in a regional style. Such houses would stand in clusters around courtyards surrounded by open space and gardens. Once houses are built using energy-saving materials and sources of renewable energy, each group of houses is fairly self-sufficient and inexpensive to run. You, like many of your neighbours, might keep poultry or livestock in your spare time, and recycle kitchen and garden wastes while growing a large part of your food. The size and shape of each living area is defined by the need to keep services within walking and cycling distance. Cheap and plentiful public transport connects people to town and city centres which offer services and luxuries like hospitals, universities, theatres. A personal car is no longer a daily necessity but an occasional luxury.

High-technology goods like cars and computers are still available in a culture of sharing rather than ownership. Local resources and local products are preferred over imported goods. Due to a significant reduction in unnecessary production and consumption, you will need to work fewer hours so that you have more time to yourself

The authors with Kumhiko Morita and his wife at their home.

for your family, leisure or public service. In such a society, a thriving Local Exchange Trading System develops; you can learn the violin in return for painting someone's kitchen or walking their dog.

Each region lives within its capacities and does not exploit other regions and the exploitation of the South by the North gradually disappears. A multitude of regional cultures flourishes. What will you have to give up? Some of the luxuries of industrial society will be curtailed. The local organic vegetables you eat might look less shiny and uniform, reminding you of the earth they grew in, and in winter you might eat more winter greens and fewer snow peas imported from Kenya (Kenyans might use that land to grow food for themselves). The higher cost of transport will curtail mass tourism but holidays at home might become more attractive and the Internet can still keep people in touch with one another over long distances.

It requires an enormous leap of the imagination to conceive of such a situation as a reality. Yet nothing in it is essentially new and the underlying principles are more sophisticated than those of the first scenario, which depends on the naive notion that economic growth is good in itself and can continue indefinitely.

We ourselves travelled lightly while researching this book. Back home, we are too old for a lifestyle revolution. We use our car for shopping instead of the costly and infrequent bus service. We grow some of our food; much of the rest comes from the global consumer economy which we have so bitterly criticised. At least the *ideas* of Living Lightly have come to permeate our home. Two of Zachary's elder sisters, Tanya and Zoe, work full-time in organisations which defend and facilitate sustainable practices around the world. Living Lightly begins as an attitude of mind.

After two years of intermittent travel and one year constant writing, can we affirm that Living Lightly presents a viable alternative to the current trend of globalisation? Can it succeed? Only the future will show. We have written about what we saw. It is in the spaces between spoken and written words that a different truth emerges. It is up to each reader to decide to what extent he or she can live a life with aspirations and values which work against the dominant consumer culture. What cheers us after our travels is that people in such varied niches are preparing for the second scenario we described above. To live lightly does not imply rejecting the marvels of our times, but using them with care. As the poet Gary Synder remarks, 'The best things in life are not things.'[2]

Notes

1   'Preparing for the Revolt' in *Development* (SID, Rome, Issue 3/1995).
2   Gary Snyder told us that he used this aphorism in a poem after seeing it carved in stone by De Wayne Williams, a desert sage.

Bibliography

• •

(We have marked with a * the books we found particularly useful for information on the theory and practice of Living Lightly.)

Albery, Nicholas (ed). *The Book of Visions: Over 500 of the best ideas from around the world* (Virgin, 1992)

*Albery, Nicholas and others. *DIY Futures: People's Ideas and Projects for a Better World* (The Institute for Social Inventions, 1996)

Allen, Paul and Todd, Bob. *Off the Grid: Managing Independent Renewable Electricity Systems.* (New Futures: CAT Publications, 1995)

*Andrews, Cecile. *The Circle of Simplicity* (HarperCollins, 1997)

Berman, Morris. *Coming to Our Senses: Body and spirit in the hidden history of the West* (Unwin, 1990)

Borer, Pat and Harris, Cindy. *Out of the Woods: Ecological Design for Timber-Frame Housing* (Centre for Alternative Technology and The Walter Segal Self Build Trust, 1994)

*Berry, Thomas. *The Dream of the Earth* (Sierra Club, 1988)

Bhave, Vinoba. *Moved by Love: The memoirs of Vinoba Bhave* (Green Books, 1994)

Blix, Jacqueline and Heitmiller, David. *Getting a Life: Real Lives Transformed by Your Money Or Your Life* (Viking Penguin, 1997)

Body, Richard. *Agriculture, the Triumph and the Shame* (Temple Smith, 1982)

Brown, Lester (ed). *State of the World* (published yearly, W. W. Norton)

Brown, L. R. and Kane, H. *Vital Signs 1994* (W. W. Norton, 1995)

Burch, Mark. *Simplicity: Notes, Stories and Exercises for Developing Unimaginable Wealth* (New Society Publishers, 1995)

Caddy, Peter. *In Perfect Timing: Memoirs of a Man for the New Millennium* (Findhorn Press, 1996)

Castro, Stephen J. *Hypocrisy and Dissent within the Findhorn Foundation* (New Media Books, 1996)

Clunies, Ross T. and Hildyard, N. *The Politics of Industrial Agriculture* (Earthscan, 1992)

Coates, Chris et al. *The Guide to Co-operative Living* (Diggers and Dreamers Publications, 1995)

Cohen, J. E. *How Many People Can the Earth Support?* (W. W. Norton, 1995)

Colborn, T. with Dumanoski, D. and Myers, J. *Our Stolen Future: Are We Threatening Our Fertility, Intelligence and Survival?* (Penguin, 1966)

Daly, H. and Cobb, J. *For the Common Good: Redirecting the Economy Toward Community, the Environment, and a Sustainable Future* (Beacon Press, 1989)

*Dominguez, J. and Robin, V. *Your Money or Your Life: Transforming your relationship with money and achieving financial independence* (Penguin, 1992)

*Douthwaite, Richard. *Short Circuit: Strengthening Local Economies for Security in an Unstable World* (Green Books, 1996)

   The Growth Illusion (Green Books, 1992)

Dunant, Sarah and Porter, Roy. *The Age of Anxiety* (Virago, 1996)

*Durning, Alan. *How Much is Enough? The Consumer Society and the Future of the Earth* (W. W. Norton, 1992)

Dwelly, Tim (ed). *Living in The Future: 24 sustainable development ideas from the UK.* (The UK National Council for Habitat II, 1996)

*The Ecologist. *Whose Common Future? Reclaiming the Commons* (Earthscan, 1993)

Ekins, Paul. *A New World Order: Grassroots Movements for Global Change* (Routledge, 1992)

Elgin, Duane. *Voluntary Simplicity: Toward a Way of Life That is Outwardly Simple, Inwardly Rich* (William Morrow, 1981: revised 1993)

*Fairlie, Simon. *Low Impact Development: Planning and People in a Sustainable Countryside* (Jon Carpenter, 1996)

Fairclough, Gerard. *Creative Compartments: A Design for Future Organisation* (Adamantine Press, 1994)

*Fern, Ken. *Plants for a Future: Edible and Useful Plants for a Healthier World* (Permanent Publications, 1997)

Fukuoka, Masanobu, *The Road Back to Nature* (1996) (order from Permanent Publications)

Gaskin, Ina May. *Spiritual Midwifery* (The Book Company, 1994)

*Ghazi, Polly and Jones, Judy. *Downshifting: The Guide to Happier, Simpler Living* (Coronet Books, 1997)

Gillet, Pierre. *Small is Difficult: The Pangs and Success of Small Boat Technology Transfer in South India* (IT Publications, 1995)

*Girardet, Herbert. *Gaia Atlas of Cities* (Gaia Books, 1992)

   Earthrise: How we can heal our injured planet? (Paladin, 1992)

Goldsmith, Edward. *The Way* (Rider 1992, revised edition Green Books 1996)

Gottlieb, Robert. *Forcing the Spring* (Island Press, 1993)

*Groh, Trauger M. and McFadden, Steven S. H. *Farms of Tomorrow: Community-Supported Farms, Farm-Supported Communities* (Bio-Dynamic Farm Ass. Inc., PO Box 550, Kinberton, PA 19442, USA. 1990)

Hart, Robert. *Forest Gardening* (Green Books, 1991)

Ho, Mae Wan. *Genetic Engineering: Dream or Nightmare?* (Gateway Books, 1998)

*Hoogendijk, Willem. 'Preparing for the Revolt' (in *Development*, 3/1995)

*Holmgren, David. *Gardening as Agriculture: A Permaculture Perspective* (Holmgren Design Services, 16, Fourteenth Street, Hepburn, 3641, Victoria, Australia, 1995)

Hollis, Arthur. *The Farmer, The Plough and The Devil: The Story of Fordhall Farm Pioneer of Organic Farming* (Ashgrove Press, 1986)

*Jacobs, Michael. *The Politics of the Real World* (Earthscan, 1996)

James, Oliver. *Britain on the Couch: Treating a Low Serotonin Society* (Century,1997)

Janson, A. M. et al. *Investing in Natural Capital* (Island Press, 1994)

*Jaynes, Julian. *The Origins of Consciousness in the Breakdown of the Bicameral Mind* (Houghton Mifflin, 1976)

*Jeavons, John. *How to Grow More Vegetables Than You Ever Thought Possible on Less than You can Imagine* (Ten Speed Press, 1995)

Jones, Emrys. *Metropolis: The World's Great Cities* (Oxford Uuniversity Press, 1990)

*Kaneko, Yoshinori. *A Farm with a Future: Living with the Blessings of Soil and Sun* (Y. and T. Kaneko, 809 Shimosato, Saitama, Japan, 1994)

Kinkade, Pat. *Is It Utopia Yet? An Insider's View of Twin Oaks Community in its 25th Year* (Twin Oaks Publishing, 1994)

*Korten, David. *When Corporations Rule the World* (Kumarian Press, 1995)

*Lang, Tim and Hines, Colin. *The New Protectionism: Protecting the Future against Free Trade* (Earthscan, 1993)

Lappé, Frances Moore and Collins, Joseph. *Food First* (Abacus, 1982)

Lerner, Michael. *Jewish Renewal: A Path to Healing and Transformation* (HarperCollins, 1995)

Liedloff, Jean. *The Continuum Concept* (Penguin, 1986)

Linsey, Andrew. *Animal Theology* (SCM Press, 1994)

*Logsdon, Gene. *At Nature's Pace: Farming and the American Dream* (Pantheon Books, 1994)

*Lovelock, James. *The Ages of Gaia* (Oxford University Press, 1995)
  The Practical Science of Planetary Medicine (Gaia Books, 1996)

*Marshall, Peter. *Nature's Web: an exploration of ecological thinking* (Simon and Schuster, 1992)

*McCamart, Kathryn and Durrett, Charles. *Cohousing: A Contemporary Approach to Housing Ourselves* (Ten Speed Press, revised 1994)

MacFadyen, J. Trevere. *Gaining Ground: The Renewal of America's Small Farms* (Ballantine Books, 1984)

*McKay, George. *Senseless Acts of Beauty: Cultures of Resistance in the Sixties* (Verso, 1966)

McKibben, Bill. *Hope, Human and Wild: True Stories of Living Lightly on the Earth* (Little, Brown, 1995)

*Metcalf, Bill (ed). *Shared Visions, Shared Lives: Communal Living around the Globe* (Findhorn Press, 1996)
  From Utopian Dreaming to Communal Reality: Co-operative Lifestyles in Australia (UNSW Press, 1995)
  'Findhorn, the Routinization of Charisma' (in *Communal Studies Journal*, vol. 13, 1993)

*Mollison, Bill. *Permaculture: A Designer's Manual* (Tagari Publications, PO Box 1, Tyalgum, NSW, Australia, 1988)

*Mollison, Bill with Slay, Reny Mia. *Introduction to Permaculture* (Tagari, 1991)

*Norberg-Hodge, Helena. *Ancient Futures: Learning from Ladakh* (Sierra Club, 1991)

Omvedt, Gail. *Dalit Visions* (Longmans Orient, 1995)

*Pratt, Simon (ed), *The Permaculture Plot: The Guide to Permaculture in Britain* (Permanent Publications, 4th edition, 1997)

*Pretty, Jules, *Regenerating Agriculture: Policies and Practice for Sustainability and Self-Reliance* (Earthscan, 1995)

    The Living Land (Earthscan, 1998)

Pye-Smith, C. and Feyerbad, G. B. with Sandbrook, R. *The Wealth of Communities* (Earthscan, 1994)

*Quinn, Daniel. *Ishmael* (Bantam 1993)

Rich, Bruce. *Mortgaging the Earth: The World Bank, Environmental Impoverishment and the Crisis of Development* (Beacon Press, 1994)

Rifkin, Jeremy. *Biosphere Politics: A new consciousness for a new century* (HarperCollins, 1992)

Roelofs, Joan. *Greening Cities: Building Just and Sustainable Communities* (The Bootstrap Press, 1996)

Roszak, Theodore. *The Voice of the Earth* (Simon and Schuster, 1992)

Ryan, John and Durning, Alan. *Stuff, The Secret Lives of Everyday Things*, (Northwest Environment Watch, 1997)

*Sachs, Wolfgang (ed). *Global Ecology: A New Arena of Political Conflict* (Zed Books, 1993)

    (ed). *The Development Dictionary* (Zed Books, 1992)

Sale, Kirkpatrick. *The Conquest of Paradise: Christopher Columbus and the Columbian Legacy* (Hodder and Stoughton, 1991)

    Rebels Against the Future (Addison-Wesley, 1995)

Schor, Juliet. *The Overworked American* (Basic Books, 1993)

*Schumacher, E. F. *Small is Beautiful* (Abacus, 1974)

*Schwarz, Walter and Dorothy. *Breaking Through:Theory and Practice of Holistic Living* (Green Books, 1988)

Seabrook, Jeremy. *Race for Riches* (Green Print, 1988)

*Seymour, John. *Retrieved from The Future* (New European Publications,1996)

    The Forgotten Arts (Dorling Kindersley,1985)

    The Fat of The Land (reissued, Metanoya Press, 1996)

    The Self-Sufficient Gardener (Corgi edition, 1994)

    with Girardet, Herbert. *Blueprint for a Green Planet* (Dorling Kindersley, 1987)

Shaffer, Carolyn R. and Anundsen, Kristin. *Creating Community Anywhere: Finding Support and Connection in a Fragmented World* (Tarcher/Perigee, 1993)

*Shiva, Vandana. *Staying Alive: Women, Ecology and Development* (Zed Books,1989)

Shoard, Marion. *This Land is Our Land* (Gaia, 1998)

*Singer, Peter. *Animal Liberation* (Jonathan Cape, 1990)

*Spangler, David. *A Pilgrim in Aquarius* (Findhorn Press, 1993)

Steiner, Rudolf. *Intuitive Thinking as a Spiritual Path* (Anthroposophic Press, 1995)

*Swimme, Brian and Berry, Thomas. *The Universe Story* (HarperCollins, 1992)

Talbott, John. *Simply Build Green: A technical guide to the ecological houses at the Findhorn Foundation* (Findhorn Press, 1995)

Thomas, Kate. *The Destiny Challenge: A Record of Spiritual Experience and Observation* (New Frequency Press, 1992)

*Thoreau, Henry David. *Walden* (Penguin Classics, 1986)

*Trainer, Ted. *The Conserver Society: Alternatives for Sustainability* (Zed Books,1995) *Towards a Sustainable Economy* (Jon Carpenter, 1996)

*Traugot, Michael. *A Short History of The Farm* (privately printed. Michael Trauger, 84, The Farm, Summertown TN 38483, USA, 1994)

*Vidal, John. *McLibel: Burger Culture on Trial* (Macmillan 1998)

*Wackernagel, Mathis and Rees, William. *Our Ecological Footprint: Reducing Human Impact on the Earth* (New Society Publishers, 1996)

*Wakefield, Stacey, and Grrrt. *Not For Rent: Conversations with Creative Activists in the UK* (Evil Twin Publications, Amsterdam and Seattle, 1995)

*Watson, David. *Urban Permaculture: A Practical Handbook for Sustainable Living* (Permanent Publications, 1993)

Watson, Lyall. *Dark Nature* (Hodder and Stoughton/Sceptre, 1995)

Weizsacker, Ernst Ulrich von. *Earth Politics* (Zed Books, 1994)

*Weizsacker, Ernst Ulrich von, Lovins, Amory and Hunter, L. *Factor Four: Doubling Wealth, Halving Resource Use* (Earthscan, 1997)

Whitefield, Patrick. *Permaculture in a Nutshell* (Permanent Publications,1993)

Willers, Bill (ed). *Learning to Listen to the Land* (Island Press, 1991)

*Zeldin, Theodore. *An Intimate History of Humanity* (Sinclair Stevenson, 1994)

Useful addresses

•••

Australia

Crystal Waters, 59 Crystal Waters, MS 16, Maleny, Q 455274 Tel: 94 4741 Fax: 4578. www.gaia.org/crystalwaters/index.html Max Lindegger, Eco-logical Solutions Ltd. email: ecosol@peg.apc.org

Holmgren Design Services, 16 Fourteenth Street, Hepburn Springs, VIC 3461. Tel: 053 48 3461.

Jill Jordan, PO Box 87 Maleny Q4552.

Canada

Adbusters, 13225 Marine Drive V4A IE6, Vancouver. Tel: 604-736 9401 email: Adbuster@adbusters.org Web: www.adbusters.org

Virtual High, PO Box 38083 Vancouver B.C. Canada V5Z 4L9: Tel: 739-5941 Fax: 739 6903. email: Brentcameron@intouch.bc.ca

Netherlands

VAKgroep, Lauwerecht 55, Utrecht 3515. Tel: 030-272-1660. e-mail: amf@amf.xs4all.nl

India

Auroville, Visitors Centre, Auroville, 605 101 India. Tel: 413 62239; Fax: 62274. e-mail: avi@auroville.org.in Web: www.auroville-india.org

K. R Datye, Ganesh Kutir, 1st Floor, 68 Prarthana Samaj Rd, Vile Parle (East), Bombay 400-057

Navdanya Centre (Dr Vanaja Ramprasad), JP Nagaram II Phase, 23rd Main (10th Cross), Door 839 B560078 e-mail: navdam@green.frlht.ernet.in

SPARC (Sheela Patel) PO Box 9389m, Bombay 400 026 Tel: 283-6743. Fax 285-1500.

Japan

Japan Organic Agriculture Association, Hongo Corporation #1001, 2-40-13 Hongo, Bunkyo-ku, Tokyo 113. Tel: +81-3-3818-3078. Fax: +81-3-5684-8103.

Seikatsu Club Consumers Co-operative Union, Marumasu Building 5F; 6-24-20 Shinjuku, Shinjuku-ku, Tokyo 160. Tel: +81-3-5285-1833. Fax: +81-3-5285-1837.

UK

British Trust for Conservation Volunteers, 36, St Mary's Street, Wallingford OX10 OEU. Tel: 01491 839766. Fax: 839646. e-mail: information @btcv.org.uk

Brockwood Park School, Bramdean, Hampshire SO24 OLQ. Tel: 01962 771744 Fax: 771875. e-mail: admin@brockwood1.win-uk.net

Centre for Alternative Technology, Machynlleth, Powys, Wales SY20 9AZ. Tel: 01654 702400. Fax: 702782. e-mail: cat@gn.apc.org Web: www. foe.co.uk/CAT

Henry Doubleday Research Association, National Centre for Organic Gardening, Ryton, Coventry CV8 3LG. Tel: 01203 303517. Fax: 639229.

Eco-village Network, The CREATE Centre, 'B' Bond Warehouse, Smaton Road, Bristol BS1 6XN. Tel: 0117 922 4391. Fax: 929 7283. email: evnuk@gaia.org Web: www.gaia.org/thegen/index.html/

Findhorn Foundation, The Park, Findhorn Bay, Forres IV36 OTZ, Scotland. Tel/Fax: 01309-690331. Fax: 691301. Web: www.gaia.org/findhorn/ t1.html

Friends of the Earth, 26 Underwood St, London N17JQ. Tel: 0171 490 1555.

Green Network Charitable Trust, 9 Claremont Road, Lexden Colchester C3 5BE. Tel and fax: 01206-546902/766005. e-mail: 100727,3110 @compuserve.com

Greenpeace, Canonbury Villas, London N1 2PN. Tel: 0171 354 5100.

Intermediate Technology, 103-5 Southampton Row, London WC1B 4HH. Tel: 0171 436 9761.

Keveral Organic Farm, St Martin's by Looe, Cornwall PL13 1PA. Tel: 01503 250215.

The Land is Ours (TLIO) Box E, 111 Magdalen Road, Oxford OX4 1RQ. Tel: 01865-722016. Web: www.envirolink.org/orgs/tlio

LETS Information Centre, Letslink UK, 2 Kent Street, Portsmouth PO1 3BS. Tel: 01705-730639. Fax: 730629. Web:www.communities.org.uk/lets

National Federation of City Farms, The Greenhouse, Hereford Street, Bedminster, Bristol BS3 4NA. Tel: 0117 923 1800 Fax: 923 1900

New Economics Foundation, Vine Court, 112-116 Whitechapel Road, London E1 1JE. Tel: 0171 377 5696. Fax: 5720. Web: http://sosig.ac.uk/neweconomics/ newecon.html

Organic Roundabout, 28 Hamstead Road, Hockley, Birmingham B19 1DB. Tel: 0121 507 1200. Fax: 0121 515 3524.

Permaculture Association, PO Box 1, Buckfastleigh, Devon TQ11 OLH. Tel: 01654 712188. e-mail: pcbritain@gn.apc.org

Permanent Publications (permaculture), Hyden House Ltd., The Sustainability Centre, East Meon, Hampshire GU32 1HR. Tel: 01730 823311 Fax: 823322. e-mail: Glen@permaculture.co.uk Web: www.permaculture.co.uk

Plants for a Future, The Field, Penpol, Lostwithiel, PL22 ONG. Tel: 01208-873554.

Radical Routes secondary co-operative, Cornerstone Housing Co-operative, 16 Sholebroke Avenue, Chapeltown, Leeds LA7 3HB. Tel. 0113 262 9365. e-mail: cornerstone@gn.apc.org.

Schumacher College, The Old Postern, Dartington TQ9 6EA. Tel: 01803 865934.

Fax: 866899.

The Soil Association, Bristol House, 40-56 Victoria Street, Bristol BS1 6BY. Tel: 0117 9290661. Fax: 9252504.

Sustainable Agriculture Food & Environment Alliance (SAFE), 38 Ebury Street, London SW1W OLU. Tel: 0171 823 5660.

Tinkers Bubble, Little Norton, Stoke sub Hamdon, Somerset TA14 6TE.

Trees for Life, address c/o Findhorn. Tel/Fax: 01309 691292. e-mail: trees@findhorn.org Web: www.gaia.org/treesforlife/

Triodos Bank, Brunel House, 11 The Promenade, Bristol BS8 3NN. Tel: 0117 973 9339.

Vegan Organic and Agriculture Network, 35 Rayleigh Avenue, Westcliff, Essex SSO 7DS. Tel: 01702 303459.

The Vegan Society, 7 Battle Road, St Leonards on Sea, East Sussex TN37 7AA. Tel: 01424 427393. Fax 717064.

The Vegetarian Society, Dunham Road, Altrincham, Cheshire WA14 4QG. Tel/Fax: 0161 928 0793. Web: www.vegsoc.org

WWOOF (Working Weekends On Organic Farms), 19 Bradford Road, Lewes, BN7 1RB. Tel: 01273 476286.

USA

Bethel New Life, 367 N.Karlov, Chicago IL 60624-1898 Tel: (312) 826-5540. Fax: (312) 826-5728

Caretaker Farm, 1210 Hancock Road, Williamstown 01267; Genesis Farm, 41A Silver Lake Rd, Blairstown NJ 07825.

Centre for Neighborhood Technology, 2125 W.North Ave, Chicago ILL 60647 Tel: (312) 278-4800.

The Cohousing Company, 1250 Addison Street #113, Berkeley, CA 94702. Tel: (510) 549-9980. Fax: 549-2140.

Earth First, PO Box 1415 Eugene, Oregon 95440 earthfirst@ igc.apc.org   Web: www.telalink.net/~zoomst/earthfirst/index.html

The Farm, 556 Farm Road, Summertown TN 38483-0090 Tel: (615) 964-3992 /4324 Fax: 2200. email: ecovillage@thefarm.gaia.org Web: www.gaia.org/farm/index.html

Fellowship for Intentional Communtity, Route 1 Box 155-WEB, Rutledge MO 63563-9720; Tel/Fax: (660) 883-5545. e-mail: fic@ic.org www.ic.org

Friends of the Earth, 530 Seventh St, SE, Washington DC 20003.

Trauger Groh, 135 Temple Road, Wilton NH 03086.

International Forum on Globalisation, 950 Lombard Street, San Francisco CA 94133. Tel: (415) 771-1102

New Road Map Foundation PO Box 15981, Seattle, WA 98115. Tel: (206) 527 0437. Web: www. slnet.com/cip/nrm/

Rocky Mountain Institute, 1739 Snowmass Creek Road, Snowmass, CO 81654-9199.

Rodale Research Centre 33 East Minor St, Emmaeus, Pennsylvania 18049.

E.F. Schumacher Society, Box 76, RD3, Jug End Rd., Great Barrington MA 01230. Tel: (413) 528-4472 Fax: (413) 528-4472; e-mail: efssociety@ aol.com

Simple Living Network, P.O. Box 233, Trout Lake, WA 98650. Tel: (509) 395-2323; 1-800-318-5725. Fax: (509) 395-2128. e-mail: slnet@slnet.com.

Travellers Earth Repair Network, services for Green travellers world-wide. POBox 4469, Bellingham WA98227. Tel/Fax: 360-738-4972.

Worldwatch Institute 1776 Massachusetts Ave NW, Washington DC 20036. Web: www.worldwatch.org

Publications in UK, US and Canada

Co-housing Journal, c/o Co-housing Network, P.O.Box 2584, Berkeley, CA 94702, USA.

Communities, Journal of Cooperative Living, Rt 1, Box 155, Rutledge MO 63563, USA.

The Ecologist, Agriculture House, Bath Road, Sturminster Newton, Dorset DT10 1DU, England. Tel: 01258-473476.

Green Futures/Forum for the Future, 22 City Road London EC1V 1JT, England.

Living Gently Quarterly, PO Box 8302 Victoria, British Columbia, Canada V8W 3R9.

Permaculture Magazine, The Sustainability Centre, Hyden House Ltd. East Meon, Hampshire, GU32 1HR, England. Tel: 01730 823311. Fax: 823322. e-mail: Hello@permaculture.co.uk

Positive News, The Six Bells, Church Street, Bishop's Castle, Shropshire SY4 5AA, England. Tel: 01588 630121. Fax: 630122. e-mail: positivenews@ btinternet.com Web: www.oneworld.org/positive-news

Resurgence, Ford House, Hartland, Bideford, Devon EX39 6EE, England. Tel: 01237 441293.

Simple Living, 2319 North 45th Street Box 149 Seattle, WA 98103, USA.

Squall, POBox 8959, London N19 5HW, England. Tel: 0171-561 1204. e-mail: squall.co.uk Web: www.squall.co.uk

Utne Reader, 1624 Harmon Place, Suite 330, Minneapolis, MN 55403-9862, USA. Tel: (612) 338-5040. Fax: (612) 338-6043.

Yes: A journal of Positive Futures, PO Box 10818, Bainbridge Island,WA 98110-0818, USA.

Index

Towards a Sustainable Economy: The Need for Fundamental Change

Reviewing this book by **Ted Trainer** in *Resurgence*, Richard Douthwaite wrote: "Trainer writes so smartly and directly that he can smarten up your thinking even if you've been pondering the topics he deals with for years. *Towards a Sustainable Economy* contains the clearest short summary of the fundamental flaws in conventional economic theory I have ever read. It's an ideal introductory textbook for anyone who is keen to know just why so much seems to be going wrong." 192pp pbk, £10.99. 1 897766 14 9

What Everybody Really Wants to Know About Money

The idiocies of orthodox economists are laid bare by **Frances Hutchinson** as she exposes their ignorance of the nature and role of money, together with their wild and foolish assumptions about human nature. She shows how, to bring about today's global capitalist free market, work has been devalued to a form of slavery, and people everywhere have been denied access to their natural and basic means of survival: the land. 224pp pbk, £12. 1 897766 33 5

The Grip of Death

An original analysis by **Michael Rowbotham** of the consequences of virtually all the money in the world being privately created by banks as a debt that we pay interest on. David Korten writes: "An essential self-education tool for anyone interestyed in creating a world that works, pushing the issues further and posing the implications more bluntlythan I have seen anywhere else." 'Grip of death' is a loose translation of the French 'mortgage'. 352pp pbk, £15. 1 897766 40 8

Beyond Optimism: A Buddhist Political Ecology

Ken Jones' outstanding analysis of the human predicament using the persuasive Buddhist combination of radical vision and down-to-earth pragmatism is described by Jonathon Porritt as "insightful and extraordinarily helpful." 224pp pbk, £9.99. 1 897766 06 8

Low Impact Development: Planning and People in a Sustainable Countryside

Instead of excluding low income people from living and working in rural areas, **Simon Fairlie** argues that planners and planning law should look favourably on low impact and environmentally benign homes and workplaces in the country-side. He makes detailed policy recommendations. Colin Ward writes: "Many of us waited a long time for this kind of challenge to the official ideology of rural housing." 176pp illus pbk, £10. 1 897766 25 4

Our books are available (post free in the UK) from Jon Carpenter Publishing, 2 The Spendlove Centre, Charlbury OX7 3PQ. Ask for our catalogue. Credit card orders may be phoned to 01689 870437 or 01608 811969.